Social Justice Pedagogy Across the Curriculum

What knowledge and tools do pre- and in-service educators need to teach for and about social justice across the curriculum in K-12 classrooms?

This compelling text synthesizes in one volume historical foundations, philosophic/theoretical conceptualizations, and applications of social justice education in public school classrooms.

- Part I details the history of the multicultural movement and the instantiation of public schooling as a social justice project.
- Part II connects theoretical frameworks to social justice curricula. Parts I and II are general to all K-12 classrooms.
- Part III provides powerful specific subject-area examples of good practice, including English as a Second Language and Special/Exceptional Education.

Social Justice Pedagogy Across the Curriculum includes highlighted Points of Inquiry and Points of Praxis sections offering recommendations to teachers and researchers and activities, resources, and suggested readings. These features invite teachers at all stages of their careers to reflect on the role of social justice in education, particularly as it relates to their particular classrooms, schools, and communities.

Relevant for any course that addresses history, theory, or practice of multicultural/social justice education and teaching diverse groups of students, this text is ideal for classes that are not subject-level specific and serve a host of students from various backgrounds.

Thandeka K. Chapman is Associate Professor of Urban Education in the Department of Curriculum and Instruction at the University of Wisconsin, Milwaukee.

Nikola Hobbel is Associate Professor of English Education, Humboldt State University.

Language, Culture, and Teaching
Sonia Nieto, Series Editor

Visit **www.routledge.com/education** for additional information on titles in the Language, Culture, and Teaching series.

Social Justice Pedagogy Across the Curriculum

The Practice of Freedom

Edited by

Thandeka K. Chapman
University of Wisconsin, Milwaukee

Nikola Hobbel
Humboldt State University

Routledge
Taylor & Francis Group

NEW YORK AND LONDON

First published 2010
by Routledge
270 Madison Avenue, New York, NY 10016

Simultaneously published in the UK
by Routledge
2 Park Square, Milton Park, Abingdon, Oxon OX14 4RN

Routledge is an imprint of the Taylor & Francis Group, an informa business

© 2010 Taylor & Francis

Typeset in Minion and Gill Sans by Swales & Willis Ltd, Exeter, Devon
Printed and bound in the United States of America on acid-free paper by
Edwards Brothers, Inc.

Library of Congress Cataloging in Publication Data
A catalog record has been requested for this book

ISBN 10: 0–415–80600–3 (hbk)
ISBN 10: 0–415–80604–6 (pbk)
ISBN 10: 0–203–85448–9 (ebk)

ISBN 13: 978–0–415–80600–8 (hbk)
ISBN 13: 978–0–415–80604–6 (pbk)
ISBN 13: 978–0–203–85448–8 (ebk)

I would like to dedicate this book to the Milwaukee PEOPLE (Pre-College Enrichment Opportunity Program for Learning Excellence) students with whom I fell in love and who brought me to their city.—T.K.C.

To Dan, with love, gratitude and respect.—N.H.

Contents

Foreword

Sonia Nieto

Social justice: it's on everyone's mind these days. From political pundits to teacher educators, from school principals to parents, and from political scientists to car salespeople, everyone has an opinion on social justice. Some are staunch advocates, others fierce opponents, but everyone seems passionate about the promise or the perils of social justice. Some consider it the *sine qua non* of a democracy. Others liken it to socialism and the end of the civilized world as we know it. But what exactly *is* social justice? And, in terms of the specific matters addressed in this text, what does social justice have to do with education?

In *Social Justice Pedagogy Across the Curriculum: The Practice of Freedom,* editors Thandeka K. Chapman and Nikola Hobbel address these questions and more. They and the other authors in this book tackle multiple layers of the concept of social justice as it applies to education, and they provide powerful examples of what it looks like in practice, particularly in schools with diverse populations. Using Freirean theories of liberatory education, basic tenets of multicultural education, important concepts of Black feminist thought, poststructural analysis, and queer pedagogy, among others, the authors weave a tapestry that is at once complex and provocative. In the process, they offer all of us—teachers, teacher educators, researchers, policy makers, and others interested in the current context of education—a comprehensive and thought-provoking look at the history of social justice, a thorough exploration of the theoretical underpinnings of the concept, and engaging stories of how it is used in classrooms.

Social Justice Pedagogy Across the Curriculum is the newest addition to the Language, Culture, and Teaching (LCT) series, a series for preservice and practicing teachers that encourages critical thought and thoughtful action in teaching and learning. If you are already teaching, no doubt many of you are working in diverse settings and searching for theories and strategies to help you connect with your students. If you are not yet teaching, most of you will probably find yourselves working in diverse communities with students whose identities—race/ethnicity, language, social class, and so forth—differ from your own. The books in the LCT series ask you to recognize that there is no "generic" student, but that instead all students come to school with their individual sociocultural realities and specific sociopolitical contexts. Through theoretical discussions, practical applications, and thoughtful questions and activities, this book will help all K-12 teachers bridge the gap between their own reality and that of their students.

While some may argue that matters such as power, privilege, identity, and diversity are peripheral to education, editors Chapman and Hobbel and the authors of the wide-ranging chapters in their book argue convincingly that without an awareness of these issues, teachers are doomed to approach their teaching, and their students, in simplistic and uncritical ways that will do little to prepare them for the complex and heterogeneous world in which we live. In fact, one could argue that it is impossible to be a teacher without taking into account such issues as gender, sexuality, language, race, social class, ability, and other individual and group differences because these are at the very heart of equitable education, and they always have been. In fact, a close look at U.S. educational history makes it obvious that few controversies have been *unrelated* to social justice in education, whether these have focused on segregated schools, bilingual education, education for youngsters with special needs, or gender-fair education, among others.

This book asks you to reflect on the role of social justice in education, particularly as it relates to your particular classroom, school, and community. Some of the authors are seasoned academics with long and distinguished careers in the field; others are newer to the academy and to public education and they bring an intensity and vitality to the field that will transform it. Regardless of who they are, all of them are convinced that all teachers—not just those who teach language, literacy, and the social sciences—need to be prepared to learn about, reflect on, and apply these concepts in their teaching. This book provides just the tools you will need to do these things. More importantly, *Social Justice Pedagogy Across the Curriculum* gives you a way of thinking about social justice that transcends methods, strategies, and lesson plans and focuses instead on education as a moral and political endeavor.

Preface

When we thought about what type of book we wanted to create, we realized that we needed to incorporate three elements: history, theory, and praxis. Many teacher educators in multicultural education/social justice teach a number of required courses that every student must complete. This means that preservice and inservice teachers enter our courses with various levels of experience with and knowledge about social justice. These courses also serve as service courses for administrators, special education professionals, community educators, and other students who wish to better understand how to teach and learn in racially, linguistically, and socially diverse spaces. Therefore, we saw a need for a book that could be used in total as a text for these types of courses, providing rich instantiations of these three aspects of social justice pedagogy. This book is our attempt to fulfill this need in teacher education programs.

In the spirit of Freirean dialogue and critical community learning, we do not wish for readers to use this book as a prescriptive manual. It is not a "how-to" text from which teachers can excerpt activities and lesson plans, but a conceptual map and set of guide posts to help teachers cultivate social justice education in their communities. We hope that these rich and diverse chapters inspire and support teachers to create the learning spaces they dare to envision.

We cannot emphasize enough that we want this book to be useful for teachers and teacher educators. Towards this purpose, we have included two special features at the end of each chapter: *Points of Inquiry* and *Points of Praxis*.

Points of Inquiry is a set of questions that can be used to guide discussions of the chapter. These questions will, we hope, help readers to synthesize and analyze the chapter with regard to individual and collective teaching situations, as well as offer directions for further study. As readers become more familiar with the book, we hope new and interesting additions to these questions will be created. We hope that teachers and students will be able to add their own questions and research to the Points of Inquiry section as well.

Points of Praxis is a set of activities and questions for students to take into their classrooms. These should not be seen as static models to fit the context of every learning environment; rather, these points should guide us in creating praxis that is appropriate to our individual schooling contexts. We hope that these activities will be taken as suggestions, not mandates. As we carry the Points of Praxis into different learning spaces, we hope that these attempts help more of us to become more comfortable turning classrooms into places where we are *doing* social justice education.

Overview

Part I. Historical Perspectives

Part I provides the reader with three different historical perspectives on the evolution of social justice education. History matters. We need to understand the complex, nonlinear, interconnected social and institutional systems that have shaped and continue to shape what is possible in public schools. History roots the growth of social justice, helping it to thrive and withstand the winds of change—bending, but not breaking. Historical study keeps us from seeing events as occurring in a vacuum of presentism, one that denies the power that people have to change the world. As we speak of the *dorje* that adorns our cover, history becomes a tool of enlightenment to help conceptualize and re-conceptualize our previous readings of the history of education in the U.S.A.

Carl A. Grant and Melissa L. Gibson's chapter (Chapter 1) is the work of maverick scholars. These authors researched the Universal Declaration of Human Rights (1945–1951) as a point of entry to discuss the language of social justice that is now common usage to describe the goals and principals of education that is a human right. Grant and Gibson balance their work between the U.S. and global contexts to display the on-going debates and conversations that have occurred with regard to what counts as good and meaningful education.

Christine Sleeter's contribution (Chapter 2) is grounded in the particular struggles of the U.S. federal government to institutionalize equitable schooling in America. Her work moves the reader beyond the ideals of equitable education to demonstrate the differences between the spirit of the law, the State's interpretations of the law, and the local implementation of the law. While Sleeter does not pose lawmakers as altruistic actors, she complicates notions of intention and compliance by examining both the means and ends of federal policies that were meant to create greater equity for all students.

Maurianne Adams (Chapter 3) then spins history in a third direction through her articulations of the various social and academic movements that have shaped social justice in education. Her chapter enlightens readers about the multiple influences that continue to work in conversation with the goals of social justice education. In this chapter, we receive a brief glimpse of the different advocacy groups that have reinforced the desire for social action and group empowerment that go beyond just informing students about justice and injustice. Because she touches upon many theories and movements, Adam's chapter also serves as an introduction to the section of the book which provides an extended explanation of how theoretical frameworks have influenced conceptualizations of social justice in education.

Part II. Theoretical Intersections

Part II is all about theory. We are theorists and believe that a sound theoretical orientation assists us in providing rationales for and making decisions about our pedagogical choices. Our use of theory encourages students to explicate the epistemologies that affect our curricular orientations, teaching philosophies, and our dispositions toward children and their families. Attaining a broad vocabulary of ideas, concepts, and experiences is a source of transformation and power. Theory helps us to explain how knowledge affects us and guides our practice as teachers and students to understand how power and privilege function in large and small institutions and social contexts. We see it as enlightening to be able to place thoughts, feelings, and behaviors into frames of reference, giving us an extended vocabulary and form of expression to explain how we teach and to understand the experiences students bring with them to learning.

We start Part II with critical pedagogy because it is a key tool for understanding issues of power, privilege, oppression, and empowerment in social justice education. These concepts formulate the critiques and questions that must be posed before agency can occur. Drawing on the works of Antonio Gramsci, Pierre Bourdieu, and Paulo Freire, Bekisizwe S. Ndimande (Chapter 4) discusses the ways in which the often unyielding institution of education can be a tool of individual and social empowerment.

Adrienne D. Dixson and Jamila D. Smith (Chapter 5) continue to explore these issues under the banner of Black feminist theory. In this chapter, they examine the ways in which Black feminist theories inform social justice education. Their discussion of Black feminist theory draws on several notable Black female scholars and a number of disciplines to contextualize and deconstruct their positions as social justice educators.

In "Can We Learn Queerly?" (Chapter 6), Lisa W. Loutzenheiser explores how queer theories and queering pedagogies are important, yet tension-filled and contested elements of teaching across difference. Moving away from single-issue approaches and identity politics as the central focus of social justice education, this chapter envisions queering pedagogies as an attempt to address the relationships between sexuality and other oppressions, particularly race and sexuality/gender identity in educational contexts.

Patricia D. Quijada Cerecer, Leticia Alvarez Gutiérrez, and Francisco Rios (Chapter 7) highlight the origins of multicultural education for social reconstruction. The authors explain how multicultural education evolved to explicitly include a critical theory perspective of pedagogy based on Paulo Freire's ideas. The authors discuss the challenges to multicultural education that have weakened educators' understandings of multicultural education and have led to myths about what it means to enact a multicultural pedagogy. In a Freirean effort to leave the reader with hope, the authors highlight scholars and programs that have successful multicultural education components.

Robert J. Parkes, Jennifer M. Gore, and Wendy Elsworth (Chapter 8) use poststructuralism to critique and support the need for social justice education. Their explanation of the theory gives readers one of the clearest articulations of post-structuralism that we have encountered. Through their discussion of categories and systems of reasoning, they challenge the reader to think about what it means to create new classroom spaces that allow students to co-construct the curriculum, share power, and envision a different society. This chapter lays bare the conflicts embedded between teaching for social justice and the institutionalized, privileged ways of knowing and presenting knowledge to the world.

Bryan McKinley Jones Brayboy and Teresa L. McCarty (Chapter 9) describe the multiple facets of indigenous knowledge and how these facets are not only attached to, but are implicit in social justice education. Using two examples from schools that have incorporated the epistemologies of their Native American students into the culture of the school and the curriculum, Brayboy and McCarty make the case that students' ways of knowing the world cannot be separate from formal schooling practices.

David J. Connor and Susan L. Gabel (Chapter 10) state some hard truths about the way people in the U.S.A. view disabilities and how the politics of race and disability are both intertwined and at odds. This chapter forces readers to evaluate both personal and institutional biases against people with disabilities. Using Disabilities Studies as a framework to explain the depth and breadth of pervasive negative stereotypes and unjust institutional policies, the authors advocate for a revolutionary perspective of people with disabilities.

Part III. Social Justice Pedagogy and Praxis

Part III of this book is arguably the most necessary. We understand that theoretical discussions of social justice education must be coupled with concrete examples of practice. Teachers and students ask how to enact social justice pedagogy in their classrooms. Where are the models? Can you give us examples? These pleas do not fall on deaf ears; however, finding teachers who practice social justice and conducting research with them is difficult. Many teachers doing this work find themselves in isolated, heavily contested spaces. These teachers face the challenges of adhering to State and district standards and assessments that now penalize teachers and students for non-conformity. For many of these teachers who are pressured to use "teacher-proof" packages and test preparation curriculum, now is not the time to expose their teaching practices to the world. Frankly, there has never been a good time to announce that you are teaching students to question their beliefs, culture, society, and the institutions that contour their lives and the lives of their families in an effort to change communities and the greater society. Although it remains a struggle to find empirical work that helps us envision our own critical classrooms, this section of the book provides the reader with documented practices from different content areas, grade levels, and educational services.

Therese Quinn (Chapter 11) shares multiple experiences working with K-12 students in art education. She asserts that the tenets of art education are an easy match to concepts of social justice because both art education and social justice focus on student expression, perspective, and relevant connections to the outside world.

Nikola Hobbel and Thandeka K. Chapman (Chapter 12) attempt to define the learning outcomes of social justice. They turn the language of traditional standards around to ask teachers to think about the goals and objectives that are embodied in social justice education and can be identified in student work. Using data from a three-week writing seminar, Hobbel and Chapman explain the dispositions, skills, and knowledge that they hope to cultivate in students through social justice education.

Korina M. Jocson (Chapter 13) describes her work with the June Jordan Poetry Contest and the work of the People's Poetry project in public high schools. The themes chosen for the poems and the emphasis on words as agency mark this project as social justice education. Jocson explains the process and the products of the collaborative project.

Eric (Rico) Gutstein (Chapter 14) shares experiences from his years of work in mathematics and social justice education. Using Paulo Freire's work to frame and rationalize his choices for teaching mathematics in new and critical ways, Gutstein demonstrates that mathematics and social justice are not incompatible.

Mary M. Atwater and Regina L. Suriel (Chapter 15) frame social justice education within the scope of critical multicultural education. Their work speaks back to power when they articulate how science can be taught through a culturally relevant lens, despite overwhelming pressure from the field to maintain traditional, disciplinary-specific forms of teaching science. Atwater and Suriel defy national and State standards that exclude issues of social and cultural contexts and student perspectives from science education.

David Stovall and Daniel Morales-Doyle (Chapter 16) also speak to power in their narrative of their work in a charter high school. Stovall and Morales-Doyle discuss the successes, perils, and barriers to doing social justice education in highly contested neighborhood spaces that are defined by race and racism and classism.

Raquel Oxford (Chapter 17) characterizes how language education can be a tool for the social justice educator. Given the close relationships between language and culture, Oxford poses language education as a means to alleviate cultural ignorance. She defines the various categories of language education to highlight issues of power and privilege in education policy, classroom practices, and teacher education that support and deny social justice language education in K-12 classrooms. Throughout the chapter, the author provides examples of classroom activities that push students to rethink their views of race and culture.

Finally, Ira Shor reminds us (Afterword) of the present context that shapes our lives. He calls us to action, asking, "Who will save school and society?" Of course, the answer is, "We will." We will engage without proselytizing, and we will care without patronizing: we will allow each other and ourselves a full humanity that demands equity, democracy, and justice for all of us.

Acknowledgments

Numerous people have made this work possible, from its early inception to its current instantiation. We would like to primarily thank Sonia Nieto, who went from inspiring our work to helping us publish it. She is a truly luminous teacher and scholar, whose grace, generosity, and loving kindness centers our work. Naomi Silverman, editor extraordinaire at Routledge, worked closely with us, guiding our instincts and choices with her rich experience and gentle humor; she deserves our deep appreciation as well.

Thank you to my mom, Bernadine S. Chapman, and my dad, Horace J. Chapman, for setting such fine examples of social justice educators and social justice advocates. Thank you to my sister, Nomathemba Chapman Pressley, my niece, Peyton, and my nephew, Jared, for giving me a psuedo-parental perspective on schools, teachers, and classrooms.

Thanks are due to my late father, Daniel Carl Hobbel, who taught me to love justice, and to my mother, Karin-Elke Hobbel, who taught me to practice pragmatism. Not to acknowledge my extraordinary students, from Petaluma, Analy, Madison, Milwaukee, Humboldt, and beyond would be to ignore those who have enlightened and inspired me the most.

Introduction

Conversations, Problems, and Action

Thandeka K. Chapman and Nikola Hobbel

The cover of this book shows the image of a *dorje*, or *vajra* in Sanskrit. In Tibetan Buddhism, this is an image symbolizing the union of relative and absolute truths, the feminine and the masculine, compassion and wisdom, spirit and commitment. Underlining this series of unions is the idea that the interaction between binaries leads to enlightenment: perhaps a lofty symbol for a textbook! Still, to us, this illustrates the potential of teaching and learning (a transformative, reciprocal, and human experience), even as it is joined to the institution of schooling (which is often dulling and dehumanizing—"drill and kill," "sit still," "wait for the bell"). We use the *dorje* to symbolize our commitment to social justice education as a tool of union and solidarity. Social justice education leads students to *embrace* and *name* their ways of knowing the world through new critical understandings of themselves, their communities, and the larger society. We believe these kinds of understanding are a form of transformation, even enlightenment, that we can all experience.

This book grew out of conversations with colleagues and friends concerning what it means to reach for social justice in K-12 classrooms. Later, these musings on *praxis*, the combination of theory and practice, reflection and action, turned into a successful conference panel. At that time, we knew several colleagues who were engaging in and writing about social justice pedagogy in K-12 learning spaces. We invited those scholars to present with us, and we asked Sonia Nieto to discuss our work. We were extremely pleased to have Professor Emerita Nieto as part of the panel, because we center our work in social justice on her powerful scholarship. Sonia Nieto has used her work in multicultural education for social justice to push scholars to think more holistically about the ties between students' heritage languages, their cultures, and (dis)connections to schooling. She has conducted significant work with preservice and practicing teachers to highlight best practices in multicultural education. Her framework for critical multicultural education culminates with the need for a social justice perspective that transforms the average classroom into a socially engaged teaching and learning environment. Because of this, Sonia Nieto's definition of social justice: *a philosophy, an approach, and actions that embody treating all people with fairness, respect, dignity, and generosity* anchors this text.

According to Nieto and Bode (2008), social justice education should do four things: 1. challenge, confront, and disrupt "misconceptions, untruths, and stereotypes that lead to structural inequality and discrimination based on race, social class, gender, and other social and human differences," 2. provide "all students with the resources necessary to learn to their full potential," 3. draw on the "talents and strengths that students bring to their education," and 4. create a "learning environment that promotes critical thinking and supports agency for social change" (2008, p. 11). These four components of social justice education stand as a comprehensive approach to teaching and learning in K-12 classrooms. Nieto and Bode's definition includes the explicit call to help students develop critical dispositions that help them to reflect on their communities and their world. By providing resources and creating rigorous learning environments, we can help each other and our students excel using both individual and cultural skill sets. This is a definition that culminates in a promise of agency, the ability to enact social change together.

Here, we offer future and practicing teachers the opportunity to engage in strengthening praxis: a reflection-in-action that grows from reciprocal learning and considering the problems, structural and otherwise, inherent in working toward transformative education. Our main goal here is to frame social justice from a gamut of perspectives: historical contexts, theoretical intersections, and practical cases. We want readers to deepen their understanding of the social movements, political events, academic concepts, and curricular components that have shaped current views of social justice pedagogy. Providing each other with the tools to locate our practice and our students' learning in multiple sociopolitical and historical contexts, we move our conversations and problems posed into action.

Educational Scholarship in Social Justice Education

In recent years the proliferation of work in social justice in education has significantly increased. In her annual "year in review" (YIR) of publications on social justice, Professor Emerita Maurianne Adams of the Social Justice in Education Program at the University of Massachusetts at Amherst and editor of *Equity and Excellence in Education* states,

> Even though Social Justice Education is a relatively new field within Education, it has been named increasingly in databases or print resources, sometimes to signal a systemic, multiple-identity approach to issues of discrimination and inequality but also sometimes as an attractive synonym for "diversity." In preparing YIR '07, we were struck by how much more difficult the job had become of winnowing articles we considered useful to teachers, teacher preparation faculty, school personnel, community educators, and people in higher education who are interested in this emergent field. The variety and interdisciplinarity of the field has always presented a challenge to this YIR effort. However, the sheer number and variability of articles using Social Justice or Social Justice Education in the title or among keywords made the YIR project more time-consuming and difficult this year than ever before.
>
> (Adams et al., 2008, p. 483)

Often what we see in social justice education literature takes the form of conceptual scholarship or critiques of traditional pedagogies, assessments, and teacher practices that inhibit social justice education—without adequately defining social justice education. Even when scholars present definitions of social justice education, their articulations seem convenient to their arguments, rather than comprehensive across contexts of inquiry.

Over the past ten years the use of the term "social justice" has been applied to the field of education to identify useful programs and curricula, document practice, and articulate outcomes for the creation of successful models. The increased use of the term "social justice" has led to a diffusion of meaning that threatens to make the concept of social justice ineffective and difficult to document through empirical research. Moreover, the field struggles to capture the everyday practices and professional dispositions of social justice teachers in ways that substantiate their practices and assist other educators in implementing their own visions of social justice education.

How We Came to Social Justice Education

Thandeka's Story

When I was 14, I started attending a magnet school that drew students from around the entire state of Illinois. During those three years, I lived and learned with kids from different racial and ethnic groups, socio-economic classes, and geographic locations. We had a state-of-the-art facility and highly experienced teachers who believed we could learn. These teachers probably would not call themselves critical educators, but their disciplinary approaches to knowledge, the questions they asked us to explore, and the conversations they engaged in with us cultivated our ability to ask deeper questions pertaining to the nature of knowledge, the axis of power and privilege, and the illusion of Truth. Coming from a small, White farming town with a small university, I experienced enlightenment, in the forms of knowledge, empathy, and skills again and again. After high school, I attended Spelman College, one of two Black colleges for women in the U.S.A. At Spelman, the use of critical theory and social justice education were explicit, deeply embedded, and essential. Embracing and being embraced by my African American culture was like having the air around me change so that I could breathe and therefore think more clearly and with more certainty. During both these tremendous experiences, I worked in various educational settings with students who did not have the access or opportunity to learn the way I have learned. Throughout my professional life, my goal to give all students the same rich learning opportunities I have had in my life has never wavered. Multicultural education for social justice is a means to reach this goal.

Nikola's Story

My early school experiences were marked by politics: I attended the John F. Kennedy bilingual school in what was then known as West Berlin, a walled city still occupied by the Allied Forces of World War II. JFKS was populated by British, German, and American students (the French maintained an officer's club as their mark of occupation). The U.S. forces made themselves most visible, running their tanks down the boulevard in front of the school, soldiers waving at us as they rumbled past. We picnicked at the shooting range, picking spent shells from banks of sand dumped in an otherwise leafy park. For me, with my German mother and American father, speaking two languages at home and in school was natural. In addition, from Kindergarten through third grade, my classmates and I had the same homeroom teacher: Helga Albrecht Thiele. This was unusual, but Helga approached the principal each year and asked to continue on with us; she told him that she loved us. When I moved to the United States, my new fifth-grade peers, upon discovering where I came from, asked me if I was a Nazi, and whether my family had dug under the wall or ballooned over it to escape. I was not offended, only nonplussed: how could people know so little about my home? How one's own contexts shape, for better or worse, one's understanding of the world has consequently marked my approach to teaching and my reflection about my own experiences and attitudes. Later, when I became a teacher, I chose to loop with my students, staying with them for years. To me, teaching and learning at its best is always marked by love: not a paternalistic love, but one of engagement with each other, our lives and our communities.

Social Justice Education and Multicultural Education

Through very different pathways, both of us come to social justice education rooted in the traditions of multicultural education (MCE). Scholars of multicultural education and critical theory have used the concept of social justice as forms of praxis in PreK-12 classrooms, education policy, and teacher education research (Baker, 1979; Bigelow, 1990; Cummins, 1986; Gay, 1978; Grant & Sleeter, 1986; Greene, 1986), and education activists have used social justice as a political charge to challenge the status quo (Anyon, 1981; Ayers, 1986; Freire, 1970; Hilliard, 1992). Although they share similar theoretical and social movement backgrounds, the two concepts differ. MCE has a host of approaches to content, practice, and whole school reform that detail the "how-to" of working with children and families. Social justice education is more about the goal of transformation rather than the journey. Multicultural education has different levels of application that show how teachers and schools are incorporating the concepts of equity and equality into their curricula. We have yet to introduce typologies to social justice education because the emphasis has been on the product and not the process (Chapman & Hobbel, 2005)—and, from a Freirean perspective, the process cannot be dictated. These two paradigms can work in concert, as we see in the higher levels of MCE: transformative multicultural education (Banks, 1993), multicultural education for social reconstruction (Grant & Sleeter, 2008). Combining the process with the product is a powerful pedagogical tool. It is our hope that this book helps more educators to combine the MCE and social justice education to create socially just classrooms; however, we emphasize that this text is not a "how-to"—it is designed to be more of a "what if?" a "why so?" and a "think about it."

The *dorje* is said to be an irresistible force: both thunderbolt and diamond, cutting any substance without being cut itself. The reason for this is, in part, because of the unity of opposites. To us, it means that we must reconcile and affirm profound, real, and ideological differences among us and still be able to critique and move towards action. Transformation may take the form of new knowledge about social justice history, theory, or practice. It may take the form of a new or deeper personal understanding of one's own practice and teaching philosophy. Perhaps it will provide someone with the vocabulary to name what he or she wishes to produce in his or her future classroom.

We are ever hopeful that you, if you do not already, come to call yourself a social justice educator—one who can be comfortable being uncomfortable, one who can be challenged and challenging, one who can reconcile and unify for the goal of transforming our schools and society.

References

Adams, M., DeJong, K., Hamilton, C., Hughbanks, C., Smith, T., & Whitlock, E. R. (2008). Review of the year's publication for 2007: Social Justice Education. *Equity & Excellence in Education, 41*(4), 482–537.

Anyon, J. (1981). Social class and school knowledge. *Curriculum Inquiry, 11*(1), 3–42.

Ayers, W. (1986). About teaching and teachers. *Harvard Educational Review, 56*(1), 49–51.

Baker, G. (1979). Policy issues in multicultural education in the United States. *Journal of Negro Education, XLVIII*(3), 253–266.

Banks, J. A. (1993). The canon debate, knowledge construction, and multicultural education. *Educational Researcher, 22*(5), 4–14.

Bigelow, W. (1990). Inside the classroom: Social vision and critical pedagogy. *Teachers College Record, 91*(3), 437–448.

Chapman, T. K. & Hobbel, N. (2005). Multicultural education and its typologies. In S. Farenga & D. Ness (Eds.), *Encyclopedia of Education and Human Development*, Vol. 1 (pp. 296–301). New York: M. E. Sharpe.

Cummins, J. (1986). Empowering minority students: A framework for intervention. *Harvard Educational Review, 56*(1), 18–36.

Freire, P. (1970). The adult literacy process as cultural action for freedom. *Harvard Educational Review, 40*(2), 205–225.

Gay, G. (1978). Multicultural preparation and teacher effectiveness in desegregated schools. *Theory Into Practice, 17*(2), 149–156.

Grant, C. A., & Sleeter, C. E. (1986). Race, class, and gender in education research: An argument for integrative analysis. *Review of Research, 56*(2), 195–211.

Grant, C. A., & Sleeter, C. E. (2008). *Turning on learning: Five approaches for multicultural teaching plans for race, class, gender and disability* (5th ed.). Hoboken, NJ: Wiley.

Greene, M. (1986). In search of a critical pedagogy. *Harvard Educational Review, 56*(4), 427–441.

Hilliard, A. (1992). Why we must pluralize the curriculum. *Educational Leadership, 49*(4), 12–14.

Nieto, S. & Bode, P. (2008). *Affirming diversity: The sociopolitical context of multicultural education* (5th ed.). Boston: Allyn & Bacon.

Part I

Historical Perspectives

Chapter 1

"These are Revolutionary Times"

Human Rights, Social Justice, and Popular Protest

Carl A. Grant and Melissa L. Gibson

Although social justice education in the U.S.A. is frequently historicized in terms of the Civil Rights Movement and twentieth-century protest movements, it also is historically tied to the twentieth-century's human rights initiatives. These human rights pioneers—the drafters of the Universal Declaration of Human Rights and the UN's Human Rights Commission members—are social justice ancestors usually ignored in our American context but whose efforts have indelibly influenced and shaped social justice efforts in the U.S.A. In fact, this history makes clear that the mid-century human rights initiatives were part of a transnational movement for social justice. Reframing social justice education in terms of human rights gives clarity to our work as social justice educators: It strengthens a vision of education as central to promoting human rights and social justice, it refocuses attention not only on civil rights but also social and economic rights, and it explicitly contests our current context of globalization and neoliberal educational reform.

> "In these days of difficulty, we Americans everywhere must and shall choose the path of social justice . . . the path of faith, the path of hope, and the path of love toward our fellow man."
> —*Inscription at the FDR National Memorial, Washington, D.C., from a campaign speech on October 2, 1932, in Detroit, Michigan*

The latter half of the twentieth century in the United States is widely recognized as a period of popular protest and uprising against social injustice. While demands for equality were not universal—as evinced, for example, by the strength of conservative Republicanism under Presidents Nixon and Reagan—this period is nonetheless marked by vocal and organized calls for greater social justice. Often—and somewhat inaccurately—this attention to justice and equality is traced back to the Civil Rights Movement of the 1950s and 1960s. Despite earlier decades' struggles for civil rights, it is the successes and failures of the mid-century that are narrated in the popular imagination as spawning later social justice movements, including the Women's Rights Movement, the Gay Rights Movement, the American Indian Movement, the Black Nationalist Movement, the labor campaigns typified by the United Farm Workers' struggles under the leadership of Cesar Chavez, and the Disability Rights Movement. These struggles continue into the twenty-first century: In the face of the continuing specter of racism and social inequality, we have seen, for example, mass protests such as the 2006 Day Without an Immigrant marches and the post-September 11 attention to protecting civil liberties and ending racial and religious profiling. Together, these make up what could be deemed a social justice movement.

This is, however, all well-trod territory. Whether looking at a high school history textbook on twentieth-century American history, Howard Zinn's (2005) *A People's History of the United States,* popular media attention to the legacies of the 1960s (e.g., Darman, 2007; Time, 1988), or even in James Banks's (2004) oft-cited history of multicultural education, the history and effects of the aforementioned protest movements are well discussed in both popular and scholarly literature. Given this well-known civil rights timeline—and given its inattention to the social justice work of earlier decades—we instead want to historicize social justice education in a new context. To do this, we will look to the Universal Declaration of Human Rights (1945–1951), which itself drew on the social justice efforts of earlier movements and time periods while also becoming an antecedent manifesto and foundation for later movements.

Born of a historical moment when the world was explicitly concerned with protecting social justice (Morsink, 1999), the Universal Declaration of Human Rights (UDHR) affords a unifying and global conception of justice. By delving into the history of the UDHR,[1] we argue that (1) this is in fact a social justice manifesto, and (2) this social justice manifesto continues to shape global discourse about justice, equity, and social responsibility. Next, we turn back to the aforementioned protest movements to show how our contemporary notions of justice and equality—however unrealized they may be—are rooted in the ideals of the UDHR. We then connect the UDHR and the social justice ideals of subsequent protest movements to contemporary ideas of social justice education. Finally, we will look at the ways that these twentieth-century conceptions of justice compel twenty-first-century attention to globalization.

Our ultimate hope is not to present a monolithic, over-simplified history of social justice—we know, for example, that another side to this story is America's elevation of property rights above all other rights (Harris, 1993; Ladson-Billings & Tate, 1995). We recognize that there are multiple social justice histories, each impartial on its own; our goal is not to present The History, but to stimulate discussion about the many roots of our work, which too often remain a mirage. As British-born economist and philosopher Friedrich Hayek's asserts, "[W]hole books and treatises have been written about social justice without ever offering a definition of it. It is allowed to float in the air as if everyone will recognize an instance of it when it appears" (Novak, 2000, p. 11). This chapter attempts to pull social justice history back down to earth.

The Universal Declaration of Human Rights as a Social Justice Manifesto

The Historical Context: Confronting Injustice and Promoting Human Rights in the United Nations

In the first half of the twentieth century, the world was confronted with injustice, aggression, and economic collapse on a massive scale. In the wake of social cataclysm—including two world wars, the Great Depression, and the dismantling of colonial empires—there was unprecedented international attention to the cause of social justice and the codification of a universal moral code (Glendon, 2001; Ishay, 2004; Morsink, 1999). In fact, Woodrow Wilson, in his 1918 "Fourteen Points Address" calling for the creation of the League of Nations, declared the need for an international body devoted to protecting and promoting social justice (Ishay, 2004). However, this call was not realized until after World War II, when the war's tragedies—including the Jewish Holocaust[2]—cemented the need for an international mandate to intervene on behalf of justice (Morsink, 1999). A few weeks after Germany's 1945 surrender, 51 nations signed the United Nations Charter, finally realizing Wilson's call (Glendon, 2001).

Explicit in the UN's Charter were four goals: to prevent future wars; to establish international justice; to promote social progress and improved standards of living; and "to affirm faith in fundamental human rights, in the dignity and worth of the human person, in the equal rights of men and women and of nations large and small" (UN, 1945, Preamble). This affirmation of human rights is often seen as a pragmatic approach to justice, a tool outlining minimum standards of human dignity, a tool whose use could move the world towards greater justice socially, economically, and politically (Appiah, 2003; Ignatieff, 2003; Koenig, 1997; Mower, 1979). While human rights themselves are certainly not *guarantees* of social justice (Gutmann, 2003), they are essential tools for working towards it (Carolan, 2000).

Indeed, the early years of the UN's existence were marked by a near-singular attention to codifying this human rights—and, by extension, social justice—agenda (Morsink, 1999). Three months after its founding, the UN articulated the Nuremburg Principles, which would be the guiding principles in the prosecution of Nazi war criminals during the Nuremburg Trials. The Nuremburg Principles—and the Convention on the Prevention and Punishment of the Crime of Genocide that grew out of them—were the UN's first human rights treaties, written in direct response to what was seen at the time as an ultimate act of social *in*justice and a cataclysmic violation of human rights, the Holocaust (Ishay, 2004; Morsink, 1999).

The next human rights initiative was undertaken during the UN's first General Assembly meeting in January 1946, when it established a Human Rights Commission whose primary task would be to author an international bill of rights (Glendon, 2001). The U.S.A.—particularly Franklin Delano Roosevelt—heavily influenced this work (Glendon, 2001; Hareven, 1968; Mower, 1979). In his "Four Freedoms" speech, FDR declared world peace to be founded on four freedoms:

The first is freedom of speech and expression—everywhere in the world. The second is freedom of every person to worship God in his own way—everywhere in the world. The third is freedom from want—which, translated into world terms, means economic understandings which will secure to every nation a healthy peacetime life for its inhabitants—everywhere in the world. The fourth is freedom from fear—which, translated into world terms, means a world-wide reduction of armaments to such a point and in such a thorough fashion that no nation will be in a position to commit an act of physical aggression against any neighbor—anywhere in the world.

(Roosevelt, 1941)

These "four freedoms" are widely seen at providing the UN's core human rights framework (Anderson, 2003; Glendon, 2001; Ishay, 2004; Johnson, 1987; Mower, 1979); in fact, protecting these "four freedoms" was explicitly named in the Atlantic Charter as a justification for U.S. involvement in World War II (Anderson, 2003). The "four freedoms" importantly hit on two central points in the consideration of human rights: one, that the rights to be protected were both civil/political and economic/social; and two, that international peace was itself a human right (Mower, 1979). What's more, these "four freedoms" reflect FDR's domestic vision of an economic and political system more just than unbridled capitalism—economic freedom meant more than the freedom of markets; it meant that individuals should be *guaranteed* a "freedom from want" (Ishay, 2004). FDR advocated for government guarantees of certain economic rights, including job protection, economic security, and the sharing of economic and scientific progress (Roosevelt, 1944). Moreover, FDR explicitly named this vision "choosing the path of social justice," as commemorated at his own memorial in Washington, DC.

It was, however, Eleanor Roosevelt as chair of the Human Rights Commission who ensured that the UN lived up to this vision (Glendon, 2001; Johnson, 1987; Mower, 1979). At the time, Roosevelt was considered by dominant American society to be an outspoken advocate for social justice and civil rights—serving as a board member of the National Association for the Advancement of Colored People (NAACP), setting up a controversial concert for Marian Anderson at the Lincoln Memorial, defying Jim Crow in Southern establishments (Anderson, 2003). She, like her husband, saw social responsibility and social justice as fundamental to world peace:

[T]he basis of world peace is the teaching which runs through almost all the great world religions: 'Love your neighbor as yourself' . . . [W]hen we center on our own home, family, or business, we neglect this fundamental obligation of every human being, and until it is acknowledged and fulfilled, we cannot have world peace.

(in Mower, 1979, p. 20)

As the founder of Human Rights Day, leader of the UDHR drafting, and international advocate for human rights, Eleanor Roosevelt left an indelible mark on our understanding of human rights and social justice (Glendon, 2001; Johnson, 1987; Morsink, 1999; Mower, 1979).

Codifying Human Rights and Social Justice in the Universal Declaration of Human Rights

> "[The UN members] believe that men and women, all over the world, have the right to live . . . free from the haunting fear of poverty and insecurity. They believe that they should have . . . more complete access to the heritage . . . of civilization so painfully built by human effort. They believe that science and the arts should combine to serve peace and the well-being, spiritual as well as material, of all men and women without discrimination of any kind. They believe that . . . the power is in their hands to advance . . . this well-being more swiftly than in any previous age."
>
> —*"The Grounds of an International Declaration of Human Rights"*
> *(UNESCO, 1949, p. 259)*

The initial work of the Human Rights Commission strongly pushed to define human rights primarily in terms of racial anti-discrimination, largely as a response to the Holocaust—a genocide fueled by overt racial and ethnic hatred (Morsink, 1999). This focus was widely supported by delegates from the Philippines, Egypt, India, the Dominican Republic, Cuba, France, the Soviet Republics, Latin America, and even Roosevelt herself (Glendon, 2001; Hareven, 1968). In fact, in its survey of the world's rights traditions, UNESCO (1949)[3] found anti-discrimination and the acceptance of difference to be one of the most common refrains.

This emphasis on anti-discrimination reflects the UDHR's grounding in empathy and morality. In fact, an early draft written by French delegate and Nobel Peace Prize-winner René Cassin was written not to take political sides in the burgeoning Cold War, but rather to articulate common international moral standards. This moral stance was clarified by Chinese philosopher and delegate P. C. Chang, who proposed the Chinese symbol *ren*—which roughly translates to "two-man mindedness" and evokes empathy and compassion—as the overarching human rights principle (Glendon, 2001). Indeed, the very will to declare human rights was, according to Lebanese delegate Charles Malik, "about an international moral will" (Glendon, 2001, p. 86).

From Wilson's initial call for the promotion of social justice to the explicit discussion of justice in its Charter, one of the UN's moral stands was focused on advocating for and working toward the ultimate goal of social justice (Ishay, 2004). Parties as diverse as Syria, who called for the inclusion of social justice in the UDHR (Glendon, 2001), and Eleanor Roosevelt, who saw the UN's mission as furthering social justice (Hareven, 1968), advocated for this vision. This is certainly *not* to say that all nations were equal advocates for social justice. To the contrary, the most powerful governments—the U.K., the USSR, the U.S.A.—strongly resisted human rights, particularly when they challenged domestic policies. In the end, however, other nations—China, Syria, India, Argentina—banded together to insist on its pre-eminence in the UN's mission (Anderson, 2003; Glendon, 2001; Johnson, 1987; Morsink, 1999; Mower, 1997).

As understood by the UN delegates, human rights led to social justice by challenging unequal hierarchies of power, amplifying the voices of the weak, and eliminating poverty, discrimination, and exploitation—the root causes of conflict (Glendon, 2001; Ishay, 2004; UNESCO, 1949). President Truman described this nexus of concerns at the signing of the UN Charter: "Experience has shown how deeply the seeds of war are planted by economic rivalry and *social injustice*" (emphasis added; Glendon, 2001, p. 238). Over forty years later, Secretary General of the UN Boutros Boutros-Ghali echoed Truman in his description of the UN's primary aim as "address[ing] the deepest causes of conflict: economic despair, social injustice and political oppression" (in Andreopoulos, 1997, p. 11). This attention to economic inequality, unequal power hierarchies, and political oppression remain the focus of twenty-first century social justice and human rights work, including within education.

What, then, are the specific rights guaranteed by the UDHR that move the world toward greater social justice? Roughly, the UDHR included two categories of rights—political/civil and social/economic—and they strongly reflected FDR's "four freedoms": "freedom of speech and belief and freedom from fear and want [have] been proclaimed as the highest aspiration of the common people" (UN, 1948b, Preamble). Furthermore, the UDHR declared the equality of all humans by guaranteeing the right to self-determination and freedom from tyranny, oppression, and exploitation. Human rights scholar Michael Ignatieff (2003) argues that these freedoms—to self-determination and from oppression— are deeply linked: "We know from historical experience that when human beings have defensible rights—when their agency as individuals is protected and enhanced—they are less likely be abused and oppressed" (Ignatieff, 2003, p. 4). *All* persons—regardless of race, nationality, creed, gender, age, religion, or any other identity status—were granted international rights to challenge injustice, barbarism, and oppression.

In its 30 articles, the UDHR outlaws slavery, servitude, torture, arbitrary arrest, detention, and interference in private matters. It affirms equal recognition and protection before the law, fair trials domestically and internationally, and innocence until proven guilty. It guarantees freedom of movement, residence, speech, religion, thought, and opinion. It also guarantees the right to asylum, to a nationality, to marry and have a family, to own property, to change one's religion, to participate in government, to social security, to work at the job of one's choosing, to be paid an equal and living wage, to organize and join trade unions, to ample rest and leisure, to an adequate standard of living (with specific reference to food, clothing, housing, medical care), to free and compulsory elementary schooling, to an education that promotes human rights and allows for self-actualization, to participate in the cultural life of the community, and to international peace (United Nations, 1948b, Articles 1–30). The UDHR attempts to protect these rights by articulating what governments must *do* and guarantee in order to foster a minimum level of social, political, and economic equality.

As is clear from this catalogue of guarantees, the UDHR conceived of human rights far more broadly than traditional Western civil rights. In what was seen as a radical departure from the Western rights tradition, which focused only on personal liberties, the UDHR included rights for economic opportunity, protection, and development (Glendon, 2001; Ishay, 2004; Johnson, 1987; Richardson, 2000). While early drafts took these largely verbatim from the 1948 Bogota Conference's Pan-American Declaration of Rights—a document in the dignitarian rights tradition rather than the civil rights tradition[4]—they also directly reflected the Roosevelts' conceptions of social justice (Glendon, 2001). For example, in FDR's 1944 State of the Union address, he outlined his "second bill of rights," which would ensure for every citizen a good education; a useful and remunerative job; a wage capable of meeting basic needs; adequate medical care; basic protection from the fears of old age, sickness, accident, and unemployment; and the right of every family to a decent home (Roosevelt, 1944).

This unlikely combination of two rights traditions on opposite sides of the Cold War battle ground—civil and political rights associated with the liberal/democratic tradition of the West and social and economic rights with the socialist/communist tradition of the East—is evidence of the Human Rights Commission's understanding of the role of social inequality in fomenting aggression. Reiterated throughout drafting were the assertions that political independence and economic sovereignty go hand in hand, that international security and civil rights depend on economic justice, and that genuine justice ensures an individual's personal *and* economic security (Glendon, 2001; Ishay, 2004; Morsink, 1999; UNESCO, 1949). In this, human rights offers a broader framework for social justice than civil rights (Anderson, 2003).

The UDHR also goes beyond civil rights in its inclusion of not merely *rights* but also *responsibilities* (Glendon, 2001; Ishay, 2004; UNESCO, 1949; Morsink, 1999). In Western rights theory, the role of the state is usually limited to ensuring that individual liberties (e.g., to speech, to property) are not compromised. However, in the UDHR, the state is responsible for actively providing for the economic and social welfare of its citizens—through the guarantees of equal wages, decent housing, and social services. Whereas the civil rights tradition might simply guarantee an individual the right to work if jobs are available, the UN's articulation of human rights would instead guarantee that any individual who wants to work *will* work and, what's more, will be given equal pay for equal work, earning enough for an adequate standard of living. In this, the government does more than protect against intrusions on individual liberty; the government guarantees a certain standard of living. This was a widely supported rights philosophy (Glendon, 2001; Ishay, 2004), one that emphasized collective responsibility. Perhaps Mahatma Gandhi (UNESCO, 1949) explained this most famously:

> I learnt from my illiterate but wise mother that all rights to be deserved and preserved came from duty well done. Thus the very right to live accrues to us only when we do the duty of citizenship of the world. From this one fundamental statement, perhaps it is easy enough to define the duties of Man and

Woman and correlate every right to some corresponding duty to be first performed. Every other right can be shown to be a usurpation hardly worth fighting for. (p. 18)

Fundamentally, human rights are not just *rights*, but responsibilities to uphold (Ishay, 2004).

Working in the "Small Places": Promoting Human Rights and Social Justice via Education

"Education shall be directed to the full development of the human personality and to the strengthening of respect for human rights and fundamental freedoms. It shall promote understanding, tolerance, and friendship among all nations, racial or religious groups, and shall further the activities of the UN for the maintenance of peace."

—*The Universal Declaration of Human Rights, Article 26.2*

The UDHR guarantees for all people the right to education. While early drafts limited this to free and compulsory elementary education, by the final Declaration, education had been given a prominent role in fostering respect for human rights. The Preamble itself names education as *the* vehicle for promoting human rights: "[T]his Universal Declaration of Human Rights . . . shall strive *by teaching and education* to promote respect for these rights and freedoms" (emphasis added; UN, 1948b). The emphasis on education as the arbiter of human rights reflects one of the many compromises made about the role of the state in protecting human rights (Glendon, 2001). Even American Secretary of State John Foster Dulles—who was one of the staunchest opponents of the entire human rights project, along with President Eisenhower, under whom he served—argued that it was the role of *education* (and not governments) to foster a human rights culture (Anderson, 2003; Hareven, 1968). In fact, UDHR drafter Cassin attributed more power to education than legal tribunals: "Legal force of itself is only a secondary safety valve: it is the education of young people and even of adults that constitutes the primary and real guarantee for minority groups faced with racial hatred that leads so easily to violence and murder" (in Osler & Starkey, 2000b, p. 94). In the view of the UDHR drafters, only education could cultivate a global human rights culture. No government, no law, and no war could cultivate respect for human dignity and difference the way that a human rights education could.

Indeed, the UNESCO philosopher's survey (1949) revealed near global unanimity that education should "facilitate the mutual understanding of the peoples of the world" (p. 269) and ready citizens for their governmental and social responsibilities, including the protection and promotion of social justice. By promoting the human right to education as something more than compulsory and free elementary education, the UDHR drafters seemed to answer educator I. L. Kandel's challenge of whether human rights education would be "education for acquiescence or education for freedom" (UNESCO, 1949, p. 223)—whether human rights education would encourage critical thought about human rights and unequal power structures or maintain allegiance to the status quo. In the end, the UDHR—with the support even of human rights opponents—came down on the side of "education for freedom."

Human Rights Muddles and the Cultural Imperialism of the UDHR

While the UDHR attempts to be a universal document guaranteeing the rights of all, there are problems with this vision of justice. For example, the UDHR is frequently critiqued for promoting a compromised vision of justice, a vision warped by Cold War politicking and, as a result, a vision that fails to protect the weak and oppressed (Anderson, 2003; Glendon, 2001; Morsink, 1999). Human rights are also critiqued for the American exceptionalism embedded in them—the American idea, present during the drafting process and continuing today, that human rights are only for export and that American life is above international rebuke (Jenkins & Cox, 2005). Additionally, the human rights framework is strongly critiqued by feminist legal scholar Catherine MacKinnon (1993) for ignoring the specific rights and needs of women.

Perhaps most worrisome, however, is the critique of the UDHR as culturally imperialist. It is increasingly common for the very notion of 'universal' human rights to be critiqued as a fundamentally Western perspective that invalidates the right to cultural and political self-determination (Burke, 2006; Glendon, 2001; Howard, 1997/8; Ishay, 2004). In addition to the argument that universal rights themselves are a Western imposition, it is also argued that the supremacy of the civil/political and social/economic rights of the individual over any kind of collective rights reflects Western priorities (Howard, 1997/8)—a bias that continues to beg justification in current discourse (e.g., Appiah, 2003; Ignatieff, 2003; Rawls, 1993). These cries of cultural imperialism were further justified when powerful UN members denied colonial territories' demands for human rights and independence (Ishay, 2004). Human rights were universal, it seemed, so long as their protection did not challenge traditional power structures.

Although the human rights framework did stem, in part, from an American vision, it was actually the other, less powerful members of the UN who became its most outspoken advocates (Mower, 1979). In fact, it was *China*—included in a UN founding conference as a token gesture—who pushed for the explicit inclusion of human rights, justice, and racial equality in the Charter. The three other conference participants—the U.S.A., the U.K., and the USSR—fought these references (Anderson, 2003). China was loudly joined by political and philosophical leaders such as Mahatma Gandhi (India), Carlos Romulo (Philippines), Charles Malik (Lebanon), Ho Chi Minh (Vietnam), Kwame Nkrumah (Ghana), Léopold Senghor (Senegal), and even African American scholar W.E.B. DuBois in declaring the need for *universal* human rights (Ishay, 2004).

The aforementioned UNESCO philosophers' survey (1949) additionally confirmed that these rights were *universal* human rights. Although the codification of rights was historically a Western undertaking (e.g., the Bill of Rights, the Declaration of the Rights of Man), UNESCO found that, "where basic human values are concerned, cultural diversity had been exaggerated . . . a core of fundamental principles was widely shared in countries that had not yet adopted rights instruments and in cultures that had not embraced the language of rights" (Glendon, 2001, p. 222). Chang, for example, strongly argued that rights were for everyone, not just Westerners (Glendon, 2001); Chung-Sho Lo (UNESCO, 1949) spoke of the Confucian responsibility of fulfilling duties to one's neighbors; and Humayan Kabir (UNESCO, 1949) discussed Islam as a model of human rights. When drafting the UDHR, the Human Rights Commission was deliberate about including these diverse voices and traditions. In fact, the earliest drafts were strongly influenced by the 1948 Pan-American Declaration of Rights and included rights from the constitutions of Scandinavia and the Soviet Republics as well as from Asian philosophy; later drafts included the perspectives of Asia and the Middle East.

However, save for South Africa, there was no African representation during these foundational meetings; most of Africa was still under colonial yoke (Morsink, 1999). By the time of the Covenants, however, independent African nations played a prominent role in writing these treaties (Hareven, 1968). What's more, 22 different postcolonial, African constitutions make explicit mention of human rights, which also figure prominently in the Charter of the Organization of African Unity (Mower, 1979). In fact, the language of human rights was central in anti-colonial and anti-imperialist struggles. Even at the 1955 Bandung Conference, one of the first gatherings of what would subsequently come to be called the "Third World," human rights were critical for *challenging*—rather than perpetuating—Western imperialism (Burke, 2006).

What is blatantly missing from the UDHR is any guarantee of minority or group rights (Burke, 2006; Howard, 1997/8; Morsink, 1999). For the postcolonial world, cultural and group rights have been intricately linked to the right to self-determination—at the heart of the Covenants. During the UDHR drafting process, there was significant pressure to guarantee minority rights. Malik even proposed including the statement, "Cultural groups shall not be denied the right to free self-development," but it was defeated by both North and South Americans (Glendon, 2001, p. 119). Eleanor Roosevelt—despite publicly recognizing "the evils that underdeveloped nations are trying to correct" (Emblidge, 2001, p. 185)—argued that minority rights didn't apply in the Americas because of what she called the "assimilationist ideal": "[P]eople who come to [American] shores do so because they want to become citizens of our countries. They leave behind certain economic, religious, and social conditions that they wish to shed and prefer to be assimilated into the new country that they are adopting" (Glendon, 2001, p. 161). In the end, the Americans won: there is no guarantee of group rights in the UDHR.

Human Rights, Popular Protest, and Social Justice in the Late Twentieth Century

A New International Language of Justice

> "There are two sides to the human rights program. Freedom of expression, freedom of worship, freedom of suffrage. But much closer to the people in the new world is the question of something to eat and a better life."
>
> —*Eleanor Roosevelt (Johnson, 1989, p. 36)*

As already detailed, the first half of the twentieth century and, in particular, the immediate post-World War II context were a time explicitly concerned with social justice. By looking to this history, we see that social justice was broadly conceived as the protection of both individual liberties and economic security in order to promote world peace. Most central to this period's conception of social justice was an awareness of inequality, brutality, and oppression, and implicit in this was the honoring and valuing of diverse cultural, political, and religious views. Finally, conceptions of justice were fundamentally guided by empathy, morality, and a sense of social responsibility. Human rights were the specific guarantees—for example, to equal pay, an adequate standard of living, or the freedom of thought—that could promote this vision of social justice the world over. In turn, this vision—which is more comprehensive than American civil rights—"lent wings to movements that would soon bring down colonial empires" (Glendon, 2001, p. xvi). Indeed, these human rights documents—by codifying an international language for describing oppression, inequality, and brutality—provided oppressed peoples with a new framework for speaking out for justice and equality. Despite modern-day critiques of human rights as culturally imperialist, the language of human rights has nevertheless fueled "colonial revolutions abroad and the civil rights revolution" in the U.S.A. (Ignatieff, 2003, p. 6).

In fact, by the 1950s, world leaders from Africa and Asia were some of the strongest proponents of human rights—as seen, for example, in their prominence at the 1955 Bandung Conference (Burke, 2006). Despite the compromises and Western worldview embedded within, the *language* of human rights was a powerful tool for challenging imperial domination and domestic discrimination: South African Moses Kotane used human rights to condemn apartheid; Ghana's Kwame Nkrumah and Senegal's Léopold Senghor referred to human rights in their calls for African independence; and the Philippines' Carlos Romulo used human rights to point to the tyranny of domestic elites (Burke, 2006). Leaders for justice the world over—from Martin Luther King, Jr. to Pope John XXIII—seized the language of human rights (Glendon, 2001).

Human Rights and the American Civil Rights Movement

> "The time has arrived for the Democratic Party to get out of the shadow of states' rights and walk . . . into the bright sunshine of human rights."
> —*Minneapolis Mayor and eventual Democratic presidential candidate Hubert Humphrey, at the 1948 Democratic National Convention*
> *(Anderson, 2003, p. 124)*

Human rights were deeply connected with the Civil Rights Movement. In the immediate post-World War II context, the NAACP looked to link the struggle for African American equality and justice at home to the global struggle against imperialism and for human rights (Anderson, 2003). As Executive Director Walter White noted in 1944, African Americans took "literally the shibboleths of the Four Freedoms . . . [and] they intend[ed] to secure and enjoy those freedoms and to put an end to the old order in which men, solely because they are colored, can be worked to exhaustion, exploited, despised, spat upon and derided by those whose chief right to sovereignty is whiteness of skin" (Anderson, 2003, p. 17). The "four freedoms"—as articulated in FDR's State of the Union address, the Atlantic Charter, and eventually the UDHR itself—went beyond civil rights by naming specific human rights, including the right to an equal and living wage, the right to an education promoting citizenship and self-actualization, the right to adequate health care, the right to move freely and to choose one's residence, the right to a decent standard of living, and the right to marry whomever one wants (UN, 1948b). These social and economic rights were a "lifeline" for those mired in the injustices of Jim Crow (Anderson, 2003, p. 137).

What's more, the UDHR drafting process revealed the power of human rights language to shame America's discriminatory practices. Throughout drafting, both the U.S.A. and the Soviet Union regularly used the language of human rights to call attention to one another's Cold War hypocrisies. The Soviets drew particular attention to the U.S.A.'s oppressive treatment of African Americans: By pointing out everything from unequal wages and segregated housing to lynchings and police brutality, the UDHR became an explicit language of rights with which the U.S.A. could be called to task. In fact, using the language of human rights, the U.S.A. was named as the same kind of discriminatory state as the burgeoning apartheid regime of South Africa (Anderson, 2003; Dudziak, 2000; Glendon, 2001; Hareven, 1968; Ishay, 2004; Johnson, 1987).

A human rights framework also supported post-World War II fights for equality. For example, returning black veterans launched the "Double V" campaign of World War II—"Victory at home, victory abroad"—in which they linked their fight for justice and democracy in Europe to the fight for African American equality at home. The NAACP also challenged Winston Churchill's 'racing' of the four freedoms of the Atlantic Charter—he claimed that these freedoms were for whites only—by demanding a seat at the negotiating table of the UN. Using the language of human rights even empowered African American leaders to challenge President Truman's belief that African Americans wanted "justice, not social equality" (Anderson, 2003, p. 2) by arguing that social and economic equality were necessary correlates for social justice.

In addition, African American organizations thrice petitioned the UN to intervene on behalf of the U.S.A.'s human rights violations against African Americans: the National Negro Congress's 1946 petition, *A Petition to the United Nations on Behalf of 13 Million Oppressed Negro Citizens of the United States of America;* the NAACP's 1947 petition, *An Appeal to the World;* and the Civil Rights Congress's 1951 petition, *We Charge Genocide.* All three petitions were an attempt to lift the struggle for racial equality and justice in the U.S.A. to an international arena, both because such an international focus might pressure the U.S.A. into taking greater action at home and because it explicitly connected the struggle for African American equality with the struggle for equality, justice, and human rights internationally (Anderson, 2003; Dudziak, 2000).

The NAACP's petition, *An Appeal to the World,* was brought before the General Assembly in 1947—before the UDHR had been drafted or approved. In it, the

NAACP highlighted the hypocrisy of both the U.S.A. and—as a result of its failings to uphold the Charter's ideals—the UN: By ignoring African Americans' denial of human rights, the UN and the U.S.A. failed to live up to the explicit declarations of human rights and racial equality outlined in the Charter and, later, the UDHR. The petition described conditions of African American life that were in clear violation of human rights, such as exclusion from elections, persecution of activists, the tolerance of lynching, sanctioned discrimination, and inadequate housing, health care, and education. The petition also directly appealed to international outrage about the Holocaust: it compared the sub-human living conditions of urban ghettoes to Jewish ghettoes; it decried the physical brutality and terrorism targeted at African Americans fighting for equal education at the same time that the U.S.A. was fighting genocide and fascism abroad; and it described American racist groups who were explicitly modeled after Nazi Storm Troopers and who used 'state's rights' to successfully defend their racism. The NAACP argued that such overt denial of human rights threatened the rights of other nations and peoples, directly opposed the work and ideals of the UN, and made a mockery of international human rights.

The final petition was submitted by the Civil Rights Congress (CRC; a Communist Party-affiliated organization; see Anderson, 2003) in 1951. *We Charge Genocide* detailed similar human rights violations as the NAACP's—including segregation, Jim Crow laws, political disenfranchisement, police and public brutality, a corrupt justice system, and statistics on quality of life differentials—but this time, it linked these violations to the Convention on Genocide:

> [A]ny of the following acts committed with intent to destroy, in whole or in part, a national, ethnical, racial or religious group, as such: (a) Killing members of the group; (b) Causing serious bodily or mental harm to members of the group; (c) Deliberately inflicting on the group conditions of life calculated to bring about its physical destruction in whole or in part; (d) Imposing measures intended to prevent births within the group; (e) Forcibly transferring children of the group to another group.
>
> (UN, 1948a, Article II)

The CRC argued that states, politicians, and organizations within the U.S.A. were engaged in "conspiracy to commit genocide" and "direct and public incitement to commit genocide" (UN, 1948a, Article III), both international crimes as laid out in the Convention on Genocide. Because the federal government took virtually no action to prevent these crimes of genocide, it was complicit, again an international crime according to the Convention. Appealing to the General Assembly as the "conscience of mankind" (Patterson, 1951, p. 57), the CRC argued that the entire project of the UN was undermined by U.S. violations of international treaties at home—what irony that the U.S.A. was complicit in genocide yet one of its Supreme Court justices presided over the Nuremburg Trials! The UN's Charter explicitly linked the prevention of war with the prosecution of genocide and the securing of human rights; failing to secure those rights in the U.S.A. not only made a mockery of the UN's mission, but it also threatened world peace.

Neither petition was ultimately successful in catalyzing a UN intervention; both were, in fact, actively silenced and stymied by UN leadership and even Eleanor Roosevelt herself, who was worried about embarrassing the U.S.A. and fueling Soviet critiques of the U.S.A. Despite this, the petitions *were* successful at publicly humiliating the U.S.A. for its civil and human rights violations (Anderson, 2003; Dudziak, 2000; Glendon, 2001). The language of human rights proved to be a powerful way, both domestically and internationally, to challenge U.S. inequities and injustices. This power was the very reason that Roosevelt and the other U.S. representatives worked so hard to *prevent* African Americans from linking their domestic struggle with human rights. Opponents knew that doing so might open the U.S.A. to international critique and intervention (Dudziak, 2000; Hobbins, 1998). Unfortunately, the tangle of Cold War politics eventually led the NAACP and other civil rights leaders to abandon this more powerful human rights platform for the limited equality afforded by civil rights alone—American politicians were unwilling to give any ground on human rights lest it seem to the world that they were admitting to the very criticisms Soviet Russia used against them (Dudziak, 2000). Historian Carol Anderson (2003) goes so far as to argue that the Civil Rights Movement ultimately failed because it *couldn't* maintain the human rights connection. In fact, she argues that persistent inequality in contemporary America is a *direct result* of the NAACP's abdication of a human rights platform. Inequality persists because of repeated human rights violations in education, health care, and housing—violations that "have just become part of the accepted day-to-day grind for black America" (p. 272).

Human Rights, Protest Movements, and Social Justice Principles

> "I have the audacity to believe that peoples everywhere can have three meals a day for their bodies, education and culture for their minds, and dignity, equality and freedom for their spirits. I believe that what self-centered men have torn down, men other-centered can build up. I still believe that one day mankind will . . . be crowned triumphant over war and bloodshed, and nonviolent redemptive goodwill will proclaim the rule of the land."
>
> —*Martin Luther King, Jr., Nobel Prize Acceptance Speech (1964)*

Human Rights as Social Justice

While the NAACP and early civil rights leaders may have abandoned human rights, later movements actually drew on human rights in their vision of social change—both explicitly in the descriptions of their work as well as implicitly in the goals of their work, most of which correspond directly to the human rights outlined in the UDHR. For example, both Martin Luther King, Jr., and Malcolm X longed to transform the Civil Rights Movement into a human rights movement (Anderson, 2003). King wrote his "Letter from a Birmingham Jail" (1963) while imprisoned for work he was doing on behalf of the Alabama Christian Movement for Human Rights and spoke eloquently about the demands of the "human rights revolution" (King, 1968), while Malcolm X argued:

> The American black man is the world's most shameful case of minority oppression. . . . How is a black man going to get "civil rights" before he first wins his *human* rights? If the American black man will start thinking about his *human* rights, and then start thinking of himself as part of one of the world's greatest people, he will see he has a case for the United Nations.
> (original emphasis; Malcolm X & Haley, 1972, p. 207)

Malcolm X echoed earlier petitions to the UN when he argued that *human* rights superceded and subsumed civil rights. What's more, civil rights could only be granted to citizens, to *humans,* and as long as the U.S.A. continued to deny African Americans their full human rights, they would remain less-than-human in the eyes of white America, remaining persecuted and oppressed.

King and Malcolm X were not alone. In its 1966 Statement of Purpose, the National Organization of Women (NOW) declared:

> We . . . believe that the time has come for a new movement toward true equality for all women in America, and toward a fully equal partnership of the sexes, as part of the *world-wide revolution of human rights* now taking place within and beyond our national borders. . . . We realize that women's problems are linked to many broader questions of social justice; their solution will require concerted action by many groups. Therefore, convinced that human rights for all are indivisible, we expect to give active support to the common cause of equal rights for all those who suffer discrimination and deprivation.
> (emphasis added; Friedan, 1966)

Feminist and NOW member Gloria Steinem (1970) even went so far as to describe her own political work not as feminist, but as humanist. Within the Gay Rights Movement, two of the most active advocacy groups orient themselves to human rights—the Human Rights Campaign and the International Gay and Lesbian Human Rights Commission, whose mission is to "secure the full enjoyment of the human rights of all people and communities subject to discrimination or abuse on the basis of sexual orientation" (IGLHRC, 2008). Even the Gay Liberation Front, an activist/protest group that sprung up as a result of the 1969 Stonewall Riots, described their mission of promoting gay rights as intricately linked with human rights:

> We see the persecution of homosexuality as part of a general attempt to oppress all minorities and keep them powerless. Our fate is linked. . . . Therefore we declare our support as homosexuals or bisexuals for the struggles of the black, the feminist, the Spanish-American, the Indian, the Hippie, the Young, the Student, and other victims of oppression and prejudice.
> (Gay Liberation Front, 1969)

In this, they not only drew on the framework of human rights but also demonstrated two principles of contemporary social justice—empathy and solidarity.

Finally, Cesar Chavez described the United Farm Workers' struggle as "seek[ing] our basic, God-given rights as human beings. . . . To the growers and to all who oppose us, we say the words of Benito Juarez: 'Respect for another's right is the meaning of peace'" (UFW, 2008, par. 120). The promise and realization of human rights were central to the UFW's labor struggles.

Cultural Pluralism as Social Justice

All of the social justice movements of the twentieth century were working towards social changes codified by the UDHR. First—and perhaps most significantly—is the commitment to cultural pluralism. Given that universal human rights originated as a means of protecting humanity from the brutality of state-sponsored racism and that the UDHR names anti-discrimination as one of its guiding moral principles, human rights are fundamentally guided by cultural pluralism (Ignatieff, 2003; Osler & Starkey, 2000a/b). Certainly, this commitment often gets watered down to tolerance, but the role of diversity in human rights is more than mere anti-discrimination. As Peter Figueroa (2000) explains,

> Citizenship (in a plural society) involves commitment to the society in its diversity; openness to, and indeed solidarity with and respect for, the different other, in particular the "ethnically" different; acceptance of the basic equal worth of all people, of the rights and responsibilities of all; and a rejection of any form of exploitation, inequitable treatment or racism. (p. 57)

A social justice commitment to diversity is about more than the mere fact of difference; rather, a social justice commitment to diversity is more akin to pluralism, or "the [civic and social] engagement that creates a common society from all that plurality" (Eck, 2006). In this, social justice—like human rights—explicitly fights against discrimination. After all, the persistence of institutional racism (and sexism, able-ism, classism, and homophobia) is a direct threat to human rights and to democracy (Ignatieff, 2003; Osler & Starkey, 2000a).

In fact, many social justice protest movements grew in response to the stubborn persistence of institutional racism. In doing so, these protest movements articulated and fought for a vision of the world where cultural pluralism was realized and where diverse voices and experiences were not only honored but also made integral to civil society. For example, the American Indian Movement (AIM) states that one prong of its mission is the restoration and revival of native cultures (Wittstock & Salinas, 2008); NOW "envision[s] a world where there is recognition and respect for each person's intrinsic worth as well as the rich diversity of the various groups among us" (NOW, 1998); and UFW's Chavez warned that, "Preservation of one's own culture does not require contempt or disrespect for other cultures" (UFW, 2008). In a pluralistic society, cultural difference and disagreement are not *threats* to a socially just civil society; rather, they *enrich* and *ensure* a civil society committed to social justice.

Voice as Social Justice

A corollary to cultural pluralism is a commitment to giving voice to the weak and the oppressed. After all, at the heart of social protest movements and the UDHR—as well as social justice education—is providing "an avenue of power for the disadvantaged" (Richardson, 2000, p. 82) by allowing the claims of victims to speak louder than the claims of oppressors and by preventing the tyranny of marginalized groups (Ignatieff, 2003; Spencer, 2000). Giving voice to the weak and oppressed is *how* human rights—and ultimately, social justice—are realized. AIM works toward this end by insisting on the rights of native peoples to interpret treaties and to address the federal government (Wittstock & Salinas, 2008), while the Human Rights Campaign actively works to elect officials who will speak on behalf of gay, lesbian, bisexual, and transgender individuals (HRC, 2008). Perhaps Martin Luther King, Jr. (1967) describes this work most powerfully: "We are called to speak for the weak, for the voiceless, for victims of our nation and for those it calls enemy." Providing the opportunity for the voices of the less powerful to be heard is one way of fighting for that fundamental human right to self-determination. In working for self-determination, human rights and social protest are "empowering the powerless, giving voice to the voiceless" (Ignatieff, 2003, p. 70).

Economic and Social Rights as Social Justice

However, the most fundamental way in which social justice movements align with a human rights framework is in their constant demands for the economic and social rights guaranteed in the UDHR: equal pay for equal work, living wages, adequate health care, social support for the impoverished, equitable and meaningful education, and reducing the gap between rich and poor, among others. Human rights cannot be divorced from social and economic arrangements—justice and rights are inextricably linked (Witkins, 1998). As political philosopher Amy Gutmann (2003) argues, "Starving people are denied their human agency. They are also being denied their dignity, and they are being degraded. They are not being treated as agents with a human life to lead" (p. xii). Social justice movements recognized this, and so they advocated for the economic and social rights of all citizens: AIM vows to "reclaim and affirm health, housing, employment, economic development, and education for all Indian people" (Wittstock & Salinas, 2008); NOW (1998) "envision[s] a world where social and economic justice exist, where all people have the food, housing, clothing, health care and education they need"; the Gay Liberation Front (1969), after the Stonewall Riots, demanded the right of homosexuals to own their businesses and run their own organizations; the UFW struggled not merely for employment security and rights but also for the protection of the physical health of farm workers (Chavez, 1989); Martin Luther King Jr. and Myles Horton launched a Poor People's Campaign in which a "multiracial army of the poor" would demand economic justice; and the Individuals with Disabilities in Education Act demanded that individuals with disabilities be afforded equal educational opportunities. All of these movements are *centrally* concerned with the litany of social and economic rights guaranteed by the UDHR.

State Action as Social Justice

Finally, these social justice movements understand the complicity of the state in perpetuating inequality—and thus the state's responsibility for eliminating inequality. As King (1967) famously declared about the war in Vietnam:

> True compassion is more than flinging a coin to a beggar; it is not haphazard and superficial. It comes to see that an edifice which produces beggars needs restructuring. A true revolution of values will soon look uneasily on the glaring contrast of poverty and wealth. With righteous indignation, it will look across the seas and see individual capitalists of the West investing huge sums of money in Asia, Africa and South America, only to take the profits out with no concern for the social betterment of the countries, and say: "This is not just."

This is precisely the perspective called for by a UN Special Rapporteur on the Right to Education when arguing that schools (a vehicle of the state), rather than trying to correct 'socially excluded' individuals, needed to recognize and address the 'statal' and systemic exclusions and discriminations that oppress students—to understand that 'socially excluded' students are made this way through state actions and inactions—and to understand that it is a *human rights obligation* to address these systemic inequalities (Alderson, 2000).

Clarifying Social Justice Education through the Universal Declaration of Human Rights

> "Teaching for social justice might be thought of as a kind of popular education— of, by, and for the people—something that lies at the heart of education in a democracy, education toward a more vital, more muscular democratic society. It can propel us toward action, away from complacency, reminding us of the powerful commitment, persistence, bravery, and triumphs of our justice-seeking forebears—women and men who sought to build a world that worked for us all. Abolitionists, suffragettes, labor organizers, civil rights activists: Without them, liberty would today be slighter, poorer, weaker—the American flag wrapped around an empty shell—a democracy of form and symbol over substance."
>
> —*Bill Ayers, "Social Justice and Teaching" (2008)*

Given the connection between human rights and social justice and the central role of education in promoting both, social justice education can be understood as fulfilling the vision of global justice and human dignity promoted by the UDHR. To make this claim, it is important to clarify social justice education—a complicated task, as the field is often critiqued for its lack of a uniform definition. As Gloria Ladson-Billings (2006) argues, social justice education is "less a thing and more an ethical position" (p. 40).

Two theories of social justice writ large are used to frame social justice education and to clarify its ethical positions. The first is John Rawls' (1971) theory of distributive justice, which, as summarized by Cochran-Smith (2008), "focuses on equality of individuals, civic engagement, and a common political commitment to all citizens' autonomy to pursue their own ideas of the good life" (p. 7). In this theory of distributive justice, *in*justice is rooted in macro-level, political/economic structures that cause exploitation and material deprivation and prevent self-actualization. The second framework is Nancy Fraser's (1997) dualism of the politics of redistribution and the politics of recognition. In this theory, there is the acknowledgment that injustice can stem not just from one's unfair exclusion from the macro-level political and economic order but also from the denial of one's lived experience, identity, and culture. Justice is not simply the redistribution of material resources but also the recognition and acceptance of diversity. Justice is about economic and political rights as well as pluralism.

Theories of social justice *education* build from these two frameworks. For example, Marilyn Cochran-Smith (2008) describes teaching for social justice as an intellectual approach to the inescapably political work of schooling. The three key components to her theory—equity of learning opportunities, respect for social groups, and teaching through tension—lead to the goal of promoting students' learning and enhancing their life chances. Teaching for social justice must connect "distributive justice, which locates equality and autonomy at the center of democratic societies, with current political struggles for recognition, which challenge the school and knowledge structures that reinforce the disrespect and oppression of social groups" (p. 12). Another articulation is North's (2006): If the ultimate goal of social justice is the restructuring of the political economy, or ensuring the UDHR's economic and political rights, then social justice education must "challenge the existing hierarchies of power, embracing difference [and] challenging cultural imperialism" (p. 510). Finally, Grant and Agosto (2008) describe social justice as the ultimate *aim* of education, where social justice is a regulative system of fairness that ensures the security of citizens, pushes for distributive equality and interrogates why distributive inequalities exist, and aims for the elimination of institutionalized domination. Social justice education is, ultimately, "education for freedom," where the promotion of basic human rights and dignity fosters social change: "Teaching for social justice is teaching that arouses students, engages them in a quest to identify obstacles to their full humanity, to their freedom, and then to drive, to move against those obstacles. And so the fundamental message of the teacher for social justice is: You can change the world" (Ayers, 1998, p. xvii). By embracing cultural differences and promoting pluralism, by challenging cultural imperialism and unequal hierarchies of power, by interrogating material inequalities and advocating for economic justice, and by equipping students with the skills necessary to be active democratic citizens, social justice education is working for a world that honors fundamental human rights. At its core, social justice education builds on Rawls's (1971) notion of self-actualization to enact an education that promotes "the full development of the human personality" (UDHR, 1948, 26.2).

In fact, social justice education attempts to realize the UDHR's vision for education—to educate about basic human rights and fundamental human dignity, to foster the dispositions and attitudes that protect human rights, and to allow for individuals' self-actualization and personal development. In realizing this vision, social justice education emphasizes equipping students with the tools necessary to fulfill their democratic responsibilities (Ayers, 2008; Cochran-Smith, 2008; Grant & Agosto, 2008), with one of the central tools being critical thinking (Applebaum, 2008; Cochran-Smith, 2008; Gutmann, 1999; Gutstein, 2005). This critical thinking is honed through curricular attention to inequality, injustice, and the violation of rights. For example, in Eric Gutstein's (2008; and see Chapter 14 in this volume) high school math classes, his students apply mathematical knowledge, such as probability, to current events. In one example, his students determined the statistical likelihood that the black defendants in the Jena 6 case could have 'randomly' received the all-white juries that they did. In social justice pedagogy, the central purpose of educational content—literacy, numeracy, scientific and historical inquiry, the arts—is to raise students' critical consciousness and to help them become advocates for justice and human rights.

This is, after all, the precise role of education laid out in the UDHR. As a former Director General of UNESCO explained, "Education for human rights and democracy in the last analysis means the empowerment of each and every individual to participate with an active sense of responsibility in all aspects of political and social life" (Spencer, 2000, p. 28). Education for human rights—like Ayers's (2008) description of social justice education as "the heart of education in a democracy, education toward a more vital, more muscular democratic society"—is committed to preparing students for a deliberative democracy that values diversity, social responsibility, and human rights. This education becomes a means of resisting systemic inequality and discrimination. In fact, this articulation of "education for freedom"—or education that encourages students to examine their world with empathy and an eye towards justice—was central to Eleanor Roosevelt's vision of human rights (Harevan, 1968). She explained this role:

> Where, after all, do universal human rights begin? In small places, close to home—so close and so small that they cannot be seen on any maps of the world. Yet they are the world of the individual person; the neighborhood he lives in; the school or college he attends; the factory, farm, or office where he works. Such are the places where every man, woman and child seeks equal justice, equal opportunity, equal dignity without discrimination. Unless these rights have meaning there, they have little meaning anywhere.
> (UN Department of Public Information, 1997, par. 7)

For Roosevelt, schools were both the seedbeds for and the ultimate realization of human rights, where citizens first learned about and first experienced human rights. This, according to Glendon (2001), is what is most striking about the UDHR: "[T]he most remarkable feature of the Declaration [is] its attention to the 'small places' where people first learn about their rights and how to exercise them responsibly—families, schools, workplaces, and religious associations" (p. 240). Without these 'small places,' human rights and social justice will never be realized.

Conclusion: Social Justice and Human Rights Education in an Era of Globalization

In the post-World War II context, the NAACP understood that white supremacy transcended national borders. The treatment of African Americans at home was intimately linked to colonial and imperial domination the world over (Anderson, 2003). Their insight into the internationalism of oppression rings even more true today. In an era of globalization—an era of the "primacy of property rights over human rights" (Sleeter, 2008, p. 144)[5]—a social justice framework has become even more critical: promoting equality, justice, and human dignity is necessary for challenging global imperialism. But when both George Bush (Office of the Press Secretary, 2007) and Bill Ayers (2008) can claim 'social justice' as central to their work, it is obvious the term needs clarification. Historicizing social justice in terms of human rights can clarify this politically contested term—as well as the ultimate aims of social justice education.

In particular, a human rights framework explicitly and importantly challenges the prevailing view that twenty-first century education is solely for market preparation and for serving the needs of capital (Grant & Grant, 2007; Lipman, 2001; Sleeter, 2008). Instead, in the language of human rights and in the aims of social justice, we see a mandate—an *international* mandate—for education that contributes to self-realization, to respect for human rights, and to a flourishing and whole life. This vision not only reframes education as a public good rather than a marketable commodity, but it also demands that education be directed toward cultivating an informed and democratic citizenry. Education for citizenship was central to Thomas Jefferson's vision of American democracy, and it remains especially crucial today. Human rights and social justice education can empower citizens to contest the marketization of their education, their democracies, and themselves (Grant & Grant, 2007). Indeed, human rights—as framed by the UDHR, as reinvigorated by the aforementioned social protest movements, and as advocated for today—explicitly challenges the primacy of capital over human dignity and social justice, instead asserting the basic human right to a living wage, an adequate standard of living, and social security, as well as the *state's responsibility to protect and provide for these rights.* Human rights become a powerful antidote to unbridled capitalism and imperialist greed.

Finally, by grounding social justice in the language of human rights, we are also reminded of the promises of our globalized world—of the interconnectedness of world citizens (Blackmore, 2000), of the possibilities of cosmopolitanism to triumph over nativism (Appiah, 2003; Parker, 2004), of the internationalism of struggles for social justice (Apple and Buras, 2006; Maran, 1999)—and of the ways that education can attend to and build on these promises through multicultural curricula and pedagogy promoting pluralism, equality, and human rights.

Whether looking at worsening living conditions for America's growing lower classes (Anyon, 2005), the increasing poverty of the world's poorest nations and citizens (Ishay, 2004), the far-reaching social and economic effects of globalization (Lipman, 2001), the enduring armed conflicts of the world, or the persistence of genocide, it is clear that we have not yet achieved the vision of social justice set out by the Human Rights Commission. Martin Luther King, Jr.'s (1967) words still ring true: "These are revolutionary times. All over the globe men are revolting against old systems of exploitation and oppression, and out of the wombs of a frail world, new systems of justice and equality are being born." We are *still* working for "the advent of a world in which human beings shall enjoy freedom of speech and belief and freedom from fear and want . . . the highest aspiration of the common people" (UN, 1948b, Preamble).

Points of Inquiry

- How did the shift from human rights to civil rights affect the discourses surrounding the rights of minority groups?
- Why is it important to provide students with a sense of history or histories when discussing social justice?
- How does the UN document on human rights align or challenge current issues of globalization, the environment, and other social issues?
- Let's look at how this chapter speaks to various content areas:
  - Social Studies: history, international education, democracy, studying the UN
  - English/Language Arts: national and international perspectives of writers' interpretations of what it means to be human, maintain a democracy, be a citizen
  - Arts/music: artistic interpretations of struggle and humanity; the role(s) the arts play in humanity and humanness, art/music history studies of period artists, art as protest
  - Science: ethical considerations for science, the history of human rights abuse in the name of science, institutional review boards (IRBs) as an example of the protection of human rights, use of scientific inquiry to resolve human rights atrocities
  - Math: statistics and data analysis of human rights abuses and their outcomes.

Points of Praxis

- Use the documents in the chapter to build a lesson plan on primary sources.
- Read human rights declarations from around the world as part of a unit of globalization.
- Read auto/biographies of the Roosevelts.
- Debate the currency of the document today.
- Apply the document to current conflicts: Who is in violation of the UN decree? Who is protecting human rights? Debate both sides of the conflict.

Notes

1 While we are focusing on the Universal Declaration of Human Rights (UDHR), there were two human rights documents written and ratified at the UN from 1945–1948: the Convention on the Prevention and Punishment of the Crime of Genocide and the UDHR. The UDHR was written as a statement of general human rights aims without reference to enforcement; its supplemental, legally binding treaties on human rights—the International Covenant on Civil and Political Rights and the International Covenant on Economic, Social, and Cultural Rights (referred to jointly as the Covenants)—were written in 1966 (Glendon, 2001).

2 The naming of Hitler's genocide of European Jewry as the Holocaust is contested. On the one hand, "holocaust" is the English translation for the Hebrew word given to this tragedy, *Shoah*—a word that, in Hebrew, came to be the proper noun naming this genocide. On the other hand, other groups subjected to genocide contest the claiming of the word "holocaust" by a single people. Out of respect for other genocides—most of which receive far less media, historical, or political attention—some refer to specific Holocausts: the Jewish Holocaust, the Rwandan Holocaust, the African Holocaust. Yet this, too, is contested, and can be seen as a means of diminishing the catastrophic consequences of anti-Semitism. We recognize both sides of this complicated debate; we understand that the naming of history has real political and social consequences. However, given the World War II context of this chapter, we will refer to this genocide as the Holocaust. Our editors disagree with this choice.

3 Concurrent to the Human Rights Commission's work on drafting an "international bill of rights," the United Nations Educational and Scientific Committee (UNESCO) set about surveying philosophers, politicians, scholars, scientists, and educators the world over in order to determine if there even were such a thing as *universal* human rights. UNESCO collected its responses and submitted them to the Human Rights Commission as evidence that there were, indeed, universal human rights; as guidance as to what those universal rights were; and as a warning about the limits of crafting a universal declaration. While the Human Rights Commission did not use UNESCO's survey in its drafting process, most of UNESCO's findings correspond to the final UDHR (Glendon, 2001; UNESCO, 1949).

4 Two distinct rights traditions are codified in rights documents. The first tradition, Western civil rights, is associated with the British, French, and American revolutionary documents; civil rights protect property, life, and liberty as well as the freedoms of speech, religion, and assembly. In this tradition, the emphasis is on "individual liberty and initiative more than equality or social solidarity and was infused with a greater mistrust of government" (Glendon, 2001, p. xvii). On the other hand, dignitarian rights—also referred to as second-generation rights—emphasize equality, fraternity, and collective responsibility, balancing individual liberties with social responsibility. The state plays an active role in guaranteeing rights as well as protecting and providing for the needy. Dignitarian rights include the right to work, to education, and to basic subsistence. This tradition is most associated with social democracies such as in Scandinavia and Latin America (Glendon, 2001; Ishay, 2004; Morsink, 1999).

5 We define globalization as the process of "increased economic, cultural, environmental, and social interdependencies and new transnational financial and political formation arising out of the mobility of capital, labor and information, with both homogenizing and differentiating tendencies" (Blackmore, 2000, p. 33). More specifically, globalization is characterized by the growing international centrality of capital markets and by the reframing of "all social relations, all forms of knowledge and culture in terms of the market," with "[a]ll human production and all sites of social intercourse, all services that a society establishes for the common good . . . potential targets for investment and profit making" (Lipman, 2001). We recognize that there are multiple globalizations, ranging from cultural and technological exchange to neo-liberal expansion (Santos, 2002; Sleeter, 2003). In all, we see two trends: Increased economic inequality and the increased possibility for trans-national social protest.

References

Alderson, P. (2000). Practicing democracy in two inner city schools. In Osler, A. (Ed.), *Citizenship and democracy in schools: Diversity, identity, and equality* (pp. 125–132). Stoke on Trent, UK: Trentham Books.

Anderson, C. (2003). *Eyes off the prize: The United Nations and the African American struggle for human rights, 1944–1955.* New York: Cambridge University Press.

Andreopoulos, G. (1997). Human rights education in the post-Cold War context. In Andreopoulos, G., & Claude, R. (Eds.), *Human rights education for the twenty-first century* (pp. 9–20). Philadelphia: University of Pennsylvania Press.

Anyon, J. (2005). *Radical possibilities: Public policy, urban education, and a new social movement.* New York: Routledge.

Appiah, K. (2003). Grounding human rights. In Gutmann, A. (Ed.), *Michael Ignatieff: Human rights as politics and idolatry* (pp. 101–116). Princeton, NJ: Princeton University Press.

Apple, M., & Buras, K. (2006). *The subaltern speak: Curriculum, power, and educational struggles.* New York: Routledge.

Applebaum, B. (2008). Is teaching for social justice a 'liberal bias'? *Teachers College Record, 110*(12).

Ayers, W. (1998). Foreword: Popular education—Teaching for social justice. In Ayers, W., Hunt, J., & Quinn, T. (Eds.), *Teaching for social justice: A democracy and education reader* (pp. xvii–xxx). New York: Teachers College Press.

Ayers, W. (2008). Social justice and teaching. Retrieved May 11, 2008, from: http://billayers.wordpress.com/2008/05/07/social-justice-and-teaching/

Banks, J. (2004). Multicultural education: Historical development, dimensions, and practice. In Banks, J., & Banks, C. (Eds.), *Handbook of research on multicultural education* (2nd ed.), (pp. 3–29). San Francisco: Jossey Bass.

Blackmore, J. (1999). Localization/globalization and the midwife state: Strategic dilemmas for state feminism in education. *Journal of Education Policy, 14*(1), 33–54.

Burke, R. (2006). "The compelling dialogue of freedom": Human rights at the Bandung Conference. *Human Rights Quarterly 28,* 947–965.

Carolan, S. (2000). Parents, human rights, and racial justice. In Osler, A. (Ed.), *Citizenship and democracy in schools: Diversity, identity, and equality* (pp. 185–192). Stoke on Trent, UK: Trentham Books.

Chavez, C. (1989). Address at Pacific Lutheran University, Tacoma, Washington. Retrieved from: http://www.ufw.org/_page.php?menu=research&inc=history/10.html

Cochran-Smith, M. (2008). Toward a theory of teacher education for social justice. Paper prepared for the annual meeting of the American Educational Research Association, April, New York City.

Darman, J. (2007). 1968: The year that changed everything. *Newsweek,* November 10.

DuBois, W.E.B. (Ed.) (1947). *An appeal to the world: A statement on the denial of human rights to minorities in the case of citizens of Negro descent in the United States of America and an appeal to the United Nations for redress.* New York: National Association for the Advancement of Colored People.

Dudziak, M. (2000). *Cold War Civil Rights: Race and the image of American democracy.* Princeton, NJ: Princeton University Press.

Eck, D. (2006). From diversity to pluralism. Cambridge, MA: The Pluralism Project at Harvard University. Retrieved from: http://www.pluralism.org/pluralism/essays/from_diversity_to_pluralism.php

Emblidge, D. (Ed.), (2001). *My Day: The best of Eleanor Roosevelt's acclaimed newspaper columns, 1936–1962*. Cambridge, MA: DaCapo Press.

Figueroa, P. (2000). Citizenship education for a plural society. In Osler, A. (Ed.), *Citizenship and democracy in schools: Diversity, identity, and equality* (pp. 47–62). Stoke on Trent, UK: Trentham Books.

Fraser, N. (1997). *Justice interruptus: Critical reflections on the "postsocialist" condition*. New York: Routledge.

Friedan, B. (1966). The National Organization for Women's 1966 Declaration of Purpose. Retrieved from: http://www.now.org/history/purpos66.html

Gay Liberation Front (1969). A radical manifesto: The homophile movement must be radicalized! Retrieved from People *with* a history: An online guide to lesbian, gay, bisexual, and trans* history: http://www.fordham.edu/halsall/pwh/1969docs.html

Glendon, M. (2001). *A world made new: Eleanor Roosevelt and the Universal Declaration of Human Rights*. New York: Random House.

Grant, C., & Agosto, V. (2008). Teacher capacity and social justice in teacher education. In Cochran-Smith, M., Feiman-Nemster, S., McIntyre, D., & Demers, K. (Eds.), *Handbook of research in teacher education* (pp. 176–200). London: Taylor and Francis.

Grant, C., & Grant, A. (2007). Schooling and globalization: What do we tell our kids and clients? What are we being told? *Journal of Ethnic and Cultural Diversity in Social Work, 16*(3/4), 213–225.

Gutmann, A. (1999). *Democratic education*. Princeton, NJ: Princeton University Press.

Gutmann, A. (2003). Introduction. In Gutmann, A. (Ed.), *Michael Ignatieff: Human rights as politics and idolatry* (pp. vii–xxvii). Princeton, NJ: Princeton University Press.

Gutstein, E. (2005). *Reading and writing the world with mathematics: Toward a pedagogy for social justice*. London: RoutledgeFalmer.

Gutstein, E. (2008). Critical multicultural approaches to mathematics education in urban, K-12 classrooms. Paper presented at the annual meeting of the American Educational Research Association, March 25, New York.

Hareven, T. (1968). *Eleanor Roosevelt: An American conscience*. Chicago: Quadrangle Books.

Harris, C. (1993). Whiteness as property. *Harvard Law Review, 106*(8), 1707–1791.

Hobbins, A. J. (1998) Eleanor Roosevelt, John Humphrey, and the Canadian opposition to the Universal Declaration of Human Rights: Looking back on the 50th anniversary of UNDHR. *International Journal, 53*, 325–342.

Howard, R. (1997/8). Human rights and the culture wars: Globalization and the universality of human rights. *International Journal, 53*, 94–112.

Human Rights Campaign (HRC) (2008). Mission statement. Retrieved from Human Rights Campaign website: http://www.hrc.org/about_us/2528.htm

Ignatieff, M. (2003). Human rights as politics and idolatry. In Gutmann, A. (Ed.), *Michael Ignatieff: Human rights as politics and idolatry* (pp. 3–98). Princeton, NJ: Princeton University Press.

International Gay and Lesbian Human Rights Commission (IGLHRC) (2008). What we do and why. Retrieved from International Gay and Lesbian Human Rights Commission website: http://www.iglhrc.org/site/iglhrc/section.php?id=25

Ishay, M. (2004). *The history of human rights: From ancient times to the globalization era*. Berkeley, CA: University of California Press.

Jenkins, A., & Cox, L. (2005). Bringing human rights home. *The Nation*, June 27.

Johnson, M. (1987). The contributions of Eleanor and Franklin Roosevelt to the development of international protection for human rights. *Human Rights Quarterly, 9*, 19–48.

King, M. (1963). Letter from Birmingham jail, April 16. Retrieved from the Martin Luther King, Jr., Research and Education Institute: http://www.stanford.edu/group/King/popular_requests/frequentdocs/birmingham.pdf

King, M. (1964). Nobel Prize acceptance speech, December 10. Retrieved from: http://nobelprizes.com/nobel/peace/MLK-nobel.html

King, M. (1967). Beyond Vietnam, April 4. Retrieved from the Martin Luther King, Jr., Research and Education Institute, http://www.stanford.edu/group/King/.

King, M. (1968). I've been to the mountaintop, April 3. Retrieved from The Martin Luther King, Jr., Research and Education Institute: http://www.stanford.edu/group/King/publications/speeches/I%27ve_been_to_the_mountaintop.pdf

Koenig, S. (1997). Foreward. In Andreopoulos, G., & Claude, R. (Eds.), *Human rights education for the twenty-first century* (pp. xiii–xvii). Philadelphia: University of Pennsylvania Press.

Ladson-Billings, G. (2006). "Yes, but how do we do it?" Practicing culturally relevant pedagogy. In Landsman, J., & Lewis, C. (Eds.), *White teachers/diverse classrooms: A guide to building inclusive schools, promoting high expectations, and eliminating racism* (pp. 29–42). Sterling, VA: Stylus.

Ladson-Billings, G., & Tate, W. (1995). Toward a critical race theory of education. *Teachers College Record, 97*(1), 47–68.

Lipman, P. (2001). Bush's education plan, globalization, and the politics of race. *Cultural Logic [on-line], 4*(1). Retrieved from: http://clogic.eserver.org/4-1/lipman.html

MacKinnon, C. (1993). Crimes of war, crimes of peace. In Shute, S., & Hurley, S. (Eds.), *On human rights: The Oxford Amnesty lectures, 1993* (pp. 83–110). New York: Basic Books.

Malcolm X, & Haley, A. (1972). *The autobiography of Malcolm X.* New York: Ballantine.

Maran, R. (1999). International human rights in the US. *Social Justice, 26*(1), 49–71.

Morsink, J. (1999). *The Universal Declaration of Human Rights: Origins, drafting, and intent.* Philadelphia: University of Pennsylvania Press.

Mower, A. G. (1979). *The United States, the United Nations, and human rights: The Eleanor Roosevelt and Jimmy Carter eras.* Westport, CT: Greenwood Press.

National Organization for Women (NOW) (1998). Declaration of sentiments for the National Organization for Women. Retrieved from: http://www.now.org/organization/conference/1998/vision98.html

North, C. (2006). More than words? Delving into the substantive meaning(s) of "social justice" in education. *Review of Educational Research, 76*(4), 507–535.

Novak, M. (2000). Defining social justice. *First Things, 108,* 11–13.

Office of the Press Secretary (2007). Fact sheet: Advancing the cause of social justice in the Western Hemisphere, March 5. Retrieved from: http://www.whitehouse.gov/news/releases/2007/03/20070305-4.html

Osler, A., & Starkey, H. (2000a). Citizenship, human rights and cultural diversity. In Osler, A. (Ed.), *Citizenship and democracy in schools: Diversity, identity, and equality* (pp. 13–18). Stoke on Trent, UK: Trentham Books.

Osler, A., & Starkey, H. (2000b). Human rights, responsibilities and school self-evaluation. In Osler, A. (Ed.), *Citizenship and democracy in schools: Diversity, identity, and equality* (pp. 91–109). Stoke on Trent, UK: Trentham Books.

Parker, W. (2004). Diversity, globalization, and democratic education: Curriculum possibilities. In Banks, J. (Ed.), *Diversity and citizenship education: Global perspectives* (pp. 433–458). San Francisco: Jossey Bass.

Patterson, W. (Ed.), (1951). *We charge genocide: The historic petition to the United Nations for relief from a crime of the United States government against the Negro people.* New York: Civil Rights Congress.

Rawls, J. (1971). *A theory of justice.* Cambridge, MA: Belknap Press of Harvard University Press.

Rawls, J. (1993). The law of peoples. In Shute, S., & Hurley, S. (Eds.), *On human rights: The Oxford Amnesty lectures, 1993* (pp. 41–82). New York: Basic Books.

Richardson, R. (2000). Human rights and racial justice: Connections and contrasts. In Osler, A. (Ed.), *Citizenship and democracy in schools: Diversity, identity, and equality* (pp. 79–90). Stoke on Trent, UK: Trentham Books.

Roosevelt, F. (1941). "Four Freedoms" speech/Annual message to Congress, January 6. Selected Public Papers of FDR, Franklin D. Roosevelt Public Archives. Franklin D. Roosevelt Presidential Library and Museum (hosted). Retrieved from: http://www.fdrlibrary.marist.edu/4free.html

Roosevelt, F. (1944). State of the Union message to Congress, January 11. In Woolley, J., & Peters, G., (Eds.), *The American Presidency Project* [online]. Santa Barbara, CA: University of California (hosted), Gerhard Peters (database). Retrieved from: http://www.presidency.ucsb.edu/ws/?pid=16518

Santos, B. (2002). Toward a multicultural conception of human rights. In Hernandez-Truyol, B. (Ed.), *Moral imperialism: A critical anthology* (pp. 39–60). New York: NYU Press.

Sleeter, C. (2003). Teaching globalization. *Multicultural Perspectives, 5*(2), 3–9.

Sleeter, C. (2008). Teaching for democracy in an age of corporatocracy. *Teachers College Record, 110*(1), 139–159.

Spencer, S. (2000). The implications of the human rights act for citizenship education. In Osler, A. (Ed.), *Citizenship and democracy in schools: Diversity, identity, and equality* (pp. 19–32). Stoke on Trent, UK: Trentham Books.

Steinem, G. (1970). Women's liberation aims to free men, too. *Washington Post,* June 7. Retrieved from: http://scriptorium.lib.duke.edu/wlm/aims/

Time Magazine, Inc. (1988). *1968: The year that shaped a generation,* January 11, 1988.

United Farm Workers (UFW) (2008). Education of the heart—quotes by Cesar Chavez. Retrieved from: http://ufw.org/_page.php?menu=research&inc=history/09.html

United Nations (UN) (1945). Charter of the United Nations. Retrieved from: http://www.un.org/aboutun/charter/index.html

United Nations (1948a). Convention on the Prevention and Punishment of the Crime of Genocide. Retrieved from: http://www.un.org/millennium/law/iv-1.htm

United Nations (1948b). Universal Declaration of Human Rights. Retrieved from: http://www.un.org/Overview/rights.html

United Nations Department of Public Information (1997). *All human rights for all: The Universal Declaration of Human Rights press kit.* Retrieved from: http://www.un.org/rights/50/carta.htm

United Nations Educational, Scientific and Cultural Organization (UNESCO) (Ed.), (1949). *Human rights: Comments and interpretations, a symposium edited by UNESCO with an introduction by Jacques Maritain.* New York: Columbia University Press.

Witkin, S. (1998). Human rights and social work. *Social Work, 43*(3),197–201.

Wittstock, L., & Salinas, E. (2008). A brief history of the American Indian Movement. Retrieved from: http://www.aimovement.org/ggc/history.html

Zinn, H. (1980/2005). *A people's history of the United States: 1492 to present.* New York: Harper Collins.

Chapter 2

Federal Education Policy and Social Justice Education

Christine E. Sleeter

This chapter argues that federal policy can serve conflicting purposes. On the one hand, it is necessary for protecting rights when states and local governments refuse to do so. Federal policy can serve as a moral compass guiding ethical decisions, a needed legal foundation for efforts to protect and defend rights, and a source of funding to augment inadequate local resources. On the other hand, policy is often ignored or shaped by powerful groups to serve their own interests, giving the illusion more than the substance of change. To explore these issues, the chapter examines three forms of policy tools beginning with the landmark Brown v. Board of Education: court cases, funding levers, and regulations. Each is discussed in terms of one or two forms of inequity, including racial segregation, language policy, disability policy, gender inequity, and social class. The chapter argues that, while the tools by themselves do not constitute a panacea since both dominant groups as well as historically oppressed groups use the same policy tools to advance their interests, educators need to be familiar with the history of their use.

I am often asked whether I think the U.S.A., like Canada, should have an explicit national policy supporting multicultural education. The question leaves me feeling ambivalent, however. As I show in this chapter, policy can serve conflicting purposes. On the one hand, federal policy is necessary for protecting rights when states and local governments refuse to do so. Federal policy can serve as a moral compass guiding ethical decisions, and a needed legal foundation for efforts to protect and defend rights. Federal policy can also provide resources to augment inadequate resources at state and local levels. On the other hand, policy is often ignored or shaped by powerful groups to serve their own interests, giving the illusion more than the substance of change. Policy can also extend regulation and control, as Popkewitz (1991) argued based on an analysis of state teacher credentialing standards. Browne-Marshall (2007) discusses this dual use of the law (establishing versus challenging inequity) very clearly:

> Laws were enacted to create slavery, deprive Blacks and other people of color of their basic human rights, and maintain a socioracial hierarchy based on a White power structure. For centuries, Blacks and their advocates of goodwill have utilized every available method to challenge a socioracial hierarchy

that would relegate those of African descent to the lowest tier of American society. (pp. xxxiii–xxxiv)

Laws and court cases became helpful for challenging oppression that laws had been used to establish.

To explore how conflicting purposes, uses, and responses to federal policy play out with respect to equity and education, and to offer examples, I will examine three (often interrelated) forms of policy tools: court cases, funding, and regulations. I will discuss each in terms of one or two forms of inequity that social movements using these tools have challenged or attempted to challenge. (The U.S.A. privileges the role of the states in educational policy, but space does not permit me to review policy at those levels, except in direct relationship to federal policy.) I will argue that understanding the potential of these policy tools is useful, but the tools by themselves do not constitute a panacea since dominant groups who benefit from existing social arrangements use the same policy tools. However, those who wish to advance equity and equality in schools need to be familiar with a history of their use.

The next section of this chapter focuses on uses of the courts to challenge racism, which subsequent federal policies challenging other forms of inequity were then able to build on. Following that is a discussion of federal funding and its use to help shape and enforce policy, with examples of language and disability that illustrate the interplay between court cases and funding. Then the chapter turns to the use of published regulations that accompany federal funding, with a focus on gender equity, to show how regulations operationalize particular meanings of equity. Court cases, funding legislation, and regulations interact, however; my separation of them is only for the purpose of looking at how each works. The chapter then examines the management of inequity (as opposed to direct challenges to inequity), with a focus on how federal policy has framed social class and education. The chapter concludes by returning to the question of whether there should be a policy for multicultural education, in light of the issues examined in the chapter.

Challenging Racial Segregation through the Courts

Litigation and legislation, especially when connected with social movement and strong moral values, can provide leverage for justice. Since the U.S. Supreme Court ruling in *Brown v. Board of Education* (1954) is popularly hailed as the basis for subsequent efforts to use the federal legal system as a tool for social justice in education, I will begin with it. The 1954 *Brown* decision (*Brown I*) overturned *Plessy v. Ferguson* (1896), which had upheld the constitutionality of racially segregated public facilities. *Brown I* established the principles that separate schools are inherently unequal, and that opportunity for education is a right that must be made available on equal terms.

Brown I did not simply emerge from the ether, but had a long history leading up to the decision. The earliest case brought by African Americans seeking access to education was *Roberts v. Boston* in 1850, which challenged Boston's policy of racially segregated schooling. The state court decided in favor of the city; the

Roberts decision subsequently served as legal precedent upholding segregation in the many cases that African Americans filed (Brown, 2004; Browne-Marshall, 2007). *Gong Lum v. Rice* (1927) extended legalized racial segregation to all non-White children, specifically Chinese Americans. Shortly thereafter, the NAACP, which had been formed in 1909, began filing lawsuits to challenge racial segregation. Initial wins involved getting African American students admitted to White graduate schools in the absence of Black graduate schools (Brown, 2004; Browne-Marshall, 2007).

Additional cases began to chip away at legalized school segregation. For example, in *Méndez v. Westminster* (1946), the segregation of Mexican American students was successfully challenged in a local court. Although Mexican Americans were officially classified as White, unofficially they experienced racial discrimination, which this court case acknowledged. The school district attempted to have the case overturned in *Westminster v. Méndez* (1947), but the Ninth Circuit Court upheld the 1946 Méndez decision. Thurgood Marshall wrote the amicus brief challenging segregation, providing arguments that later helped support the *Brown I* case. The Méndez ruling, coupled with pressure from communities of color, spurred the California state legislature to remove passages from the state's education code that had legalized racial segregation (Valencia, 2005).

As Browne-Marshall (2007) explains, the decision in *Brown I* rested largely on evidence of psychological damage African Americans experienced due to school segregation, which violated equal protection of citizens under the Fourteenth Amendment of the Constitution. The philosophical *Brown I* of 1954 was followed in 1955 by the action-oriented *Brown II*, in which the NAACP "called for immediate integration of public schools" (Browne-Marshall, p. 30). However, the Supreme Court decided that school districts could develop their own desegregation plans, and although they were to proceed with "all deliberate speed," it was up to local districts to decide what that would mean.

Ironically, the ambiguous language used in the action-oriented decision in *Brown II* gave White-dominant school boards license to resist desegregation actively, which they did. For example, Prince Edward County in Virginia closed its public schools for five years rather than desegregate them, providing its White students with financial support to attend private schools. This stalling practice was not ruled unconstitutional until 1964 in *Griffin v. County School Board of Prince Edward County*, and the policy became a precursor to contemporary school choice policies in effect today. Kansas City, Missouri, redrew its attendance zones around neighborhood schools, but the combination of residential segregation and the district's policy of granting transfer requests meant that only token desegregation actually took place (Moran, 2005).

According to Brown (2004), racial segregation was dismantled minimally until a good fifteen years after *Brown I*. Then three events converged to prompt action: (1) expiration of "all deliberate speed" in the form of decisions such as *Griffin* (1964), (2) organized pressure from the Civil Rights movement, and (3) passage of the Civil Rights Act of 1964, which established federal funding as a tool for enforcing action, an important tool discussed in the next section.

During the 1960s and early 1970s, lawsuits prompted court decisions that continued to clarify what counts as school segregation and legal remedies for addressing it. For example, in *Swann v. Charlotte-Mecklenburg* (1971), the Supreme Court established a formula for acceptable racial balance, and upheld busing as a remedy to achieve that balance. For African American communities, this ruling upheld a practical strategy that could be used to desegregate the schools despite the prevalence of housing segregation. In many cities throughout the North, such as Rockford, Illinois, Chicago, Boston, and Milwaukee, busing became the primary remedy for school segregation in the face of extensive and on-going residential segregation. In *Larry P. v. Riles* (1972) a federal district court ruled that California cannot place students in classes for the mentally retarded on the basis of culturally biased tests, thereby providing African American parents with a tool to challenge placement procedures they saw as unfair to their children. In *Cisneros v. Corpus Christi Independent School District* (1970), a circuit court extended *Brown I* to Mexican Americans. School districts had dodged desegregation of schools serving Mexican American students who were classified as White by claiming that they did not experience racial discrimination. As Contreras and Valverde (1994) point out, this ruling was significant because it recognized Mexican Americans as an ethnic minority that does experience racial discrimination, and that is, therefore, entitled to protections under the *Brown* decision—a claim that Mexican American communities had been making but that school districts had been ignoring.

Whites were actively resisting desegregation by moving to suburbs where they established White enclaves and White schools. For example, even though Kansas City's desegregation plan resulted in only token integration, thousands of Whites moved out of the city into a suburban ring. As Moran (2005) explained, "Between 1960 and 1980, the suburbs experienced substantial growth, more than doubling their school enrollments and adding nearly 500,000 new residents, 97% of whom were White" (p. 1938). In the context of White flight to the suburbs, application of *Brown I* in many urban areas shifted to metropolitan busing programs, which African American parents experienced with mixed feelings. Morris (2001) examined this situation with respect to St. Louis, where African American plaintiffs had accused the Board of Education of racial discrimination in *Liddell v. St. Louis Board of Education* (1975, 1979). The plaintiffs lost the case at the local level, but the Eighth Circuit Court of Appeals reversed the decision. The St. Louis Board of Education then accused the suburban schools of contributing to the problem by facilitating White flight. A settlement was reached under which the suburban schools would voluntarily desegregate by accepting African American transfer students from the city, White suburban students could transfer to city schools that would be refurbished, and suburban schools would hire African American teachers. Morris interviewed African American educators to find out their perceptions of this remedy. The African American educators expressed concerns about the stigmatizing of Black teachers throughout discussions of the plan, the plan's effect of "creaming" the most academically talented African American students from the urban schools, and their concern that African American children were the main ones riding buses predicated on the dubious contention that they would learn better in White schools than Black schools. Further, over the long run, citizens of St. Louis were taxed to support the plan more than suburban citizens were taxed. Morris argued that how desegregation was ultimately handled placed much more of a burden on the Black community than on White communities that were the perpetrators of racial segregation.

Whites have continued moving out of urban areas into suburbs as well as resisting desegregation in other ways, such as challenging busing programs (Fennimore, 2001). In the context of both White resistance and a global recession beginning in the late 1970s (Browne-Marshall, 2007), the Supreme Court shifted away from protecting remedies for a legacy of racism to enforcing a "colorblind" application of rules that assume structural racism to have largely disappeared. Beginnings of this shift were evident in *Milliken v. Bradley* (1974), when the Supreme Court ruled "that suburban Detroit school districts could not be forced to participate in a metropolitan-wide school desegregation remedy unless it was established that school officials in these districts—and not the housing market that envelopes the districts—had conducted racially discriminatory acts that then led to the pervasive cross-district segregation"; African American plaintiffs would have to prove "that the suburban school district boundary lines had been deliberately drawn on the basis of race" (Wells, Duran & White, 2008, p. 2538). In essence, *Milliken* sealed the segregated fates of urban districts by evoking White flight to suburbs that could not be held accountable for desegregating the nearby urban schools.

After *Milliken*, the Supreme Court agreed to hear far fewer cases involving racial discrimination, and, in the cases it agreed to hear, became less likely to support challenges to racial discrimination than it had been earlier. The Court's stance on affirmative action is a good example. Affirmative action came from Executive Order 11246, issued by President Lyndon Johnson in 1965, requiring "government contractors to take 'affirmative action' in hiring minority employees" (Browne-Marshall, 2007, p. 39). The thinking behind this was that racism was so deeply entrenched that it would not disappear without sustained effort toward meeting goals; affirmative action was gradually extended to school admissions policies. In *Regents of the University of California v. Bakke* (1978), the Supreme Court struck down an affirmative action program used for admission into medical school, arguing that a race-conscious admission policy is constitutional only if it serves a compelling state interest and does not unduly harm people who are outside the protected group. The university had argued that the admissions program helped recruit potential Black doctors who might serve in high-needs areas. The plaintiff, however, argued that taking race into consideration prevented White applicants from competing for admission equally, and the university could not discriminate against applicants on the basis of race to remedy a shortage of Black doctors that the university had not created (Browne-Marshall, 2007).

As Wells et al. (2008) argue, in addition to narrowing its interpretation of the scope of racism, the Supreme Court gave increasingly less weight to the growing body of social science research evidence on the impacts of racism. Based on syntheses of research, Wells, Holme, Atanda, and Revilla (2005) and Wells et al. (2008) show that while school experiences for students in desegregated settings have often been tumultuous, on the balance, desegregation has had a positive impact on African American school achievement and later ability to navigate a predominantly White world, as well as on improving White attitudes about African Americans.

In recent years, Supreme Court decisions have further weakened efforts to dismantle structural racism and its effects on education. Two decisions involved the University of Michigan in 2003. In *Grutter v. Bollinger* the Court recognized educational benefits to maintaining diversity on college campuses, particularly when doing so helps the university to attain its mission and goals. However, in *Gratz v. Bollinger* the Court declared the University's use of race in admission unconstitutional, arguing that the policy went too far in attempting to redress a legacy of racism by disadvantaging White applicants. In two decisions in 2007—*Parents Involved in Community Schools v. Seattle School District No. 1* and *Meredith v. Jefferson County Board of Education*—the Court rejected using race to assign students to schools when White parents sued because their children were denied access to the school of their choice.

Thus, as these cases illustrate, over about 30 years the Supreme Court shifted from supporting policies to dismantle a legacy of structural racism impacting one-third of U.S. citizens to supporting colorblindness when individual Whites claimed to be harmed by such policies, even while Whites who do see race have fled to White suburbs. The Court had played an invaluable role in establishing a legal basis for equity, but at the same time, relying on courts limits what can be done. Decisions shift according to who is on the Court at any given time, and what kind of arguments they are willing to accept in the context of the times. As Wells et al. (2005) summed up their analysis of legal efforts to challenge racial segregation, "the school desegregation policies and efforts that existed in these schools were better than nothing, but simply not enough to change the larger society single-handedly" (p. 2143).

Structural racism, particularly in the form of racially segregated schooling, was the first form of inequity to be addressed at the federal level, limited though the subsequent success may be. Court cases can be ignored. Those who benefit from existing institutional arrangements—Whites in the case of institutional racism—can simply ignore Court rulings if there are no sanctions for not following them. Funding and regulations attached to the funding are useful tools for enforcing compliance with Court decisions, a process that is examined in the next section.

Volunteer and Compliance Uses of Funding

Resources exert either a carrot or a stick function. Funding tied to compliance acts as a stick in that institutions that do not comply with the law are punished by withholding funds. Funding that school districts and states can apply for voluntarily to enable new initiatives acts as a carrot. These metaphors are commonly used in discussions of federal funding that is tied to social change policies, evoking the image of a farmer dangling a carrot in front of a stubborn horse, while wielding a whip if the horse does not move toward the carrot. Both volunteer and compliance funds have been used at the federal level to promote equity policies, although not very systematically. This section briefly examines their use for desegregating schools based on race, and for protecting education rights of language minority students and students with disabilities.

Based on a historical analysis of how the federal government has at various times used funds to expand educational opportunity, Hirschland and Steinmo (2003) argue that it has done so in a patchwork fashion. The current 10% of school budgets provided by the federal government is a very small amount that minimizes potential federal impact. Further, as Smith (2000) points out, states can choose to relinquish federal funds, thereby refusing to comply with the law. Therefore, the extent to which states and local districts enact equity depends on commitments of people at the local level. However, federal policy is still a useful enforcement tool in economically struggling districts that need funds to serve specific populations of students.

The practice of tying funds to compliance with federal equity law is rooted in Title VI of the Civil Rights Act of 1964, which prohibits discrimination on the basis of race, color, religion, sex, or national origin in any program receiving federal funding. Exactly what counts as discrimination has been clarified through regulations and court cases quite unevenly. As Pollock (2005) points out,

> Civil rights laws, federal regulations developed by the department to 'implement' civil rights laws, and internal policy guidance became more specific and detailed as they developed, having first offered basic protection to students from discrimination on the basis of race and gradually developing more specific provisions to protect language minorities from academic discrimination, girls from sexual harassment and inequity in athletic resources or academic opportunities, and finally, 'the disabled' from inattention to their conditions or academic needs. (p. 2119)

Title VI mandates that school districts must comply with nondiscrimination law in order to receive federal funds, including funds from the Elementary and Secondary Education Act.

The Office of Civil Rights (OCR) was created in 1967 to enforce it. Initially the charge of OCR was centered on racial discrimination, but as equity legislation expanded, so did OCR's mission. Since 1965, Congress has passed the Elementary and Secondary Education Act (ESEA), authorizing federal funds for public schools. With oversight of OCR, the federal Department of Health, Education and Welfare (HEW) established guidelines to determine the degree to which school districts were in compliance with racial desegregation rulings, and OCR began to conduct on-site investigations to determine whether districts were following the guidelines that would enable them to receive federal funds. It has often taken local complaints or lawsuits, however, to prompt federal action.

For example, in an examination of the application of this process to Kansas City, Moran (2005) points out that it was not until HEW was sued in 1973 (in *Adams v. Richardson*) that it began to review school desegregation plans seriously and pressure districts to comply with the law. At that time, school districts were increasingly strapped for cash. As federal funding grew to make up roughly 10% of Kansas City's school district budget, interest in compliance grew dramatically, especially when HEW actually withheld $1.6 million from the district in 1975 until it submitted an acceptable school desegregation plan. Moran argues that pressure in the form of federal funding was necessary to make the district respond, and that "without the prodding of OCR and the threat of forfeiting the district's federal funding, several of these reforms would not have been initiated" (p. 1949).

Voluntary funding has less impact than compliance funding mainly because programs supported by voluntary funds tend to be temporary and optional. However, voluntary funds can sometimes prompt school districts to innovate or serve students in ways they might not otherwise. A good example was the Ethnic Heritage Studies Act, which was part of ESEA between 1974 and 1980. This Act provided federal funds that public school districts and universities could apply for in order to develop curriculum materials to use in teaching ethnic studies. It funded over 2,000 reports, print and audiovisual materials, and instruction kits (Gentile, 1994). (My first encounter with multicultural education was through a locally developed curriculum resource for Seattle teachers in desegregated schools, that was funded through this legislation.) Unfortunately, the Ethnic Heritage Studies Act was terminated under the Reagan administration.

Below, I examine how voluntary and compliance forms of funding were combined for educating language minority students and students with disabilities. State authorization of bilingual education dates back to the mid-1800s, when many states authorized use of European languages such as German, French, Swedish, and Spanish as media of instruction in schools for European immigrants. However, nativist movements during the first half of the twentieth century repressed bilingualism; volunteer funding to finance teaching English was offered to states through the Bureau of Nationalization and the Bureau of Education right after World War I. By 1923, 34 states mandated English-only in schools (Ovando, 2003).

In the early 1960s, Cubans who fled Castro's Revolution pressed for bilingual schools in anticipation of returning to Cuba. They established a successful bilingual program at an elementary school in Florida (Coral Way Elementary School), which stimulated development of other bilingual programs elsewhere. In 1968, in response mainly to Cuban parents and educators, Congress authorized voluntary funding for bilingual education programs in the form of the Bilingual Education Act, passed initially as Title VII of ESEA. Ovando (2003) points out that the light skin and middle-class status of many of these Cubans meant that they did not experience the racism that Mexicans have subsequently experienced when pressing for the same kinds of language programming. Under the Bilingual Education Act of 1968, school districts could apply for competitive grants in four areas: resources for education programs, training for teachers and teacher aides, development and dissemination of materials (including coursework in the history and culture of minority groups), and parent involvement projects. The 1968 Act had few guidelines, leaving districts on their own to define what counts as bilingual education (Stewner-Manzanares, 1988). However, the birth of bilingual education programs encouraged Mexican American and Indigenous educators, particularly those in the Southwest, who saw hope that schools would begin to respond constructively to their own children. As Ovando (2003) points out, community activism and litigation by many Spanish-speaking parents prompted school districts to take advantage of Bilingual Education Act funds to establish programs.

In 1974, the Supreme Court applied the Civil Rights Act of 1964 to language minority students in *Lau v. Nichols*, which declared that classes taught in English without providing assistance for learning English deny language minority students an equal opportunity; districts must provide assistance (namely, teach English and also offer content instruction in a language students can understand while they are learning English) if at least 25 students of a given language background are enrolled. To prod compliance with the law, the Office of Civil Rights began to pressure school districts to provide meaningful instruction for language minority students. Subsequent reauthorizations of the Bilingual Education Act were tied to *Lau*, with funds intended to both help school districts develop programs that comply with *Lau*, and define much more specifically what counts as bilingual education. The 1974 reauthorization of the Bilingual Education Act "defined a bilingual education program as one that provided instruction in English and in the native language of the student to allow the student to progress effectively through the educational system"; although it favored transition to English, it did not exclude native language maintenance programs (Stewner-Manzanares, 1988). In addition, the 1974 reauthorization provided more funding for capacity-building by establishing regional support centers, consultants, teacher trainers, and research programs. The 1984 reauthorization awarded grants for various program structures designed to move students and their families toward English language proficiency. The extent to which native language could be used in programs funded through the Bilingual Education Act was always hotly contested (Stewner-Manzanares, 1988).

Bilingual Education Act funds were a form of voluntary funding, and only a small proportion of language minority students were ever served through them. Development and support of programs devolved mainly to the states, where it has been difficult to track the extent to which students have received appropriate language programming, mainly because of lack of agreement on program terminology and lack of data. In 1997, Baker and Hakuta reported that, according to a national survey, "reading and math were taught in programs using bilingual education in less than half of first and third grade classrooms serving limited English proficient students" (p. 1). Instruction offered in English, or assisted by aides who translate for students, was more common. They estimated that only about one-third of English learners nationwide were enrolled in a bilingual or English as a Second Language program.

Families can sue the state (and many have done so) for failure to comply with *Lau*. One such suit, *Castañeda v. Pickard* (1981), clarified obligations of school districts receiving federal funding. *Castañeda v. Pickard* was filed against the Raymondville Independent School District in Texas by the father of two Mexican-American children, who claimed that the district was discriminating against them by placing them in a classroom that was segregated based on ethnicity and race, and by failing to establish sufficient bilingual programming to assist them in learning English so they could participate equally in English-based instruction. Ultimately, the Fifth Circuit Court of Appeals ruled in favor of the Castañedas. The "Castañeda test" requires schools to "implement a program based on sound educational theory, designate enough resources and teachers to serve ELLs, and discontinue a program if it is not producing results" (Ragan & Lesaux, 2006). In 1991, the Office of Civil Rights further clarified that students redesignated as fluent in English "must be able to achieve academic parity with their native English speaking peers. They must have access to the same curriculum, and have similar rates of drop out and retention" (Ragan & Lesaux, 2006). Although equal access and parity have not been achieved, the clarification of state obligations that are tied to funding has provided a tool that advocates for language minority children have used.

Regulations governing federal funding and service to language minority students began to shift during the Reagan administration. According to Ovando (2003), Secretary of Education William Bennett pressed to allow English-only programs to count as a portion of what the Bilingual Education Act would fund. The Reagan administration also rescinded *Lau* remedies that had been established under the Carter administration. Nationally, growing English-only sentiment was fueling anti-bilingual education efforts, such as Proposition 227, which passed in California in 1998. Regulations were further loosened under *No Child Left Behind*, which shifted the focus from provision of language services to monitoring student achievement in English.

Currently, districts receiving federal funding must submit the number and percentage of children who attain English proficiency over the year, the number who are meeting state academic content requirements, and progress made by those redesignated as fluent in English in meeting state academic content requirements for two years after redesignation. States must also establish "annual measurable achievement objectives" that set specific targets for acquisition of English language proficiency, redesignation rates, and academic achievement of English learners. Once a language minority student has been enrolled in U.S. schools for more than a year and classified as an English Language Learner (ELL), he or she is to be assessed in the same manner and frequency as native speakers of English. *No Child Left Behind* allows for native language testing of ELLs, but with a maximum time limit of five years and only on a case-by-case basis after three years (Ragan & Lesaux, 2006). Although federal policy has shifted from protecting language rights toward rapid acquisition of English (Black, 2006), and although many states have gutted bilingual services, as Pollock (2005) points out, Civil Rights law has

> gradually given language-minority students an entitlement to detailed academic attention . . . schools cannot throw English language learners (ELLs) into English-only classrooms without making specific provisions for their language development needs . . . the very legal prescription of a right to attention to ELLs' academic needs prompts lawyers to seek concrete academic opportunities for students learning English. (p. 2131)

Whereas funding to support the education of language minority students has been inconsistent, a combination of compliance and voluntary legislation has been used quite systematically to build capacity for equitable schooling for students with disabilities. Parents of children with disabilities used *Brown I* as a basis on which to sue school districts for excluding their children from quality education programs. *Mills v. Board of Education* (1972) and *Pennsylvania Association for Retarded Children v. Commonwealth of Pennsylvania* (1972) are two of the more commonly cited such cases that established legal rights of children with disabilities to equal protection to a free and appropriate public education. At the same time, Congress had been authorizing volunteer funds that school districts could apply for in order to develop programs for children with disabilities. For example, PL 85–926, passed in 1958, authorized funds for universities to train teachers for the mentally retarded; this was extended in 1963 to other disability areas. PL 90–538, passed in 1968, authorized funds for projects designed to provide comprehensive services to handicapped preschool children and their families (Ysseldyke & Algozzine, 1982).

Disability rights advocates joined the Civil Rights movement's emphasis on historically marginalized groups claiming voice and a right to organize on behalf of their own needs (Linton, 1998). The Civil Rights Act of 1964 did not mention people with disabilities, so the American Coalition of People with Disabilities (a national disability rights organization) pressed to extend civil rights legislation. As a result, Section 504 of the 1973 Rehabilitation Act prohibits discrimination on the basis of disability in any program receiving federal funds. The Office of Civil Rights oversees enforcement of Section 504, which provided the basis for major school reform addressing disability.

PL 94–142, the Education for All Handicapped Children Act of 1975, established both a stick to enforce compliance through the threat of withholding federal funds, as well as volunteer funding for states. (This Act was later renamed the Individuals with Disabilities Education Act.) Its purpose was to ensure that "all handicapped students have the right to a free, appropriate public education to meet their particular needs. Simply placing students in classes or programs for the handicapped is not enough; schools must ensure that the instruction delivered is appropriate to the needs of each learner" (Ysseldyke & Algozzine, 1982, p. 155). This requirement meant that states receiving federal funds must develop placement options for students in the "least restrictive environment" staffed with qualified teachers, placement decisions and identification of students' needs must involve parents, and states must establish detailed plans elaborating on exactly how all of this is set up and monitored. Local education agencies or school systems are responsible for identifying, locating, and evaluating children who need special education services, but states are responsible for seeing that local plans comply with requirements. As McLaughlin and Thurlow (2003) explain, a central compliance feature is the written individualized education program (IEP) that serves as a contract delineating exactly what services are to be delivered to each child and who is accountable for providing the services. Services might include things in addition to teachers such as transportation, interpreters, readers, speech therapy, occupational therapy, and assistive technology.

To help states reform and improve their systems for compliance and develop coordinated programs that support compliance (such as personnel development, research, and dissemination of information), the various iterations of the Education for All Handicapped Children/Individuals with Disabilities Education Act also established competitive funding that states could apply for. During the mid-1980s through the 1990s, the amount of competitive funding was substantially increased to support systemic change, school-to-work transitions, professional development for teachers, and improved accountability for meeting student achievement standards (Cobb & Johnson, 1997). As Danielson and Malouf (1994) pointed out, this combined use of compliance and voluntary funding attempts to build broad-based involvement in creating ways of educating students with disabilities, rather than simply creating top-down mandates that might be resisted.

Similar to the shift governing language minority students, in 1997 and again in 2004, the Individuals with Disabilities Education Act was modified to emphasize monitoring student achievement rather than providing services. Assessment measures are to be lined up with state assessments used in general education, as much as possible, and performance of students with disabilities is to be reported in as much detail as is performance of non-disabled students.

Regulations surrounding allocation of funds have become increasingly detailed. For example, Goals 2000, passed in 1994, required that state plans for educating students with disabilities include teacher training, strategies for involving parents and the community in grassroots reform efforts, and strategies for assisting districts and schools in meeting needs of students with disabilities who have dropped out. Since regulations are so integral to funding, we will now focus on this policy tool.

Federal Regulations

When legislation is passed, published regulations define and operationalize its meaning for implementation. The Office of Civil Rights is charged with enforcing equity legislation according to details spelled out in the regulations.[1] Thus, regulations both define what is to change, as well as set limits around what federal intervention does and does not require be changed. This section examines uses as well as limits of federal regulations through the example of gender equity.

The women's movement of the 1960s and 1970s pressed for equal protection in many areas, linking equity in education to equity in employment. As Deckard (1983) put it, "Equal opportunity in education is a prerequisite to equal job opportunity" (p. 406). Culminating years of work by feminist groups to combat sex discrimination in education, in 1972, Title IX was added to the Elementary and Secondary Education Act that authorizes federal funds for schools (Stromquist, 1993). Title IX specifies that "No person in the United States shall, on the basis of sex, be excluded from participation in, be denied the benefits of, or be subjected to discrimination under any education program or activity receiving Federal financial assistance." Regulations spelling out what that means were published initially in 1975, and have been periodically revised and expanded upon since that time. The regulations address the following areas: general matters related to institutional policies, notification of students and employees, and grievance procedures; admission into institutions; treatment of students once they are admitted, with particular attention to housing and facilities, courses and other activities, counseling, financial aid, health insurance, student marital or parental status, and athletics; and employment policies and procedures.

The thrust of Title IX was strengthened by passage of the Women's Educational Equity Act in 1974 and provisions addressing gender equity in the Vocational Educational Amendments Act of 1976, both of which authorized volunteer funding for programs and initiatives to combat gender discrimination in schools, augment teacher education, and offer adult education; and by technical assistance centers funded through the Civil Rights Act of 1964 to provide school districts with assistance in complying with civil rights legislation related to race, national origin, and language (with later addition of gender). Like equity regulations for language minority students and students with disabilities, Title IX was required to be publicized so that teachers, students, parents, alumni, and employees would be aware of rights and obligations. Organizations such as the Project on Equal Education Rights of the NOW Legal Defense Fund printed and distributed copies of informational fliers, which provided educators and activists with a basis for gender equity work in schools, as well as students with information about their rights.

Many of the initial regulations in Title IX are sufficiently specific and direct that they prompted significant changes. For example, the 1975 regulations state that,

> Courses or other educational activities may not be provided separately on the basis of sex. An institution may not require or refuse participation in any course by any of its students on that basis. This included physical education, industrial, business, vocational, technical, home economics, music, and adult education courses.
>
> (*Federal Register*, June 4, 1975, p. 24128)

This regulation banned practices such as assigning girls to cooking and sewing classes, and boys to shop classes. Schools not only stopped automatically making such assignments, but some constructed creative alternatives to serve and appeal to both sexes, such as domestic arts classes that feature an array of projects.

Other initial regulations were less clear and more controversial. For example, sexual harassment is not directly mentioned in the Title IX regulations; it took Supreme Court rulings such as *Franklin v. Gwinnett County Schools* (1992) to establish that sexual harassment constitutes discrimination that is not permitted under Title IX. The Office of Civil Rights issued a detailed sexual harassment guide in 1997, which it revised in 2001, following Supreme Court decisions in *Gebser v. Lago Vista Independent School District* (1998) and *Davis v. Monroe County Board of Education* (1999), to spell out forms of harassment that count, including harassment of students by school personnel as well as by other students, same-sex harassment, and harassment based on sexual orientation (U.S. Department of Education, 2001). For schools and universities, this requirement has meant that definitions of sexual harassment need to be publicized, and professional staff must be trained in recognizing, reporting, and not perpetrating it.

Athletics has been particularly controversial. The Office of Civil Rights spelled out an initial interpretation of regulations for college athletics in 1975, but colleges and universities argued that it was too vague, so OCR wrote a revision in 1979. The revision came to be known as the "three-prong test" of an institution's compliance (institutions need to comply with at least one prong): (1) providing athletic opportunities that are substantially proportionate to the student enrollment, OR (2) demonstrating a continual expansion of athletic opportunities for the underrepresented sex, OR (3) fully and effectively accommodating the interest and ability of the underrepresented sex. While this clarification provided more guidance, the larger problem is that athletics represents a huge business in many universities, and men's sports—especially football and basketball—continue to be much more lucrative than women's sports. The existence of different ways to measure proportionality has helped universities to continue to support men's more than women's sports while presenting themselves as in compliance (Anderson, Cheslock & Ehrenberg, 2006). According to Anderson et al. (2006), while college athletic opportunities and scholarships for women expanded considerably after 1972, most institutions are still not in compliance. On the average, while by 2002 women comprised 55% of all college students, they were only 42% of varsity athletes. Many smaller institutions with a high proportion of female students find it difficult financially to provide both the minimal number of men's sports required by the National Collegiate Athletic Association (NCAA) and women's sports that are proportional to women's attendance at the institution. But a much bigger issue is that many colleges and universities continue to favor men's sports because they are so lucrative. As Kennedy (2007) argued, while one can argue that lucrative sports could help fund expansion of a university's offerings, especially its offerings to women, universities do not necessarily see Title IX as an opportunity for cultivating women's athletics, so its reach is continually resisted.

Title IX continues to face additional on-going challenges that illustrate the limits of regulations. One challenge has been the omission of several significant concerns. Curriculum was explicitly left out of Title IX regulations due largely to protests from textbook companies, even though at the time Title IX was written, the existence of sexism in textbooks and the significance of curriculum to learning gender stereotyping had been documented (Stromquist, 1993). Sexual orientation is not mentioned in Title IX at all; protections extended to students and staff on the basis of sex do not extend to sexual orientation. Gay, lesbian, and bisexual students have, however, been able to use the Equal Access Act, which was passed in 1984 to protect religious groups from discrimination when forming extracurricular clubs in schools, to also protect Gay/Straight Alliances (Lugg, 2003).

A second challenge has been enforcement. The Office of Civil Rights has never been funded to a degree that would enable it to be a strong enforcer of equity legislation and regulations, but under administrations that hold low value for equity, it has been severely underfunded. As with attempts to reverse racism, far too little federal enforcement in the face of societal resistance has made federal equity legislation weak (Stromquist, 1993).

A third challenge has been active political attempts to curtail Title IX through interpretations of regulation wording or through rewording the regulations. In *Grove City v. Bell* (1984), the Supreme Court ruled that Title IX applies only to those programs receiving federal funding, not to the institution as a whole, thereby exempting most athletic programs. After four years of struggle and over a Presidential veto, in 1988 Congress passed the Civil Rights Restoration Act, clarifying that Title IX applies to *all* programs at any institution receiving federal funding. In 2006, the Bush administration announced changes in the wording of Title IX to make it easier to offer single-sex classes, activities, and schools. The new wording specifies that these be non-vocational classes, and that their purpose be "related to the achievement of an important objective such as improving the educational achievement of students, providing diverse educational opportunities or meeting the particular, identified needs of students. If a single-sex class is provided, the important objective must be implemented in a manner that treats male and female students even-handedly" (U.S. Department of Education, 2006). This change, however, was strongly opposed by feminist organizations that are concerned about lack of protection from sex segregation based on gender stereotyping, in the context of a wider society that still structures much activity around gender stereotypes, and inconclusive research regarding the benefits of all-girls' schools (Klein, 2005).

Overall, regulations provide a useful, if limited, tool for working for institutional change. What they actually cover does not constitute the entire scope of discrimination, and implementing them requires making shifts in the culture of institutions, which entails changing behavior of individuals. Reflecting on the impact of federal regulations on sex discrimination, Klein and colleagues (1985) emphasized the importance of a broad range of actors, including sex-equity assistance organizations as well as teachers and administrators trained in sex equity, since they are the ones who actually interact daily with students (see also Klein et al., 1994).

But despite their limitations, federal regulations are useful. In a discussion of OCR and its work for race equity, Pollock (2005) argues that lack of regulatory detail about what constitutes racial discrimination, in contrast to abundant detail outlining other forms of discrimination, has greatly hindered the ability of the OCR to take on racism. She compares regulations protecting against racial discrimination with those protecting against disability discrimination. For race, according to Pollock, "Title VI decreed in 1964 that 'No person in the United States shall, on the ground of race, color, or national origin, be excluded from participation in, be denied the benefits of, or be subjected to discrimination under any program or activity receiving Federal financial assistance'" (p. 2120). Subsequent clarifications prohibited recipients of federal funds, "'on the basis of race, color, or national origin,' from denying an individual any 'service' or 'benefit' provided under the recipient's program; providing any service or benefit that is 'different' from that provided to others under the program; or subjecting an individual to 'separate' treatment in any matter related to his or her receipt of any service or benefit" (pp. 2120–2121).

For disability, by comparison, recipients of federal funding must adhere to a much more detailed set of regulations. Pollock explains that recipients

> must provide "handicapped" students with educational opportunities both "equal" and "effective" in comparison with those provided the non-"handicapped" student: the "educational needs of handicapped persons" must be met "as adequately as the needs of nonhandicapped persons are met". . . . Accordingly, law and regulation for protecting disabled students require schools to assess disabled students, hold meetings on their needs and educational goals, plan individualized programs for their education, and follow these programs to the letter. If a parent thinks that her child is disabled, for example, she has a civil right to have a professional assessment of him; if this assessment determines the child is not disabled, she has a civil right to challenge this assessment with an outside moderator. If assessors determine that a child is disabled, the child then has a civil right to have an individualized plan designed to assist him in his school work and the right to have that plan followed. Disabled students, thus, are actually entitled by civil rights law to have attention paid to the details of their academic development [through the] Individual Education Plans (IEPs). (pp. 2130–2131)

As Pollock argues, the work of OCR has shifted away from race and toward disability, partly because parents of children with disabilities have learned to use the detailed regulations to argue on their behalf. While federal regulations do little to clarify what constitutes racial discrimination, regulations are very detailed as to what constituted discrimination against students with disabilities. Well-educated parents who are White and middle class, in particular, have been able to bring to bear their resources to get OCR to advocate for their own children, thus shifting its work away from needs of families with less education, income, or racial privilege.

Federal Policy and Management of Inequity

This chapter has focused largely on the potential of federal litigation and legislation for working toward equity and social justice in education. At the same time, these policy levers have also been used to manage rather than challenge inequity. Social class is an example. We will examine social class and education with respect to litigation, then funding.

The U.S. Supreme Court has not taken a stand that challenges social class discrimination in education. Perhaps the best-known case at a state level was *Serrano v. Priest* in California, which involved three rulings between 1971 and 1977. In 1968, a case was filed by lawyers representing John Serrano, challenging systems of school financing that depended largely on the wealth of school districts. In *Serrano I*, lawyers argued that school districts with the same tax rate should have the same amount of money to spend on education, regardless of the wealth of the district (Powers, 2004). A Superior Court ruled that California's system of financing public education through local property taxes violated the state's equal protection clause by allowing for wide disparities in the quality of schooling available to children. The California legislature then established a funding formula that would equalize funding for recurring expenses (i.e., expenses other than infrastructure and capital), which was supported in *Serrano II*. As Coon (1999) points out, however, limiting attention to recurring expenses left intact significant inequalities that are tied to family income, notably capital expenses for things like building, infrastructure, and technology.

However, *Serrano* also had limited impact due to a Supreme Court ruling in *San Antonio Independent School District v. Rodriguez* (1973). This case was brought about by parents suing the school district for violation of the Equal Protection clause of the 14th Amendment by allowing school funding to depend on the wealth of the district. The Supreme Court rejected the parents' claim, arguing that education is not explicitly protected by the U.S. Constitution. *Serrano III* involved a challenge to the California state legislature's response to Proposition 13 that froze property taxes. The Superior Court ruled that the state's equalization system complies with the law, but adjusted the formula used to equalize school funding for inflation (Powers, 2004). In reality, school districts remained widely unequal in terms of resources such as qualified teachers, the condition of school buildings, and the quality and supply of books. These inequalities led to the lawsuit *Williams v. State of California*, which was settled in 2005, and requires counties to monitor and address resource inequities across school districts. Brochures explaining the *Williams* case to parents and other citizens, and forms to use to file complaints, are available (see for example, http://www.decentschools.org/settlement_action.php). For the purpose of this chapter, however, it is important to underscore that cases such as these have been settled at the state level only.

Federal funding to address poverty in education was taken on most visibly during the "War on Poverty" under President Johnson. The two largest poverty programs funded at the federal level, beginning in 1965, are Title I of ESEA and Head Start. Head Start, which resulted from pressures by civil rights activists during the 1960s, authorizes funds for a range of services to preschool children in poverty to ready them for schooling (Anyon, 2005). Head Start essentially provides a range of services to preschool children and their parents that more affluent families already have access to. Evaluation studies of the impact of Head Start on children are mixed, partly because the quality of programs has been mixed, although evaluations tend to find at least modest positive gains for children who have participated in Head Start in comparison to those who have not (see for example Jung & Stone, 2008; Nathan, 2007). An alternative to Head Start would be to ensure that states provide a full range of preschool services to all children. In a comparison of student outcomes of Head Start with student outcomes of state-sponsored pre-kindergarten, using matched samples of children in Georgia, Henry, Gordon, and Rickman (2006) found the children in pre-kindergarten to do slightly better, due probably to program differences in areas such as priorities, models, and monitoring. They suggest that universal state-sponsored pre-kindergarten might be a more equitable policy.

Title I authorizes voluntary funds to states and local educational agencies that have high concentrations of children in poverty to provide supplemental remedial education services. The intent of Title I when it began in 1965 was to provide resources that would enable schools to close the achievement gap between children in poverty and children from more affluent communities (Borman, 2005). Since its inception, Title I has gone through revisions in the nature of programs that qualify, criteria and standards for evaluating programs, and oversight, which is beyond the scope of this chapter to describe (see Borman, Stringfield, & Slavin, 2001). Based on an analysis of evaluations of Title I since its inception, Borman (2005) points out that although there is a good deal of variability in the extent to which it improves student academic performance due to large differences in program quality, and although early evaluations found most Title I interventions to be largely ineffective, by the mid-1980s, programs had become somewhat effective in boosting the achievement of children in poverty. However, when effects of Title I supplementary programs are compared with effects of comprehensive whole-school reform of high-poverty schools, the comprehensively reformed schools "outperformed 55% of the Title I schools" (Borman, 2005, p. 11). Borman concludes that there are limits to what federal funding mechanisms can be expected to do, since what matters more is how schools use the resources that are available to them.

Federal funding related to social class has been designed largely to compensate for a "culture of poverty" (Brosio, 1994, p. 482), or "disadvantage," the term still used to designate who these programs serve.[2] Neither is directed toward challenging social class stratification in education. Unlike race, gender, and disability, federal education policy never framed poverty as a result of a system of discrimination. Civil rights legislation, based on the larger Civil Rights Act, initially framed race, disability, and gender discrimination in institutionalized terms, although that framing shifted to individual acts of discrimination, especially under Republican administrations. Social class, however, was not included as a protected category under the Civil Rights Act, and in the course of policy-setting, social class was never framed in terms of a system that maintains wealth inequality. As Brosio (1994) points out, even though the various funding programs that began under the War on Poverty helped many people, they did not address structures that create and perpetuate poverty. As Brosio put it, "The absence of class-consciousness . . . and the failure to get at the socioeconomic heart of inequity . . . have permitted the American phenomenon of looking to educational reform as an ameliorative strategy for the generally recognized storm and stress caused by the anarchic, powerful, capitalist economy" (p. 483).

Because most people in the U.S.A. understand social class mainly as a result of individual differences in initiative, ability, or effort rather than as a system involving collective use of power, social class is perhaps the strongest example of where federal policy manages inequity rather than challenging it. Ironically, although OCR is currently most active in disability work (Pollock, 2005), the creation of special education can be viewed as managing inequity as well. Skrtic (1995) argues that schools, organized as loosely coupled bureaucracies, allow for minimal and symbolic compliance with equity legislation and litigation by converting demands for fundamental change into incidental change. Special education has served this purpose by siphoning off the students schools do not serve well into special programs that are decoupled from the rest of the organization, thereby providing an often-limited means for serving such students while at the same time buffering schools and teachers from having to change the nature of regular classroom instruction. Problems such as the continuing overrepresentation of students of color in special education tend to be framed as special education problems, when they actually reflect on-going failure of general education to serve diverse students well. Skrtic points out that special education legislation's detailed regulations produce mechanisms for labeling students as disabled and establishing procedures for ensuring compliance and provision of services, but without actually changing the nature of general education itself.

Conclusion

I began this chapter by expressing ambivalence about whether I believe the U.S.A. should have a national policy supporting multicultural education. This is not an entirely theoretical question. Recently I began participating in discussions regarding whether the state should adopt a policy requiring all practicing, licensed teachers to be trained to use culturally responsive pedagogy. On the surface, that might seem like a good idea in that teachers who currently have little or no preparation for such teaching would experience it. However, such a policy would also involve compromises. In order to enforce it, regulatory details would need to spell out exactly what counts as compliance, which would entail defining exactly what culturally responsive pedagogy is, and what counts as acceptable training. But among professionals who work deeply in these areas, there is no single agreed-upon definition, nor a well-established process for effective professional development. An unwanted but anticipated result of such a policy would be that innovative approaches for helping teachers learn to teach students of color or from poverty backgrounds more effectively, but that do not match adopted criteria, would be used less, or would serve as supplements to programs that comply with the law. Another unwanted but anticipated result would be that once professional development programs that meet criteria are in place, many educators would consider the problem of teacher training for culturally responsive pedagogy to be solved.

In that light, let us turn to the question of a national policy for multicultural education. Federal policy is helpful for establishing rights of students. One could propose that, as a condition of receiving federal funding, education institutions must demonstrate that the students they serve have full access to teachers and other professionals who can demonstrate knowledge and skill in working them well, which includes building on the knowledge, cultural backgrounds, and linguistic resources that students bring; and that students have access to multicultural curricula. It would be up to states and local education agencies to demonstrate how they are ensuring students' rights to such professionals, but it could be required that any agencies demonstrate links between their compliance plans, and research in areas such as culturally responsive pedagogy, funds of knowledge, or multicultural curriculum. Volunteer funding could be made available for the development of multicultural education teacher and leader development projects, and for evaluation of the impact of such projects on classrooms, schools, and students.

Social justice educators have a rich legacy of litigation and legislation on which to build. Winning court cases and passing laws (especially laws with funding to make things happen) matters. Making available resources that can be used to further knowledge and documentation of practice may be preferable to mandating specific practices, however, unless there is convincing and clear evidence that warrants mandated practices.

Points of Inquiry

- How do these federal policies reflect the society at the time?
- How can social justice educators use federal policy to gain "carrot" funds/resources for their classrooms? What current grants, scholarships, and programs are available to teachers and schools?
- Why are compliance funds necessary? Are they less effective than voluntary funds for moving teachers and schools toward multicultural education for social justice?
- What does the research say on the need for teacher compliance and ground-level buy-in for implementing new programs in public schools?
- What do you see as the greatest un-met multicultural social justice need in education in your community? To what extent do existing policies speak to this need? In what ways might existing policies be strengthened? What new policies might be needed?

Points of Praxis

- Students read primary sources such as the IDEA, the Bilingual Education Act, NCLB, and Title XI

  - Create an education summit of the school or several schools
  - Have students decide what's missing, should be changed, should be removed to create a current document(s)
  - Send new document to the Secretary of Education and the President.

- Students create a website for parents and students to review their rights in schools.
- Students do an oral history study that focuses on a particular policy change in schools, such as women who were affected by Title XI.

Notes

1 The Office of Special Education and Rehabilitation Services (OSERS), also located in the U.S. Department of Education, administers the Individuals with Disabilities Education

Act, while OCR monitors non-discrimination compliance specified in Section 504 and the Americans with Disabilities Act. These functions are interrelated, and ideally are coordinated.

2   See, for example, current wording of Title I: Improving the Academic Achievement of the Disadvantaged, on the U.S. Office of Education website: http://www.ed.gov/policy/elsec/leg/esea02/pg1.html

References

Anderson, D. J., Cheslock, J. J. & Ehrenberg, R. G. (2006). Gender equity in intercollegiate athletics: Determinants of Title IX compliance. *Journal of Higher Education, 77* (2). 225–250.

Anyon, J. (2005). *Radical possibilities.* New York: Routledge.

Baker, S. & Hakuta, K. (1997). Bilingual education and Latino civil rights. Civil Rights Project/Derechos Civiles Proyecto, Los Angeles, UCLA. Retrieved February 4, 2009 at: http://www.civilrightsproject.ucla.edu/research/latino97/Hakuta.pdf

Black, W. R. (2006). Constructing accountability performance for English Language Learner students: An unfinished journey toward language minority rights. *Educational Policy 20*(1), 197–224.

Borman, G. D. (2005). National efforts to bring reform to scale in high-poverty schools: Outcomes and implications. *Review of Research in Education 29,* 1–28.

Borman, G. D., Stringfield, S. & Slavin, R. E. (2001). *Title I, Compensatory education at the crossroads.* Mahwah, NJ: Lawrence Erlbaum.

Brosio, R. A. (1994). *A radical democratic critique of capitalist education.* New York: Peter Lang.

Brown, F. (2004). The first serious implementation of Brown: The 1964 Civil Rights Act and beyond. *Journal of Negro Education 73*(3), 182–190.

Browne-Marshall, G. J. (2007). *Race, law, and American society.* New York: Routledge.

Cobb, B. & Johnson, D. R. (1997). The Statewide Systems Change Initiative as a federal policy mechanism for promoting educational reform. *Career Development for Exceptional Individuals 20*(2), 179–190.

Contreras, A. R. & Valverde, L. A. (1994). The impact of Brown on the education of Latinos. *Journal of Negro Education 63*(3), 470–481.

Coon, A. (1999). Separate and unequal: Serrano played an important role in development of school-district policy. *FindLaw.* Retrieved January 2, 2008 from: http://library.findlaw.com/1999/Dec/1/129939.html

Danielson, L. C. & Malouf, D. B. (1994). Federal policy and educational reform: Achieving better outcomes for students with disabilities. *Special Services in the Schools 9*(2), 11–19.

Deckard, B. S. (1983). *The women's movement.* New York: Harper & Row.

Fennimore, B. S. (2001). Historical white resistance to equity in public education: A challenge to white teacher educators. In S. H. King & L. A. Castennel (Eds.), *Racism and racial inequality: Implications for teacher education* (pp. 43–50). Washington, DC: American Association of Colleges for Teacher Education.

Gentile, N. (1994). *The Ethnic Heritage Studies Act curriculum materials guide.* Philadelphia, PA: Balch Institute for Ethnic Studies.

Henry, G. T., Gordon, C. S. & Rickman, D. K. (2006). Early education policy alternatives: Comparing quality and outcomes of Head Start and state prekindergarten. *Educational Evaluation and Policy Analysis 28*(1), 77–99.

Hirschland, M. J. & Steinmo, S. (2003). Correcting the record: Understanding the history of federal intervention and failure in securing U.S. educational reform. *Educational Policy* 17(3), 343–364.

Jung, S. & Stone, S. (2008). Sociodemographic and programmatic moderators of early Head Start: Evidence from the National Head Start Research and Evaluation Project. *Children and Schools* 30(3), 149–157.

Kennedy, C. L. (2007). The athletic directors' dilemma: "$$$ & women's sports." *Gender Issues* 24, 34–45.

Klein, S. S. (2005). Title IX and single-sex education. Feminist Majority Foundation. Retrieved May 1, 2008 from: feminist.org/education/pdfs/SingleSex.pdf

Klein, S. S., Russo, L. N., Tittle, C. K., Schmuck, P. A., Campbell, P. B., Blackwell, P. J., Murray, S. R., Dwyer, C. A., Lockheed, M. E. Landers, B. & Simonson, J. R. (1985). Summary and recommendations for the continued achievement of sex equity in and through education. In Klein, S. S. (Ed.). *Handbook for achieving sex equity through education* (pp. 489–519). Baltimore, MD: Johns Hopkins Press.

Klein, S. S. Ortman, P. E., Campbell, P., Greenberg, S., Hollingsworth, S., Jacobs, J., Kachuck, B., McClelland, A., Pollard, D., Sadker, D., Sadker, M., Schmuck, P., Scott, E. & Wiggins, J. (1994). Continuing the journey toward gender equity. *Educational Researcher* 23(8), 13–21.

Linton, S. (1998). *Claiming disability*. New York: New York University Press.

Lugg, C. A. (2003). Faggots, lezzies and dykes: Gender, sexual orientation, and a new politics of education. *Educational Administration Quarterly* 39(1), 95–134.

McLaughlin, M. J. & Thurlow, M. (2003). Educational accountability and students with disabilities: Issues and challenges. *Educational Policy* 17(4), 431–451.

Moran, P. W. (2005). Too little, too late: The illusive goal of school desegregation in Kansas City, Missouri, and the role of the federal government. *Teachers College Record* 107(9), 1933–1955. http://www.tcrecord.org ID Number: 12149 (date accessed: February 12, 2008).

Morris, J. E. (2001). Forgotten voices of Black educators: Critical race perspectives on the implementation of a desegregation plan. *Educational Policy* 15(4), 575–600.

Nathan, R. P. (2007). How should we read the evidence about Head Start? Three views. *Journal of Policy Analysis and Management* 26, 673–689.

Ovando, C. J. (2003). Bilingual education in the U.S.: Historical development and current issues. *Bilingual Research Journal* 27(1), 1–24.

Pollock, M. (2005). Keeping on keeping on: OCR and complaints of racial discrimination 50 years after *Brown*. *Teachers College Record* 107(9), 2106–2140.

Popkewitz, T. S. (1991). *A political sociology of educational reform*. New York: Teachers College Press.

Powers, J. M. (2004). High-stakes accountability and equity: Using evidence from California's public schools accountability act to address the issues in *Williams v. State of California*. *American Educational Research Journal* 41(4), 763–796.

Ragan, A., & Lesaux, N. (2006). Federal, state, and district level English language learner program entry and exit requirements: Effects on the education of language minority learners. *Education Policy Analysis Archives* 14(20). Retrieved March 2, 2008 from: http://epaa.asu.edu/epaa/v14n20

Skrtic, T. M. (1995). Special education and student disability as organizational pathologies: Toward a metatheory of school organization and change. In T. M. Skrtic (Ed.), *Disability and democracy* (pp. 190–232). New York: Teachers College Press.

Smith, B. J. (2000). The federal role in early childhood special education policy in the next century: The responsibility of the individual. *Topics in Early Childhood Special Education 20*(1), 7–13.

Stewner-Manzanares, G. (1988). The Bilingual Education Act: Twenty years later. National Clearinghouse for Bilingual Education Occasional Papers, no. 6. Retrieved March 2, 2008 from: http://www.ncela.gwu.edu/pubs/classics/focus/06bea.htm

Stromquist, N. P. (1993). Sex-equity legislation in education: The state as promoter of women's rights. *Review of Educational Research 63*(4), 379–407.

U.S. Department of Education (2001). Revised sexual harassment guidance: Harassment of students by school employees, other students, or third parties. Retrieved May 1, 2008 from: http://www.ed.gov/offices/OCR/archives/pdf/shguide.pdf

U.S. Department of Education (2006). Secretary Spellings announces more choices in single-sex education. Retrieved May 1, 2008 from: www.ed.gov/news/pressreleases/2006/10/10242006.html

Valencia, R. R. (2005). The Mexican American struggle for equal educational opportunity in *Mendez v. Westminster*: Helping to pave the way for *Brown v. Board of Education*. *Teachers College Record 107*(3), 289–423.

Wells, A. S., Duran, J. & White, T. (2008). Refusing to leave desegregation behind: From graduates of racially diverse schools to the Supreme Court. *Teachers College Record 110*(12). http://www.tcrecord.org ID Number: 14553 (date accessed: March 14, 2008).

Wells, A. S., Holme, J. J., Atanda, A. K. & Revilla, A. T. (2005). Tackling racial segregation one policy at a time: Why school desegregation only went so far. *Teachers College Record 107*(9), 2141–2177. http://www.tcrecord.org ID Number: 12156 (date accessed: March 7, 2008).

Ysseldyke, J. E. & Algozzine, B. (1982). *Critical issues in special and remedial education.* Boston: Houghton Mifflin.

Chapter 3

Roots of Social Justice Pedagogies in Social Movements[1]

Maurianne Adams

Most, but not all of the pedagogies explored in this chapter have emerged out of grass-roots, community, and/or academic traditions that were nourished, over many decades, by each other as well as a variety of other approaches developed in different historical contexts. These distinctive traditions have provided us with the materials for a coherent body of social justice education practice, which can be summarized in a series of principles of practice. This chapter links principles of SJE with a new appreciation of the decades of experimentation and practice, in multiple and diverse communities of educators and activists, that have resulted in a coherent body of SJE pedagogy.

> We know that . . . changing *what* we teach, means changing *how* we teach.
>
> (Culley & Portuges, 1985)

> [T]he pedagogical process is the most significant determinant of the quality of the educational opportunities students actually receive in the classroom.
>
> (Gay, 1995)

Popular phrases such as "walking the talk," "practicing what we teach" (Martin, 1995) or "walking the road" (Cochran-Smith, 2004; Horton & Freire, 1991) capture the challenge of *doing* what we *say* or *practicing* what we *preach* in everyday life, let alone providing classrooms in which student experiences are congruent with the intentions of the curriculum. Paulo Freire, for whom education is the practice of freedom (alluded to in the subtitle for this volume), calls this *praxis*, to emphasize the integration of theory and practice, reflection and action, content and process. This integration presents a special challenge for social justice educators, for whom the curriculum and subject matter are often contested and the conventional "lecture and listen" pedagogical methods are often not effective.

Frameworks for Social Justice Education Practice

As social justice educators, we juggle multiple goals. We plan for interactions that are respectful and safe (not necessarily easy or comfortable) as we engage students in discussions that challenge established worldviews and elicit feelings as well as

intellect. We are aware of participants' advantaged or targeted social identity positions in relation to social justice course content, and anticipate that they will
respond differently based on their varying experiences, social identity positions,
and cognitive levels. We believe that we ignore participant beliefs, feelings, and
assumptions at our peril. It is our aim to help them practice honest personal reflection based on credible sources for their views on social justice topics, and to develop
the skills of critical thinking toward a better informed and more comprehensive
view of their complex social roles and responsibilities as social agents.

As social justice educators we develop courses in which the perspective (whatever
the specific curricular content) calls into question the relations of power and privilege, pays careful attention to the inequalities experienced by disadvantaged and
marginalized social identity groups in the U.S.A., and identifies recurrent and
continuing patterns of disadvantage experienced by peoples of color and peoples
identified as immigrants or the children of immigrants, by people who do not have
social class privilege or gender privilege or do not conform to social norms of gender or sexuality, who are disabled, young and old.

The two epigraphs to this chapter focus the attention of social justice educators
on *how* we do *what* we do. They ask that we not only rethink and revise our course
content from a social justice perspective, but they ask also that we think carefully
about how we design and plan our approach to teaching and facilitation, that we
anticipate the likely reactions of our students and participants, as well as our own
likely reactions to their reactions, and that we strive to achieve congruence between
our message and our method. This is the focus for this chapter.

Most, but not all of the pedagogies explored in this chapter have emerged out of
grassroots, community, and/or academic traditions that were nourished, over
many decades, by each other as well as a variety of other approaches developed in
different historical contexts. These distinctive traditions have provided us with the
materials for a coherent body of social justice education (SJE) practice, which can
be summarized by the following principles of practice—principles that we will
return to at the end of this chapter with a renewed appreciation of the decades of
experimentation and practice, in multiple and diverse communities of educators
and activists, that have resulted in a coherent SJE pedagogy.

1. SJE pedagogies balance the emotional and cognitive components of the learn-
    ing process.
2. SJE pedagogies acknowledge and support the personal (the individual stu-
    dent's experience) while illuminating the systemic (theories of the interactions
    among social groups and social systems).
3. SJE pedagogies pay attention to social relations and dynamics within the class-
    room.
4. SJE pedagogies utilize reflection and experience as tools for student-centered
    learning.
5. SJE pedagogies value awareness, personal growth, and change as outcomes of
    the learning process.
6. SJE pedagogies acknowledge and seek to transform the many ways in which

identity-based social position and power, privilege, and disadvantage, shape participant interactions in the classroom and everyday contexts.

Several of the pedagogical principles noted above and associated with today's social justice educational practice are rooted in yesterday's activist grassroots communities, such as the experiential, community-based education practiced at Highlander Folk School (Horton, 1998; Horton & Freire, 1990) and the consciousness-raising encouraged in the 1964 Mississippi Freedom Schools (Howe, 1984; Rachal, 1998). Although consciousness-raising became a core pedagogy in the early women's movement (Evans, 1979; Sarachild, 1974), it is also recognizable in earlier Civil Rights community education and simultaneously in Freire's literacy procedures. Thus a focus on personal awareness, to take only one element of SJE pedagogy, has several points of origin and illustrates the interactions that have taken place among similar community-based, experiential- and activist-oriented pedagogies that have developed in parallel albeit distinct movement traditions. The focus on personal awareness has origins also in the school-based Intercultural and Intergroup pedagogies of the 1920s and 1950s and in the student-centered pedagogies of early multicultural education school reform efforts (J. A. Banks, 1996; Suzuki, 1984).

I highlight these confluent, parallel, and/or interconnecting pedagogical traditions to emphasize the complex roots of social justice pedagogies—both in traditions of protest, consciousness-raising, and activist community education which in some cases influenced each other, and also in the more formal school-based antibias and intercultural, intergroup education whose goals were the elimination of stereotype and equitable intergroup relationships. This chapter focuses upon the complexly intersecting pedagogical legacies of these grassroots social movements with the more formal school curricula, that flow into and enrich each other, sometimes from sources that are difficult to document but which need to be honored as having cumulatively enriched and shaped today's social justice and diversity classrooms, workshops, and community-based pedagogies. These present-day pedagogies, whether from activist, community-based historical origins or from school-based traditions, come together in a practice that we today call *social justice education.*

My own practice is located within a higher education tradition called "Social Justice Education"[2] (SJE) which invokes an intellectual tradition, body of knowledge, conceptual framework, range of social diversity and social justice issues, and attention to pedagogical process (Adams, Bell, & Griffin, 1997, 2007), that differentiate it from the traditions generally known as "Multicultural Education" (MCE) (Grant & Chapman, 2008). The SJE intellectual tradition draws explicitly upon scholar/activists such as Fanon (1967, 1968), Memmi (1965), and Freire (1970/1994). Its body of knowledge includes history, social science, and identity development, based upon differently historically situated yet interlocking manifestations of systemic oppression (racism, classism, religious oppression, sexism, heterosexism, transgender oppression, ableism, ageism, and adultism) (Bell, 2007; Young, 1990). The SJE conceptual frameworks describe "Isms" (such as racism, classism, sexism) as manifestations of a system of oppression, characterized by the pervasive and self-perpetuating dynamics of domination and subordination (whether primarily rooted in systems of racism, sexism, classism, or some other manifestation of oppression). Within this understanding of the overall social system, specific manifestations of oppression are analyzed at different sites or levels—that is, the individual, institutional, systemic—and also conscious or unconscious levels (Hardiman, Jackson, & Griffin, 2007). This SJE approach also is characterized by focused attention on *process* (in the classroom, *process* and *pedagogy* are often used interchangeably) with careful attention to the appropriateness of pedagogical or change processes to identified levels (individual, institutional, systemic), or to the goals and objectives (awareness, information, action, institutional change, systemic action), and/or to the readiness, awareness levels, and contexts of the participants. Most often, however, SJE practice is focused at the individual level (individual students or groups of students) in formal settings (school classrooms) with the goals of awareness, knowledge, and personal action (Adams et al., 2007; Adams & Love, 2005). Although social justice education *pedagogies* have over the years been practiced in K-12 and inservice teacher settings (Johnson, Bernal, Weideman, & Knight, 2002), much of the practice is located in higher education or in popular, community, and adult education settings, directed to social group identity-based oppressions (race, ethnic and language-based, gender-normative, heteronormative, age and ability, class and religion).

How does this tradition differ from the Multicultural Education tradition—especially as multicultural educators increasingly focus on social justice goals and objectives, and theorize racism within a larger framework of systemic oppression that also includes gender, class, and (dis)ability (Grant & Chapman, 2008; Nieto & Bode, 2008; Sleeter & Grant, 2008)? The narrative told by the founders of multicultural education emphasizes the historical significance in 1954 of *Brown v. Board of Education*, the ensuing bitter and sometimes violent neighborhood conflicts as well as curricular and pedagogical innovations that accompanied school desegregation, and the challenges posed by access to quality education and academic achievement for many if not most children of color (Banks, 2006, 2008; Grant & Chapman, 2008). Although multicultural education is for *all* children in K-12 settings (Nieto & Bode, 2008; Sleeter & Grant, 2008), the focus of attention remains primarily on race-, and secondarily on class-, gender-, and/or disability-based patterns of disadvantage and exclusion (Grant & Chapman, 2008, vol. 1). For multicultural educators, pedagogy is one among several essential tools of educational transformation, sometimes taking a back-seat to more immediately pressing issues of curricular reform, standards-based state curricula, testing, the achievement gap, detracking, and other issues of K-12 school reform and educational policy (see, for example, Nieto & Bode, 2008).

In contrast, SJE is rooted in more activist, grassroots social movements which have nurtured a more experiential, nonformal pedagogy as the preferred strategy for an affective, interactive approach to learning. The SJE approach serves a curriculum whose goals include personal awareness of social justice issues, openness to different perspectives on complex social questions, recognition of the everyday here-and-now examples of violations of social justice, and motivation to take action to create social change. SJE pedagogies can be found in formal and informal settings—schools as well as communities—and they engage a wide range of issues, including racism, ethnocentrism, classism, sexism, heterosexism, gender oppression, religious oppression, ableism, ageism, and adultism. The range of social justice issues (often called "Isms" for short) illustrates the view held by social justice educators that there are many sources of inequality and injustice, that these manifestations of oppression often interact with each other, that inequality or injustice cannot be eliminated by focus on one form of oppression solely, and that there is no hierarchy of importance among these forms of oppression. Although one or another manifestation of oppression may be more visible in a specific context, all are salient to those groups that experience advantage as well as disadvantage on the basis of a specific "ism" (Hardiman et al., 2007).

The congruence and mutually generative practices that have historically contributed to a broadly based SJE pedagogy in service of the goals described above, have helped to challenge the tradition in schools of teacher-centered pedagogies in favor of student-centered, interactive, dialogic alternatives to classroom norms. Although the pedagogical traditions described in this chapter have their distinct histories and bodies of current practice, from the perspective of a composite SJE practice, what is striking is their convergence in an active, engaged, student-centered educational approach. This approach supports a subject matter that is neither neutral nor objective, that often is contested, and that explores complex, nuanced social justice questions that are not subject to right/wrong answers. It invites perspectives shaped by personal experience, where the personal is infused with the political and systemic. These approaches, however various their originating sources, share the premise that learning is subjective, that teachers and learners are socially positioned with reference to the curriculum and each other, and that their subject positions will shift in relation to different dominant or subordinate groups, histories, legacies, and situated perspectives. Taken together, these traditions endorse a SJE set of practices that are interactive and experiential, and an SJE learning environment in which shared experiences, mutual perspective-taking, and dialogic interaction are key elements in learning.

The traditions explored in this chapter include (1) Freirean critical pedagogies; (2) social identity and cognitive development frameworks; (3) laboratory, T-group, and organizational frameworks for intergroup, intercultural, and international training models; (4) Black studies, ethnic studies, multicultural education, and teacher education; (5) experiential education; and (6) feminist pedagogies. The list is far from exhaustive, and does not include key pedagogical traditions taken up in detail in chapters 4–10 of this volume, namely critical theory, Black feminist, indigenous, and queer theory, and social justice pedagogy derived from critical multiculturalism and poststructuralism.

1. Critical Pedagogical Frameworks: Paulo Freire

Although the relation of Freire's pedagogy to SJE is treated at length elsewhere in this volume (see chapters 4 and 8), Freire's work is so foundational as to require acknowledgment in this chapter as well. Central to Freire's approach is the process of dialogic inquiry whereby peoples who are oppressed arrive at the understanding, through a facilitated process of questions based on "codes" and generative themes, that their oppression is not part of the natural order of things but rather the result of powerful social interests that have been historically constructed—and as such, that oppressive social power can be dismantled and changed. A Freirean teacher is a problem-poser who asks thought-provoking questions, based on photographs or objects ("codes") that will elicit descriptions of current inequality, and who encourages students to ask their own questions. Through problem-posing, students learn to question answers rather than merely to answer questions. In this pedagogy, students experience education as something they do, not as something done to them (Shor, 1993, p. 26).

This process of identifying external historical and socially constructed sources of oppression has its internal dimension as well, namely the recognition by those who have been oppressed, that "They are at one and the same time themselves and the oppressor whose consciousness they have internalized. . . . Only as they discover themselves to be 'hosts' of the oppressor can they contribute to the midwifery of their liberating pedagogy" (Freire, 1970, pp. 32–33).

One key element in Freire's pedagogy, of tremendous value to social justice educators, is his opposition to "banking education" which involves "deposits" of predigested knowledge in students as if they were "'receptacles' to be 'filled' by the teacher":

> In the banking concept of education, knowledge is a gift bestowed by those who consider themselves knowledgeable upon those whom they consider to know nothing. Projecting an absolute ignorance upon others, a characteristic of the ideology of oppression, negates education and knowledge as processes of inquiry. . . . [B]y considering their ignorance absolute, [the teacher] justifies his own existence.
>
> (Freire, 1970, p. 53)

In opposition to this teacher–student, expert–novice dichotomy which Freire argues serves the subordination and dehumanization of its objects, is a reciprocal process of problem-posing, "the posing of the problems of human beings in their relations with the world" (1970, p. 60), described as a dialogic inquiry through which "both are simultaneously teachers and students" (1970, p. 53). Problem-posing involves "a process in which all grow. . . . [T]he problem-posing educator constantly re-forms his reflections in the reflection of the students. The students—no longer docile listeners—are now critical co-investigators in dialogue with the teacher" (1970, pp. 61–62). This is "education as the practice of freedom—as opposed to education as the practice of domination" (1970, p. 62), a formulation that affirms Freire's insistence that *how* one learns is inseparable from *what* one learns, carrying its own undercurrent message either of equality (but not sameness), reciprocity, and mutuality, or of domination and subordination.

Discussion that follows of the pedagogies practiced in the grassroots, community-based schools during the Civil Rights Movement, will note the extraordinary parallelism between the learner-centered, experiential approaches enacted in the Mississippi Freedom Schools of the 1960s (inspired in part by Highlander Folk School) and Freire's approach (not published in English until 1970 [Horton & Freire, 1991; Rachal, 1998]). Subsequent to the publication of *Pedagogy of the Oppressed* (1970) and other works by Freire, the convergence of Freirean, critical pedagogy with other communities of practice has been striking (see, for example, Smith-Maddox & Solórzano, 2002; Weiler, 1991).

The Freirean influence on nonformal SJE practice also appears in the pedagogies of theater, inspired by Boal's *Theater of the Oppressed* (1985), to create spaces for actor/audience dialogues about oppression and liberation, using fluid, permeable scenarios that dramatize oppression with openings for "spec-actors" (active spectators) to engage in this slice of real life (whether or not active spectators know that this is theater rather than "real life"). Boal's *Games for Actors and Non-actors* (1992) provides instruction and detail for activities, games, and structured exercises "designed to uncover essential truths about societies and cultures without resort, in the first instance, to spoken language" (p. xix) to generate instances of oppression and possibilities for political awareness and liberation (Kershaw, 1992; Mindell, 1995). Dramatization of social justice issues or problems happen in shared space rather than behind the proscenium arch, *agent provocateur* actors mingle with the spectators to stimulate reactions, and the audience does not realize, in most cases, that they are an audience. New pedagogies emerge as the games and activities designed by Boal and colleagues become incorporated into social justice courses through the use of dramatized social justice scenarios, problem/resolution simulations, and case studies (Rohd, 1998; Schutzman & Cohen-Cruz, 1994).

2. Social Identity and Cognitive Development Approaches

The affective dimension of social justice education—that is, the feelings, perspectives, and personal experiences that students and participants bring to bear on *what* social justice educators teach—provides one important reason for questioning traditional notions of *how* we teach. One pedagogical tradition that has helped social justice educators to theorize and understand the ways in which learners in SJE classrooms are likely to make different meanings of their experiences (although they may appear to have had the same experiences and to share the same social identities) is the tradition based upon models of racial identity development (Cross, 1971; Jackson, 1976; Sherif & Sherif, 1970). These models originated n the context of Civil Rights and Black Power challenges to racism and to racial identities that accepted the status quo. The models described changes in racial consciousness that could not only mobilize social change (Hurtado, 1997; Sherif & Sherif, 1970), but also guide the efforts of educators, behavioral scientists, and activists to design, facilitate, and assess effective learning environments for anti-racist curricula (Cross, 1991; Jackson, 2001).

For educators in the 1980s who came to define their practice as "SJE" (and I identify with the SJE community of practice) these theories of racial identity development provided the basis for other identity-specific development models which helped us design and facilitate SJE curricula concerning different manifestations of oppression at personal, institutional, and systemic levels (Hardiman et al., 2007).

Social identity *development* models, whether focusing upon racial, sexual, class, or gendered identities or the intersections among them, described cognitively organized personal responses to oppression in the social environment (and also, internalized "within" every person) as strategies by which individuals accept, resist, or redefine their experiences of oppression as well as their hopes for liberation, through an evolving (raced, gendered, classed, etc.) personal identity and epistemology (Cross, Smith, & Payne, 2002; Wijeyesinghe & Jackson, 2001). The social identity development models provided conceptual organizers to highlight and explain the processes of developing a consciousness that accepts, resists, or redefines experiences of oppression in personal relations, small groups, social institutions, and/or culture (Hardiman & Jackson, 1992, 1997; Jackson, 2001). In addition to developmental models that focus on racial identity (Cross, 1991; Hardiman, 2001; Helms, 1995; Jackson, 2001; Tatum, 1992), social identity models include "coming out" models of gay liberation (Cass, 1996: Cox & Gallois, 1996), feminist identity models in the women's movement (Bargad & Hyde, 1991; Downing & Roush, 1985), and ethnic and racial identity development models that reflect the ethnic/racial complexities of identity for immigrant communities of color (Duany, 1998; Hurtado, Gurin, & Peng, 1994; Kim, 2001). More recently, intersectional approaches (using postmodern metaphors such as fluidity, co-construction, indeterminancy, braiding) have captured the ways in which identity is simultaneously or interactively raced, classed, gendered, and sexed (Chan, 1995; Cramer & Gilson, 1999; Das Gupta, 1997; Hurtado, 1997).

Social identity development models share several key assumptions: (1) individuals of all social identity groups are affected by pervasive and interacting multiple oppressions, and may respond to situations differently, depending on their consciousness levels and worldview; (2) one's social identity changes through personal experiences that contradict or cause dissonance with one's present worldview; (3) individual interactions within groups as well as between groups are affected by developmental differences in the (un)conscious awareness of oppression; and (4) stage, phase, or worldview are metaphors for differentiating levels of consciousness or experiences of identity.

These social identity development models also help social justice educators make sense of our own unexamined assumptions and worldviews, as well as designing and facilitating learning environments that take into account our students' current worldview. What "develops" is a person's increasingly informed, differentiated, and inclusive understanding of within group and between group commonalities and differences, the relationship of inequality and difference to broader societal legacies of advantage and disadvantage, and a personalized awareness of how these understandings help to make sense of one's everyday experiences of inequality and difference. Beverly Tatum uses the metaphor of a spiral staircase: "As a person ascends a spiral staircase, she may stop and look down at a spot below. When she reaches the next level, she may look down and see the same spot, but the vantage point has changed" (Tatum, 1992, p. 12).

Social justice educators also make use of the developmentally related *cognitive development models* to anticipate and plan for entrenched modes of thinking that are also often mistaken for overt "resistance" among participants in social justice classes. The emotional attachments to familiar beliefs and thought processes rooted in trusted home, school, and religious communities often compound the cognitive and conceptual challenges experienced by participants in social justice classes (Bidell, Lee, Bouchie, Ward, & Brass, 1994; King & Shuford, 1996).

Cognitive development models describe pathways by which learners' meaning-making can evolve from simple, dichotomous, either/or thinking to thinking that is complex, critical, and can deal with contradictions, divergent perspectives, and the challenges posed by inequality and injustice or by different perspectives based on different social contexts and experiences (King & Kitchener, 1994; Perry, 1981). Cognitive development involves evolving capacities and skill in thinking abstractly as well as coordinating the abstract with the concrete or person, to trust one's own judgment rather than relying on external authority, and to gain confidence in dealing with doubt, uncertainty, contradiction, or independent inquiry (Baxter-Magolda, 1992; Belenky, Clinchy, Goldberger, & Tarule, 1986; King & Kitchener, 1994).

3. Laboratory, Training-Group, and Organizational Frameworks

Similar to the cognitive psychology frameworks described above, the study of group dynamics and intergroup processes, pioneered in the 1940s by interracial community leaders and experimental social psychologists, offers a third framework for SJE pedagogy. Kurt Lewin, a German Jewish refugee from Nazism, had studied intergroup prejudice and developed action research focused on community settings in the 1940s and had observed the effectiveness of using simulations and role plays within small-group interactions to elicit interpersonal feedback and group awareness. From these observations, he and colleagues developed a set of group-based procedures called "laboratory training" that examined interracial and other intergroup conflicts and provided opportunities to "get into the shoes of the other" (Benne, 1964; Lippitt, 1949).

Laboratory training uses structured, facilitated (but sometimes leaderless) group interactions (also called training-groups or "T-groups") to enable participants to learn about themselves in group-based social situations that focus on the following elements of group process. Reflection-enhancing strategies such as *processing* and *feedback*—terms anchored in the T-group literature—have become central to many SJE pedagogies. *Feedback* helps participants hear how other people respond to them and thus understand their impact on others across differences of culture, social identity, and social status. *Processing* enables participants to make personal meanings of feedback from other participants which may be open to more than one interpretation. Feedback and processing, used together, help surface interpersonal, cross-culture, intergroup miscommunication in classroom settings, and bring undercurrents of conflict and criticism out into the open where they can be constructively addressed. Small group simulations and structured interactions provide specific, socially situated examples of otherwise elusive abstractions about racism, classism, and other oppressions that can then be interpreted and analyzed ("processed") from multiple perspectives. In the discussions of community-based workshops, consciousness-raising, and Intergroup Dialogue that come later in this chapter, the specifically social justice applications of these T-group processes will be apparent.

The laboratory and T-group approaches offer pedagogies that are effective for multicultural group dynamics in diverse communities, whether grassroots communities or multicultural work groups. These approaches have also informed school-based intergroup, intercultural, and international training efforts, dating in some cases from the 1920s or the 1940s. School-based intercultural programs were developed to address ethnic/religious pride and understanding for the (initially European) immigrants arriving in large numbers between 1880 and 1923, many if not most poor, rural, speaking languages other than English. Subsequently, in the context of 1940s, further intergroup programs were developed to defuse the racial prejudice and violence that had erupted in newly integrated (Northern and Midwestern) neighborhoods and workplaces, as war-time industrialization brought black workers and their families into northern neighborhoods and work-forces (J. A. Banks, 1996). These 1940s intergroup programs focused on schooling as a major site for anti-bias education and interracial understanding but also reached beyond the schools into families and neighborhoods. Teachers were encouraged to experiment with active, dynamic pedagogies to engage students as well as their families, as schools because primary sites for anti-racism and anti-bias education, with classrooms structured to enable students to directly experience democratic decision-making across differences of culture, religion, ethnic or racial backgrounds (J. A. Banks, 1996).

In recent years, there has been considerable pedagogical experimentation and research into educational outcomes by social justice educators within Intergroup Dialogue (IGD) programs that have been designed to meet specific local audiences and purposes in schools, colleges, workforces, government, the military, neighborhoods, and communities (Schoem & Hurtado, 2001; Stephan & Vogt, 2004). IGD has recently gained notice as a way to help participants bridge their social and cultural difference and inequalities as well as to resolve intergroup conflicts (Gurin, Dey, Hurtado, & Gurin, 2002; Nagda, Gurin, & Lopez, 2003). It offers structured, facilitated, face-to-face, interactive learning experiences between participants representing two or more social identity groups for a sustained exploration of their histories, commonalities, and differences, in the context of their positions of relative advantage and disadvantage (Zúñiga, Nagda, Chesler, & Cytron-Walker, 2007). The pedagogical processes of IGD have been shown to foster intergroup communication, resolve conflict, build bridges, enhance mutual understanding, and forge action coalitions and networks among participants from different racial, ethnic, gender, sexuality, class, religious, and/or national backgrounds. They build on the

SJE pedagogical foundations described thus far in this chapter—personal narratives of social group experience, opportunities to reflect on what has been said and heard, interactive small and large group learning activities, in the context of information (from readings, films, or lecturettes) about historical and systemic legacies of power and privilege.

4. Black Studies, Ethnic Studies, Multicultural Education

Historical surveys of Multicultural Education (MCE) stress the intellectual and curricular indebtedness of MCE to Black and Ethnic Studies, as distinct from the intercultural and intergroup education movements described above (J. A. Banks, 1996; 2006; see Suzuki, 1984, for a different view of the tradition). MCE shares with Black Studies and Ethnic Studies a curricular mandate to correct the historical record and stereotyped representations of African Americans and the Black experience in the curricula taught to all U.S. schoolchildren, and thus shares a curricular emphasis with Black Studies and Ethnic Studies (Banks, 2008). MCE equity pedagogies within K-12 schools were enriched by Black and Latino/a Civil Rights activists who brought an experiential, activist pedagogy into these curricula, fused ethnic minority pride with social action, and insisted that education address real-world problems of racial inequality and injustice (Cole, 1991; Moses & Cobb, 2001; Nieto & Bode, 2008). The nonformal education pioneered during 1964 in the Freedom Schools in Mississippi—with explicit focus on Black history, social empowerment, and the real-world experiences of participants—transformed not only the curriculum but also the pedagogy, incorporating experiential activities, school- and community-based scenarios of privilege and disadvantage, simulations for speaking truth to power, and testimonials linking the personal to the political (Howe, 1984; McWhorter, 1969; Rachal, 1998). They established a powerful critique of traditional pedagogies in schools and universities, questioning "*what* is taught in the liberal arts curricula of America's colleges and universities; *to whom* and *by whom* it is taught; *how* it is taught; and *why* it is taught" (Cole, 1991, p. 134).

These movement-based experiential and activist pedagogies reflect SJE because they are supported and strengthened by Freire's vision of agency and empowerment. Bob Moses, who had pioneered the nonformal community schools during the 1964 Mississippi summer, has continued in the same vein, developing a reality-based, experiential and activist teaching and learning process that "starts where the children are, experiences that they share" and then asks that they reflect, form abstract conceptualizations from their reflection, and test the conceptualizations against their experience (Moses & Cobb, 2001, p. 119). This circular process of "clocking" one's learning echoes Kolb's learning-style model as applied by social justice educators (Anderson & Adams, 1992; Kolb, 1984), in this case imagined by the children as a circle or clock (noon is the experience, quarter past the reflective meaning-making, half past the conceptual work) which "is not only experiential, but *culturally* based" (Moses & Cobb, 2001, p. 120).

It is important to note how this SJE pedagogy continues in math and science education, where innovative incorporation of real-life stories and problem-posing draws on the social, political, and cultural capital of students ignored by traditional teaching and problem-solving approaches (Barton & Upadhyay, 2010 in press; Giecek, 2007; Gutstein, 2006; Leonard, 2008; Nasir & Cobb, 2007; see chapters 14 and 15, this volume). These SJE approaches draw on personal and community experiences as part of the "data" for schooling, generate theories from everyday instances that are readily available, and insist that theory be tied to action—approaches that come into SJE reinforced by a Black feminist tradition (Bunch & Powell, 1983; James & Farmer, 1993) "that places daily life at the center of history" (Russell, 1983, p. 272) and in which "the classroom is the first step in [students'] own transformation" (Coleman-Burns, 1993, p. 141). (See discussion of Black feminist pedagogies, see Chapter 5 this volume).

Many of the elements of Black/Ethnic/MC curricula—such as the commitment to personal and cultural experience as the source of meaningful classroom examples, the social relevance of what is to be learned and how it might be applied, and a critical or oppositional stance to received knowledge—have become hallmarks of "culturally relevant teaching" in the pedagogies of educators/theorists identified with multicultural education as well (Gay, 2000; Irvine, 2002; Villegas & Lucas, 2002). First explored by Suzuki in the early 1980s (1984), *culturally relevant teaching* has evolved as a pedagogy that affirms everyone's membership in a larger community, envisions teaching as a way to give back to one's community, and uses a Freirean "mining" rather than "banking" approach to teaching. The constituent components of fostering and then practicing culturally responsive teaching are described and illustrated in step-wise detail by Villegas & Lucas (2002), who ask inexperienced social justice instructors to learn about students and their communities, cultivate the practice of culturally responsive teaching, and create a community of learners.

Multicultural education theorists and practitioners such as Suzuki (1984), Banks and Banks (1995), Nieto and Bode (2008), and Sleeter and Grant (2008) have enormously enriched the possibilities for transformative curricula in K-12 schooling (see Grant & Chapman, 2008, volume I). They invoke Freire's call for a critical pedagogy based on the student's experiences and viewpoints, not an imposed culture. They bring an analysis of social inequality and institutional power to their discussions of effective classroom pedagogical practice.

Increasingly, the personal experiences of teachers as well as students have become pedagogical texts in their own right. They embody first-person narratives—often from specific racial, ethnic, class, disability, and gender perspectives, not only for the purposes of recognition and connection (Nieto, 2003, 2005), but more notably as a source of inspiration (Berlak & Moyenda, 2001; Ensign, 2005; Oyler, Hamre, & Bejoian, 2006; Peña, 2005). This inspiration, buttressed by detailed pedagogical narratives and descriptions, has taken social justice pedagogical practice across the curriculum (Kumashiro, 2004; Ouellett, 2005).

There are a number of explicit, detailed descriptions of how to implement SJE pedagogies that have been written specifically for teacher and faculty practice (for example, Adams et al., 2007; Adams & Love, 2005; Enns & Sinacore, 2005; Hackman, 2005; Kumashiro, 2000, 2002, 2004; Marshall & Oliva, 2006). New work describes strategies for "Action for Social Justice in Education" (Griffiths, 2003) or for "Developing social justice allies" (Reason, Broido, Davis, & Evans, 2005). Sometimes these pedagogies focus upon strategies and materials for teaching by, to, for, and about underrepresented groups in education—students and teachers of color (Berlak & Moyenda, 2001; Bolgatz, 2005; Johnson et al., 2002; Tusmith & Reddy, 2002); gay, lesbian, bisexual, transgender students and teachers (Griffin, 2003; Kumashiro, 2002; McCarthy, 2005); disabled students and teachers (Oyler et al., 2006; Pliner, 2004); and class, classism, and privilege (Anderson, Cavanaugh, & Lee, 2000; Collins & Yeskel, 2005; Giecek, 2007; Heintz & Folbre, 2000; Liu, Robles, Leondar-Wright, Brewer, & Adamson, 2006; Pittelman, 2005; Yeskel, 2008). And sometimes white researchers and practitioners have used teaching narratives and personal stories to describe the language and dynamics of advantage, privilege, and colorblindness (Bell, 2003; Rodriguez & Villaverde, 2000).

5. Experiential Education Frameworks

Through all of the pedagogies discussed thus far—social identity development, laboratory and T-group, intergroup, Black Studies and multicultural education—there is a common thread of great significance to SJE, namely, that "all learning is experiential" (Joplin, 1995) and that most formal, traditional classrooms focus far too much on the teacher's delivery of course content at the expense of the learner's direct immersion in the learning process. Experiential education is a legacy of John Dewey (Hunt, 1995; Kolb, 1984), who used the term "reflective experience" to refer to the linkage by which the personal and social meanings of experience interact and become one (Hunt, 1995); a linkage which constitutes the core focus for experiential educators as well as the experiential components of other SJE pedagogical sources already discussed.

An experiential pedagogical process usually starts from a structured experience and focuses the learner's reflections upon that experience, in that "Experience alone is insufficient to be called experiential education, and it is the reflection process which turns experience into experiential education" (Joplin, 1995, p. 15). Joplin's "action–reflection" cycle consists of a "challenging action," which is preceded by a "focus" and followed by a reflective "debrief" (Joplin, 1995). The connections between the experience–reflection–debrief process highlighted in experiential pedagogies and T-group processes in the laboratory traditions as well as the "codes" and "generative themes" in the Freirean tradition, are not accidental. Although rooted in altogether different communities of practice, they share the insight that all learning involves reflection on experience.

There are numerous forms and variants of experiential education—extracurricular fieldwork, role-plays and simulations embedded in the curriculum, semesters abroad or in the workplace. Their influences on SJE pedagogy include encouraging students to visit each other's religious or neighborhood or support-group "turfs," structured out-of-class interviews to explore ethnic or religious or sexual/gendered diversity within extended families or immediate neighborhoods, ethnographic research in communities or cities, as well as role-plays, dramatizations, or simulations to enact and convey experience (Griffin & Mulligan, 1992)—as in the critical tradition stimulated by Freire and Boal and discussed above. The field of outdoor experiential education (or outdoor adventure) has proven both challenging and fruitful for SJE practice—challenging because of its associations with leisure, expensive equipment, and race/class privilege in which the "knapsack of privilege" becomes more than just a metaphor (McIntosh, 1998), but fruitful because of the opportunities presented by the growing participation of urban youth of color and women in outdoor experiential, trust-, community- and confidence-building programs (Warren, 2005). Some hands-on, physically active cooperative exercises developed within outdoor experiential education have made their way into social justice education practice, as ice-breakers and as community-building activities (Adams et al., 2007; Pfeiffer & Jones, 1974).

The core principles and practices (Proudman, 1995) of experiential education, however, also lead to questions of social status and social position concerning "the embodied location of experience and the social organization of the process" (Bell, 1995, p. 9):

> We talk about concrete experience, but I do not know what this means. To me experience "exists" through interpretation. It is produced through the meanings given it. Interpretations of lived experiences are always contextual and specific. Experiences are contingent; interpretations can change. . . . Perhaps remembering an experience recomposes it so that its meaning changes.
>
> (Bell, 1995, pp. 10, 15)

Experiential educators are themselves engaged in a search for core SJ principles (Koliba, O'Meara, & Seidel, 2000) as social identity, social status, and social position become visible concerns within communities of experiential educators (Warren, 1996), in tandem with the questions of experienced and positionality posed by feminist educators as discussed in the section that follows (see Applebaum, 2008).

6. Feminist Pedagogies

The centrality of pedagogy and process to the women's movement can be seen in accounts of its origins in feminist consciousness-raising among women activists in the Student Nonviolent Coordinating Committee (SNCC) and Students for a Democratic Society (SDS) who drew on consciousness-raising as an established strategy within the Civil Rights Movement (Evans, 1979; Howe, 1984). Florence Howe traces her own understanding that "all education is political" and her experiments with teaching that "turns upside down" the traditional roles of teacher and learner, back to her experiences teaching in Mississippi's 1964 Freedom Schools (Howe, 1984). Howe describes a pedagogy designed to raise the consciousness among Black students, a pedagogy that begins on the level of the students' everyday lives and those things in their environment that they have either already experienced or can readily perceive, and builds up to a more realistic perception of

American society, the conditions of their oppression, and political alternatives offered by the Freedom Movement (Howe, 1984, p. 10).

This is the consciousness-raising process that, as explored in the Women's Movement, surfaced women's personal experiences as a legitimate source of knowledge and also a critique of established knowledge, generated new analyses of domination and subordination, and served the emergence of feminist theory (Sarachild, 1974).

Consciousness-raising served both as a liberatory process from the unexamined acceptance of patriarchal norms and as a generative source for the data that constitutes a feminist critique and feminist standpoint. Within the Women's Movement, the process started from the telling of women's individual stories, and moved to discussion of commonalities of experience in areas such as childhood, jobs, motherhood, relationships, politics, economic arrangements. Consciousness-raising involved a "process of transformative learning" that awakened personal awareness, led to critical self-reflection and analysis, discovered group commonality among a "class" of situations, and provided "an ongoing and continuing source of theory and ideas for action" (Sarachild, 1974, p. 147). Decades later, consciousness-raising remained a key feminist strategy (Hart, 1991; Larson, 2005), with its postmodern emphasis on "personal stories [which] gain new readings both by the teller and by the other group members" (Damarin, 1994, p. 35)—and its connections to Freire's use of visual or verbal "codes" to identify generative themes which enable participants to pose problems and develop a shared consciousness of their social, economic, political situation:

> to know through dialogue with them both their *objective situation* and their *awareness* of that situation. . . . [W]e must pose this existential, concrete, present situation to the people as a problem which challenges them and requires a response. . . . We must realize that their view of the world, manifested variously in their action, reflects their *situation* in the world.
>
> (Freire, 1970/1994, pp. 76–77)

This pedagogy is also connected to the use of counter-stories within Critical Race Theory (Solórzano & Yosso, 2002). These influences run in both directions, as feminist educators and critical (race) theorists continue to enrich each other's practice in a convergence that has led to powerful new SJE pedagogical practice (see, for example, Enns & Sinacore, 2005; Fernandez, 2002; Weiler, 1991).

Other areas of congruence include cooperative, interactive, and dialogic pedagogies, derived from intergroup, anti-racist, and Freirean sources, within feminist pedagogies developed to address the research findings concerning women's silence in traditional classrooms (Lewis, 1993; Sadker & Sadker, 1992; Sandler & Hall, 1982) or build upon the relational and emotional dimensions of women's socialization and experience (Belenky et al., 1986). Clearly, the feminist affirmation of student-based, active learning in collaborative small groups has converged with pedagogical traditions of Freirean, critical, intergroup, and experiential practice (Smith-Maddox & Solórzano, 2002).

Feminist pedagogies do not necessarily agree about whether or how instructors should or should not draw upon their positional power to maintain classroom norms—while also not abuse their power to speak for others. Toward this end, feminists have pointed to two sources of power asymmetry in the classroom based on the instructor's institutional power, status, and authority on the one hand, and on her identity-status position relative to the race, gender, class, age, or other social identity statuses inhabited by her students.

The feminist themes of process, voice, positionality, safety, power, and authority are related in feminist pedagogies to validating women's feelings and emotions. The "connected" way of knowing described by Belenky et al. (1986) combines feeling with thought, and emotion with ideas. Believing that "the central role for the emotions in feminist education is their function in helping us explore feminist beliefs and values," Fisher (1987) uses student experiences as a basis for improvisation, simulation, dialogue, and questioning, in order to integrate emotion with thought. This valuing of emotion and feelings has led social justice educators to appreciate a process orientation as well.

Silence may not be the result of "voicelessness" so much as a result of "not talking in their authentic voices. . . . What they/we say, to whom, in what context . . . is the result of conscious and unconscious assessments of the power relations and safety of the situation" (Ellsworth, 1994, p. 313). In SJE, classroom safety is integrally tied to respect and the expression of emotion, especially emotions perceived as negative, such as fear, discomfort, threat, pain, anxiety, hostility, and anger. Throughout the SJE literature, running as a strong undercurrent, is the view that participants must feel that their comments will be treated with respect whether or not the faculty member or the class agrees with them, whether or not they are expressed dispassionately or with understandable emotion.

Conclusions

I want to conclude on a personal note, remembering how I first came to SJE in the 1960s as a traditionally trained classroom teacher, adept in the lecture-and-listen method in which "classroom discussion" too often meant "read the teacher's mind." With like-minded colleagues, I spent decades of sometimes creative, sometimes seat-of-the-pants trial and error, working toward an effective social justice education body of pedagogical practice. With my colleagues I was reaching for something that was not teacher-centered instruction, but also was not unstructured flow of feeling, nor confrontational displays of outrage or political correctness. This effort was informed by a search for useable, relevant pedagogical resources and models from earlier communities of social justice practice. It became clear that we could draw upon generations of skilled, knowledgeable predecessors who also had struggled to develop effective social justice pedagogies that expressed congruence between values, course content, and teaching-learning processes. The impressive and courageous work of generations of anti-racist educators, grassroots educators in the Civil Rights Movement, intercultural and MCE educators, feminists in the Women's Movement, experiential educators and T-group facilitators, educators working with social identity and cognitive development approaches—many of them acknowledged in this chapter—offered support, exemplars, and a leg-up for the work that as recently as a dozen years ago was still being pooh-poohed in the academic establishment as if it were merely a "touchy-feely" and solely intuitive approach.

Since then, things have turned around mightily. In the last few years, respectful use of the terms "social justice" and "social justice education" has increased exponentionally, although not always with the precision one might wish. In the 2006 American Educational Research Association (AERA) national conference program, I counted 112 paper titles or sessions using these terms, and by 2008, there were many more. Similarly, in our collaborative annual efforts within the SJE journal *Equity & Excellence in Education* to create a "Review of the Year's Publication [in] Social Justice Education," we have each year noted a virtual doubling of the previous year's output in book, chapter, and journal article titles using "social justice" and "social justice education" (for example, see Adams, DeJong, Hamilton, Hughbanks, Smith, & Whitlock, 2008). Although at times the term sounds like a virtuous or well-meaning add-on, the widespread use of *social justice education* also suggests an effort to invoke a systemic approach to questions of inequality and disadvantage and to provide the critical and analytic perspectives and personal engagement that I believe are the indispensable attributes of a *social justice*, as distinct from a *diversity* approach.

The communities of practice who developed the pedagogies explored in this chapter, through decades of innovative experiment and analysis in grassroots, community, and classroom locales, suggest that today's social justice educators are nourished by the rich accumulation of wisdom from many streams of practice. These distinctive and confluent traditions have given today's practitioners a coherent body of social justice education practice, which I believe can be usefully summarized by the following principles of practice:

1. *SJE pedagogies balance the emotional and cognitive components of the learning process:* They acknowledge and build on the role of emotion in learning. They pay attention to classroom norms and guidelines to maintain respectful and safe group interactions.
2. *SJE pedagogies acknowledge and support the personal (the individual student's experience) while illuminating the systemic (theories of the interactions among social groups and social systems):* They call attention to the here-and-now of the individual student's experiences and/or individual interactions in classroom settings to illustrate that the workings of social systems are produced through an accumulation of concrete, real-life examples. This is teaching that acknowledges the personal experiences of the learner, and challenges learners to connect their experiences to the larger historical patterns or systems of social experience.
3. *SJE pedagogies pay attention to social relations and dynamics within the classroom:* They help participants name behaviors that emerge in group dynamics, understand the here-and-now of group processes, and improve interpersonal,

intercultural communications, without blaming or judging individuals for misinformation or culturally different styles of interacting. They draw participant attention to social relations in the classroom as examples of framing concepts such as stereotype, privilege, and disadvantage.

4.   *SJE pedagogies utilize reflection and experience as tools for student-centered learning:* They use the student's worldview and experience as the starting point for dialogue or problem-posing. Facilitators as well as participants make conscious use of reflection and experience as tools for interactive, student-centered learning.

5.   *SJE pedagogies value awareness, personal growth, and change as outcomes of the learning process:* They balance different learning styles and are explicitly organized around goals of social awareness, knowledge, and social action, although proportions of these three goals change in relation to student interest and readiness. Facilitators reward and acknowledge the awareness, personal growth, and efforts of learners to work toward change that take place in the classroom, understood as outcomes of the learning process.

6.   *SJE pedagogies acknowledge and seek to transform the many ways in which identity-based social position and power, privilege and disadvantage, shape participant interactions in the classroom and everyday contexts:* Facilitators or instructors are not exempt from the implications of these analyses of social position and power, in that facilitators and instructors are themselves, as participants, implicated in the dynamics of the SJE learning process.

The ideas and possibilities presented here may seem overwhelming to someone just starting out as a social justice educator, or socialized and skilled primarily within the traditional lecture-and-discussion mode of higher education. For both the novice and the experienced social justice educator, it is encouraging to know that these principles of social justice pedagogical practice not only are embedded in a long tradition of social justice practice, but also that they restate core principles of effective college teaching (Chickering & Gamson, 1987; Hatfield, 1995; Meyers & Jones, 1993; National Council for the Social Studies, 2002). In its most recent iteration, the National Council for the Social Studies has articulated pedagogical standards that closely approximate the principles of practice enumerated here, and which include the following statements:

> Social studies teachers should . . . support learners' intellectual, social, and personal development. . . . [F]it the different approaches to learning of diverse learners. . . . [E]ncourage student development of critical thinking, problem solving, and performance skills. . . . [E]ncourage social interactive, active engagement in learning, and self-motivation. . . . [F]oster active inquiry, collaboration, and supportive interaction in the classroom.
> (National Council for the Social Studies, 2002, I, 51)

The work reviewed in this chapter reminds us that when, as instructors, we make the effort to teach to *all* of our students—acknowledging that *all* means a range of invisible and visible social group differences based on race, ethnicity, national origins, first language, class, gender, sexuality, ability, and age—in that moment we are reaching for social justice pedagogies. Social justice pedagogies such as these are the tools used by instructors who acknowledge that effective teaching for all students means the development of practices that will engage and include the broad social, cultural, and linguistic diversity of U.S. students in subjects that are personally meaningful to them. It is our hope that in the chapters that follow, the various approaches to SJE pedagogies will provide support and encouragement as well as inspiration and new possibilities for novice and experienced social justice educators alike.

Points of Inquiry

- How can we help our students develop Freire's "critical consciousness"?
- Who is the learner? What are her/his processes of understanding and meaning-making?
- What are the effects of different classroom contexts and social groupings, or of different dynamics in group or interpersonal communication and interaction in the classroom or community?
- How do other theories and frameworks help us better understand the origins and complexity of SJE?
- What do you feel is compelling about SJE?
- What do you feel is daunting or deters you from SJE?
- How do you see the issues discussed in the chapter as affecting your learning? Your teaching? Your ways of interacting with people?

Points of Praxis

- Try to incorporate these cognitive development strategies used in SJE into your classroom:

  ○ *presentation of the self:* Allow students to have opportunities to disclose their attitudes, beliefs, and behaviors for the purposes of feedback and learning;

  ○ *feedback:* Share the information provided by other group participants that enables the learners to understand the impact of what they say or do;

  ○ a *learning environment or climate*: Create learning environments that are designed to maximize trust and minimize defensiveness so that participants can change language and behavior that is inappropriate;

  ○ *cognitive organizers or map or models:* Provide and model organizers that are derived from research and theory to help participants to organize and generalize from experiences within the group; and

○   *opportunities for experimentation, practice, and application:* Organize activities and support new experiences to try out and practice new patterns of thought and behavior, in order to transfer them to back-home situations (adapted from Golembiewski & Blumberg, 1977; Pfeiffer & Jones, 1974).

• Practice feminist pedagogies:

○   Be aware of issues of power and privilege that are manifested through the social and institutional structures that affect your learning environment;

○   Be considerate of students' feelings and temperaments;

○   Create safe and affirming learning spaces;

○   Be aware of "silencing" that occurs in your classroom.

Notes

1   This chapter is based upon Adams (2007), Pedagogical frameworks for social justice education, in M. Adams, L. A. Bell, & P. Griffin (Eds.), *Teaching for diversity and social justice*, 2nd ed. (New York: Routledge), pp. 15–33.
2   Here I am referring to a community of practice in the School of Education at the University of Massachusetts Amherst, which reaches back to work we were developing in the 1970s, formalized into a graduate program in 1985. Much of this work has been described by the colleagues and former students who contributed chapters to Adams, Bell, & Griffin (1997, 2007) (Eds.), *Teaching for diversity and social justice* (1st and 2nd ed.). For current program information, see www.umass.edu/sje/overview.html

References

Adams, M. (2007). Pedagogical frameworks for social justice education. In M. Adams, L.A. Bell, & P. Griffin (Eds.), *Teaching for diversity and social justice* (pp. 15–34), (2nd ed.). New York: Routledge.

Adams, M., & Love, B. J. (2005). Teaching with a social justice perspective: A model for faculty seminars across academic disciplines. In M. L. Ouellett (Ed.), *Teaching inclusively: Resources for course, department & institutional change in higher education* (pp. 586–619). Stillwater, OK: New Forums.

Adams, M., Bell, L. A., & Griffin, P. (Eds.). (1997). *Teaching for diversity and social justice: A sourcebook.* New York: Routledge.

Adams, M., Bell, L. A., & Griffin, P. (2007). *Teaching for diversity and social justice* (2nd ed.). New York: Routledge.

Adams, M., DeJong, K., Hamilton, C., Hughbanks, C., Smith, T., & Whitlock, E. R. (2008). Review of the year's publication for 2007: Social Justice Education. *Equity & Excellence in Education, 41*(4), 482–537.

Anderson, J., & Adams, M. (1992). Acknowledging the learning styles of diverse student populations: Implications for instructional design. In L. L. B. Border, & N. V. N. Chism (Eds.), *Teaching for diversity.* New Directions for Teaching and Learning, no. 49 (pp. 19–33). San Francisco: Jossey-Bass.

Anderson, S. Cavanagh, J., Lee, T., & Institute for Policy Studies (2000). *Field guide to the global economy* (revised and updated). New York: New Press.

Applebaum, B. (2008). "Doesn't my experience count?" White students, the authority of experience, and social justice pedagogy. *Race, Ethnicity, & Education, 11*(4), 405–414.

Banks, C. A. M. (1996). The intergroup education movement. In *Multicultural education, transformative knowledge, and action: Historical and contemporary perspectives* (pp. 251–277). New York: Teachers College Press.

Banks, J. A. (1996). The African American roots of multicultural education. In *Multicultural education, transformative knowledge, and action: Historical and contemporary perspectives* (pp. 30–45). New York: Teachers College Press.

Banks, J. A. (2006). *Race, culture, and education: The selected works of James. A. Banks.* New York: Routledge.

Banks, J. A. (2008). *Teaching strategies for ethnic studies* (8th ed.). Boston: Allyn & Bacon.

Banks, J. A., & Banks, C. A. M. (Eds.). (1995). *Handbook of research on multicultural education.* New York: Macmillan.

Bargad, A., & Hyde, J. S. (1991). Women's studies: A study of feminist identity development in women. *Psychology of Women Quarterly, 15,* 181–210.

Barton, A. C., & Upadhyay, B. (Eds.). (2010). Special theme issue: Teaching and Learning Science for Social Justice. *Equity & Excellence in Education, 43*(1). In press.

Baxter-Magolda, M. B. (1992). *Knowing and reasoning in college: Gender-related patterns in students' intellectual development.* San Francisco: Jossey-Bass.

Belenky, M. F., Clinchy, M. B., Goldberger, N. R., & Tarule, J. M. (1986). *Women's ways of knowing: The development of self, voice, and mind.* New York: Basic Books.

Bell, L. A. (2003). Telling tales: What stories can teach us about racism. *Race Ethnicity and Education, 6*(1), 8–25.

Bell, L. A. (2007). Theoretical foundations for Social Justice Education. In M. Adams, L.A. Bell, & P. Griffin (Eds.), *Teaching for diversity and social justice* (pp. 1–14), (2nd ed.). New York: Routledge.

Bell, M. (1995). What constitutes experience? Rethinking theoretical assumptions. In R. J. Kraft, & J. Kielsmeier (Eds.), *Experiential learning in schools and higher education* (pp. 9–17). Dubuque, IA: Kendall/Hunt.

Benne, K. D. (1964). History of the T-Group in the laboratory setting. In L.P. Bradord, J. Gibb, & K.D. Benne (Eds.), *T-Group theory and laboratory method: Innovation in re-education* (pp. 80–136). New York: John Wiley.

Berlak, A., & Moyenda, S. (2001). *Taking it personally: Racism in the classroom from kindergarden to college.* Philadelphia, PA: Temple University Press.

Bidell, T. R., Lee, E. M., Bouchie, N., Ward, C., & Brass, D. (1994). Developing conceptions of racism among young white adults in the context of cultural diversity coursework. *Journal of Adult Development, 1*(3), 185–200.

Boal, A. (1985). *Theater of the oppressed* (C. A. McBridge, & M-O. L. McBridge Trans.). New York: Theatre Communications Group.

Boal, A. (1992). *Games for actors and non-actors* (A. Jackson, Trans.). New York: Routledge.

Bolgatz, J. (2005). *Talking race in the classroom.* New York: Teachers College Press.

Bunch, C., & Powell, B. (1983). Charlotte Bunch and Betty Powell talk about feminism, blacks and education as politics. In C. Bunch, & S. Pollack (Eds.), *Learning our way: Essays in feminist education.* Trumansburg, NY: Crossing Press.

Cass, V. C. (1996). Sexual orientation identity formation: A western phenomenon. In R. P. Cabaj, & T. S. Stein (Eds.), *Textbook of homosexuality and mental health.* Washington, DC: American Psychiatric Press.

Chan, C. S. (1995). Issues of sexual identity in an ethnic minority: The case of Chinese American lesbians, gay men, and bisexual people. In A. R. D'Augelli, & C. J. Patterson, *Lesbian, gay, and bisexual identities over the lifespan: Psychological perspectives.* New York: Oxford University Press.

Chickering, A. K., & Gamson, Z. (1987). Seven principles of good practice. *AAHE Bulletin, 39,* 3–7.

Cochran-Smith, M. (2004). *Walking the road: Race, diversity and social justice in teacher education.* New York: Teachers College Press.

Cole, J. B. (1991). Black studies in liberal arts education. In J. E. Butler, & J. C. Walter (Eds.), *Transforming the curriculum: Ethnic studies and women's studies* (pp. 131–147). Albany, NY: State University of New York Press.

Coleman-Burns, P. (1993). The revolution within: Transforming ourselves. In J. James, & R. Farmer (Eds.), *Spirit, space and survival: African American women in (white) academe* (pp. 139–157). New York: Routledge.

Collins, C., & Yeskel, F., with United for a Fair Economy and Class Action. (2005). *Economic apartheid in America: A primer on economic inequality and insecurity.* New York: New Press.

Cox, S., & Gallois, C. (1996). Gay and lesbian identity development: A social identity perspective. *Journal of Homosexuality, 30*(4), 1–30.

Cramer, E. P., & Gilson, S. F. (1999). Queers and crips: Parallel identity development processes for persons with nonvisible disabilities and lesbian, gay, and bisexual persons. *Journal of Gay, Lesbian, and Bisexual Identity, 4*(1), 23–37.

Cross, W. E. (1971). The Negro-to-Black conversion experience: Toward a psychology of Black liberation. *Black World, 20*(9), 13–27.

Cross, W. E., Jr. (1991). *Shades of Black: Diversity in African-American identity.* Philadelphia, PA: Temple University Press.

Cross, W. E., Jr., Smith, L., & Payne, Y. (2002). Black identity: A repertoire of daily enactments. In P. B. Pedersen, J. G. Draguns, W. J. Lonner, & J. E. Trimble (Eds.), *Counseling across cultures* (pp. 93–107), (5th ed.). Thousand Oaks, CA: Sage Publications.

Culley, M., & Portuges, C. (1985). *Gendered subjects: The dynamics of feminist teaching.* Boston: Routledge & Kegan Paul.

Damarin, S. (1994). Equity, caring and beyond: Can feminist ethics inform educational technology? *Educational Technology, 34*(2), 34–39.

Das Gupta, M. (1997). "What is Indian about you?": A gendered, transnational approach to ethnicity. *Gender & Society, 11*(5), 572–596.

Downing, N. E., & Roush, K. L. (1985). From passive acceptance to active commitment: A model of feminist identity development for women. *The Counseling Psychologist, 13*(4), 695–709.

Duany, J. (1998). Reconstructing racial identity: Ethnicity, color, and class among Dominicans in the United States and Puerto Rico. *Latin American Perspectives, 25*(3), 147–172.

Ellsworth, E. (1994). Why doesn't this feel empowering? Working through the repressive myths of critical pedagogy. *Harvard Educational Review, 59*(3), 297–234.

Enns, C. Z., & Sinacore, A. L. (Eds.). (2005). *Teaching and social justice: Integrating multicultural and feminist theories in the classroom.* Washington, DC: American Psychological Association.

Ensign, J. (2005). A story of complexity: Identity development, difference, and teaching for social justice. In R. A. Pena, K. Guest, L. W. Matsuda (Eds.), *Community and difference: Teaching, pluralism, and social justice.* New York: Peter Lang.

Evans, S. (1979). *Personal politics: The roots of women's liberation in the Civil Rights Movement and the New Left.* New York: Random House.

Fanon, F. (1967). *Black skin, white masks.* New York: Grove Press.

Fanon, F. (1968). *The wretched of the earth.* New York: Grove Press.

Fisher, B. (1987). The heart has its reasons: Feeling, thinking, and community-building in feminist education. *Women's Studies Quarterly, 15*, 47–58.

Fernandez, L. (2002). Telling stories about school: Using critical race and Latino critical theories to document Latina/Latino education and resistance. *Qualitative Inquiry, 8*(1): 45–65.

Freire, P. (1970/1994). *Pedagogy of the oppressed.* New York: Continuum.

Gay, G. (1995). Mirror images on common issues: Parallels between multicultural education and critical pedagogy. In C. E. Sleeter, & P. L McLaren (Eds.), *Multicultural education, critical pedagogy, and the politics of difference* (p. 172). Albany: SUNY.

Gay, G. (2000). *Culturally responsive teaching: Theory, research, & practice.* New York: Teachers College Press.

Giecek, T. S., with United for a Fair Economy (2007). *Teaching economics as if people mattered: A curriculum guide to today's economy.* Boston: United for a Fair Economy.

Golembiewski, R. T., & Blumberg, A. (1977). *Sensitivity training and the laboratory approach: Readings about concepts and applications.* Itasca, IL: F.E. Peacock.

Grant, C., & Chapman, T. K. (2008). *History of multicultural education* (6 vols). New York: Routledge.

Griffin, C., & Mulligan, J. (Eds.). (1992). *Empowerment through experiential learning: Explorations of good practice.* London: Kogan Page.

Griffin, P. (Ed.). (2003). LGBTQ issues in K-12 schools. [Special theme issue.] *Equity & Excellence in Education, 36*(2).

Griffiths, M. (Ed.). (2003). *Action for social justice in education: Fairly different.* Philadelphia, PA: Open University Press.

Gurin, P., Dey, E. L., Hurtado, S., & Gurin, G. (2002). Diversity and higher education: Theory and impact on educational outcomes. *Harvard Educational Review, 72*(3), 330–366.

Gutstein, E. (2006). *Reading and writing the world with mathematics: Toward a pedagogy for social justice* New York: Routledge.

Hackman, H. (2005). Five essential components for social justice education. *Equity & Excellence in Education, 38*(2), 103–110.

Hardiman, R. (2001). Reflections on white identity development theory. In C. L. Wijeyesinghe, & B. W. Jackson (Eds.), *New perspectives on racial identity development: A theoretical and practical anthology* (pp. 108–128). New York: New York University Press.

Hardiman, R., & Jackson, B. W. (1992). Racial identity development: Understanding racial dynamics in college classrooms and on campus. In M. Adams (Ed.), *Promoting diversity in college classrooms: Innovative responses for the curriculum, faculty, and institutions.* San Francisco: Jossey-Bass.

Hardiman, R. & Jackson, B. W. (1997). Conceptual foundations for social justice courses. In M. Adams, L.A. Bell, & P. Griffin (Eds.), *Teaching for diversity and social justice: A sourcebook* (pp. 16–29). New York: Routledge.

Hardiman, R., Jackson, B., & Griffin, P. (2007). Conceptual foundations for social justice education. In M. Adams, L. A. Bell, & P. Griffin (Eds.), *Teaching for diversity & social justice* (pp. 35–66), (2nd ed.). New York: Routledge.

Hart, M. U. (1991). Liberation through consciousness raising. In J. Mezirow et al. (Eds.),

Fostering critical reflection in adulthood: A guide to transformative and emancipatory learning. San Francisco: Jossey-Bass.

Hatfield, S. R. (Ed.). (1995). *The seven principles in action: Improving undergraduate education.* Bolton, MA: Anker.

Heintz, J., & Folbre, N. (2000). *The ultimate field guide to the U.S. economy: A compact and irreverent guide to economic life in America.* New York: New Press.

Helms, J. E. (1995). An update of Helms's White and People of Color Racial Idenitity models. In J. G. Ponterotto, J. M. Casas, L.A. Suzuki, & C. M. Alexander (Eds.), *Handbook of multicultural counseling* (pp. 181–198). Thousand Oaks, CA: Sage.

Horton, M., & Freire, P. (1991). *We make the road by walking: Conversations on education and social change* (reprint ed.). Philadelphia, PA: Temple University Press.

Horton, M., with J. & H. Kohl (1998). *The long haul: An autobiography.* New York: Teachers College Press.

Howe, F. (1984). Mississippi's Freedom Schools: The politics of education. In F. Howe (Ed.), *Myths of coeducation: Selected essays, 1964–1983* (pp. 1–17). Bloomington, IN: Indiana University Press.

Hunt Jr., J. S. (1995). Dewey's philosophical method and its influence on his philosophy of education. In K. Warren, M. Sakofs, & J. S. Hunt, Jr. (Eds.), *The theory of experiential education.* Dubuque, IA: Kendall/Hunt.

Hurtado, A. (1997). Understanding multiple group identities: Inserting women into cultural transformations. *Journal of Social Issues, 53*(2), 299–328.

Hurtado, A., Gurin, P., & Peng, T. (1994). Social identities—a framework for studying the adaptations of immigrants and ethnics: The adaptations of Mexicans to the United States. *Social Problems, 41*(1), 129–151.

Irvine, J. J. (2002). *In search of wholeness: African American teachers and their culturally specific classroom practices.* New York: Palgrave.

Jackson, B. W. (Ed.). (1976). *Black identity development.* Dubuque, IA: KendallHunt.

Jackson, B. W. (2001). Black identity development: Further analysis and elaboration. In C. Wijeyesinghe, & B. W. Jackson (Eds.), *New perspectives on racial identity development: A theoretical and practical anthology* (pp. 8–31). New York: New York University Press.

James, J. & R. Farmer (Eds.). (1993). *Spirit, space and survival: African American women in (white) academe.* New York: Routledge.

Johnson, K. A., Bernal, D. D., Wiedeman, C. R., & Knight, M. G. (2002). Special issue: The struggle for equity and social justice education: Theories, policies, and practices. *Equity & Excellence in Education, 35*(3).

Joplin, L. (1995). On defining experiential education. In K. Warren, M. Sakofs, & J. S. Hunt, Jr. (Eds.), *The theory of experiential education.* Dubuque, IA: Kendall/Hunt.

Kumashiro, K. K. (2000). Toward a theory of anti-oppressive education. *Review of Educational Research, 70*(1), 25–53.

Kumashiro, K. K. (2002). *Troubling education: Queer activism and antioppressive pedagogy.* New York: Routledge-Falmer.

Kershaw, B. (1992). *The politics of performance: Radical theatre as cultural intervention.* New York: Routledge.

Kim, J. (2001). Asian American identity development. In B. W. Jackson, & C. Wijeyesinghe (Eds.), *New perspectives on racial identity development: A theoretical and practical anthology* (pp. 67–90). New York: New York University Press.

King, P. M., & Kitchener, K. S. (1994). *Developing reflective judgment: Understanding and promoting intellectual growth and critical thinking in adolescents and adults.* San Francisco: Jossey-Bass.

King, P. M., & Shuford, B. C. (1996). A multicultural view is a more cognitively complex view: Cognitive development and multicultural education. *American Behavioral Scientist, 40*(2), 153–164.

Kolb, D. A. (1984). *Experiential learning: Experience as the source of learning and development.* Englewood Cliffs, NJ: Prentice-Hall.

Koliba, C., O'Meara, K., & Seidel, R. (2000). Special issue: Social Justice Principles for Experiential Education. *National Society of Experiential Education Quarterly, 26*(1).

Kumashiro, K. K. (Ed.). (2004). *Against common sense: Teaching and learning toward social justice.* New York: RoutledgeFalmer.

Larson, L. M. (2005). The necessity of feminist pedagogy in a climate of political backlash. *Equity & Excellence in Education, 38*(2), 135–144.

Leonard, J. (2008). *Culturally specific pedagogy in the mathematics classroom: Strategies for teachers and students.* New York: Routledge.

Lewis, M. G. (1993). *Without a word: Teaching beyond women's silence.* New York: Routledge.

Lippitt, R. (1949). *Training in community relations.* New York: Harper & Brothers.

Liu, M., Robles, B, Leondar-Wright, B., Brewer, R., & Adamson, R., with United for a Fair Economy. (2006). *The color of wealth: The story behind the U.S. racial wealth divide.* New York: New Press.

McCarthy, L. (2005). Recent issues in social justice education. [Special theme issue.] *Equity & Excellence in Education, 38*(2).

McIntosh, P. (1998). White privilege: Unpacking the invisible knapsack. In *Beyond heroes and holidays: A practical guide to k-12 anti-racist, multicultural education and staff development* (pp. 79–82). Wellesley: Network of Educators on the Americas.

McWhorter, G. A. (1969). Deck the ivy racist halls: The case of black studies. In A. L. Robinson, C. C. Foster, & D. H. Ogilvie (Eds.), *Black studies in the university: A symposium.* New Haven, CT: Yale University Press.

Marshall, C., & Oliva, M. (Eds.). (2006). *Leadership for social justice: Making revolutions in education.* Boston: Pearson.

Martin, R. J. (1995) (Ed.). *Practicing what we teach: Confronting diversity in teacher education.* Albany, NY: SUNY Press.

Memmi, A. (1965). *The colonizer and the colonized.* Boston: Beacon Press.

Meyers, C., & Jones, T. B. (1993). *Promoting active learning: Strategies for the college classroom.* San Francisco: Jossey-Bass.

Mindell, A. (1995). *Sitting in the fire: Large group transformation using conflict and diversity.* Portland, OR: Lao Tse Press.

Moses, R. P., & Cobb, C. E., Jr. (2001). *Radical equations: Math literacy and civil rights.* Boston: Beacon Press.

Nagda, B. A., Gurin, P., & Lopez, G. (2003). Transformative pedagogy for democracy and social justice. *Race, Ethnicity and Education, 6*(2), in press.

Nasir, N. S., & Cobb, P. (2007). *Improving access to mathematics: Diversity and equity in the classroom.* New York: Teachers College Press.

National Council for the Social Studies (2002). *National Standards for Social Studies Teachers.* Volume I, revised. Silver Spring, MD: National Council for the Social Studies.

Nieto, S. (2003). *What keeps teachers going?* New York: Teachers College Press.

Nieto, S. (2005). *Why we teach.* New York: Teachers College Press.

Nieto, S., & Bode, P. (2008). *Affirming diversity: The sociopolitical context of multicultural education* (5th ed.). Boston: Allyn & Bacon.

Ouellett, M. L.(Ed.). (2005). *Teaching inclusively: Resources for course, department & institutional change in higher education.* Stillwater, OK: New Forums.

Oyler, C., Hamre, B., & Bejoian, L. M. (2006). Special issue: Narrating disability: Pedagogical imperatives. *Equity & Excellence in Education, 39*(2).

Peña, R. (2005). Water is clear like me: A story about race, identity, teaching, and social justice. In R. A. Peña, K. Guest, & L. W. Matsuda (Ed.), *Community and difference: Teaching, pluralism, and social justice* (pp. 1–24). New York: Peter Lang.

Perry, W. G. (1981). Cognitive and ethical growth: The making of meaning. In A. Chickering (Ed.), *The modern American college* (pp. 76–116). San Francisco: Jossey-Bass.

Pfeiffer, J. W., & Jones, J. E. (Eds.). (1974). *Handbook of structured experiences for human relations training* (Vols. 1–2 revised ed.). La Jolla, CA: University Associates.

Pittelman, K., & Resource Generation. (2005). *Classified: How to stop hiding your privilege and use it for social change.* Brooklyn, NY: Soft Skull Press.

Pliner, S. (2004). Special issue: Universal instructional design and higher education. *Equity & Excellence in Education, 37*(2).

Proudman, B. (1995). AEE adopts definition. *The AEE Horizon, 15,* 1, 21.

Rachal, J. R. (1998). We'll never turn back: Adult education and the struggle for citizenship in Mississippi's Freedom Summer. *American Educational Research Journal, 35*(2), 167–198.

Reason, R. D., Broido, E. M., Davis, T. L., & Evans, N. J. (Eds.). (2005). *Developing social justice allies* (Vol. 110). San Francisco: Jossey-Bass.

Rodriguez, N. M., & Villaverde, L. E. (Eds.). (2000) *Dismantling white privilege: Pedagogy, politics, and whiteness.* New York: Peter Lang.

Rohd, M. (1998). *Theatre for community, conflict and dialogue: The hope is vital training manual.* Portsmouth, NH: Heinemann.

Russell, M. G. (1983). Black-eyed blues connections: From the inside out. In C. Bunch, & S. Pollack (Eds.), *Learning our way: Essays in feminist education.* Trumansburg, NY: The Crossing Press.

Sadker, M., & Sadker, D. (1992). Ensuring equitable participation in college classes. In L. L. B. Border, & N. V.N. Chism (Eds.), *Teaching for diversity.* New Directions for Teaching and Learning, no. 49. San Francisco: Jossey-Bass.

Sandler, B. R., & Hall, R. M. (1982). *The campus climate revisited: Chilly for women faculty, administrators, and graduate students.* Washington, DC: Project on the Status and Education of Women, Association of American Colleges.

Sarachild, K. (1974). Consciousness-raising: A radical weapon. In Redstockings (Ed.), *Feminist revolution* (pp. 144–150). New York: Random House.

Schoem, D., & Hurtado, S. (Eds.). (2001). *Intergroup dialogue; Deliberative democracy in school, college, community, and workplace.* Ann Arbor, MI: University of Michigan Press.

Schutzman, M. & Cohen-Cruz, J. (1994). *Playing Boal: Theatre, therapy, activism.* London: Routledge.

Sherif, M., & Sherif, C. (1970). Black unrest as a social movement toward an emerging self-identity. *Journal of Social and Behavioral Sciences, 15*(3), 41–52.

Shor, I. (1993). Education is politics: Paulo Freire's critical pedagogy. In P. McLaren, & P. Leonard (Eds.), *Paulo Freire: A critical encounter* (pp. 25–35). New York: Routledge.

Sleeter, C. E., & Grant, C. A. (2008). Education that is multicultural and social reconstructionist. In C. E. Sleeter, & C. A. Grant (Eds.), *Making choices for multicultural education: Five approaches to race, class, and gender* (6th ed.). New York: Macmillan.

Smith-Maddox, R., & Solórzano, D. G. (2002). Using critical race theory, Paul Freire's problem-posing method, and case study research to confront race and racism in education. *Qualitative Inquiry 8*(1), 66–84.

Solórzano, D., & Yosso, T. (2002). Critical race methodology: Counter-storytelling as an analytical framework for education research. *Qualitative Inquiry, 8*(1), 23–44.

Stephan, W. G., Vogt, W. P. (Eds.). (2004). *Education programs for improving intergroup relations: Theory, research, and practice.* New York: Teachers College Press.

Suzuki, B. H. (1984). Curriculum transformation for multicultural education. *Education and Urban Society, 16*(3), 294–322.

Tatum, B. D. (1992). Talking about race, learning about racism: The application of racial identity development theory in the classroom. *Harvard Educational Review, 62*(1), 1–24.

Tusmith, B., & Reddy, M. T. (Eds.). (2002). *Race in the college classroom: Pedagogy and politics.* New Brunswick, NJ: Rutgers University Press.

Villegas, A. M., & Lucas, T. (2002). *Educating culturally responsive teachers: A coherent approach.* Albany, NY: SUNY Press.

Warren, K. (Ed.). (1996). *Women's voices in experiential education.* Dubuque, IA: Kendall/Hunt.

Warren, K. (2005). A path worth taking: The development of social justice in outdoor experiential education. *Equity & Excellence in Education, 38*(1), 89–99.

Weiler, K. (1991). Freire and a feminist pedagogy of difference. *Harvard Educational Review 61*(4), 449–474.

Wijeyesinghe, C., & Jackson, B. W. (Eds.). (2001). *New perspectives on racial identity development: A theoretical and practical anthology.* New York: New York University Press.

Yeskel, F. (Ed.). (2008). Special theme issue: Class in education. *Equity & Excellence in Education, 41*(1), 1–148.

Young, I. M. (1990). *Justice and the politics of difference.* Princeton, NJ: Princeton University Press.

Zúñiga, X., Nagda, B. A., Chesler, M., & Cytron-Walker, A. (2007). *Intergroup dialogue in higher education: Meaningful learning about social justice.* ASHE Higher Education Report: *32*(4). Hoboken, NJ: John Wiley.

Part II

Theoretical Intersections

Chapter 4

Critical Theory as Social Justice Pedagogy

Bekisizwe S. Ndimande

Education is not a neutral phenomenon that takes place in an ideological vacuum. Rather, education is characterized by social and political contestations that have led to educational inequalities, especially among marginalized communities. This chapter argues about the role and importance of critical theory in combating educational and social inequalities that are perpetuated through school curriculum and educational policy and practice. This, I argue, is important to help our educational institutions achieve the goal of teaching toward social justice education. First, I explain the origins of critical theory, its proponents, and its meaning and understanding of school curriculum in the twenty-first century. Second, I discuss the relationship between critical theory and social justice education. Put differently, I argue about the contributions and the importance of critical theory in creating a socially just curriculum that can eliminate the long-standing educational inequalities in our public schools.

For many decades, the history of classroom curriculum in the United States and in other nations such as South Africa, Brazil, Namibia, the United Kingdom, and so forth, has been characterized as a curriculum content that has produced and reproduced social inequalities (Apple, 1979; Bowles and Gintis, 1976; Freire, 1970; Giroux, 1983; Kallaway, 1984; Nkomo, 1990; Young, 1971; Zeichner and Dahlstrom, 2001). The school curriculum, in its positivist and behaviorist forms, treated knowledge as something to be managed, adhered to, and followed rigidly and uncritically, and consumed unchallenged as if this knowledge represented the universal "truth" for all students in the classroom. The knowledge production itself was problematic, as was the case with school textbook content (Apple, 1993; Loewen, 1995) which created canons of "truths" and historical distortions taught and accepted without much debate in the classroom. By and large these have been the dispositions of the mainstream curriculum which lacked or failed to recognize the different environmental experiences of children (Dewey, 1938) as well as the different sociopolitical contexts in which public schools exist.

However, our curriculum has witnessed a gradual yet significant shift from the positivist and behavioral approach over the past few decades (Beyer and Apple, 1998). This shift has created a new approach to the teaching of curriculum content in schools; for instance, the shift to transformative education created a language of possibilities for teachers and students to engage the content of the curriculum by questioning the schools' official knowledge and by problematizing the meaning of school curriculum in broad terms (Freire, 1970; Apple, 1993). This shift is an antithesis to the traditional regurgitation of the curriculum content as if it represented undisputed truths and opinions. Unlike the top-down, rigid, and prescriptive positivist approach to curriculum in previous decades, this was the beginning of a critical and transformative evaluation of classroom curriculum in which critical theorists grounded their focus and concern on what is being taught in public schools, why was that particular knowledge taught, whose perspectives it represented, and questioned the underrepresentation of the subaltern groups in the curriculum. Through this shift, critical scholars have increasingly called for social justice education and multicultural education (Banks and Banks, 1995; Delpit, 1995; Grant and Sleeter, 1996; Ladson-Billings, 1994; Nieto & Bode, 2008) in order to transform the curriculum to serve all students equitably in schools.

I focus this chapter on two distinct areas of discussion about critical theory and social justice education. First, I explain the origins of critical theory, its proponents in social sciences and the field of education, but the discussion is situated broadly within the discourse of educational research.[1] In discussing this I foreground the shortcomings of the positivist and behaviorist approaches in the framing of curriculum and classroom learning as an impetus for seeking an alternative theory that provides critical engagement with the classroom curriculum discourse. Second, I explore the relations between critical theory and social justice education by discussing the importance of both critical theory and social justice education in school transformation and policy reform in the twenty-first century. Simply put, I argue about the contributions and the importance of critical theory in creating a socially just curriculum so that all students can be rewarded equitably in the school system that has been historically characterized by inequalities in educational outcomes.

Impetus toward Critical Theory in School Curriculum

It is impossible to provide a nuanced analysis of critical theory and its role in educational transformation before explaining the forms of rationalities, ideas, and the corpus of knowledge production preceding it. Prior to the development of critical theory as a field in the social sciences in the mid-twentieth century, positivism and behaviorism dominated educational institutions in the United States and in other countries. Augusto Comte, one of the popular advocates for positivism, argued that authentic knowledge comes through a positive affirmation of theories using scientific experiments and empirical inquiry (Comte, 1957), basically denouncing metaphysics and the dominance of theology in human thoughts. Positivism itself has to be understood within the backdrop of a paradigm shift at the time, namely, from what came to be called the Dark Ages to the Enlightenment era in Western Europe. During the Enlightenment movement intellectuals argued that in order to understand nature and society, strict scientific measures were necessary and would contribute to better human relations and better understanding of the world. Therefore, positivism was a philosophy that grounded its analysis on scientific measurements of truth since the "truth" was perceived as dissociated from personality and social environment.[2]

This "culture of positivism" became a social force in that its logic of scientific methodology, prediction, and technical control came to carry the intellectual currency and was perceived superior to hermeneutic principles that guided social sciences.[3] As a result, some academic disciplines began to focus more and more on "tangible evidence" so they could join the dominant academic discourse and be perceived as authentic members of the academy that valued "true" science. For instance, in the field of psychology, behaviorism, one of the branches of psychology, began to place more emphasis on experimental science, rather than introspection of truth and environmental influence. Therefore, positivism would play an integral part of knowledge construction in most academic disciplines in the early twentieth century.

Inevitably, the school curriculum would not be immune to the influence of positivism. This can be traced back to influential figures such as Frederick Taylor, Franklin Bobbit, Edward Thorndike, Ralph Tyler, Edward Ross, and many others, who proposed curriculum ideas rooted on a positivist framework.[4] Kliebard (1995) provides strong arguments to illustrate how these individuals' curriculum proposals were influenced by the scientific discourse largely based on the standardized techniques of production as well as the factory style of management. Ralph Tyler, whose work would become the dominant model in schools at the time, framed his ideas along the behaviorist discourse—i.e. the individual child behavior in the classroom, rather than the environment in which those individuals lived.[5] Based on this philosophy, Tyler's curriculum model makes a strong case on curriculum expertise, which he claimed to be useful in improving learning in public schools.[6]

Because of the positivist influence on curriculum, the categories that shape students' learning experiences and mediate their relationship between school and the larger society have had little to do with the value of critical thinking and social commitment (Giroux, 1997). According to Giroux, the objectification of knowledge is parallel to the objectification of the students themselves:

> There is little in the positivist pedagogical model that encourages students to generate their own meanings, to capitalize on their own cultural capital, or to participate in evaluating their own classroom experiences. The principles of order, control, and certainty in positivist pedagogy appear inherently opposed to such an approach. (p. 25)

Indeed, the biases inherent in positivism necessitated an alternative theory, an alternative discourse, and a paradigm shift in knowledge production. As pointed out by McLaren and Giarelli (1995), a number of scholars in the field of social sciences had to pursue an alternative form of scientific research and empirical analyses whose aim was to offer a nuanced and more meaningful description of the world than positivism. This paradigm shift created an intellectual space for more radical and transformative ways of theorizing about curriculum, decisions on the curriculum content, and teaching pedagogies in the public school system. It is, therefore, against this backdrop that critical theory was perceived as an alternative theory through which school curriculum and classroom pedagogy would be conceptualized and understood in the early twentieth century.

Defining Critical Theory

Defining any kind of theory can be difficult and problematic given the significance and meanings attached to theory (Thomas, 2007: p. 21) especially as it pertains to the contexts in which it is applied and the arguments it invokes. By definition, critical theory is a broad field that includes contributions from the Frankfurt School, Marxist and neo-Marxist traditions, theories of democracy, feminist tradition, postcolonial theories, among others (Popkewitz, 1999; Torres, 1999). While critical theory identifies, associates, and traces its original roots to the German Marxist Frankfurt School in the 1920s, its uses and evolution in various discourses that challenged the essentializing and biased positivist framework have had slight variances across different fields in the social sciences.[7] In this chapter I use the term *critical theory* as situated within the educational field context which gained momentum in the early 1970s and throughout the 1990s in the United States and Europe, which had an influence on educational scholars in other countries as well. Critical theory in this discussion is informed by the work of intellectuals and theorists such as Antonio Gramsci (in Henderson, 1988; Hoare & Smith, 1971); Paulo Freire (1970); Louis Althusser (1971); Michael Apple (1979); Samuel Bowles and Herbert Gintis (1976); Michael Young (1975); Henry Giroux (1983), Pierre Bourdieu (1984); Peter McLaren and Thomas Popkewitz (1995); and Ira Shor (1992) among others.

The critical theory literature that emerged around this time brought a different view of school curriculum, education policies, and pedagogical practices. Unlike the positivist social efficiency discourse, critical theory centered the school and classroom curriculum on human emancipatory discourse and democracy. This new discourse included debates about the impact of categories such as class, race, gender, culture, and ability on educational outcomes. Geneva Gay (1995), one of the pioneering intellectuals in the field of social justice education, states that critical theory is among the theories of social emancipation that carried the principles of social justice initiatives in the twentieth century. As a critical discipline, it aimed at re-examining the sociocultural realities in school at society, seeking possible answers to the perpetual social inequalities. According to Gay:

> Critical theory deals with practice and perspective, understanding and control, and the dialectical relationship between theory and practice. Its ultimate value commitment is human emancipation. Its intentions are to expose contradictions in culture, to explain how curriculum perpetuates the socioeconomic class structures and patterns of exploitation and subjugation present in society at large, and to strive passionately and compassionately for a new social order of egalitarianism in schools and society. (p. 26)

Similarly, Gordon (1995) views critical theory as an alternative, a dissenting voice from the biases of traditional schooling instituted by positivist and behaviorist research. For Gordon (1995) "Critical theory is the critique of domination. It seeks to focus on a world becoming less free, to cast doubt on the claims of technological scientific rationality, and then to imply that present configurations do not have to be as they are—that it is possible to change reality, and that conditions may already exist that can make such change possible" (p. 190).

Critical theory would become significant as a theoretical lens in analyzing issues of social diversity and multicultural education in the United States in the mid-twentieth century. Research (Banks and Banks, 1995; Perry and Fraser, 1994) pointed to an increasing cultural diversity in the United States by the turn of the nineteenth century. Writing in the early 1990s, Perry and Fraser (1994) assert: "Today this nation's people is more diverse than ever" (p. 3.). In the *Handbook of Research on Multicultural Education*, Banks and Banks (1995) argue that to transform the school system, educators must engage in in-depth knowledge about the influence and contributions of all groups and be able to find ways of providing a meaningful integration of this increasing diversity of our classrooms. This is even more important when we consider the global trends in human relations, i.e. how various nations across the world have been influenced by the global connectedness, including the global market in which we live.

However, this progressive rationale about school curriculum has been challenged by the neoliberal and neoconservative politics that often propose conservative policies for the purpose, I argue, of retaining the dominant status quo. The emphasis on standardized testing (McNeil, 2000); the call for a return to core knowledge (Hirsch, 1996), and the support for markets in education and school "choice" policies (Chubb and Moe, 1990), are but a few examples of the neoconservative and neoliberal resistance to changes toward social justice education. Therefore, using critical theory, I lay out an argument concerning why educators and policy makers should strive to implement curriculum, school policy, and classroom practices that are inclusive for all students in our diverse classrooms.

Critical Theory and Social Justice Education

Critical analysis is necessary and crucial in school organization, school policy implementation, and classroom curricula so that our public schools can become more oriented toward social justice projects and reject the neoconservative impulses that have characterized public education for decades. These sets of theories can help teachers and researchers collaborate in creating the language of possibility and create curriculum policy and classroom pedagogy geared towards equal educational opportunities. For this purpose, I would like to focus on the problems of school segregation and resource gaps as well as problematic classroom discourse in most public schools.

School Segregation and Resource Gap

One of the most fundamental principles toward social justice education is to provide all students with equal access to quality education. In doing so, social justice has to oppose various policies that hinder the educational success of students of color, for instance, such as school segregation. School segregation has historically privileged some and denied other students, particularly white students and students of color, respectively. The discriminatory laws of Jim Crow in the U.S.A., especially in the U.S. South, was part of the segregation policy that led to huge educational disparities among white and students of color, particularly black students. Although this may seem as an event of the past given the struggles of the Civil Righs Movement to end segregation and transform our social institutions, the reality is that these discriminatory practices are still present in many U.S. public schools in the twenty-first century and this should be a cause for concern for all of us involved in the education of our children (Kozol, 1991).

In what he calls the resegregation of American public schools, Orfield (2004) laments the systemic segregation of American public schools even as the nation celebrated the fortieth anniversary of *Brown vs Board of Education Topika, Kansas* in 2004. This, Orfield argues, has been exacerbated by the residential segregation which is also driven by the socio-economic status of people living in those neighborhoods. Because of these inherent social inequalities, schools in wealthy neighborhoods tend to be rewarded differently compared to those of poor neighborhoods. While some may argue that this phenomenon has nothing to do with the racial school segregation that was opposed by the Civil Rights Movement in the 1960s, I posit that since access to money is historically correlated to race, poor schools tend to be overwhelmingly those that serve people of color.

Jean Anyon (1981), who conducted a research study on five different elementary schools to contrast social class settings and educational outcomes in different neighborhoods of New Jersey, found that there was an extreme outcome difference between children who went to working-class schools and those who went to middle- or upper-class schools. Anyon's research discovered that the curriculum and instruction in those five schools varied from school to school, hence making it very hard for students to attain a similar social status or a social status different from what the school aimed to allocate to them. For example, her study found that on one hand in working-class schools, the curriculum and pedagogy were more likely to steer students to blue collar jobs when they graduated from high school with little or no chance of going to college. On the other hand, middle- or upper-class schools' curriculum encouraged students to go to college and prepared them for high-paying jobs; thus it was more likely that students from these schools would attain a middle- or upper-class social status. By virtue of the curriculum, students were thus stratified to future social class status aligned to the culture and classroom pedagogy of their specific schools.

Jonathan Kozol (1991) visited segregated public schools in poor neighborhoods across the country and concluded that segregated schooling is one of the major causes that perpetuate social inequalities. He argued that segregation is the source of disparities in school funding. Gaps in funding among districts and neighborhoods are significant between large, predominantly minority city districts and nearby, predominantly white suburban districts (Books, 2007). As Kozol and Books point out, there is a strong correlation between inadequate funding and educational opportunities. This becomes one of the consequential factors in access to quality education and future educational success. In essence, Anyon (1981); Kozol (1991); and Books (2007) conclude that current school segregation continues to produce and reproduce outcome inequalities based on the amount of resources available to public schools of certain neighborhoods and it is often the case that poor neighborhoods receive less because of the federal and state taxes connected to school funding (Books, 2007) and the parents' financial inability to support their resource-strapped public schools.

Critical theory informs us that school segregation in the first place is wrong. It helps us understand the sociopolitical inequalities that have been caused by the racialized policies and structural inequalities in the nation. Although school desegregation has its own problems, as I show later in this chapter, it is highly desirable in a diverse nation like the U.S.A. To create a socially just system of education we need teachers and researchers who would oppose any form of school segregation and mobilize with communities to set in place measures that can expedite desegregation and provide equitable funding to all schools.

Nieto (2006) contends that in order to create better education for all students, we should eliminate what she calls the "resource gap" in our public schools. Nieto maintains that we should provide students with all resources necessary to learn to their potential. Indeed, as Nieto argues further, working toward social justice education also means adopting the conscientious decision to end social poverty by creating educational access to all students, a social justice project that traces its roots to the turn of the nineteenth century and gained further momentum with the Civil Rights Movement of the 1960s.

Problematic Classroom Discourse

The fact that most schools have desegregation in the United States doesn't automatically translate to curriculum and pedagogical amelioration in those schools.[8] Desegregated schools have deep-seated problems too, regarding what happens inside the classroom and how individuals are treated or the nature of the curriculum offered in those schools. Research reveals that in racialized and class-structured societies, individual's learning is either constrained or enhanced by the nature of the curriculum and how it is presented in classrooms that have students from diverse backgrounds. Further, research has found that it is often the case that students who come to the same school, but from different sociocultural backgrounds, achieve differently even if they receive the same instruction.

Bourdieu (1984) and Grant and Sleeter (1996) make strong cases concerning the absence of equal educational achievement between working-class and middle-class students in desegregated schools. The difference between what is regarded as everyday knowledge and school knowledge comes to the fore in these settings.[9] For students from middle-class backgrounds, their everyday knowledge is congruent to school knowledge, thus they have the advantage of possessing the cultural capital legitimized and deemed necessary in school.[10] Based on research conducted in a desegregated school setting, Grant and Sleeter (1996) found that "While all children come to school with a fund of cultural capital, they do not all come with the cultural capital valued by the white middle class, and that is the cultural capital on which school knowledge—high status knowledge—is built" (p. 55).

Graham Vulliamy's (1976) "What Counts as School Music" is another good example that demonstrates how curriculum materials (re)produce social class inequalities, thus contributing to social stratification and hierarchy. Vulliamy researched what happens inside schools that may exacerbate racial and social inequalities. He chose to examine what was usually defined as school knowledge and how that knowledge was taught in a classroom setting. In this case he looked at music as a school subject. He found that the only music type that was legitimized by the school was referred to as "avant garde," which was regarded by the school as "serious" music, simply because it, according to the school, originated from the European "serious tradition." Important to note here that this happened at a time of tremendous revolution in music; for instance, this was the time when jazz music had gained popularity. Yet the school still regarded jazz as some kind of "popular music" drawing from African cultures, therefore not congruent to the school curriculum. Whitty (1985) argues that this is a form of cultural bias and that the schools were guilty of an unjustifiable practice which could result in the pedagogy of exclusions for students who were not from the dominant culture.[11]

A few years ago I discovered that my 15-year-old nephew in South Africa did not know how to write or read in our mother tongue, IsiZulu, because his school did not teach any indigenous language at an early stage (Ndimande, 2004). The school policy mandated the teaching of mother tongue only after grade six. This is rather disturbing in a nation where the identities of indigenous peoples were marginalized by the dehumanizing Bantu education for many years under apartheid. Besides, it is ironic in a South African context where 79% of the population speaks IsiZulu as a first language and yet the school does not recognize the importance of this language and its role in the learning process. Obviously, the elevation of English over IsiZulu creates a problematic cultural bias in the school curriculum that very likely leads to the further marginalization of other children's cultures.[12]

Consider a different learning environment described by Noffke (1998) where teachers in classrooms that served predominantly African American students made a concerted effort to implement curricular material and engage in teaching methods that were relevant to all the students in order to make the everyday knowledge be part of the school knowledge. This effort led to the recognition of students of color's cultural identities and histories through social justice oriented curriculum content. Unlike my nephew, Thuto's, school that introduces his culture in sixth grade, Noffke's (1998) observations show the importance of culturally relevant pedagogy as well as its early introduction: "Both the fourth and fifth graders began their work with discussion of the local African American community and its resources. The fourth grade went on to study aspects of the geography and history of Africa, while the fifth graders focused their attention on what would now be called African American history" (p. 106).[13]

The discussion in this chapter illustrates the importance of social justice education and the role of critical analysis in eliminating hegemonic practices such as social stratification through schools, school segregation and funding inequities, biased curriculum content, and other hegemonic practices that exist in the public school system. I argue here that since critical theory is a critique of domination

(Gordon, 1995), a social theory of social emancipation and for social justice (Gay, 1995), it is best situated to be used as a theoretical lens to interrupt such inequalities in schools and help propose democratic strategies that can help all students succeed in schools. If such educational inequalities persist, it is unthinkable to believe that methods of instruction alone, albeit important, could simply solve the educational problems, without really taking a critical evaluation of what is actually taught, how it is taught, and how the school knowledge is created or rather how it has been manipulated and controlled by the dominant group. Hence critical theory seeks to engage a broad collaboration among teachers, parents, and professional educators to interrogate this educational hegemony by conscientizing us to pay more attention to the complicated dynamics of race, culture, class, gender, ability, and sexuality.

Paulo Freire (1970), one of the renowned scholars of critical theory, writes about problematic curriculum content and pedagogy that tends to marginalize oppressed groups. He argues that the curriculum of the oppressed is characterized by biased knowledge toward the ruling class, i.e. it is biased toward the groups with power to select their everyday knowledge and social perspectives to be central to classroom content. Using critical theory as a lens, Freire argues that a school curriculum devoid of historical or distorted reality has led to the dehumanization of people, people who are "made" to lose sense of their history and identity. This serves to create a stratified society where power is not shared equally among communities. In this context, argues Freire, the rulers, those he called the oppressors, are found subjugating others, those he called the oppressed.

Because of these pervasive inequalities, Freire makes a strong case that students whose cultures are not represented in the curriculum content may perceive themselves as less legitimate and undeserving of leadership roles in the classroom. This perpetuates low self-esteem and even promotes ignorance of their cultural heritage. On the contrary, Freire proposes liberatory education that engages students to challenge the curriculum content and create critical possibilities to change the world. Liberatory education does not assimilate people, but helps them to support broader struggles for cultural, political, economic, gender, and social recognition.

In *Pedagogy of the Oppressed*, Freire (1970) states that the pedagogy of the oppressed is the pedagogy of people engaged in the fight for their own liberation. Here is one of Freire's crucial tenets about education for social justice: "No pedagogy which is truly liberating can remain distant from the oppressed by treating them as unfortunates and by presenting for their emulation models from among the oppressors. The oppressed must be their own example in the struggle for their redemption" (p. 39). Schools should be places for sociopolitical and economic and intellectual independence, not dehumanize those with less power and treat them as objects. Social justice education has the duty to interrogate the dichotomy of subjects versus objects on curriculum and pedagogy so that all students are treated equitably in classrooms and are encouraged to be critical thinkers, thus to get involved in what Freire called the processes of "reading the world."

For Freire, and others, no curriculum can serve as a course for social justice if the institution treats students as objects who are empty vessels waiting to be filled by the knowledge from the teacher. As Shor (1992) further points out, a critical curriculum is the one that would encourage students' questions in the classroom, not to perpetually use a top-down approach where the teacher fills in the empty jugs that students bring in class. According to this approach, the teacher should help students develop their intellectual and emotional powers so they are able to use this knowledge to reflect on their everyday experience and relations with the broader social structures. This is a true critical education that can stimulate a dialogue for discussion and help students to be able to argue from various perspectives given the diversity in which we live.

Conclusion

I have shown in this chapter that social justice education is crucial for educators, students, policy makers, and educational researchers since education is not simply a neutral process that serves all students equally in the classroom. The process of schooling and what actually goes on in the classroom is complicated and often mediated by conflict and contestation (Apple, 1995). This simply suggests that education does not always provide equal educational opportunities to every individual child. Classroom curriculum in many countries has been characterized by this contestation, contradictions, and inequalities.

Prior to the emergence of critical theory, school knowledge and school research was characterized by a positivist and behavioral approach, a paradigm in the early twentieth century that traces its roots to the Enlightenment era. The problem with positivism, in general, is that it treated all its research, including the human aspects, as something that needed to be subject to scientific measurement. For positivism, scientific knowledge was deemed original from positivist affirmation of scientific experiments and empirical inquiry. In this approach, human background and social environment, let alone the diversity of experiences, are not considered in the creation of knowledge, i.e. the assembling of it. In fact, people's social environments and relations to social structures were ignored. This led a growing number of social scientists to view positivism as somehow problematic and as a result they began to search for an alternative paradigm that could consider the complexities of human life and different human experiences within the social structures.

Given the growing distrust of positivism, critical theory emerged as an alternative to positivism. Although it started in the Frankfurt School of social sciences, it soon became popular within the field of education in the 1970s to examine the issues of socio-economics, class struggles, gender gaps, and racism in education. Unlike positivism, critical theorists understood the dialectical relations between theory and practice (Gay, 1995). Its conceptual and empirical frameworks allowed critical theory to commit to social justice issues, democratic goals, and human emancipation (Gay, 1995). It is against this background that critical theory sought to problematize how school policies and curriculum content discriminated against and marginalized minority students in schools. Although some of the early critical thought was inherently essentializing, the important work of neo-Marxist sociology of education still remains crucial to uncover the educational inequalities in schools.

With the increasing diversity in our schools, and the fight against neoconservatism and neoliberalism, critical theory has remained one of the important theories to be used in policy and curriculum to improve the education system in public schools. Building a socially just nation means ending segregation in schools that is based on race. It also means providing equitable funding to all public schools. Critical theory helps us ask questions about the nature of our classroom knowledge and evaluate the effects of the dominant discourse in schools. Critical theory for social justice takes on Freire's call for an education that recognizes the students' identities, what he called a liberatory education where students are being treated as subjects rather than objects in their education. Indeed critical theory for social justice education helps us look beyond just classroom education to school-wide access, better school funding, and the rationales behind these decisions. It is the goal of critical education to return equity and justice in learning institutions by conscientizing teachers about the importance of students' cultural background in learning and ensure that students' worldviews are recognized in schools. Above all, it is education that uses critical theory to interrogate and interrupt the conservative macro and micro elements in schools and to help nurture citizens who are committed to steer our education in an appropriate direction, a direction that will bring social justice to all.

Points of Inquiry

- How does critical pedagogy embrace multicultural education for social justice?
- What factors make it difficult to teach using critical pedagogy?
- How can social justice educators help students to help themselves, without imposing their ideals on children?

Points of Praxis

- Students map the goods and services in their community:

    ○ Compare the students' maps from different geographical areas;
    ○ Compare their maps with nearby suburban areas and rural areas.

- Students research the wealth gap in the U.S.A. Plot the numbers of Americans who make various increments of annual income. Compare these numbers to racial, geographical, and historical contexts.
- Students critique their own textbooks: pictures, stories, examples, etc. What values are promoted? Who is represented? Who is not? Why?

Notes

1 I do want to acknowledge that there are different forms of theoretical traditions that define themselves as critical theory. As Popkewitz and Fendler (1999, p. xiii) point out,

these traditions, although all committed to critical projects, have different views on the definition of power or the meaning of history.

2 McLaren and Giarelli (1995) note a paradoxical relationship between positivism and the Enlightenment movement. They contend that the Enlightenment era, despite its historical biases, did interrupt other forms of oppression, such as the centralization of power and dogmatism, and by supporting rationality, freedom, and democracy, something positivism would not do.

3 See Giroux (1997) *Pedagogy and the politics of hope*, particularly chapter 1.

4 Kliebard (1995) offers a detailed discussion of different proposals for curriculum development in the United States, including a critique of individuals whose influential ideas were modeled on "input—output" factory style.

5 His model was based on the four basic principles, namely, the formulation of educational objectives, selection of learning experiences, organization of those experiences, and evaluation. See Tyler (1946) *Basic principles of curriculum and instruction.*

6 While Tyler's ideas were applauded and implemented widely in the United States and in other countries as a model for curriculum in schools, his ideas were also criticized for framing theories about children based on behavioral psychology, which has its roots in positivism. See Huebner (1966) and Kliebard (1970) for criticism of the "Tyler Rationale."

7 See Torres (1999) especially on p. 91.

8 It is important to remember that school desegregation is not similar to school integration. School desegregation simply means bringing students of different sociocultural backgrounds in close physical proximity rather than interrogating the quality of contact among these students, see Ndimande's (2005) analysis of this phenomenon in the South African context.

9 Everyday knowledge is that knowledge used at home and everyday life, whereas school knowledge is used in school. For middle-class children everyday knowledge is more or less the same as school knowledge because it is what most schools tend to legitimize as an official knowledge of the school. See Grant & Sleeter (1996) *After the school bell rings*, p. 55.

10 In a Bourdieuan sense, cultural capital refers to forms of language, ways of understanding, acting, and the forms of social tastes that is acceptable by the dominant culture. These enhance one's social status in a social field of power. See Pierre Bourdieu (1984) *Distinction.*

11 I do want to mention Willis (1977), Cole (1988), and others who have provided nuanced arguments challenging conclusions inherently based on correspondence theories. While Willis's work, in particular, is important in critical theory in terms of the role of agency and to show that "message sent is not necessarily message received," it is also crucial to understand the role of social structures such as schools and their involvement in (re)producing social inequalities, as shown by research in this discussion.

12 I do not mean to suggest the jettisoning of English in South African public schools. However, I merely want to underscore the significance of all languages in schools. I do concur with Delpit (1995) that it is also important for students who come from disadvantaged socioeconomic backgrounds to be immersed in the dominant discourse of the schools in order to gain access to the cultural capital they will need for social mobility, yet, as Delpit also warns, poor children should not be stripped of their cultural identities.

13 Noffke's (1998) research was an analysis of multicultural projects between the years 1920 and 1940 in the United States which is still relevant in the twenty-first century classroom.

References

Althusser, L. (1971). *Lenin and philosophy and other essays.* New York: Monthly Review Press.

Anyon, J. (1981). Social class and school knowledge. *Curriculum Inquiry*, vol.11, no.1, Spring, pp. 3–42.

Apple, M. W. (1979). *Ideology and curriculum*. London: Routledge & Kegan Paul.

Apple, M. W. (1993). *Official knowledge: Democratic education in a conservative age*. New York: Routledge.

Apple, M. W. (1995). *Education and power*. (2nd ed.). New York: Routledge.

Banks, J. A., & Banks, C. A. M. (Eds.). (1995). *Handbook of research on multicultural education*. New York: Simon & Schuster Macmillan.

Beyer, L. E., & Apple, M. W. (Eds.). (1998). *The curriculum: Problems, politics, and possibilities*. (2nd ed.). New York: SUNY.

Books, S. (2007). Mechanics of unfairness: How we undercut poor children's educational opportunity. Paper presented in the Faculty of Education at the University of Pretoria, October 10.

Bourdieu, P. (1984). *Distinction: A social critique of the judgment of taste*. Cambridge, MA: Harvard University Press.

Bowles, S., & Gintis, H. (1976). *Schooling in capitalist America: Educational reform and the contradictions of economic life*. New York: Basic Books.

Chubb, J., & Moe, T. (1990). *Politics, markets, and America's schools*. Washington, DC: Brookings Institute.

Cole, M. (Ed.). (1988). *Bowles and Gintis revisited*. New York: Falmer Press.

Comte, A. (1957). *A general view of positivism*. New York: Robert Speller.

Delpit, L. (1995). *Other people's children*. New York: The New Press.

Dewey, J. (1938). *Experience and education*. New York: Collier Macmillan.

Freire, P. (1970). *Pedagogy of the oppressed*. New York: Continuum.

Gay, G. (1995). Curriculum theory and multicultural education. In J. A. Banks, & C.A.M. Banks (Eds.), *Handbook of research on multicultural education* (pp. 25–43). New York: Simon & Schuster Macmillan.

Giroux, H. A. (1983). *Theory and resistance in education*. South Hadley, MA: Bergin & Garvey.

Giroux, H. A. (1997). *Pedagogy and the politics of hope: Theory, culture, and schooling*. Boulder, CO: Westview Press.

Gordon, B. M. (1995). Knowledge construction, competing critical theories, and education. In J. A. Banks, & C. A. M. Banks (Eds.), *Handbook of research on multicultural education*. (pp. 184–143). New York: Simon & Schuster Macmillan.

Grant, C. A. & Sleeter, C.E. (1996). *After the school bell rings*. Washington, DC: Falmer Press.

Henderson, H. (1988). *Prison letters: Antonio Gramsci*. Chicago: Pluto Press.

Hirsch, E. D., Jr. (1996). *The schools we need and why we don't have them*. New York: Doubleday.

Hoare, Q., & Smith, G. N. (1971). *Selection from the prison notebooks of Antonio Gramsci*. New York: International Publishers.

Huebner, D. (1966) Curricular language and classroom meaning. In J. B. Macdonald, & R. R. Leeper (Eds.), *Language and meaning*. Washington, DC: Association for Supervision and Curriculum Development.

Kallaway, P. (Ed.). (1984). *Apartheid and education: The education of Black South Africans*. Johannesburg: Ravan Press.

Kliebard, H. M. (1970). The Tyler Rationale. *School Review*, vol.78, no.2, pp. 259–272.

Kliebard, H.M. (1995). *The struggle for American curriculum* (2nd ed.). New York: Routledge.

Kozol, J. (1991). *Savage inequalities: Children in America's schools*. New York: HarperCollins.

Ladson-Billings, G. (1994). *The dreamkeepers: Successful teachers of African American children*. San Francisco: Jossey-Bass.

Loewen, J. W. (1995). *Lies my teacher told me*. New York: Simon & Schuster.

McLaren, P. L., & Giarelli, J. M. (Eds.). (1995). *Critical theory and educational research*. New York: SUNY Press.

McNeil, L. M. (2000). *Contradictions of school reform: Educational costs of standardized testing*. New York: Routledge.

Ndimande, B. S. (2004). [Re]Anglicizing the kids: Contradictions of classroom discourse in post-apartheid South Africa. In N. K. Mutua, & B. B. Swadener (Eds.), *Decolonizing research in cross-cultural contexts: Critical personal narratives* (pp. 197–214). Albany, NY: SUNY Press.

Ndimande, B. S. (2005). Cows and goats no longer count as inheritances: The politics of school "choice" in post-apartheid South Africa. Unpublished doctoral dissertation (Ph.D.), University of Wisconsin-Madison.

Nieto, S. (2006). Creating new visions for teacher education: Educating for solidarity, courage, and heart. Paper presented at the American Association of Colleges for Teacher Education (AACTE), January 30, San Diego, CA.

Nieto, S., & Bode, P. (2008). *Affirming diversity: The socio-political context of multicultural education*. (5th ed.). Boston: Allyn & Bacon.

Nkomo, M. (1990). (Ed.). *Pedagogy of domination: Toward a democratic education in South Africa*. Trenton, NJ: Africa World Press.

Noffke, S. E. (1998). Multicultural curricula: "Whose knowledge?" and beyond. In L. E. Beyer, & M. W. Apple (Eds.), *The curriculum: Problems, politics, and possibilities* (pp. 101–116), (2nd ed.). New York: SUNY Press.

Orfield, G. (2004). The American experience: Desegregation, integration, resegregation. In M. Nkomo, L. Chisholm, & C. McKinney (Eds.), *Reflections on school integration* (pp. 95–124). Cape Town, Human Science Research Council.

Perry, T., & Fraser, J. W. (Eds.). (1994). *Freedom's plow: Teaching in the multicultural classroom*. New York: Routledge.

Popkewitz, T. S. (1995). Foreword. In P. McLaren, & J. M. Giarelli (Eds.). *Critical theory and educational research* (pp. xi–xxii). New York: SUNY Press.

Popkewitz, T. S. (1999). Introduction: Critical traditions, modernism, and the "posts." In T. S. Popkewitz, & L. Fendler (Eds.), *Critical theories in education: Changing terrains of knowledge and politics* (pp. 1–13). New York: Routledge.

Popkewitz, T. S., & Fendler, L. (Eds.). (1999). *Critical theories in education: Changing terrains of knowledge and politics*. New York: Routledge.

Shor, I. (1992). *Empowering education: Critical teaching for social change*. Chicago: University of Chicago Press.

Thomas, G. (2007). *Education and theory: Strangers in paradigms*. Maidenhead, U.K.: Open University Press.

Torres, C. A. (1999). Critical theory and political sociology of education: Arguments. In T. S. Popkewitz, & L. Fendler (Eds.), *Critical theories in education: Changing terrains of knowledge and politics* (pp. 87–115). New York: Routledge.

Tyler, R. W. (1946). *Basic principles of curriculum and instruction*. Chicago: University of Chicago Press.

Vulliamy, G. (1976). What counts as school music? In G. Whitty, & M. F. D. Young (Eds.), *Explorations in the politics of school knowledge* (pp. 19–34). Driffield, U.K.: Nafferton Books.

Whitty, G. (1985). *Sociology and school knowledge: Curriculum theory, research and politics*. London: Methuen.

Willis, P. (1977). *Learning to labor: How working class kids get working class jobs.* New York: Columbia University Press.

Young, M. F. D. (1971). *Knowledge and control: New direction for the sociology of education.* London: Collier-Macmillan.

Zeichner, K., & Dahlstrom, L. (2001) (Eds.). *Democratic teacher education reform in Africa: The case of Namibia.* Windhoek, Namibia: Gamsberg Macmillan.

Chapter 5

"Jump at Da Sun"

Black Feminist Influences on Social Justice Pedagogy

Adrienne D. Dixson and Jamila D. Smith

In this chapter, we examine the ways in which Black feminist theories inform social justice education. Drawing from a diverse body of Black feminist scholarship, specifically theories in sociology, history, literary criticism, and political science, we explore how Black women understand and make sense of knowledge. This exploration, we suggest, can be applied to an understanding of Black women teachers' pedagogy.

> "Last year, when I entered the university setting, I heard a lot of talk about social justice, but was unsure of its form and function. As a product of African American schools for the majority of my education, entering a major university as the only Black woman was new for me. And while the social justice phrase kept being tossed around; I noticed none of my required readings were by or about people of color. I knew there was no justice in that."
>
> Jamila D. Smith

Introduction

A 1999 study conducted by the U.S. Department of Education found that a majority of public school teachers felt unprepared to work with students who are from socially and culturally diverse backgrounds (Department of Education, 1999). By the year 2000, Foster (1993) noted that students of color would comprise nearly 53% of all public school students. She also suggested that given this changing student demographic, a significant percentage of new teachers would need to be teachers of color. Irvine (Irvine and James 1998) suggests that teachers of color are needed not just to fulfill "role model and diversity needs," which is an argument often made to support the recruitment of more people of color into teaching. Rather, she argues that the role that Black teachers serve in the lives of African American students is more akin to that of mentors rather than role models. According to Irvine, role modeling is not as dynamic and interactive as mentoring—mentoring requires the student and teacher to have a substantive relationship with each other. Given the underachievement of students of color in public schools, particularly African American and Latino students, this notion of mentoring (among other strategies) becomes important in looking for ways to make the school experience more successful for this population of public school students. Finally, and perhaps what might be more pressing is the need for teachers who are responsive to students on academic, cultural, and emotional levels.

In this chapter, we examine the ways in which Black feminist theories inform social justice education. We situate our discussion of social justice education within the larger framework of multicultural education. Within the context of Black feminist theory, we draw from a diverse group of Black feminist scholars. Primarily, we tie our discussion of social justice education by drawing on Black feminist theories in sociology, literary criticism, history, education, law, and political science. In this chapter, we discuss some of the key concepts of multicultural education as well as outline the foundational concepts of Black feminist theories. Specifically, we find Patricia Hill Collins's scholarship helpful because she articulates a Black feminist epistemology. That is, Collins's scholarship is one of the first articulations of how Black women create and make sense of knowledge. We outline the basic tenets of Collins's text as well as attempt to shed light on how this work may be applied to studying and understanding Black women teachers' pedagogy. Second, we draw on the scholarship of Joy James (1997, 1999) because it offers an analysis and critique of the "racial uplift" ideology. Black feminist scholars often cite the racial uplift ideology as a motivation for the work of such Black women activist-scholars as Anna Julia Cooper, Mary McCleod Bethune, and others. Finally, we draw on bell hooks's notion of "engaged pedagogy" to examine how Black feminism theory can be applied to teaching at the K-12 level.

Definitions and Multiculturalism

There are many definitions of social justice. Adams, Bell, & Griffin (2007) describe their vision of social justice as, "We envision a society in which individuals are both self-determining (able to develop their full capacities) and interdependent (capable of interacting democratically with others). Social justice involves social actors who have a sense of their own agency as well as a sense of social responsibility toward and with others, their society, and the broader world in which we live" (pp. 1–2). While these are not simple goals to attain, they are possible if creating change is a foundation for one's actions. Their definition for social justice education is one that "enables people to develop the critical analytic tools necessary to understand oppression and their own socialization within oppressive systems, and to develop a sense of agency and capacity to interrupt and change oppressive patterns and behaviors in themselves and in the institutions and communities of which they are a part" (p. 2). We agree that marginalized and oppressed peoples must understand oppression and recognize how they may unwittingly participate in practices that marginalize and/or oppress others; however, we believe social justice is more than changing behaviors but changing the very institutions themselves.

Adams et al. suggest that while the dynamics of race, gender, religion, sexuality, native language, among other characteristics, have been used as exclusionary tactics for years, a social justice pedagogy focuses on ways to make them inclusive. By drawing on history, movements such as the Civil Rights Movement, the Women's

Movement, the New Left movement, among others, one is not only able to learn from past experiences, but also to understand the importance of social justice in preventing their recurrence. They write, "As we encounter today a period in many ways like the 1960s, we need to recognize the seeds and lessons for similar activist movements now and in the years ahead. We can also learn from studying connections among movements that may not have been as clearly visible as they are now in hindsight" (p. 5). Asking "In whose interest do prevailing systems operate?" will help examine both oppression and power and to understand and begin to deconstruct the notion of privilege. When education is placed on the continuum of multicultural education, Sonia Nieto (1992) says that it can function as: antiracist education, basic education, social justice, and critical pedagogy (p. 208). In this way, Nieto agrees with Adams et al.'s (2007) perspective of social justice and multicultural education as a process. She writes, "Multicultural education must be accompanied by 'unlearning' conventional wisdom as well as dismantling the policies and practices that disadvantage some students" (p. 218). She goes on to discuss the role of teachers and parents in "unlearning" these practices. This act of unlearning is consistent in various definitions and examples of social justice as well as multicultural education. In order to "do the work" of social justice, one must first acknowledge any forms of racist, sexist, ableist, and other oppressive behaviors and begin to work toward disrupting those practices.

Multicultural Education, Social Justice Pedagogy and Black Feminism

Within the broad field of teacher education, there is mounting interest in understanding what motivates and influences teachers' curricular and pedagogical decisions. Early research on teacher knowledge focused primarily on identifying teacher behaviors and strategies that facilitated increased achievement among students (Brophy & Good, 1987; Shulman, 1987). Shulman notes that these attempts have tended to look very narrowly at the teaching of skills and "generic relationships" and thus, have been less fruitful. He suggests that a line of research that explores the "wisdom of practice" that can in turn be interpreted into "potentially codifiable knowledge" is preferable (p. 12). While Shulman's work has opened the door to identifying the "wisdom of practice," more questions have emerged within this area of research.

Attendant to this growing concern with teacher knowledge, are the ways in which it is influenced, in part, by their racial and/or cultural backgrounds.[1] Moreover, there is evidence that teachers' beliefs about their own racial/cultural backgrounds impact their effectiveness with students of color (Au & Jordan, 1981; Hilliard, 1991; Irvine, 1990; Ladson-Billings, 1995; Ladson-Billings & Henry, 1990; Mohatt & Erickson, 1981). In light of the achievement gap between students of color and White students, particularly in U.S. public schools, it becomes increasingly more important to examine teachers' identities, and their influence on pedagogy and curricula, in an effort to address this gap and implement more culturally relevant pedagogical strategies.

There is a growing body of literature that examines the ways that African American teachers and, specifically, African American women teachers make sense of their pedagogy and the curriculum vis-à-vis their race/culture and gender (Beauboeuf-Lafontant, 1997, 1999, 2002; Dingus, 2008; Dixson, 2003; Dixson & Dingus, 2007; Foster, 1993). Although a number of professional educational organizations, colleges, and schools of education agree that a diverse teaching force is important given the burgeoning number of students of color in America's public schools, understanding what teachers of color bring to the classroom, other than their racial/cultural background, has yet to be fully explored and articulated. Furthermore, what we know about teaching, and in particular, the best practices in core academic subjects, have been gleaned primarily by studying teachers from one cultural/racial group: White Americans. Siddle Walker (2000) suggests that historical research on African American teachers can help uncover an African American epistemology of teaching that heretofore has gone virtually unnoticed in the educational literature, save the groundbreaking work by a relatively small number of scholars. While the historical research is important to the extent that it provides a historical context for African American education, contemporary research that examines the pedagogy of African American teachers has significant implications as well in terms of reckoning the historical record with current practices.

The research that has explored Black women's pedagogy specifically is important because it helps to highlight the function of gender in Black teacher's pedagogy (Beauboeuf-Lafontant, 1999, 2005; Dixson, 2003; Foster, 1995; hooks, 1994; Jeffries, 1994; Wade-Gayles, 1993). In particular, this exploration of gender is not just for gender's sake, but also to explore how Black women teachers' gender identities inform their pedagogy in relation to working for social change and social justice. While others have written on the feminization of teaching and the equity issues involved (Fultz, 1995a), some research has explored how being a woman is a necessary and important part of the pedagogy of the women they studied (Beauboeuf-Lafontant, 1997; Dixson, 2003; Foster, 1993; Casey, 1993; Weiler, 1988). Situating Black women teachers' pedagogy within a Black feminist framework is important because it gives us a more complex understanding of their mission and beliefs (Collins, 1990). However, we do not want to suggest that all Black women teachers would or do subscribe to Black feminism or that only Black women can engage in a social justice pedagogy. We do suggest, however, that Black women teachers, as in the words of sociologist Patricia Hill Collins, have a unique "angle of vision" on our own lives (and our pedagogy) that may be necessary in understanding exactly what we bring to educational research and practice. In addition, we believe, given Black women's subjugated position, that Black feminist theories might significantly inform social justice pedagogy.

Black Feminist Thought

Sociologist Patricia Hill Collins describes Black feminist thought as "facing the complex nexus of relationships among biological classification, the social construction of race and gender as categories of analysis, the material conditions accompanying these changing social constructions and Black women's consciousness about these themes" (p. 22). Collins bases her definition of Black feminist thought on what she describes as a "Black women's standpoint" as a perspective that expresses "those experiences and ideas shared by African-American women that provide a unique angle of vision on self, community, and society—and theories that interpret these experiences"(p. 22). Thus, for Collins, Black feminist thought "encompasses [the] theoretical interpretations of Black women's reality by those who live it" (p. 22). *Black Feminist Thought: Knowledge, Consciousness and the Politics of Empowerment* (1990) is Collins's comprehensive and influential text on Black feminist ideology. Collins challenges historically held stereotypes about Black women. Specifically, she highlights the ways in which Black women, both scholars and in the academy and activists, have resisted the images of the Mammy, the Matriarch, and the Jezebel that she argues prevail in not only popular, mainstream media, but also in political discourse particularly as they pertain to economic policies (welfare, welfare-to-work) and other domestic policy issues.

While Black women are certainly a diverse group, Collins argues that, "we all share the common experience of being African-American women in a society that denigrates women of African descent" (p. 22). Out of this common experience, she identifies seven core themes that frame Black feminist thought: (1) work, family, and Black women's oppression; (2) controlling images of Black women (the Mammy, Matriarch, and the Jezebel); (3) the power of self-definition; (4) motherhood; (5) activism; (6) sexual politics; (7) sexual politics and Black women's relationships. In addressing the diversity of Black women's experiences, Collins notes that social class differences, ethnicity, urbanization, age, sexual orientation, and regional differences all account for the variance in Black women's responses to these core themes. Moreover, in conceptualizing how Black feminist theory informs social justice pedagogy, Collins's seven core themes speak to overarching issues of marginalization that while exacerbated by the intersection of race, class, and gender, also shape the experiences of others who are marginalized. That is, using Black women's responses to the inequitable distribution of labor in the private and public sphere (mothering in particular), sexualized stereotypes, resistance behaviors, sexual orientation, can provide insight into how normalized practices and grand policies impact those who are often the most vulnerable. It is also important to understand the resistance strategies that Black women employ as a way to imagine and enact similar strategies for other groups. For example, Andrea Collins, a Black woman teacher in a Midwestern school district, used the contradictions in the rhetoric and practice of U.S. democracy to teach her students about the history of gender and class discrimination and oppression. In a lesson on the U.S. Constitution, Ms. Collins pointed out to the students that only propertied men, and in particular, propertied White men, initially had the full benefits of U.S. citizenship (Dixson and Dingus, 2008).

Collins also outlines a particular orientation to understanding and knowledge that she argues is unique to African American women. She suggests that because African American women have had to struggle against White male interpretations of the world in order to articulate our standpoint, we can describe Black feminist thought as subjugated knowledge. As a result, Black women feminist scholars have had to look to alternative sites (music, behavior, literature, daily conversations) to articulate and explore the core themes of Black feminist ideology (p. 202).

Black Feminist Epistemology

Collins outlines four areas of a Black feminist epistemology:[2] Concrete experience as a criterion of meaning; the use of dialogue in assessing knowledge claims; the ethic of caring; and the ethic of personal accountability. These criteria inform social justice pedagogy in part because they seek to challenge the master narrative and validate the experiences of marginalized groups. In addition, these criteria challenge teachers and scholars to move beyond viewing knowledge as "neutral" and "objective" but contextualized and situated.

Concrete Experiences as a Criterion of Meaning

As Collins explains, "For most African-American women, those individuals who have lived through the experiences about which they claim to be experts are more believable and credible than those who have merely read or thought about such experiences" (p. 209). Thus, we can believe that someone is an expert about a particular issue because she has lived through it. Similarly, within the context of social justice pedagogy, it is important that people of color and others who are marginalized, speak for themselves about their experiences. This does not suggest that White people cannot speak about or against the oppression of people of color, rather, it suggests that their perspective on its impact and meaning cannot be seen as the only valid perspective.

The Use of Dialogue in Assessing Knowledge Claims

Collins argues that dialogue promotes a connectedness between two subjects engaged in dialogue that is essential in the knowledge validation process and that this connectedness has African roots (p. 212). She further argues that this connectedness through dialogue promotes a sense of community that humanizes those involved in dialogue. In our efforts to attain social justice, dialogue does not imply that communication will result in equality. It does, however, serve as a tenet for change. This notion of dialogue and connectedness is aligned with the Freirean notion of conscientization that emerges out of dialogue about issues facing the oppressed and developing strategies to change their circumstances.

The Ethic of Care

Collins identifies three interrelated components of the ethic of care—individual uniqueness, appropriateness of emotions in dialogue, and the capacity for empathy. Individual uniqueness suggests that creativity and the ability to express one's self has primacy over "looking like everybody else." Similarly, Collins argues that appropriateness of emotions in dialogue makes it acceptable for a speaker or participant in a dialogue to become "emotional" when expressing her thoughts on a particular issue or the validity of an argument (p. 216). The capacity for empathy is the third component of the ethic of care. From a social justice pedagogical perspective, these ideas are crucial to engaging students in looking for strategies to challenge oppression. It is important to recognize that although individuals are part of a group, they also have unique experiences and ideas that can add complexity to understanding oppression. In addition, discussing one's experiences can be an emotional experience and using those emotions to explain and describe the impact of their experiences can be an effective way to inspire others to participate in resistance movements. Moreover, discussions about oppression often make people express anger, disappointment, and frustration. Teaching students how to harness their emotions and to respect and understand how others might feel about their experiences should be an important aspect of social justice pedagogy. Understanding the oppressive forces at work during the early part of my doctoral work would have enabled me to resist and speak out against the lack of reading material on people of color. Instead of discussing my emotions, I fell victim to silence, in fear of being labeled the "angry, Black student."

The Ethic of Personal Responsibility

As the final dimension of a Black feminist epistemology, the ethic of personal responsibility is perhaps one of the most important. As Collins states, "not only must individuals develop their knowledge claims through dialogue and present them in a style proving their concern for their ideas, but people are expected to be accountable for their knowledge claims" (p. 218). Collins argues for the need for an alternative epistemology. She states that, "The existence of a self-defined Black women's standpoint using a Black feminist epistemology calls into question the content of what currently passes as truth and simultaneously challenges the process of arriving at that truth" (p. 219). This dimension encompasses the previous three. While experience, dialogue, and emotion are essential to a Black feminist epistemology, accountability is fundamental to social justice pedagogy. Collins believes in resisting the "truth" of how the Black woman has been defined, while simultaneously remaining critical of the process of defining ourselves.

Other Dimensions of Black Feminist Ideology

Social Class Considerations

Although Collins argues that teaching for Black women is a site for political activism, James (1997) argues that most educators, or those whom she describes as "institutional educators," are likely to avoid activism that jeopardizes their teaching careers. She finds Collins's claims that teaching has "intrinsic progressivism" as problematic because teaching may in fact be a "de-radicalized political site" (p. 142). James and others have argued that Black teachers have traditionally been situated in the Black bourgeoisie (Fultz, 1995c; Higginbotham, 1989). She argues that as a result, some Black women teachers may have participated in and contributed to the schism among the Black middle-class and poor Blacks. She also argues that Collins's call to Black women scholars to "lift as we climb" does not radicalize teaching but in effect re-inscribes class differences. James asks, "What type of activism?" (p. 141). James's critique is important as a necessary check against how other factors may mediate gender and race. Her critique is also an important gauge of the extent to which Black women teachers are truly working to disrupt oppressive conditions.

Black Women Activists/Educators

Much of the work done by Black women for the liberation of Black people has all too often gone unrecognized. While some will acknowledge that Black women are the "backbone" of Black society, others lament that we are in fact the "mules" for everyone (Hurston, 1942/1996). In *Transcending the Talented Tenth* (1997), James not only offers an analysis of the racial uplift ideology, but she also addresses the issue that Black women's activism is routinely missing from historical accounts (p. 53). James argues that as progressive as Du Bois's gender politics were, he still contributed to the erasure of Black women's contribution to the struggle for racial equality. Anna Julia Cooper, worked tirelessly on issues of racial and gender oppression, yet Du Bois never formally recognized her efforts. He quoted Cooper on at least two occasions yet failed to give her the honor of naming her (p. 44). According to James, Cooper's call for the uplift of the race "from the bottom up" in which she focuses on the conditions of poor and working-class women comes a full decade before Du Bois's "Talented Tenth" concept (ibid.). Her famous refrain, "when and where I enter" is the speech from which Du Bois borrows the first sentence for his "The Damnation of Women" essay. Yet he does not even credit her by name, but rather refers to her as "As one of our women writes" (p. 44). She is rendered anonymous and the full import of her gender analyses goes unheard. Although Black women scholars have recovered Cooper's scholarship, it is disappointing that given Du Bois's stature in Black society, he chose not to work in concert with Cooper toward Black equality.

Ida B. Wells-Barnett is best known for her anti-lynching crusade. However, before she embarked on her crusade against lynchings, Wells-Barnett earned her living as a teacher. She was educated in missionary schools and became a teacher to help her father raise her siblings after the death of her mother. Unfortunately, very little is known about Wells-Barnett's classroom experiences. We do know, however, that she was unhappy as a teacher and found her true calling as a journalist and later as an activist.

Wells-Barnett exposed the fallacy of a representation of Black men as "sexual predator" and argued in fact that Black women were in more danger of being raped by White men than White women were by Black men. She has (and did) as a result, come under attack by not only Whites who disagreed with her stance, but more recently by Black feminist/womanist scholars (James, 1997, p. 62). Some of these scholars argue that Wells-Barnett refused to acknowledge that in fact some (albeit a small number) Black men raped White women (Smith, 1989; Walker, 1983). However, James counters that Wells-Barnett never in fact stated that *no* Black man ever raped a White woman, but that in *many* of the cases where a Black man had been accused of raping a White woman, the accusation was false. Wells-Barnett was uncompromising in her stance against lynching. Her "burgeoning" feminism was manifest in her refusal to accept the circumscribed roles open to women of her time. She openly challenged unfair and inaccurate sexual and gender politics that elevated White women and made it wholly impossible for Black women to claim and protect their virtue. Yet she, like Cooper, languished in obscurity, having been ignored by her peers and other historians. She laments in her diary the fact that her peer, Carter G. Woodson, does not mention her anti-lynching work in a Negro history book he published in 1930 (ibid.).

James reminds us of Wells-Barnett in these terms,

> Wells-Barnett bequeathed a legacy of skepticism concerning state-accounts of and prosecution of racialized sexual violence through the press, police and courts; of risk taking in investigative journalism; and of willingness to directly confront the state and elite society to stop violence. This legacy influenced later generations of women such as Rosa Parks and Ella Baker.
>
> (James, 1997, p. 81)

She goes on to caution us to be vigilant in how we "imagine and image" historical African American women activists-intellectuals and that what we do in this regard "shapes visions of contemporary antiracist radicalism and black female leadership." She encourages us to be careful of discrediting the radical women activists who are our foremothers, for if we are not careful, we will lose sight of the "radical black praxis" and will ultimately validate "nonradical elites" as the most viable form of leadership (p. 81). James's critique is important not to bifurcate our leadership but rather to make certain that Black leadership is an organic endeavor. Black teachers' roles in this effort are crucial not only to help shape an informed community, but as we also broadly conceive of leadership, Black teachers inherently encompass that role in the Black community.

Black Feminist Pedagogy

bell hooks and Teaching to Transgress. bell hooks, in *Teaching to Transgress: Education as the Practice of Freedom* (1994), discusses her efforts to testify to the effects of education as a liberatory endeavor. Through reflections on her experiences as a teacher and a student, hooks offers important insights on and critical analyses of what a liberatory, "engaged pedagogy" looks like in the classroom. hooks challenges the notion that teaching, whether it is in the elementary or college classroom, is a "dull, less valuable" profession. hooks further offers that the pleasure of teaching is an act of resistance, a performative act through which change, invention, and spontaneous shifts encourage students to become more engaged participants in their own learning (p. 11). It is also through these essays that we are able to "piece together" a concrete example of a Black feminist pedagogy.[3]

hooks very poignantly credits her passion and interest in teaching to a large extent to the Black women teachers she had growing up in the segregated South. She discusses her teachers' "commitment to nurturing intellect so that we could become scholars, thinkers and cultural workers—black folks who used our 'minds'" (p. 2). For hooks, her teachers were enacting a revolutionary pedagogy that she argues was "profoundly anti-colonial." She describes her teachers' work as a mission and in order to fulfill that mission, the teachers, mostly Black women, made sure that they knew their students. Her teachers, as others have described Black women teachers, were active citizens in her community (Collins, 1990; Foster, 1997; Ladson-Billings, 1995). Learning and teaching in hooks's all-Black school was joyful and full of "messianic zeal" enacted to transform her mind.

Like Thompson suggested in her discussion of the Black feminist ethic of care in which the pragmatic orientation to survival is based on confronting racism, hooks describes her teachers as having a liberatory mission to educate their students to resist racism and White supremacy. She admits that though these teachers did not identify as feminists, they were committed to and insisted on young Black women achieving academic excellence and thinking critically. For hooks, these teachers' efforts were an example of anti-sexist practice that had a profound effect on her teaching. Similarly, the teachers in one study Dixson conducted, although teaching in diverse classrooms that had students from a variety of cultures, believed it was their specific duty to make certain that the African American students in their classrooms were armed with strategies to resist racism (Dixson, 2003; Dixson and Dingus, 2008). Aware that they could not always protect them from the racism they may in fact experience in other teachers' classrooms, especially from some White women's classrooms, these teachers believed that they were giving their students some tools to resist and act against efforts to under-educate them (Interview notes, Fall 1999). While these strategies were shared with African American female and male students, the teachers also believed that as educated Black women, it was their duty to mentor their young Black female students. Very much in the tradition of othermothering,[4] these teachers did not seek to undermine their female students' mothers, but rather, to complement what was being taught at home. Further, where they believed that the mother was not able to impart such training, i.e., because of absence, drug addiction, or the mother's own struggles to survive, the teacher, in consultation with mothers or other caregivers, sought to "pick up the slack"(Interview notes, February 2000).

At this point, I would like to highlight briefly some other aspects of liberatory teaching that hooks believes are part of her teaching. hooks situates her pedagogy in a Black feminist tradition that has been shaped by the Black women teachers of her youth and informed by the scholarship of and mentoring relationship with Brazilian educator and philosopher and key originator of social justice pedagogy, Paulo Freire, who is discussed at length in Chapter 4. I will relate some of the aspects of liberatory teaching that hooks outlines to what I believe are aspects of a Black feminist pedagogy as witnessed through my observations of and interactions with the Black women teachers in my study. It is important for me to state very clearly that with this work, I am not attempting to suggest a template for Black feminist pedagogy. Rather, I am hoping to offer a suggestion of what it (Black feminist pedagogy) could be and how we can understand Black women's teaching through its lens and the lens of multicultural education as social justice.

hooks states that her interpretation of feminist pedagogy is a blending of Freire's work and thoughts and the influences of the Black women teachers of her youth. hooks credits the notion of "engaged pedagogy" with Freire's critique of the banking system of education. Freire describes the banking system as one in which teachers believe that teaching is simply giving students information to memorize and store for later use (Freire, in hooks, p. 14). Synthesizing Freire's notion of *conscientization*, or critical awareness and engagement, hooks encourages her students to be active participants in their learning and affirms their status as experts of their own knowledge and learning. She suggests that teachers must stress to their students that education is dialectical—we must actively work for liberation not just passively accept what happens. By the same token, hooks advises teachers to make the classroom a place wherein students' experiences are valued and affirmed. hooks rejects the notion that suggests that students of color invoke the "authority of experience," giving accounts of personal experiences to illustrate racism and other forms of marginalization to silence White students (in discussions about diversity, race, and racism), rather she celebrates what she calls the "passion of experience" and believes that teachers must bring their "passion of experience" into the classroom as well.

hooks's analysis also addresses the issue of presence in the classroom, both physical and spiritual. She rejects the notion that it is possible and desirable to create a split between the body and spirit. Further, she suggests that teachers (Black women teachers) always be aware that their mere presence in a "system that has not become accustomed to your presence or to your physicality" is crucial (p. 135). The importance of the presence manifests in how we physically interact with our students. In the classroom, hooks urges teachers to move among their students. In an elementary classroom this may not be an issue, but the physicality of our relationship with our students is important to consider. For hooks, walking with students, standing next to them, even a touch on the shoulder, are simplistic ways in which teachers can "work beyond the limits of the body" (p. 138).

hooks's work offers us some concrete examples of how Black feminist pedagogy is enacted in a classroom and aligned with the goals of multicultural education for social justice. A synthesis of experiences and philosophies, hooks suggests that a liberatory pedagogy situated in Black feminist theory is dynamic, empowering, and dialectical. Students and teachers are encouraged to be active participants who share their knowledge and experiences. For hooks physical boundaries are fluid but not abusive—teachers move about the classroom and share the classroom "space" with their students. This example is encouraging and helps us envision Black feminist pedagogy in the classroom regardless of the grade level.

Conclusion

We have explored the ways in which Black feminist theories may inform social justice pedagogy. We have highlighted the scholarship of Black women scholars in order to synthesize and then explore the aspects most applicable to social justice pedagogy. In addition, we have addressed some of the limitations of Black feminist ideology in relation to social and economic class issues. We do not support the notion that only Black women can understand oppression, like Collins, however, we believe that given the limitations of traditional feminist research that either decontextualizes Black women's teaching, or uses an analysis that fails to capture and communicate the complexity of Black women's experiences, it is important that we exercise our "insider status" and bring our experiences to the fore as a way of translating them across contexts. We hope this emerging scholarship that places Black women teachers as subjects is exciting and informative especially as it pertains to imagining new, socially just pedagogies.

Points of Inquiry

- In whose interests do "prevailing systems," such as education, operate to maintain exclusion?
- Why does hooks advocate for going beyond the body?
- How is teaching a radical act? A personal act? A profession? And oppressive act?
- Can men be feminists? Can Black men be Black feminists?

Points of Praxis

- Students read Black women's poetry and prose.
- Students read the works of women around the world. Compare the similarities and differences in their circumstances with regard to class, religion, geography, culture, generation.

Notes

1   We are purposefully blending race and culture as the categories are more discursive than absolute. Michael Omi and Howard Winant (1994) argue that given that race is not a biologically sound construct, it might be more useful to discuss difference in terms of culture or ethnicity rather than race. We agree with Omi and Winant on the issue of race as an invalid biological construct; however, we understand that race is often conflated with culture. To simplify our argument, and for the purposes of this chapter, we will use both terms interchangeably.

2   In her second edition of Black Feminist Thought (2000), Collins abandons the term Afrocentric when describing a Black feminist epistemology. Collins abandons the term primarily because of disagreements with its creators regarding issues of gender and sexuality. In addition, she argues that the term is too value-laden to be useful (p. xii). Collins believes, however, that Afrocentricity, broadly defined, still has merit. We tend to disagree with Collins's decision to abandon the term. Abandoning the term is inconsistent

with Black feminist thought in the sense that Black women are encouraged to redefine words, ideas, locations, etc. into that which is useful and empowering for us. Collins's dismissal of the term appears to be a contradiction.

3   Carol Boyce Davies (1990) uses the metaphor of a "quilting narrative" to describe Black women's writing. With "piecework" representing the ideas that we take in a "piecemeal" fashion from our mothers, our sisters, and our experiences with others. We are borrowing the concept to suggest that from the various essays in hooks's collection (and her other writings), we are able to "piece together," like a quilt, some aspects of a Black feminist pedagogy that may be helpful for us as we explore Black women's teaching. We do not limit our "quilting" to hooks's work. We would submit that this entire effort represents our attempt at "quilting" together some perspectives on Black feminism and Black women's teaching that we hope are a useful heuristic.

4   Othermothering is a tradition in the Black community whereby Black women help to care for and, in many instances, raise children who may or may not be related to them biologically. For a more extensive explanation of othermothering, see, Stanlie James and Abena P. A. Busia, (Eds.), *Theorizing Black Feminisms: The Visionary Pragmatism of Black Women*, 1993.

Bibliography

Adams, M., Bell, L.A., & Griffin, P. (2007). *Teaching for diversity and social justice* (2nd ed.). New York: Routledge.

Au, K., & Jordan, C. (1981). Teaching reading to Hawaiian children: Finding a culturally appropriate solution. In H. T. Trueba, G. P. Guthrie, & K. H. Au (Eds.), *Culture and the bilingual classroom: Studies in classroom ethnography* (pp. 139–152). Rowley, MA: Newbury House.

Beauboef-Lafontant, T. (1997). Teach you the way I see us: Concepts of self and teaching of African-American women teachers committed to social justice. Paper presented at the American Educational Research Association, March 24–28, Chicago, IL.

Beauboeuf-Lafontant, T. (1999). A movement against and beyond boundaries: "Politically relevant teaching" among African American teachers. *Teachers College Record, 100*(4, Summer), 702–723.

Beauboeuf-Lafontant, T. (2002). A womanist experience of caring: Understanding the pedagogy of exemplary Black women teachers. *Urban Review, 34*(1, March), 71–86.

Beauboeuf-Lafontant, T. (2005). Womanist lessons for reinventing teaching. *Journal of Teacher Education, 56*(5), 436–445.

Boyce Davies, C. (1990) *Out of the Kumbla: Caribbean women and literature.* Trenton, NJ: Africa World Press.

Brophy, J., & Good, T. (1987). *Looking in classrooms.* New York: Harper & Row.

Casey, K. (1990). Teacher as mother: Curriculum theorizing in the life histories of contemporary women teachers. *Cambridge Journal of Education, 20*(3), 301–320.

Case, K. I. (1997). African American othermothering in the urban elementary school. *The Urban Review, 29*(1), 25–39.

Casey, K. (1993). *I answer with my life.* New York: Routledge.

Clark, S. (1962). *Echo in my soul.* New York: Dutton.

Clayton, M. S. (1979). Meet Joan Yvonne Polite. *Today's Education, 68* (November–December), 30–33.

Collier-Thomas, B. (1982). The impact of Black women in education: An historical overview. *Journal of Negro Education, 51*(Summer), 173–180.

Collins, M. (1992). *Ordinary children, extraordinary teachers.* Charlottesville, VA: Hampton Roads.

Collins, M., & Tamarkin, C. (1990/1982). *Marva Collins' way: Returning to excellence in education.* New York: Putnam.

Collins, P. H. (1990/2000). *Black feminist thought: Knowledge, consciousness, and the politics of empowerment.* New York: Routledge.

Coppin, F. J. (1913). *Reminiscences of school life and hints on teaching.* Philadelphia: AME Book Concern.

Coursey, L. N. (1974). Anita J. Turner—Early Black female physical educator. *Journal of Health Physical Education Recreation, 45*(3), 71–72.

Crenshaw, K. (1995). Mapping the margins: Intersectionality, identity politics, and violence against women of color. In K. Crenshaw, Gotanda, N., Peller, G., & Thomas, K. (Eds.), *Critical race theory: The key writings that formed the movement* (pp. 357–383). New York: The New Press.

Dingus, J. E. (2008). "Our family business was education": Professional socialization among intergenerational African-American teaching families. *International Journal of Qualitative Studies in Education, 21*(6), 605–626.

Dixson, A. D. (2003). "Let's do this!": Black women teachers' politics and pedagogy. *Urban Education, 38*(2), 217–235.

Dixson, A. D., & Dingus, J. E. (2007). Tyranny of the majority: Re-enfranchisement of African American teacher educators teaching for democracy. *International Journal of Qualitative Studies in Education, 20*(6), 639–654.

Dixson, A. D., & Dingus, J. E (2008.) In search of our mothers' gardens: Black women teachers and professional socialization. *Teachers College Record, 110*(4), 805–837.

Etter-Lewis, G. (1993). *My soul is my own: Oral narratives of African American women in the professions.* New York: Routledge.

Fields, M. G. with Fields, K. (1985). *Lemon swamp: A Carolina memoir.* New York: The Free Press.

Fordham, S. (1988). Racelessness as a factor in Black students' school success: Pragmatic strategy or pyrrhic victory? *Harvard Educational Review, 58*(1), 54–85.

Foster, M. (1990). The politics of race: Through the eyes of African-American teachers. *Journal of Education, 172*(3), 123–141.

Foster, M. (1991a). "Just got to find a way": Case studies of the lives and practice of exemplary Black high school teachers. In M. Foster (Ed.), *Readings on equal education: Qualitative investigations into schools and schooling, 11,* 273–309. New York: AMS Press.

Foster, M. (1991b). Constancy, connectedness, and constraints in the lives of African American teachers. *NWSA, 3*(Spring), 233–261.

Foster, M. (1993). Othermothers: Exploring the education philosophy of Black American women teachers. In M. W. Arnot, & K. Weiler (Eds), *Feminism and social justice in education: International perspectives* (pp. 101–123). Washington, DC: Falmer Press.

Foster, M. (1995). African American teachers and culturally relevant pedagogy. In J. A. Banks, & C. A. McGee Banks (Eds.), *Handbook of research on multicultural education* (pp. 570–581). New York: Macmillan.

Foster, M. (1997). *Black teachers on teaching.* New York: The New Press.

Fultz, M. (1995a). African-American teachers in the South, 1890–1940: Growth, feminization, and salary discrimination. *Teachers College Record, 96*(3), 544–568.

Fultz, M. (1995b). Training teachers and African-American education in the South, 1900–1940. *Journal of Negro Education, 64*(2), 196–210.

Fultz, M. (1995c). African-American teachers in the South, 1890–1940: Powerlessness and the ironies of expectations and protest. *History of Education Quarterly, 35*(4), 401–422.

Giddings, P. (1984). *When and where I enter: The impact of Black women on sex and race in America.* New York: William Morrow.

Gilligan, C. (1982). *In a different voice.* Cambridge, MA: Harvard University Press.

Goodson, I. (1988). Teachers, life histories and studies of curriculum and school, *The making of curriculum: Collected essays.* Philadelphia: Falmer Press.

Guy-Sheftall, B. (Ed.). (1995). *Words of fire: An anthology of African American feminist thought.* New York: The New Press.

Harley, S. (1982). Beyond the classroom: Organizational lives of Black Female educators in the District of Columbia, 1890–1930. *Journal of Negro Education, 51,* 254–265.

Hart, E., & Ostovich, M. (1995). Educator Mary McLeod Bethune. *New Moon, 2,* 19–21.

Haskins, J. (1971). *Diary of a Harlem schoolteacher.* New York: Grove Press.

Hendrix, K. G. (2001). "Mama told Me . . .": Exploring childhood lessons that laid a foundation for my "endarkened" epistemology. *Qualitative Inquiry, 7,* 559–577.

Higginbotham, E. (1989). Beyond the sound of silence: Black women in history. *Gender and History, 1*(Spring).

Hilliard, A. (1991). Do we have the "will" to educate all children? *Educational Leadership, 49*(1), 31–36.

Hine, D. C. (Ed.). (1990). *Black women in U.S. history.* Brooklyn: Carlson.

Hine, D. C. (1998). *A shining thread of hope: The history of Black women in America.* New York: Broadway Books.

Holland, D., Lachicotte, W., Skinner, D., & Cain, C. (1998). *Identity and agency in cultural worlds.* Cambridge, MA: Harvard University Press.

hooks, b. (1981/1995). Black women: Shaping feminist theory. In B. Guy-Sheftall (Ed.), *Words of fire: An anthology of African-American feminist thought* (pp. 270–282). New York: The New Press.

hooks, b. (1994). *Teaching to transgress: Education as the practice of freedom.* New York: Routledge.

Howe, F. (1973). Sexism, racism, and the education of women. *Today's Education, 62*(5), 47–48.

Hunter, T. W. (1997). *To 'joy my freedom: Southern Black women's lives and labors after the Civil War.* Cambridge, MA: Harvard University Press.

Huntzinger, V. M. M. (1995). Portraits in Black and White: A micro and macro view of Southern teachers before and after the Civil War. Paper presented at the American Educational Research Association, April 18–22, San Francisco.

Hurston, Z. N. (1942/1996). *Dust tracks on the road: An autobiography.* New York: HarperPerennial.

Ihle, E. L. (1986). *Black girls and women in elementary education: A history of Black women's education in the South, 1865–Present* (Non-classroom guide UD 025 515–516). Harrisonburg, VA: James Madison University.

Irvine, J. J. (1989). Beyond role models: An examination of cultural influences on the pedagogical perspectives of Black teachers. *Peabody Journal of Education, 66*(4), 51–63.

Irvine, J. J. (1990). From plantation to school house: The rise and decline of Black women teachers. *Humanity & Society, 14*(3), 244–256.

Irvine, J. J. (Ed.). (2002). *In search of wholeness: African American teachers and their culturally specific classroom practices.* New York: Palgrave.

Irvine, J. J. F., & James, W. (1998). Warm demanders: Culturally responsive pedagogy of African American teachers. *Education Week, 17*(35).

James, J. (1997). *Transcending the Talented Tenth: Black leaders and American intellectuals*. New York: Routledge.

James, J. (1999). *Shadowboxing: Representations of black feminist politics*. New York: St. Martin's Press.

James, S. M., & Busia, A. P. A. (Eds.). (1993). *Theorizing Black feminisms: The visionary pragmatism of Black women*. New York: Routledge.

Jeffries, R. (1994).The trickster figure in African-American teaching: Pre- and post-desegregation. *Urban Review*, 26, 280–304.

Jenoure, T. (2000). *Navigators: African American musicians, dancers and visual artists in academe*. Albany: State University of New York Press.

Jones, L. (1999/1963). *Blues people: Negro music in White America*. New York: Quill William Morrow.

King, D. K. (1988/1995). Multiple jeopardy, multiple consciousness: The context of a Black feminist ideology. In B. Guy-Sheftall (Ed.), *Words of fire: An anthology of African-American feminist thought* (pp. 294–318). New York: The New Press.

King, J. E., & Ladson-Billings, G. (1990). Dysconscious racism and multicultural illiteracy: The distorting of the American mind. Paper presented at the American Educational Researchers Association, April, Boston, MA.

Ladson-Billings, G. (1995). Toward a theory of culturally relevant pedagogy. *American Educational Research Journal*, 32(3), 465–491.

Ladson-Billings, G., & Henry, A. (1990). Blurring the borders: Voices of African liberatory pedagogy in the United States and Canada. *Journal of Education*, 172(2), 72–88.

Mohatt, G., & Erickson, F. (1981). Cultural differences in teaching styles in an Odawa school: A sociolinguistic approach. In H. T. Trueba, G. P. Guthrie, & K. H. Au (Eds.), *Culture and the bilingual classroom* (pp. 105–138). Rowley, MA: Newbury House.

Murray, A. (2000/1976). *Stomping the blues*. New York: Da Capo Press.

Nieto, S. (1992). *Affirming diversity: The sociopolitical context of multicultural education*. New York: Longman Press. (5th ed., with P. Bode, 2008, Boston: Allyn & Bacon.)

Omi, M., & Winant, H. (1994). *Racial formation in the United States: From the 1960s to 1990s*. New York: Routledge.

Perkins, L. M. (1980). Black women and the philosophy of "race uplift" prior to emancipation (Working paper). Cambridge: Radcliffe College.

Reed, J. (1960). Marriage and fertility in Black female teachers. *Black Scholar*, 1(3–4), 22–28.

Shulman, L. (1987). Knowledge and teaching: Foundations of the new reform. *Harvard Educational Review*, 57(1), 1–22.

Sims, M. J. (1982). Inquiry and the urban classrooms: A female African-American teacher in search of truth. *Theory into Practice*, 31(Fall), 342–349.

Smith, W. D., & Chunn, E. W. (Eds.). (1989). *Black education: A quest for equity and excellence*. New Brunswick, NJ: Transaction Publishers.

Taylor, U. Y. (1998). Making waves: The theory and practice of Black feminism. *Black Scholar*, 28(2), 18–28.

Thompson, A. (1998). Not the color purple: Black feminist lessons for educational caring. *Harvard Educational Review*, 68(4), 522–554.

United States Department of Education. (1999). Teachers' feelings of preparedness. *Indicator of the Month*, December.

Wade-Gayles, G. (1993). *Pushed back to strength: A Black woman's journey home*. Boston: Beacon.

Walker, A. (1983). 'But yet and still the cotton gin kept on working . . .'. *Black Scholar*, 14, 13–17.

Walker, V. S. (2000). Valued segregated schools for African American children in the South, 1935–1969: A review of common themes and characteristics. *Review of Educational Research, 70*, 253–286.

Weiler, K. (1988). *Women teaching for change: Gender, class and power.* South Hadley, MA: Bergin & Garvey.

White, D. G. (1999). *Too heavy a load: Black women in defense of themselves, 1894–1994.* New York/London: W.W. Norton.

Chapter 6

Can We Learn Queerly?
Normativity and Social Justice Pedagogies

Lisa W. Loutzenheiser

In 1996, I published an article "Smear the Queer" in Feminist Teacher *(Loutzenheiser, 1996) about the climate of schooling for lesbian, gay, and bisexual youth (LGB). I wrote about the statistics of risk and curricular othering of LGB bodies, the conditions and climate for LGB students, and the fear of teachers who wished to address homophobia. Here, I revisit the assumptions and pedagogies upon which the 1996 article was built with the intention of reanalyzing "Smear the Queer" theoretically and in relation to a reworked notion of praxis. This chapter explores how queer theories and queering pedagogies are important, yet tension-filled and contested elements of teaching across difference. Moving away from single-issue approaches and identity politics as the central focus of social justice education, this chapter envisions queering pedagogies as an attempt to address the relationships between sexuality and other oppressions, particularly race and sexuality/gender identity in educational contexts*

> Until schools are willing to acknowledge structural heterosexism and change the culture of the school to include the concerns and cultures of many students. Gay, lesbian, and bisexual youth will continue to struggle against invisibility and isolation with all its consequences, and heterosexual students will continue to forgo an inclusive education. Schools will continue both figuratively and literally, to play "Smear the Queer." Ultimately, we all lose because we continue to educate generations of school children to be ignorant about others and relegate others to the bottom of the pile.
>
> Loutzenheiser, 1996, "How schools play smear the queer"

Introduction

In 1996, as a new graduate student, I published an article "Smear the Queer" in *Feminist Teacher* (Loutzenheiser, 1996) about the climate of schooling for lesbian, gay and bisexual youth. I wrote about the statistics of risk and curricular othering of LGB bodies, the conditions and climate for LGB students and the fear of teachers who wished to address homophobia and heterosexism.

The quote that opens this chapter is the very last paragraph of the 1996 article and in some ways points the way forward. At the end of my graduate career, I wrote a chapter called "If I talk about that, they will burn my house down" (2001), where I addressed more directly the "The possibilities and tensions of queered, anti-racist pedagogy." Now, in 2009, as a faculty member, I again revisit pedagogies of normativity and social justice, this time with the intention of reanalyzing "Smear the Queer" (*STQ*) in light of what has changed and what has stayed the same, both theoretically and in relation to praxis. In the chapter I will offer a reworking of praxis, acknowledging that within education, the starting point for praxis is a Freirean (1970) sense of bringing theory to bear upon practice.

It is useful to lay out the definitions of homophobia and heterosexism as constructs within which this discussion will occur. Homophobia refers to a fear or hatred of homosexuality, especially in others, but also in one's self (internalized homophobia). The term heteronormativity is utilized to establish an understanding of the pervasive and systemic assumption of heterosexuality as norm. Michael Warner (1993) utilizes heteronormativity to describe the manner in which "heterosexual culture thinks of itself as the elemental form of human association, . . . as the indivisible basis of all community, and the means of reproduction without which society wouldn't exist" (p. xix). Warner is arguing for the uncovering of the norming of heterosexuality, the space in classrooms where the assumption is that students, teachers, and parents are always already heterosexual.

I am preoccupied with the spaces of race and sexuality in education, and why queer theory and race theories rarely find a space to draw each upon the other. I wonder how we might plan, design, and theorize teaching and learning from the complex spaces that education and pedagogy occupy. In revisiting the 1996 article and the assumptions and pedagogies upon which it was built, this chapter explores how queer theories and queering pedagogies are important, yet tension-filled and contested elements of teaching across difference. Moving away from single-issue approaches and identity politics as the central focus of social justice education, this chapter envisions queering pedagogies as an attempt to address the relationships between sexuality and other oppressions, particularly race and sexuality/gender identity in educational contexts.

Whose Tolerance, Whose Social Justice?

Concepts such as tolerance, teaching for diversity and social justice are both useful and problematic as they have been used and co-opted to such a degree that it is difficult to ascertain precisely how the words are being defined, overuse having all but evacuated their meaning. And while there has been much discussion about what social justice and tolerance are, it may be useful here to also examine the historicity of the phrases and their current linkages to liberal and neoliberal agendas.

The development of "tolerance" as an avenue to work for equity and difference has its roots in religious movements that advocated "tolerance" of other religions and religious movements. According to Brown (2006) schools along with churches, the state and secular civic groups "promulgate tolerance" (p. 2), which "shores up troubled orders of power, repairs state legitimacy, glosses troubled universalisms, and provides cover for imperialism" (pp. 9–10). The etymology of tolerance is one avenue to explore its place in education. To tolerate (Dictionary.com) means:

1. to allow the existence, presence, practice, or act of without prohibition or hindrance
2. to endure without repugnance; put up with.

The root of *tolerate* implies deviation from the norm, the norm being the dominant group, which can only exist if there is an Other. That is, it creates a binary system: the good students must have the bad student to be recognizable as good; the heterosexual norm only exists if there is a queer or non-heterosexual. Within a tolerance framework, dominant norms remain at the centre. When teaching tolerance there is a reliance on a pedagogy that focuses on the center or the status quo and has as its main purpose the alleviation of individual prejudice. Within tolerance is a desire for an individualistic, utopian view of a color-blind, sexuality-blind society that hails what Brown argues is an unproductive and liberal notion embedded in "generalized language of antiprejudice and . . . the good society yet to come" (p. 5). A pedagogy that relies upon the possibility of the good-society-to-come, builds upon individual intent and action, while leaving undisturbed the political nature of tolerance, racism, and heterosexism (to name only two), and its connections to culture, the state, laws, policies, and educational discourses.

The difficulty of writing about social justice pedagogy stems from the very phrase "social justice," as it is not often, or clearly, defined (Novak, 2000). What is it that is meant when one speaks of social justice? of pedagogy? And to complicate the issues further, what is meant by queer pedagogy as social justice? What pedagogical meanings, and whose understanding of justice is an author hailing?

The early history of the term social justice can be traced to the Catholic Church and its social teachings, originating with Jesuit priest Luigi Taparelli (building on Thomas Aquinas) who is credited with having coined the term "social justice" in 1840 (Zajda, Majhanovich, & Rust, 2006). The ways that social justice are understood are rooted in the epistemological desires that each paradigm advocates. This includes a reliance on Catholicism's early social teachings (Novak, 2000); the individualistic rendering of John Rawls's (1971) notion of the reasonable citizen, and a liberal understanding that demands that "we all just get along"; a critically and socially reconstructionist, rights-based philosophy that demands justice, equity, and equal opportunity (Ladson-Billings, 1995; Young, 2000), and a discourse-infused deconstruction of anti-oppressive theories (Kumashiro, 2001; Loutzenheiser, 2006). One way to engage with this quagmire of words, as I will do throughout this chapter, is through an unlayering of the multiple epistemological assumptions and pedagogies that define and direct social justice and education.

Queer: Contested Space and in Tension

Queer as a term, as opposed to gay, lesbian, or bisexual, purposefully disrupts the notion that identity is fixed or immutable. It includes the desire to highlight the existence of, and interrupt silent assumptions about heterosexuality as normal, and homosexuality as Other. In the classroom and in schools, this form of 'ultimate' naming around which individuals are organized and ostracized, too often results in groups of students being viewed as universalized singular "others."

While the term *queer* has often been used as a pejorative, individually and collectively, it has been reclaimed as a pedagogy, a politics, and a theory which dislodges the requirements of fixed sexual identities such as gay or lesbian, and subsequently, heterosexual. This invites an opening up of spaces where our commonsense understandings of sex and sexuality are left messy and productively problematic. For educators, this affords the possibility of discussing sexuality as a site of social change in ways that demand attention is paid not only to sexuality, but also to the intersectionality of race, gender, and sexuality.

Returning to the Game

When I wrote *STQ,* my goal was to help uncover the ways that the structures of schools fed into the harassment and discrimination that students were encountering. In this uncovering, I was hoping to open up possibilities for change. In *STQ,* I state:

> students have made the importance of teaching students and their teachers about the wide spectrum of sexualities abundantly clear to me. Otherwise . . . we give all students the message that "the homosexual" is Other: to be feared, odd, fundamentally different. This act of Othering causes many gay, lesbian, and bisexual young people to feel that their sexuality makes them essentially unlike, separate, and forever outside the culture of their peers. (p. 59)

While the call to alter the Othering that occurs in classrooms remains a goal and a desire this paragraph reveals a number of assumptions that frame my work, most notably, the desire and belief in a pedagogical endpoint. In this pedagogical moment I was able to argue that if we understood enough about LGB youth and the manner in which schools worked with issues of sexuality, then a plan could be developed that would be inclusive of all LGB teens.

In this article, a belief in the possibility of correcting the otherness LGB is present.[1] While it is clear in the article that to Other youth in a manner that positions them as always outside is undesirable, there is also the suggestion that odd or different is negative. The desire to correct difference is rooted in the possibility of a describable solution and identity as ultimately alterable and a yearning for similarity. Advocating for similarity marks an uncritical acceptance of assimilation as the goal for LGBTTIQ as "just the same as," or wishing to be the same as the dominant centre. As I discuss in more detail below, the moves towards questioning normativity and embracing difference, while acknowledging a lack of static identities are hallmarks of queer theories and queer pedagogies. The paragraph quoted above ends with the sentence: "Othering causes isolation and depression, which in turn can lead to suicide," a popular statistical correlation that may lead the reader into problematic conclusions about the nature of risk and LGBTTIQ[2] identified youth.

Who Are LGBTTIQ/Queer Youth?

In this section, I offer a discussion of the statistics about queer youth and education that were available in 1996, and those reported currently, within an analysis of how risk discussions are both vital and counter-productive in moving towards pedagogies that interrogate normativity. In an attempt to contextualize the conversation, the stories of two youth will be introduced and then returned to through an exploration of risk discourses.

Vignette I[3]

J. is a 15-year-old student at Case High School in a larger urban center. She remembers feeling different from other children as early as first grade, and has few fond memories of elementary school. J. will tell anyone who asks that she doesn't remember her early grades. Occasionally she talks about being teased by others because she wanted to play any game that involved a ball; that was, until R. shoved her down, called her names she did not understand, and with all the other kids watching tried to pull her pants up to her chin. They laughed at her and that was the last time she played with the boys; instead she stayed to herself.

By the time J. was in grade 7, she was often cutting school and could be found smoking, drinking, hanging out and hooking up with friends during school hours. Her parents each worked long hours and she did not see very much of them. Now 17-years-old, J. has brown hair with startling eyes. She perpetually has a hoodie drawn up over her head and hanging down into her eyes, ear phones either in or dangling from her ears. Before last year, J. was silent in class. Always sitting in the back, rarely talking, scraping by with passing marks because teachers almost forgot she was there. Now, the few times she shows up for class, she is argumentative and confrontational with teachers, looking for any excuse to storm out of class or get thrown out. She feels angry all of the time and if she doesn't take it out on her teachers or her parents, she takes it out on herself. The only class in school that J. really likes is art, and as far back as she can remember adults have been telling her to stop drawing and pay attention. Although she has never told anyone, J. would love to go to art school, but since she is failing tenth grade, again, she does not see much chance of that.

Who Are the Youth We Call LGBTTIQ and How Are We Discussing Them?

In *STQ*, I examined how:

> Some of the most disturbing and shocking statistics concern the suicide and attempted suicide rates of gay, lesbian, and bisexual teens. While schools are not the only community institutions responsible for helping these young people, the suicide rates alone must spur educators to tackle these issues, if only to save a single child sitting in your classroom. (p. 59)

Again, it is not inaccurate or unimportant to expose the high rates of suicide among some LGB youth. In fact, it is instructive to discover that the statistics have remained unchanged. Yet, as the statistics are exposed, it is also important to keep in mind that statistics are a) manipulatable, b) reliant on a pathologized and "at-risk" model of who LGBTTIQ youth might be, and c) discuss youth as an essential-ized group when it is clear youth exceed boundaried identities in myriad ways. That is, youth are never just youth, never only LGBTQ identified youth, but claim and reject multiple identities that intersect with, complicate, and refute these designa-tions. Talburt (2008) notes: "young people, through their cultural practices, have complicated categories of gender and sexuality to the extent that adult queer theo-rists can often not catch up with them" (p. 102). I am arguing that it is important to know and understand the reported rates of risk and harassment of youth in schools and still be able to problematize the over-reliance on such discourses to motivate educators to act. Within such discourses, there is a single essentialist version of risk that homogenizes queer youth into one hopeless category (Harbeck, 1995). Goldstein et al. (2007) examine the way that the "safe schools" approach places queer youth in the role of victim, individualizes the problems of queer youth, nor-malizes heteronormativity, and fails to acknowledge the general inadequacies of the safe schools model to address issues of sexuality and heternormativity. Further, vic-tim discourses fail to disrupt the heterosexual/homosexual binary (Bryson & De Castell, 1993) and ignore the intersections of identity (Lugg, 2003).

With these discourses in mind, I ask myself why I relied on a "but kids are dying" discourse to open up space or normalize a discussion of sexual identity in schools. Why do those discourses offer permission for teaching and learning to occur?

In 1996, I reported that:

> *thirty percent* of all youth suicides are committed by gay, lesbian, and bisexual youth. They are three to five times more likely to attempt suicide than their het-erosexual peers and more likely to succeed when they do (Kourany). Gay, les-bian, and bisexual teens are not only at risk when it comes to suicide, but they are more likely to use and abuse drugs, be kicked out of their homes and end up the street (Buce & Obolensky; Krucks; Remafedi; Uribe & Harbeck). It is vital for teachers and teacher educators to understand the kinds of stresses and dif-ficulties that gay, lesbian, and bisexual youth face.
>
> ("Smear the queer," p. 59)

The ways we think of and construct at-risk youth need to be problematized in part because the "demographic criteria, such as sexual orientation, do not automatically imply suicide risk" (Rutter & Soucar, 2002, p. 297), meaning that statistics do not always offer substantiation for an overly broad group hypothesis. Recent studies suggest that concerns about suicidality remain with reports of approximately 28% of bi and gay young men reporting a suicide attempt (Remafedi, French, Story, Resnick, & Blum, 1998) and youths with same-sex orientation are more than two times more likely than their same-sex peers to attempt suicide (Russell & Joyner, 2001). Russell and Joyner (2001) also note that the linkages between sexual orientation and suicide may also be mediated "by critical youth suicide risk factors, including depression, hopelessness, alcohol abuse, recent suicide attempts by a peer or a family member, and experiences of victimization" (p. 1276) and "the overwhelming majority of sexual minority youths—84.6% of males and 71.7% of females with same-sex sexual orientation—report no suicidality at all" (p. 1280). Understanding that the linkages between sexual orientation and suicide are less clear-cut is one example of the ways in which risk and statistics research has begun to establish a more complex analysis, which may point the reader toward a more complicated rendering of LGBTTIQ students.

Vignette 2

R. will graduate this June with honors from Northern High School, just across down from J's Case High School. Upon first meeting him, one is struck by his tall lanky build and wide grin and easy manner. R. was raised in a household with two parents and considers himself middle class. He has been active at school and in his community, volunteering at his church and with a soccer team for younger children. R.'s early memories of school are positive, and school was a safe, fun place where his achievement and behavior were rewarded. R.'s favorite subject is history, and R. remains a voracious reader. His parent A. is the person he looks to as a role model and R. hopes to also become a doctor. He is in all honors classes at school, and while somewhat balanced, has to keep a day-timer going to keep his schedule straight.

R. realized he liked boys more than girls early on. Some of his friends know, but it's not the first thing he tells people. In fact, no one every really talks about the issues in school or out, unless it was hearing the words " fag" or "that's so gay, " in the hallways. The exception to this is one of the English teacher's, Mr. Brown, who declares the sexuality of each and every author he uses in class. It is almost as if he was told at some point that this was one way to talk about "it"; it, of course, being the incorporation of gay and lesbian content. But his embarrassingly serious pronouncements have become a joke, with students looking at each other and laughing each time he does it. R. feels uncomfortable every time he hears about it, and the one time he was in class when Mr. Brown did this, R. wanted to crawl under his desk. R. has begun to think of himself as queer, since it is messy and doesn't ask you to choose who you were each and every day. It seems as if teachers feel so uncomfortable with the idea of queer students that the possibility they exist in their school is foreign. Perhaps if it is discovered, they seem to be saying, it ought be kept quiet. The very use of the word "gay", much less queer makes the adults squirm and change the subject.

Harassment and Risk

The statistics quoted in *STQ* cited 40% of LGB students were experiencing physical violence at school with an equal number saying that the school environment negatively impacted their schoolwork. The National Gay and Lesbian Task Force study at that time reported that 90% of LGB[4] adults were subject to verbal or physical harassment, and 20% of lesbians and 50% of gay men reported that they were victims of hate crimes at school. LGBTTIQ students still feel as if they do not belong in school (Rostosky, Owens, Zimmerman, & Riggle, 2003). The reliance on categorizations of LGBTTIQ youth as "at-risk," essentialist renderings of youth, and the loci of responsibility for change are interconnected and all rely on similar understandings of change in which the focus is on the individual, rather than a heteronormative context.

More recent studies draw a correlation between still extraordinarily high numbers of youth enduring harassment at school and their academic underachievement. This research may move us away from students-as-problem, to school culture and the structural interplays between school climate and students most in need of consideration. These studies point out that factors that have linked individual risk to LGBTTIQ or queer status are more directly related to school climate and the experience of harassment. Harassment is linked to lower school achievement, higher rates of dropping out, increased substance abuse, suicidality and high-risk sexual behaviors (Rivers, 2000).

However, LGBQ[5] youths experiencing low levels of victimization at school were found to be statistically similar to their heterosexual peers, and LGBQ youths in the high-victimization group evidenced substantially more health risk behavior, compared with heterosexual youths in the high-victimization group (Bontempo & D'Augelli, 2002). Remafedi et al. (1998) also found that those victimized by peers at school were more likely to have disciplinary problems.

Other recent literature has also attempted to further complicate the picture of risk. Murdock and Bolch (2005) point out that the academic achievement was impacted for some LGB youth. In a move toward complicating risk discourses they also discuss the fact that most LGB youth are "ok." Of the 101 youth in this study, there were only 14 adolescents in the "Highly Vulnerable" group and these were the students who had poor adaptation (p. 167).

Returning to J. and R.

When you read the vignette about J., what images did you conjure up in your mind's eye? Would it change the view of J. if you knew her name is Jane at school and Jing at home. She does not remember much of her early years. Jing was not adopted until she was 5, and the first years outside of China were a blur of new family, new language, and new surroundings. Her parents were born in the U.S.A., and work hard at well-paying jobs that they both enjoy. Jing was the name she came to the U.S.A. with and her parents chose to keep it; the first day of school her teacher decided Jing was too hard and said they would call her Jane. Because that was how she was introduced to schooling, it was how she thought she was supposed to be addressed and it stuck.

At this juncture, Jing has sex with boys and girls but most of the time she is high or drunk and therefore is not sure if she likes both or just does it because they are there. Even though she does a lot of things that her parents wouldn't like, she knows that the idea of coming out, which she has heard from the mostly white people on television, doesn't really fit with her family's perspectives.

Jing wants to do well at school, wants not to be angry all the time, but she can't figure out how or why she is so mad. Jing does not need or want any help from the school about her feelings for girls; she just accepts that as who she is and what she wants. But she does wish there were more adults at school who cared about who she was, who taught something about the history and literature of Chinese-Americans, that there were more advanced art classes, and that her teachers would stop expecting her to be good at math. Mostly she wishes that somebody could help her understand why she is angry and why life is so much a blur before coming to the United States.

Upon first reading Jing's story how did you envision her race, ethnicity, family background? How did you fill in the blanks of her educational story and why? Jing might be understood as fitting into the at-risk discourses; what is lost in working with Jing when an essentialized notion of Jing is how she is understood?

In the vignette of R. or Ricky, it is easy to see a young man who seems to be thriving, if silent. He is not likely to join a Gay-Straight Alliance (GSA) if one were offered at his school, and he is quite happy to straddle the worlds between his parents, church, and school. He is a high achieving student who seems not to engage in the behaviors that are characterized as "at-risk." Ricky still has the desire to fit in, like most teens, and has begun to experience low level harassment from a couple of the other boys at school because he does not often date or engage in the routine conversations about girls and their bodies. He knows he could ask his best friend, Miranda, to go on dates with him and it would be thought that he and they were doing the expected. Ricky feels as if he just can't fake it and should not have to. But the comments of the other guys about his being a fag and a pussy are becoming uncomfortable. Ricky knows he is seen as the good, accomplished student with lots of friends and is not an outsider. The teasing (Ricky would never call it harassment), if it increases, or if Ricky tries to tell someone about it, will make him an outsider, and he does not want that. Soon Ricky will have to make a decision about how to handle what was an occasional comment, and is becoming more frequent name-calling and a few shoves here and there. The prom is next month; maybe he should just invite Miranda and be done with it?

What Ricky points out to educators is that a story of what it means to be a LGBT-TIQ identified youth in school is neither a story of complete risk or complete success. For youth who identify as LGBTTIQ, or are perceived to fall outside the gender performances of their peers and are therefore labeled as such, the world of school is a complicated space where normativity rules. The struggle against normativity and school climates that support the status quo can lead to situations where the non-normativity body must be complicit in his oppression. How can we begin to think of school and schooling in such a way where the norm is not constantly recentered?

Complicating the Game

What is Pedagogy?

Pedagogy is theoretically contested; a concept or idea that some say has lost its usefulness. Pedagogy is tangled up in sites of tension; how one understands pedagogy exposes how one thinks of the purposes of schooling, and the role of curriculum. Even as I argue that there are multiple pedagogies, there remains an assumption among many educators that there is a commonsense definition of pedagogy that is ascribed to by many, if not all. Pedagogies, I will argue, speak to a process, rather than concrete measurable application. This indeterminate pedagogy, particularly as the discussion moves into queering pedagogy, questions a pedagogy of the normal that offers seductive "tidy stories of happiness resolution and the certainty of life as if life were something to be overcome and mastered with little disturbance as possible" (Britzman, 1995, pp. 79–80). What might it mean to turn normalcy on itself and create pedagogies "whose grounds of possibility require risk, uncertainty and implication" (Britzman, 1995, p. 81)? Britzman's articulation of pedagogy rejects theories of teaching and learning that can be synthesized into a "bag of tricks" or scripted linear lesson that will necessarily produce a similar product each time it is delivered.

Thinking about inclusion

As gay, lesbian, and bisexual students move through the hallways waiting for the next shove up against a locker, or sit in classrooms anticipating the next slur, they hear few positive reflections of themselves. School curriculum rarely mentions gay lesbian, or bisexual people or issues. . . . The students rarely have role models because gay, lesbian, and bisexual teachers are afraid to come out in the classroom for fear of harassment or of losing their jobs. The end result is greater isolation for the students and more internalization of the sense of Other.

("Smear the queer," p. 62)

In *STQ*, I suggested that inclusion of LGB peoples into the curriculum, and the visibility of LGB role models were solutions to the isolation that students felt in schools. Similarly, I seem to argue that role models and inclusion in the classroom might lessen the Othering that was occurring in schools. Curricular inclusion often begins with the belief that the mere incorporation of queerly identified curriculum and pedagogy will automatically contribute to the development of higher self-esteem, increased achievement, and educational equity. This model lacks meaningful, integrated planning; the unit or essential questions are not altered and the critical analyses of the roles of gender, race, and/or sexuality can be left unexplored; rather, LGB content is added into existing lessons and units. The desire for inclusivity (rather than integration) adds in content that includes women, people of color, and/or queer peoples without contextualizing or building interconnectedness with the rest of the content.

The scarcity of integration and over-reliance on one or two day lessons that are not tied to the rest of the curriculum, results in a lack of analytic depth in relation to the systemic, which "trivializes the history under examination" (Noddings, 1997, p. 59). The end result is often an Othering, which separates out the bodies in question, but does not complicate their relationship to the dominant. Alternatively, educators often note the similarity of these Others to the normative, while reifying their difference. What has become increasingly clear to me since writing *STQ* is the pivotal role of the school culture and the discourses that circulate within and outside of schools. "In these ways, gay, lesbian, and bisexual students begin to see and hear positive images of themselves in the classroom, rather than something odd or bad" ("Smear the queer," p. 60). Here, I lament the lack of role models, and rightfully question the negative othering of students. However, the call for role models, not unlike other calls for teachers to "come out," leaves the responsibility for change in the hands of individuals, and in this case those who may be most vulnerable in that space. The reliance on role models, then, places responsibility on the bodies of those who face harassment, and away from educators and policy makers who stand on the sidelines applauding the work of the role models but do little more to alter school climate.

The above quote also has assimilative underpinnings that assume that LGBTTIQ youth ought to desire to emulate (hetero)normality, assuming an identity that does not fall too far outside the comfortable gay and lesbian body. The comfortable gay body is one that is recognizable and visible as who LGBTTIQ people ought to be (e.g., Ellen DeGeneres), not too far outside the bounds of acceptability.

Safe Schools

It is not surprising that I would have advocated for "safety" for LGBTTIQ students in school. In *SMQ*, I state:

> schools offer few forums for discussion about gay men, lesbians, and bisexuals. The combination of harassment and invisibility leads to an isolation that feels huge and reinforces some students' beliefs that they are isolated at school. Not only do they feel physically at-risk, but they do not feel safe to be themselves, nor have anyone to speak with about their concerns.
>
> ("Smear the queer," p. 61)

Embedded in my recommendation of safe spaces and a preliminary acknowledgement of systemic responsibility, I fall back on the assumption that safe schools will look the same for all LGBTTIQ identified youth. In North American contexts, safe schools has evolved into a catchphrase to encompass all of the policy intended to create diverse climates within schools, encourage inclusive environments (Parents and Friends of Lesbians and Gays, 2006), recognize the potential for violent incidence (Day & Golench, 1997; Dwyer, 1998; British Columbia Confederation of Parent Advisory Councils, 2003) and limit bullying, harassment, and intimidation within the school environment (British Columbia Ministry of Education, 2007). Walton (2004) argues that there is a "conspicuous absence of homophobic bullying from safe schools agendas" (p. 25). I am suggesting that homophobia, heteronormativity, and gender normativity are conspicuously absent from curricula and reform, as well as underscoring silent regulation. That is, safe schools programs are able to construct bullying curricula in such a manner as to fold anti-homophobia into it and negate an explicit requirement for direct action to alter school climate and/or limit discussion or pedagogies that address heterosexist or homophobic harassment.

Safe schools discourse focuses on individual behaviors, the subsequent consequences for individual students (Walton, 2004), and individual change in the form of students involved with Gay-Straight Alliances and charismatic teachers or administrators. The programs label the bully as perpetrator and those bullied as victim (never both), rather than focusing on the systemic problems that contribute to the development of the bully and the assumed superiority of the bully, which often relates to privilege and power. Folding homophobic and heterosexist bullying into the larger bullying curricula fosters an erasure of the systemic causes of violence, the systemic perpetuation of privilege, and heteronormativity. Goldstein et al. (2007) note that "by individualizing the harassment of queer youth, schools abdicate their responsibility for challenging power structures and culture that privilege heterosexuality over homosexuality" (p. 185). Further, the focus on the individual perpetuates the notion that problems within schools result from those individuals who do not conform to societal norms, rather than the oppressive dominance of such systemic norms on the construction of the individuals.

The Recalcitrance of Neoliberalism

It may be useful at this juncture to place inclusion, safe schools, role models,and at-risk discourses within an interrogation of their neoliberal aims. Wendy Brown (2006) notes "that Liberalism's excessive freighting of the individual subject with self-making, agency and a relentless responsibility for itself also contributes to the personalization of politically contoured conflicts and inequalities" (p. 17). Further, liberalism and neoliberalism privilege a "certain culture . . . [a] modern Western [one]" (Zizek, 2008, p. 662), which is, I would argue, largely a white, heterosexual and able-bodied one. How do we begin to understand neoliberalism and how does it impact education settings? Leitner, Peck, and Sheppard (2006) offer a useful definition of neoliberalism "as a socially produced, historically and geographically specific, crisis-driven, conjunctural, and definitionally incomplete phenomenon . . . . a distinctive political-economic philosophy . . . dedicated to the extension of the market and market-like forms of governance, rule and control across all spheres of life" (p. 28). From this, an analysis of market pressures in education begins to form, from Keynesian standards and accountability, to focusing on meritocracy and the individual to make change. The resulting impact of pedagogical decisions to shore up the status quo of heteronormativity and reforming the individual bear out the ideal that "neoliberalism is an ideology, a politics" (Giroux, 2005, p. 12). Similarly, the consumable "good" LGB individual student or teacher reinforces the market-driven consumption of individual success. This is who Duggan (2003) notes as the "greater acceptance of the most assimilated, gender-appropriate, politically mainstream portions of the gay population had already occurred [at the time of 9/11]— in politics, media representations, and the workplace" (p. 44). In education, consumption occurs as assimilation. The greatest example of which may be "add-and-stir," "role-model" driven inclusive curricula, which substantiates Duggan's (2003) claim that

> Along with this move toward "multicultural" diversity within the neoliberal mainstream, some proponents of "equality politics" moved away from the civil rights lobbies and identity politics organizations to advocate the abandonment of progressive-left affiliations, and the adoption of a neoliberal brand of identity/equality politics. These organizations, activists, and writers promote "color-blind" anti-affirmative action racial politics, conservative-libertarian "equality feminism," and gay "normality." (p. 44)

The advocation and purported realization of colorblindness has been offered as one example of the era of "post-identity"; here, I am not speaking to the ideas of non-essentialized, partial, intersectional, and complicated renderings of positionality and subjectivity. Rather, there is a simultaneous claim to a post-racial, post-queer world (Green, 2002); where identity constructs are argued to have been torn down with the election of President Obama, and increase in rights for LGBTTIQ peoples that is constantly in tension with neoliberal moves of identity reinforcement and normalcy. One has to wonder: who is making the claims to post-anything and to what end or purpose? In education, the idea that educators, students, or schools are beyond race or sexuality seems both preposterous and impossible; yet the desire for the post-identity moment re-instills the individualism and mosaic or "we can all get along" narrative that unburdens institutions of their systemic responsibility. One possible resistance to the re-emergence of identity politics in a manner that reinforces the status quo is to directly challenge the essentializing and assimilative potential of LGBTTIQ. Using *queer, queered, and queering* when thinking of pedagogy might be of use.

While writing *STQ*, I acknowledged that LGB students could be other than white, middle-class and able-bodied; still, imbedded in the text was a norm that spoke of LGB as the norm except when its otherness was explicitly and problematically marked. For example, when stating "these stresses are only exacerbated if the student is of color, working class, disabled, or goes against traditional gender roles" (p. 60), I was raising the potentiality of non-white LGB bodies but at the same moment, in only marking the race of non-white queers I was preoccupied with essentialized LGB student bodies, whose primary identification was LGB even if he or she was multiply oppressed. The marking of race as only non-white both shores up the Us (normal)/Them (non-normal) binary, and relegates the "gay experience" necessarily and rightfully the same for all who might consider themselves or be considered under a LGB identification. One further example is the suggestion in *STQ* that being "out" was also similarly defined and obviously desired by all groups. I write that "Students who identify as gay, lesbian, or bisexual, especially those who are *out* at school, are in jeopardy . . . ultimately making the schooling experience for many gay, lesbian and bisexual youth difficult and often dangerous" (p. 60). However, I do not discuss the ways that *out* functions at times as neither desirable nor as emancipatory or liberating for all students.

McCready (2001) outlines the ways in which Black males rejected GSA's or other LGB or queer organizations at school, noting a different manner of wanting to be understood within their own communities. Ross (2005) suggests that the closet is a raced metaphor because Black communities may be supportive of Black gay men even though there was never a public dialogue without any public exchange of explicitly spoken information, which might be read as an insult to the audience as there is an unspoken acknowledgment of gay men in the community. Ross argues that forcing an acknowledgment through coming out criticizes the Black community for an unproven ignorance.

Again, Duggan (2003) is helpful in thinking through the reasons why intersectionality might be threatening to neoliberalism. She notes. "By drawing close connections between the agenda of color-blindness and . . . the linkages between race and sexualities and the desire of neoliberal politics to smooth the way for a normalcy that refuses to challenge the status quo" (p. xii). I wonder what it would mean to petition a queer theory that requires interrogations of whiteness alongside that of queerness. That is, interrogations of the normativity of the hetero and the white alongside the other we cite in the homo and the "of color." What if the call to question normativity and hail fluidity accepts that normativity encompasses whiteness as racialized space?

Queering Contested Space

Not unlike social justice, the term queering occupies a contested and tension-filled space. Its use, reuse, and appropriation by myriad groups is a useful case study in how neoliberalism folds progressive language back in on itself. It can start with attacks from the Right, such as the following from the family research council:

> For those who aren't familiar with Queering, it focuses extensively on "re-educating parents" who object to teaching children about homosexual families, "affirming 'sissy boys,'" and eliminating "Mother's Day" and "Father's Day" from the classroom. Other chapters encourage the use of music to indoctrinate kids (with pro-homosexual songs like "Mama, What's a Dyke?"), and the drive to include gay-friendly literature in grade school, particularly the type that "affirms the comfortable friendships between young boys and adult homosexual men."
>
> (http://www.frc.org/, May 29, 2009)

Here, queering is cast as rearticulating the project of those who would change schooling as a threat to parental rights. Its ideology is one in which parents control the market rights over where their children go to school and what is taught, and if they do not like the methods they can use the rules of supply and demand, and vote with their feet.

In the use of *queer* and *queering* within pedagogies, I am calling for an analysis that extends beyond binaries of gay and straight, queer and not queer. As Talburt (2005) notes "I use the word queer to gesture toward less predictable identities and practices than L, G, B, and T commonly signify"(p. 87). *Queer* not only denotes a rejection of the fixed identity constructions of gay, straight, bisexual, or transgendered, it also calls into question the normativism of heterosexual. The focus of this use of queer and queer theories is to interrogate the ways that heteronormativity maintains the status quo of sexuality, gender identity, race, and unequal power relations, in relation to the identities of youth, teachers, parents, and schools. Within pedagogy, it is useful to think of pedagogy as that which Berlant and Warner (1995) discuss as "commentary." They suggest: "it is not useful to consider queer theory a thing, especially one dignified by capital letters. We wonder whether *queer commentary* might not more accurately describe the things linked by the rubric, most of which are not theory?" (p. 343). Luhmann (1999) links this notion of queering to pedagogy when she argues that

> What is at stake in queer pedagogy is not the application of queer theory onto pedagogy, nor the application of pedagogy for the dissemination of queer theory and knowledge. What is at stake are the implications of queer theory and pedagogy for the messy process of learning and teaching, reading and writing. (p. 151)

If we think of queering and queer pedagogy as a process of commentary, of uncovering, of teaching and learning, does it encourage educators' refusal to pin down pedagogy as linear and, as suggested in an earlier section, scriptable?

Even in the call for understanding normativity and deconstructions of gender and sex, queer theories and queer pedagogies have been often rightfully criticized as ignoring race, leading to a theoretical silence as work such as that by Gloria Anzaldúa (1987), Francisco Valdes (1999), are, especially in education, seldom taken up. Anzaldúa (1991), for example, spoke of queer as a working-class, Latina long before queer theories were introduced. She argued: "the new mestiza queers have the ability, the flexibility, the malleability, the amorphous quality of being able to stretch this way and that way. We can add new labels, names and identities as we mix with others" (p. 279). More than the erasure and loss of ideas, what if by citing queer as white, middle class and able bodied, the divisions are not only reinforced but carry an additional weight of citationality forward?

Yet it is not as if race (with whiteness as part of the conversation) can, or should, be separated from sexuality. Ferguson (2005) reminds us that "sexuality is not extraneous to other modes of difference. Sexuality is intersectional. It is constitutive of and constituted by racialized gender and class formations" (p. 88). And it is from this position that any discussion about queering must begin. The queering of pedagogy and curricula is not a call for the classroom to *become* gendered, racialized, and (hetero)sexualized; rather, it is a pedagogical tool to uncover and analyze the ways in which the classroom is already sexualized, heterosexualized, and racialized. Queer also encourages interrogations of identity categories through which we seem drawn to organize. It is the work of these theories to disrupt the uncritical usage of categorizations and labeling, to require interrogations of when these constructions are useful and when they further stereotype, or merely encourage a lack of complexity in favor of ease of understanding. Queered (pedagogy) rejects the neoliberal championing of the stability of the status quo, the return to the individual as moral center as the focal point of change, the reification of hetero (normativity) and whiteness as that which drives school policy and the ways of teaching and learning.

Queer pedagogy may offer a resistance to the neoliberal if it, too, can avoid the neoliberal backlash and reappropriation. Queer theory was, in many ways, a rejection of the identity politics of lesbian, gay, and bisexual social movements, carving out a space for mutability of identity and a commitment to interrogations of normativity. Yet, just as queer became understood as not LGBTTIQ, but a different ideology altogether, it began its neoliberal turn. Currently, there is a drive to reappropriate queer as the umbrella term for LGBTTIQ, returning it to the identity politics fold where queer pedagogies become the pedagogies of inclusion and safe schools. In theory, research, and schools there is resistance to the reabsorption of queer, in part because youth have argued that identities are not as boundaried as LGBTTIQ (MacIntosh, 2007; Talburt, 2004). In part, the project of this chapter has been to articulate queered or queering such that the production of normalcy can be interrogated and the unlayering of neoliberal production and repetition begun (Britzman, 1995).

Queer Pedagogy in the Realm of the Superhero

In *STQ*, I make a number of recommendations about how to change schools. I suggest:

- To make school environments more welcoming . . . educators can implement such changes as altering curriculum, changing the school environment, and training pre-service and supervising teachers. (pp. 59–60)
- Schools can begin with small steps. When you list categories of comments (racist, sexist) that are not acceptable in the classroom, add "homophobic" and define homophobia if students do not understand it. (p. 61)
- Teachers and teacher educators should no longer make assumptions about their own students' sexuality. (p. 61)

None of the suggestions are entirely off, but in making recommendations such as these, I am not acknowledging the local context of school and schooling. The reader could infer that I am either offering an entry point or an end point. As entry point, the ideas here offer a place to get started, but are overly formulaic and likely not to open up the types of indeterminate critical spaces a queering pedagogy might suggest. They do not offer opportunities to "deconstruct binaries central to Western modes of meaning making, learning, teaching and doing policies. . . subvert the processes of normalization" (Luhmann, 1999, p. 151). If they are read as ending points the desire to queer pedagogy has failed before it began, as both queer pedagogy and I take as a premise the impossibility of solutions.

While we may hope for a list of recommendations, a toolbox, or a place for answers about how to go about doing this work, I am suggesting that it is productive *not* to offer a list such as I did in *STQ*. Not only because of the points made above, but because it is in the process and possibility of uncovering and deconstructing in the local contexts of teachers, administrators, schools, and communities that queering pedagogy may have an opportunity to affect change.

What might it mean for queering teaching to acknowledge that racism and heterosexism and other forms of oppression are always already in play? As Delgado (1995) argues, racism is "normal, not aberrant" (p. xiv) and becomes "naturalized" or as some of us would say "normalized." Ladson-Billings (1995) goes further, suggesting that "sexism, patriarchy, heterosexism, able-ism, classism, linguisticism, and other forms of hierarchy that come from dominance and oppression are also normal." Critical race theorists, including Brayboy (2006), Ladson-Billings and Tate (1995), Gillborn (2006), Dixson and Rousseau (2006) and many others suggest a rejection of color-blindness, neutrality and theoretically require a critique of liberalism. Additionally, as I have argued elsewhere, it is impossible to engage pedagogies that have been termed multicultural, anti-oppressive, anti-racist, queer without always interrogating the simultaneously interlocking constructions we have come to call identity.

The desire to move toward the everyday interrogation across constructions is not without controversy. In part, the conflict centers on what is at the heart of or is the purpose of an analysis. Those who focus on sexuality and those who focus on race are rightfully concerned that if the unit of analysis is not race, or sexuality, then that very important and necessary analysis will become or remain invisible. This is not surprising as there is a continuing and ongoing history of race and/or non-normative sexualities becoming lost, hidden, or subsumed under other monikers, such as diversity or social justice. Utilizing a single unwavering center of analysis model often creates the secondary issue as an add-on, rather than creating an integrated analysis of how race and sexuality work hand in hand to reinforce both racism and heteronormativity.

The fear of losing one's place at the table can only begin to be rectified with theoretical understandings that demand that interlinkages and multiple sites of oppression are imbued throughout every analysis. What if the unit of analysis is contingent, fleeting, but always connected to notions of normativity and subordination? This does not disrupt the centrality of race and/or sexuality as key, but imbues the analysis with an understanding that one identity impacts the other, and likely reinforces the status quo. Highlighting the intersections does not remove the necessity to uncover and analyze the racism within queer communities or the heteronormativity within communities of color. It is important to note that these problems are no more or less evident than in the mainstream communities, requiring a similar level of analysis across, among, and between these identity constructions that denote so much and so little.

I suggest that interlinkages and inter-group subjectivities do, at times, recenter the forces of normativity that other groups are working against. There is always work to be done across groupings—the places where white queer theorists leave racism invisible, where non-sexual minority, post-colonial scholars render hetero-normativity as the status quo, or where critical race scholars focus on the United States within an often black–white binary.

Similarly, an anti-oppressive queer theory requires an interrogation of the role of normativities in relation to sexuality and gender, in conjunction with gender expectations, racial and ethnic imaginaries, and class within fluid and contingent contexts. I am arguing for a contingent notion of identity that offers particular use-fulness to pedagogy and the design of curricula. Drawing upon Butler (1992), the idea of *contingent primacy* understands that an imaginary construction of identities is always already present (Loutzenheiser, 2006). Contingent primacy acknowledges that even when one identity is, or has, primacy or is exposed as meaningful in a ped-agogical or curricular moment, the knowledge that more complicated and fluid constructions are produced around us, our schools, and the systems within which we live is also a fundamental part of the analyses. It is an understanding that this contingency is grounded in social, political, and historical contexts.

The desire, then, is for an ongoing set of interrogations of theories and analytical lenses through which we interpret race, sexuality, and other forms of injustice. It is a call for theories that begin to account for the ways in which constructions and dis-courses of that which we name race and sexuality benefit from understanding their interlinkages, while simultaneously interrogating the commonsense and tradi-tional frames into which they are embedded. Each relies on a rejection of liberal notions of self, and turns to an analysis of normativities. Theories that attend to both the materiality of race and sexuality in contemporary educational realms, and examinations of identity as unfixed and multiple, suggest the productive nature of theoretical dialogues across paradigmatic lines.

Conclusions and Queer Pedagogy in the Realm of the Superhero

> Even as I argue and advocate for a queering of pedagogy, I am brought back to the neoliberal project that attempts to pull such a praxis into erasure, produc-ing instead a particular visibility that can be consumed by the reader of this chapter or for educators writ large. I revisit the cautions of Britzman (1998) and Bryson and De Castell (1993) who noted, more than a decade ago, that to incorporate queer theory might not result in any ultimate queering of peda-gogy. In fact, they foreshadowed the neoliberal backlash and appropriation we see in this current pedagogical moment.

Yet even in this desire for queering of pedagogy, which this chapter has discussed at length, I wonder about the ways in which we hail the liberatory superhero who can do it all, that can learn how to be a perfectly queer educator with an end point sim-ilar to her/his LGBT predecessor. That is, in our search for ways to queer teaching and learning do we remain committed to a pedagogy that is utopian in its liberatory and emancipatory goals, even in its fluidity? Are we relying on the queer superhero to sweep in and teach us all how to "reach" queer youth, or to improve schooling in relation to anti-oppressive education? If we are, indeed, replacing one pedagogy seeped in the right (critical) answers for another, as opposed to believing in the impossibility of an outcome based on the queering of pedagogy, then this very queering that is attempted becomes reabsorbed into the goals of neoliberalism. I want to resist this and ask for something less known, or perhaps, not known at all. A place with fewer insides and outsides that exceeds educators' learned desire for a tidy narrative that can be taught as the I to the Other.

I am left with questions such as, How do educators engaged in queering teaching and learning resist the impulse to normalize? How is it that both those who would advocate for a queering, as I have described, and those who are wedded to an assimilative status quo can each feed into a neoliberal return? Weems (2007) argues that the pressures of pedagogy and curricular reforms can lead to a recuperation of

> heteronormative assumptions about education, and educational discourse in which queer theorizing is relegated to issues of sexuality, sexuality is confined to (deviant) identities and where queer scholars are put in their supposedly "proper" place, e.g., speaking only to/from/about sexual (minority) identities. (p. 196)
>
> Here, she warns of the box of the "good gay" that places queer in its place where it can foster the least amount of change. I would argue that GSAs might be a good example of this trend. In some spaces, GSAs have individualistic goals and objectives, focused on improving schooling for LGBTTIQ youth, while others have queer intentions. Still, even with their queering ways, GSAs themselves are an example of proper place where queering is confined to sexually minority youth and their allies (MacIntosh, 2007).

The question becomes: Are there spaces within the queering of pedagogy that allow educators and students to resist the call of the emancipatory, and exceed the push to normalization? I want to think that those spaces can be created within processes of reform that explore the paradigmatic and epistemological underpinning of work from the present and the past. In revisiting of *SMQ*, I am calling for the revisiting of our own theories and assumptions as we progress (or regress) through social and political moments. I am suggesting that a rereading of the past through present lens offers space to question our ongoing assumptions about theory, truth, and the processes of reform and the reworking of praxis.

Points of Inquiry

- Loutzenheiser mentions Ellen DeGeneres as "a comfortable gay body" "not too far outside the bounds of acceptability." What aspects of queering are acceptable, normalized? What research can you find that underscores, refutes, and/or changes Loutzenheiser's argument?
- How have queer theorists changed, challenged, and confirmed each others' work over time? What reasons can you determine for these changes?

- What, in your own words, does it mean to engage in a queering peda-gogy? What aspects of school context and culture could it possibly address? What critiques can you muster?

Points of Praxis

- GSAs are generally considered a positive advance in the life of schooling (at least from a progressive standpoint). How do GSAs operate to con-firm a particular notion of queer? How might they, at your site, confirm marginalization rather than address it in the way that the author suggests?
- The author offers a notion of queering pedagogy, one that is not pre-scriptive nor proscribed. In such an instance, how can you locate this kind of praxis at your site? What questions might you and your students pursue in order to begin, even contingently, to answer such a complex call to action?
- Consider the two vignettes in the chapter. How are issues of sexual/gen-der identity and difference addressed in the various aspects of school life at your site? Consider curriculum, clubs, rules, etc. How does the incor-poration and/or marginalization intersect with the politics of race, class, gender, ability, and the like?

Notes

1 It is also notable that, at the time of writing this article I problematically omit any reference to transgender youth.
2 Lesbian Gay Bisexual, Transgender, Two-spirit, Intersex and Questioning. I want to both acknowledge the importance of including multiple groups within this identifying phrase and acknowledge the wide differences in educational experiences between and amongst different sexual and gender minority categories. Throughout the chapter I attempt to use LGB, or LGBTTIQ as the authors of the report or the era of the article demands.
3 The vignettes are fictional amalgamations of students with whom I have worked or researched.
4 A reminder to the reader that acronym use follows the author or study specifications.
5 This study did not include transgender youth.

References

Anzaldúa, G. (1987). *Borderlands: The new mestiza = la frontera*. San Francisco: Aunt Lute.
Anzaldúa, G. (1991). To(o) queer the writer: Loca, escrita y chicana. In B. Warland (Ed.), *Inversions: Writing by dykes, queers and lesbians* (pp. 249–263). Vancouver: Press Gang.
Berlant, L., & Warner, M. (1995). What does queer theory teach us about x? *PMLA, 110*(3), 343–349.
Bontempo, D. E., & D'Augelli, A. R. (2002). The relationship between suicide risk and sexual orientation: Results of a population-based study. *Journal of adolescent health, 30*(5), 364–374.

Brayboy, B. M. J. (2006). Toward a tribal critical race theory in education. *Urban Review, 37*(5), 425–446.

British Columbia Confederation of Parent Advisory Councils. (2003). *Call it safe: A parent guide for dealing with harassment and intimidation in secondary school.* Victoria, BC: British Columbia Ministry of Education.

British Columbia Ministry of Education. (2007). *Social justice 12: Integrated resource package.* Retrieved from: http://www.bced.gov.bc.ca/irp/drafts/sj12_draft.pdf.

Britzman, D. P. (1995). Is there a queer pedagogy? Or, stop reading straight. *Educational Theory, 45*(2), 151–165.

Britzman, D. P. (1998). *Lost subjects, contested objects.* Albany, NY: State University of New York Press.

Brown, W. (2006). *Regulating aversion: Tolerance in the age of identity and empire.* Princeton, NJ: Princeton University Press.

Bryson, M., & De Castell, S. (1993). Queer pedagogy: Practice make im/perfect. *Canadian Journal of Education, 18*(2), 285–305.

Butler, J. (1992). Contingent foundations. In J. Butler & J. W. Scott (Eds.), *Feminists theorize the political* (pp. 3–21). New York: Routledge.

Day, D. M., & Golench, C. A. (1997). Promoting safe schools through policy: Results of a survey of Canadian school boards. *Journal of Educational Administration, 35*(4), 332–247.

Delgado, R. (1995). Introduction. In R. Delgado (Ed.), *Critical race theory: The cutting edge* (pp. xiii–xvi). Philadelphia: Temple University Press.

Dixson, A. D., & Rousseau, C. K. (2006). And we are still not saved: Critical race theory in education ten years later. In A. D. Dixson & C. K. Rousseau (Eds.), *Critical race theory in education: All god's children go a song* (pp. 31–56). New York: Routledge.

Duggan, L. (2003). *The twilight of inequality: Neoliberalism, cultural politics, and the the attack on democracy.* Boston: Beacon Press.

Dwyer, J. G. (1998). *Religious schools v. Children's rights.* Ithaca, NY: Cornell University Press.

Ferguson, R. A. (2005). Of our normative strivings: African American studies and the histories of sexuality. *Social Text, 23*, 85–100.

Freire, P. (1970). *Pedagogy of the oppressed.* New York: Herder and Herder.

Gillborn, D. (2006). Critical race theory and education: Racism and anti-racism in educational theory and praxis. *Discourse: Studies in the Cultural Politics of Education, 27*(1), 11–32.

Giroux, H. (2005). The terror of neoliberalism: Rethinking the significance of cultural politics. *College Literature, 32*(1), 1–19.

Goldstein, T., Russell, V., & Daley, A. (2007). Safe, positive and queering moments in teaching education and schooling: A conceptual framework. *Teaching Education, 18*(3), 183–199.

Green, A. I. (2002). Gay but not queer: Toward a post-queer study of sexuality. *Theory and Society, 31*(4), 521–545.

Harbeck, K. (1995). Addressing the needs of lesbian, gay, and bisexual youth and their advocates. In G. Unks (Ed.), *The gay teen* (pp. 125–134). New York: Routledge.

Kumashiro, K. (2001). "Posts" Perspectives on anti-oppressive education in social studies, English, mathematics and science classrooms. *Educational Researcher, 30*(3), 3–12.

Ladson-Billings, G. J. (1995). Toward a theory of culturally relevant pedagogy. *American Educational Research Journal, 32*(3), 465–491.

Ladson-Billings, G. J., & Tate, W. F. (1995). Toward a critical race theory of education. *Teachers College Record, 97*(1), 47–67.

Leitner, H., Peck, J., & Sheppard, E. (2006). *Contesting neoliberalism: Urban frontiers.* New York: Guilford Press.

Loutzenheiser, L. W. (1996). How schools play smear the queer. *Feminist Teacher, 10*(2), 59–64.

Loutzenheiser, L. W. (2001). If I talk about that, they will burn my house down: The possibilities and tensions of queered, anti-racist pedagogy. In K. Kumashiro (Ed.), *Troubling intersections of race and sexuality: Queer students of color and anti-oppressive education* (pp. 195–215). Landham, MD: Rowman & Littlefield.

Loutzenheiser, L. W. (2006). Working fluidity, materiality and the educational imaginary: A case for contingent primacy *Journal of the Canadian Association of Curriculum Studies, 3*(2), 27–39.

Lugg, C. A. (2003). Sissies, faggots, lezzies, and dykes: Gender, sexual orientation, and a new politics of education. *Educational Administration Quarterly, 39*(1), 95–134.

Luhmann, S. (1999). Queering/querying pedagogy? Or, pedagogy is a pretty queer thing. In W. Pinar (Ed.), *Queer theory in education* (pp. 141–156). Mahway, NJ: Lawrence Erlbaum.

McCready, L. (2001). When fitting in isn't an option, or why Black queer males at a California high school stay way from project 10. In K. Kumashiro (Ed.), *Troubling intersections of race and sexuality: Queer students of color and anti-oppressive education* (pp. 37–54). Landham, MD: Rowman & Littlefield.

MacIntosh, L. B. (2007). Does anyone have a band-aid? Anti-homophobia discourses and pedagogical impossibilities. *Educational Studies, 41*(1), 33–43.

Murdock, T. B., & Bolch, M. B. (2005). Risk and protective factors for poor school adjustment in lesbian, gay, and bisexual (lgb) high school youth: Variable and person-centered analyses. *Psychology in the Schools, 42*(2), 159–172.

Noddings, N. (1997). Social studies and feminism. In E. W. Ross (Ed.), *The social studies curriculum: Purposes, problems and possibilities* (pp. 59–70). Buffalo: NY: State University of New York Press.

Novak, M. (2000). Defining social justice. *First Things First, 108,* 11–13.

Parents and Friends of Lesbians and Gays. (2006). *From our house to the school house: Safe schools for all students.* New York City: PFLAG.

Rawls, J. (1971). *Theory of justice.* Cambridge, MA: Harvard University Press.

Remafedi, G., French, S., Story, M., Resnick, M. D., & Blum, R. (1998). The relationship between suicide risk and sexual orientation: Results of a population-based study. *American Journal of Public Health, 88*(1), 57–60.

Rivers, I. (2000). Social exclusion, absenteeism and sexual minority youth. *Support for learning, 15*(1), 13–18.

Ross, M. B. (2005). Beyond the closet as raceless paradigm. In E. P. Johnson, & M. G. Henderson (Eds.), *Black queer studies: A critical anthology* (pp. 161–189). Durham, NC: Duke University Press.

Rostosky, S. S., Owens, G. P., Zimmerman, R. S., & Riggle, E. D. B. (2003). Associations among sexual attraction status, school belonging, and alcohol and marijuana use in rural high school students. *Journal of Adolescence, 26*(6), 741–751.

Russell, S. T., & Joyner, K. (2001). Adolescent sexual orientation and suicide risk: Evidence from a national study. *American Journal of Public Health, 91*(8), 1276–1281.

Rutter, P. A., & Soucar, E. (2002). Youth suicide risk and sexual orientation. [Feature]. *Adolescence, 37,* 289–299.

Talburt, S. (2004). Constructions of LGBT youth: Opening up subject positions. *Theory Into Practice, 43*(2), 116–121.

Talburt, S. (2005). Queer research and queer youth. *Journal of Gay and Lesbian Issues in Education, 3*(2/3), 87–93.

Talburt, S. (2008). Queer imaginings. *Journal of LGBT Youth, 5*(3), 99–103.

Tolerate. (n.d.). Dictionary.com Unabridged (v 1.1). Retrieved May 26, 2009, from: Dictionary.com website: http://dictionary.reference.com/browse/tolerate

Valdes, F. (1999). Theorizing "Outcrt: Theories: Coalitional method and comparative jurisprudential experience—racecrits, queercrits and latcrits. *University of Miami Law Review, 53*, 1265–1322.

Walton, G. (2004). Bullying and homophobia in Canadian schools: The politics of policies, programs, and educational leadership. *Journal of Gay and Lesbian Issues in Education, 1*(4), 23–36.

Warner, M. (1993). Introduction. In M. Warner (Ed.), *Fear of a queer planet: Queer politics and social theory* (pp. vii–xxxi). Minneapolis, MN: University of Minnesota Press.

Weems, L. (2007). Un/fixing the fiend: Queering pedagogy and dangerous desires, *Educational Studies, 41*(3), 194–211.

Young, I. M. (2000). *Inclusion and democracy.* New York: Oxford Unversity Press.

Zajda, J., Majhanovich, S., & Rust, V. (2006). Education and social justice: Issues of liberty and equality in the global culture. In J. Zajda, S. Majhanovich, V. Rust & E. M. Sabina (Eds.), *Education and social justice* (pp. 1–12). Dordrecht, the Netherlands: Springer.

Zizek, S. (2008). Tolerance as an ideological category. *Critical Inquiry, 34*(4), 660–682.

Chapter 7

Critical Multiculturalism
Transformative Educational Principles and Practices

Patricia D. Quijada Cerecer, Leticia Alvarez Gutiérrez, and Francisco Rios

Multicultural education is a field of inquiry that has long historical roots and contemporary conceptions that connect to principles of critical education that can inform social justice pedagogy; however, the field has been challenged by efforts in the mainstream to foster superficial, liberal (but still assimilationist) approaches to diversity in education. We begin this chapter with a discussion of the main purposes of education in the U.S.A. Then we provide a brief historical overview of how multicultural education evolved to present day. Third, we detail the principles of critical education already evident in multicultural education theory. Fourth, we acknowledge factors associated with the problem of implementing multicultural and critical education theory into practice. We then discuss the key principles of critical multicultural education and discuss its respective connections to teaching for social justice. Finally we end with a series of provocative questions and a call to action.

> One thing we know for sure. Globalization impacts every community, in every country, in all countries; it is devouring traditions, it is devouring cultures, and it is devouring people. This is teaching us that life is about having, life is about working, instead of life being about being. And education doesn't escape this. . . . What is the role of a teacher in what we call neoliberalism . . . Mexico's political system [for example] is bound to conditions of the IMF [International Monetary Fund] and World Bank . . . and this has changed the meaning of education.
> (translated excerpt from film, *Granitos de Arena*, Friedberg, 2004)

This excerpt of the film *Granitos de Arena* illuminates the impact of globalization (the push of nations toward a single, unified international culture, political structure, social system, etc.) and neoliberalism (an economic policy of unrestrained capitalism within a globalized free market) on the teaching profession. It explicitly demonstrates how public education is becoming privatized, embodied in a corporate philosophy and processes that aim at the standardization of schooling. Importantly, in the film, teachers take to the streets to protest neoliberal government policies that threaten public education on Mexico. This film poignantly illuminates teaching as an activist profession. Unfortunately, the teachers lose this battle and return to teaching. The teachers become consciously aware of the importance of building coalitions and relationships with the community as a means to gain collective support, something they failed to do.

Granitos de Arena documents how teachers attend to the impact of public policies, especially neoliberalism, on education, and the film illustrates how teachers can take an activist stance on such issues. When we in the U.S.A. frame teaching as politically neutral, and when we understand teachers as mere technicians of curriculum and instruction, we diminish the possibilities of social justice in action. This dominant discourse of education as politically neutral, we argue, undermines attempts to integrate the most progressive dimensions of multicultural theory into practice.

The social justice teachers in *Granitos de Arena* exemplify how issues of injustice unfold and impact children when policies push public education toward privatization. The teachers demonstrate in their work how the principles of social justice—*equity, activism, social literacy*, as defined by Ayers, Quinn, and Stovall (2009)—are operationalized. Motivated by concerns that those who have the least would be unfairly excluded from schooling (*equity*) these teachers behaved in ways that demonstrated their understanding of the need for social action to bring about change (*activism*). Informing themselves about how public policy impacts schooling practices, these educators acted on their political understanding (*social literacy*). We discuss and define these three principles in more depth later in this chapter. We intend to illuminate throughout the chapter how social justice pedagogies can be informed by those who aspire toward a critical multiculturalism.

This chapter is organized in the following way. First, we discuss the main purposes of education in the U.S.A. Then we move to provide a brief historical overview of how multicultural education evolved to present day. Third, we provide an overview of principles of critical education already evident in multicultural education theory. Fourth, we provide an overview of the problem with implementing multicultural and critical education theory into practice. We then discuss the key principles of critical multicultural education and discuss its respective connections to teaching for social justice. Finally, we end with a series of provocative questions and a call to action.

Purposes of Education

Current debates around education are usually about specific programs or policies (bilingual education, vouchers, testing, etc.) but underlying them is one basic question: What are the purposes of education in the U.S.A.? We argue there is no one general purpose that dominates and guides all practice. This is evident in the diversity of aims in schools and classrooms and most noteworthy in how the complex roles of teachers have been defined. In general, there appear to be four purposes that guide education. The first is to prepare students for the workforce. This purpose seems to dominate currently and guide educational practice. Competing in the global market manifests itself in students developing technical skills that can be marketed. Yet the assessments implemented in schools today do not gauge skills that will be transferred in the workforce, demonstrating how this dominant purpose of education is contradictory. This purpose is exemplified in school districts where principals refer to themselves as CEOs, and/or where parents and students are called "customers." A second purpose is to prepare students as humans or individuals. This is illustrated in Maslow's self-actualizing theory and Piaget's cognitive approach that advocate for a child-centered purpose of schooling. Preparing students to be "good citizens" marks a third purpose of education. These efforts illuminate that the purpose of education is to support the status quo. The cultural representation of a "good American" citizen fuels assimilationist practices and a philosophy similar to those advocated by E. D. Hirsch, Linda Chavez, and Diane Ravitch who advocate for a common curricula around a common (Eurocentric) culture, promoting an uncritical form of nationalism. The fourth purpose is to prepare students as critically thinking citizens who question, contest and transform the status quo in pursuit of social justice ideals via a deeper notion of democracy and patriotism.

Some purposes of education have more influence at a particular political moment than others (e.g., education for work, citizens prepared to maintain the status quo currently). That is, some purposes may impact individual's lives and opportunities more so than others. Less evident are approaches to education that have as their foundation a desire to implement a democratic aim that engages students in critical discussions about social inequalities. These approaches assert that citizens have an obligation and responsibility to disrupt oppression while acting to move our nation toward a more just orientation. They assert a challenge to the status quo as part of what it means to be educated. Paulo Freire illuminates how,

> There is no such thing as a neutral educational process. Education either functions as an instrument which is used to facilitate the integration of the younger generation into the logic of the present system and bring about conformity to it or it becomes the "practice of freedom"—the means by which men and women deal critically and creatively with reality and discover how to participate in the transformation of their world.
>
> (Freire, 1973, p. 73)

How we answer these questions about the broad purpose of education sets the context for how multicultural education is understood and implemented.

Historical Context of Multicultural Education

To understand the emergence of multicultural education it is important to illuminate the historical work and advocacy, especially by scholars of color early on, that provided a foundation and served as a catalyst for the emergence of multicultural education and critical multiculturalism. James Banks (2004) provides one such historical perspective, which we briefly describe here.

The first phase emerged in the 1880s and is referred to as the Early Ethnic Studies Movement (Banks, 2004). This movement centered on fostering ethnic identification and its relationship to social action. Prominent scholars such as W.E.B. Du Bois, Carter G. Woodson, Manuel Gamio, and Carlos Bulosan led the Early Ethnic Studies Movement. In the 1940s the Intergroup Education Movement

(IEM) emerged, marking the second phase (Banks, 2004). The IEM expanded on the issues addressed in phase one by also acknowledging how racism, discrimination, and prejudice operated in individual-to-individual relationships in U.S. society. Gordon Allport, Lloyd Cook, Hilda Taba, Kenneth and Mamie Clark, and other scholars and activists were central forces in this movement. While the IEM began to produce new scholarly work examining the development of democratic racial attitudes and values, a shortcoming is that it did not examine racism and discrimination from an institutional or structural perspective (i.e., how public policies, practices, and processes, such as school segregation, created and exacerbated prejudice and discrimination).

Shortly after the IEM, in the 1960s, the Modern Ethnic Studies Movement emerged as the third phase (Banks, 2004). The Modern Ethnic Studies Movement centered its efforts on illuminating how ethnic and racial oppression negatively impacted people of color and their communities. This movement also produced scholarly work on how individuals and communities actively resisted ethnic and racial oppression. Rudy Acuña, Harry Kitano, Betty Lee Sung, Vine Deloria, and many other scholars/activists provided the leadership for this movement. In the 1970s, phase four emerged as the Modern Movement in Multicultural Education (Banks, 2004). The emergence of this movement centered on illuminating and dismantling institutional and systemic discrimination. During this movement attempts were made to integrate ethnic studies content into the K-12 curriculum and teacher education programs. During the Modern Movement, definitions and understandings of equity-based advocacy were expanded from ethnicity to include class, gender, sexual orientation, and disability dimensions (and their intersections—race *and* class, gender *and* disability, etc.).

Critical Multiculturalism emerged as the fifth phase of this movement (Banks, 2004). It was during this phase that scholars pushed to assert multicultural education as a more complex, organic, and dynamic field of inquiry. However, during this time period it became apparent that institutions and individuals began appropriating multicultural education for both conservative and liberal ends. Thus, the term was often found in mission statements, diversity plans, and marketing philosophies, yet its implementation often lacked the critical, activist elements that served as its genesis. Given this, critical multiculturalism emerged to re-center multicultural education within a transformative political agenda, challenging relations of power and privilege, and seeking social and structural change. In essence it emerged as a way to critique how people "do" multicultural education.

In general, given the weak ways in which most educational institutions and most practitioners in schools implement multicultural theory into policies and practice, critical multiculturalism plays an important role in reappropriating multicultural education. Christine Sleeter illuminates how multicultural education has been detracted from its original goals and advocacy toward social justice by stating the following,

> The primary issue was one of access to a quality education. If we're not dealing with questions of why access is continually important, and if we're not dealing

with issues like why we have so much poverty amid so much wealth, we're not dealing with the core issues of multiculturalism. I know it may sound trite, but the central issue remains one of justice.

(Sleeter, 2000–2001)

This critique is important especially as we examine our current political climate which pushes away from any but the most superficial approaches of multicultural education.

Current Political Climate

Currently the political climate of U.S. educational institutions is drowning in the present version of the Elementary and Secondary Education Act, renamed the No Child Left Behind (NCLB) Act by the Bush administration,[1] policies that perpetuate the narrowing of the school curriculum (including scripted teaching) and codify Eurocentric values resulting in the marginalization of individuals and historically oppressed communities. Further attempts are being made to challenge diversity content from that curriculum. For example, in Tucson, Arizona, legislation was proposed to abolish Ethnic Studies programs in K-12 (see http://instech.tusd.k12.az.us/Raza/index.asp). While this state proposition was defeated,[2] these political efforts demonstrate how the very climate of politics and society contests multicultural education being implemented in K-12 schools. This issue demonstrates also how schools are a microcosm or a reflection of the broader political society and climate. These efforts unfortunately reinforce superficial approaches to multicultural education that fuel stereotypes of subordinated others, advance shallow understandings of difference, marginalize the experiences of oppressed people in the curriculum, and approach the study of people who have been marginalized as passive—as opposed to active—agents of their experiences (Yosso, 2002).

While much progress has been made in developing and refining theories of multicultural education, minimal strides have been made in putting progressive, activist multicultural theory to practice. The operationalization of such approaches to multicultural education are often contested or blocked by legislation such as NCLB. These efforts to block multicultural education are becoming more salient as we move toward institutionalizing a Eurocentric and standardized curriculum and assessments and use these as a gauge for learning. Society is moving toward neoliberal notions in which the broad purposes of education are being defined as preparation for work and moving away from holistic, critical ways of engaging in education for civic engagement, and for being.

Critical Education Elements within Multicultural Education Theory

We reassert that the foundational elements of multicultural education have always spoken to and advocated for multicultural education within a critical education trajectory (see Chapter 4). These are evident in the theories, concepts, and practices described, primarily by academicians, who have advanced the work of the field of multicultural education since its inception. While a thorough accounting is not provided here (see Chapman & Hobbel, 2005, for one such overview of key multicultural theories), it is essential to understand how at least the three most well-known theories are linked to principles of critical education.

For many scholars in the field, James Banks offered the first foundational theory of multicultural education and it has had a productive history. Stemming from the important work being done in ethnic studies, he described four levels of curriculum integration (Banks, 1975/2009). Moving from the most superficial and surface level, Banks discussed a "contributions" approach whose focus is primarily to highlight the heroes/sheroes of a particular diversity group. The "additive" approach focuses on adding in content, concepts, and themes into the curriculum, usually as separate from the existing curriculum, usually during heritage week/month. The "transformative" approach focuses on an overhaul of the entire curriculum to assure that the curriculum illustrates the interaction of various histories, social issues, concerns, worldviews, etc. of different identity groups and, by doing so, advance multiple perspectives on the curriculum. Most important for this discussion is Banks's identification of the final level: "social action." At this level, the one that Banks challenges educators to aspire toward, the curriculum begins with pressing social problems, develops students' critical thinking and decision-making around those problems, and then works to implement solutions to those problems as part and parcel of the academic curriculum. Thus, evident in this discussion of curriculum integration are ideas of problem-posing, critical reflection, and social action—all central tenets of critical education.

Later Banks (2003) situated these levels of curriculum integration into larger goals around multicultural education. The five goals he identified were content integration (when/how educators use content from other identity groups to advance concepts, theories, etc.), knowledge construction processes (the degree to which educators help students to recognize the social nature of knowledge production and thus the biases inherent in that production), prejudice reduction (how educators work to minimize prejudice, stereotype, bias, and discrimination as an explicit part of the curriculum), equity pedagogy (how educators can use a variety of teaching styles that speak to the diverse learning styles of students as culturally influenced), and an empowering school culture and social structure (identifying structural constraints to students' having an opportunity to participate fully in school without unfair treatment based on race, class, gender, disability, language, etc.). Thus, Banks continues to take a broader view of what multicultural education includes, making explicit its anti-discriminatory aims as well as its willingness to implicate institutional structures for their role in perpetuating social and academic inequality.

Christine Sleeter and Carl Grant (1988/2009) detailed the "choices" educators make in implementing a multicultural perspective with special attention to race, class, and gender. Sleeter and Grant believe that educators should at least understand the theoretical underpinnings and conceptual assumptions, strengths, and weaknesses, and curricular, pedagogical, and schooling implications of the approaches they choose. Implicit is the idea that an approach can be context-specific (some choices are better for some social and educational situations than others), and that if the approach to multicultural education is "not working," efforts should not be abandoned; rather, the approach should be changed. Underlying each of these approaches to multicultural education are differing political orientations ranging from assimilation to liberal pluralism, and even to radical reformations of schools and society (Chapman & Hobbel, 2005).

Sleeter and Grant also describe the main goal of an education that is "multicultural and social reconstructionist" as promoting social-structural equality and cultural pluralism, with the intent to help students become citizens willing to engage in the work of eliminating social inequalities. The teaching of critical thinking skills around pressing social issues, rooting the curriculum in students' real, lived experiences with oppression, developing social action skills, employing democratic principles in the classroom, and involving parents and community members in the education process are all included. The explicit connection to principles of critical education is evident. Additionally, the idea that there are multiple meanings of what constitutes multicultural education is consistent with critical discourse efforts to undermine essentializing (that is, stereotypical and narrow) notions of aspects of diversity.

Sonia Nieto (1992/2004) approaches her discussion of social justice principles differently in her work *Affirming Diversity: The Sociopolitical Context of Multicultural Education*. From the beginning, Nieto works to question and counter deficit perspectives around diversity and explicitly situates the work of multicultural education within a social and political context. Conceptually, multicultural education includes the following principles: it is anti-racist/anti-discriminatory; it is basic (as important as math, reading, writing, etc.); it is for all students; it is pervasive (involves all elements of schooling); it is a process; it is for social justice; and it is critical pedagogy.

Evident in these last two principles is the direct link to critical education. That multicultural education is in advance of social justice implies that learning must connect critical thinking with action and includes the need to think of schooling (and living) in ways that are more expansive and inclusive. Asserting that multicultural education is critical pedagogy, Nieto points to the fact that every educational decision reflects a particular ideological and political stance. It also involves the need to question and critique implicit assumptions, underlying myths, established "truths," and persistent practices.

That the pursuit of principles of critical education are indeed part and parcel of academic scholarship in the field was further supported by Bennett's (2001) review of research around multicultural education. In this review, Bennett identified four postulates that undergird the extant research in multicultural education: curriculum reform (knowledge is constructed and contested; a Eurocentric curriculum constitutes cultural racism), equity pedagogy (all children can learn; education should help them reach their potential; teachers' and students' cultural locations/identities influence teaching and learning), multicultural competence (the reduction of racism/prejudice is possible and desirable; individuals can develop a multicultural worldview and function comfortably in other cultural contexts), and social equity. The social equity postulate includes the assertions by multicultural scholars that social change is necessary to disrupt educational inequities and reframe education to bring about equity in access, participation, and achievement. Also evident in the research is the assertion that social change is possible and consistent with basic democratic values and the American creed. It is no wonder that Gay (1995) asserts that multicultural education and critical pedagogy "both employ a language of critique, and endorse pedagogies of resistance, possibility, and hope" (p. 156).

If, as we argue, the foundational elements of multicultural education have critical education elements embedded within, why has the field been critiqued by those who espouse a critical educational perspective? McCarthy (1988) points out that multicultural education's roots do not spring from a critical activist wellspring, as we have suggested above, but rather from a liberal pluralist[3] ideology designed to quiet those discontented with the educational state of affairs via narrow reforms directed at tinkering with the curriculum. As McCarthy describes it:

> Multiculturalism is a body of thought which originates in the liberal pluralist approaches to education and society. Multicultural education, specifically, must be understood as part of a curricular truce, the fallout of a political project to deluge and neutralize Black rejection of the conformist and assimilationist curriculum models solidly in place in the 1960s. (p. 267)

Thus for McCarthy, the very heart of multicultural education can be understood as an attempt to placate the educational discontent voiced by students and communities at the margins while making the least change possible.

To be sure, some have come to understand multicultural education from a liberal pluralist stance based on a misreading of the extant literature, or based on their own interests to maintain a narrow focus on curriculum and away from an examination of institutional structures, oppression, white supremacy, social change, resistance, and radical critique of power and privilege. That there are liberal pluralist orientations within the field of multicultural education cannot be contested. Even multicultural educator Nieto (1994) acknowledged that "the most common understanding of multicultural education is that it consists largely of additive content rather than of structural changes in content and process" (p. 7).

Another explanation for the critique is what Gay (1992) points to as the gap between the theory of multicultural education and its practice. Thus, multicultural education as practiced in the main tends to trivialize difference. Ladson-Billings (2009) describes it this way:

> Although scholars such as James Banks, Carl Grant, and Geneva Gay began on a scholarly path designed to change schools as institutions so that students might be better prepared to reconstruct the society, in its current practice iteration, multicultural education is but a shadow of its conceptual self. Rather

than engage students in provocative thinking about the contradiction of U.S. ideals and lived realities, teachers often find themselves encouraging students to sing "ethnic" songs, eat ethnic food and do ethnic dances. Consistently, manifestations of multicultural education in the classroom are superficial and trivial "celebrations of diversity." (p. 33)

Therefore, it seems that the most salient critique of multicultural education is with its implementation.

The Problem of Practice

Historically, the development of multicultural education theory has integrated critical education elements.. However, the focus of most criticism that has served as the springboard for those who hold a critical multicultural education perspective is with "practice," which often evidences an ideology of liberal pluralism. This has even led to the call to abolish attempts at multicultural education altogether (Tellez, 2002), because teachers end up implementing multicultural education so superficially that it violates the integrity of those it was supposed to serve.

We assert that the problem of practice has its origins *in some combination* of the following: problems with the academic field of inquiry, problems in teacher preparation (including the overrepresentation of White, female, heterosexual, monolingual, middle-class women), problems in schools and with teachers, and problems rooted in the broader sociopolitical context. We share these challenges in hopes that those interested in pursuing social justice pedagogy can be purposeful and thoughtful in advancing practices consistent with the principles that it endorses.

Problems in the academic field of inquiry largely fall around the failure of scholars who make practice and policy recommendations but fail to link them back to the theoretical foundations of the field. Grant and Sachs (1995) argued that too often multicultural scholarship "is concerned with 'a normative politics of cultural difference' in the form of practical concerns for teachers and administrators" (p. 89), but which fails to articulate the theories of Banks, Sleeter and Grant, Nieto and others. The result is the promotion and/or interpretation and implementation of superficial approaches to multicultural education practices. Additionally, the bulk of research in the field has focused on curriculum and pedagogical concerns (and, to a lesser degree, school organization), with less attention to multicultural education aimed at addressing social, structural inequalities of either the school or the broader society (Grant & Sachs, 1995). The implicit message is that attending to curriculum and pedagogical concerns is the most important effort one can make to pursue an education that is multicultural.

In addition, multicultural education as a field of inquiry also struggles with providing direction to educators regarding some fundamental questions about diversity; questions that advocates of social justice pedagogy must likewise confront. Among these questions are the following: How can multicultural scholars make more explicit the importance of moving beyond liberal conceptions to more radical conceptions of diversity: from a focus on culture as static toward culture as dynamic, from analysis of individuals and their actions as the central level of analysis toward an analysis of social groups and institutional structures, and from celebrating difference toward the teaching about oppression and active agency in resistance as a democratic right and responsibility (Chapman & Hobbel, 2005)? How can we assure educators that their multicultural (and social justice) efforts lead to increased academic achievement even as assessed on traditional measures of learning? How do we help each other and our students understand that connections across difference in pursuit of productive alliances are never easy, automatic, or uncontested, especially when the goal is social change (O'Donnell, Pruyn, & Chávez Chávez, 2004)?

One question of special note that multicultural education scholars and social justice educators must address is which social groups are included under the diversity umbrella (Ladson-Billings, 2004). As described, much of the foundational work for multicultural education came from scholars doing ethnic studies, focusing primarily on concerns about race and ethnicity. The result is that many in the field continue to equate multicultural education with race and ethnicity issues exclusively—a focus challenged by critical multiculturalists. Others have expanded the diversity umbrella to include nationality, class, gender, disability, spiritual practice, age, and sexual orientation, which, along with race and ethnicity, make up "the big nine" social identity groups (Brazzel, 2007). Others point to the intersections of these identities as an important consideration (i.e., race with gender, class with gender, etc.). Still others argue that other forms of social identity related to heritage language, citizenship status, regional affiliation, and so on should also be included. Thinking clearly about this question will help social justice educators pursue approaches consistent with its multicultural education underpinnings.

A plethora of factors have been identified for the superficial understandings preservice teachers garner from their teacher education programs. These include structural decisions (where/when multicultural education is taught in the program and the broader university experience), field experiences, education faculty demographics, preservice teacher profiles, etc. (see Sleeter, 2001, for a comprehensive discussion of multicultural education challenges in teacher education). Any movement toward authentic multicultural education will require sustained attention to programmatic issues of content, structure, and quality of teacher preparation, including specific program practices (McDonald & Zeichner, 2009). This will not be easy in the current climate of control and accountability evident in teacher education.

The practice problem also falls on schools and teachers. With respect to the former, some schools have adopted mission statements, curricula, classroom management programs, and school-wide funding priorities (to name a few) that work against critical multicultural education and social justice approaches. With respect to teachers, the lack of preparation means that sometimes teachers just do not know how to create multicultural education or do not want to offend anyone in their undeveloped attempts to do so. The result is the pursuit of "business as usual" (Sleeter & Grant, 2009). Some teachers simply choose not to pursue multicultural education in meaningful ways since it jeopardizes their privilege or requires them to come to grips with their biases, prejudices, and racism—never easy for a person to accomplish. With respect to multicultural education from a critical education lens, some teachers do not believe they should raise issues of oppression, resistance, racism/sexism/homophobia, and the like since it is too political.

Finally, teachers' work is nested within the broader context of the culture of education and the nation-state. With respect to the former, Ladson-Billings (2009) notes that the culture of education as an institution is simply too "nice" to sustain efforts at a critical approach to education. In the introduction we argued that while the culture of the teaching profession elsewhere includes social activism, this is most rare in the U.S.A. With respect to the nation-state, the fault is also within broader social systems, especially neoliberalism, with its focus on standardization, accountability, and privatization. For example, Bohn and Sleeter (2000) have articulated the ways in which standards and assessments have been used to institutionalize a Eurocentric curriculum. What gets tested is what gets taught; so multicultural education at all but the most superficial levels (along with such basics as art, physical education, and music) is left by the wayside. Other issues impacting multicultural education include differential funding for schools that leaves some schools significantly underfunded, unwillingness of the courts to foster greater integration in schooling, and a majoritarian discourse espousing the need for race-, class-, and gender-blind approaches to educational policies and practices.

These tensions, questions, and critiques are a vital source that can strengthen the field overall, not undermine it. As Sleeter and Delgado-Bernal (2004) describe it, these critiques by critical educators should not serve to "move multicultural education away from its core conceptual moorings, but rather to anchor the field more firmly in those moorings" (p. 240). Likewise, we assert that social justice educators must confront many of these similar challenges in ways that respond genuinely to its theoretical and conceptual principles.

Critical Multiculturalism

Liberal, uncritical multicultural education has been criticized for promising to transform schools and their contexts but not actually making any significant impact on the daily schooling experiences of marginalized students. It has failed to challenge majority students' attitudes about their role in society, change monocultural schooling practices (May, 1999), examine differences while making an explicit link to power, provide a critical analysis of racism, and prepare students for social activism (Sleeter & Delgado-Bernal, 2004). Instead critics charge that multicultural education has only superficially challenged power relations in the form of "tolerance" which, in turn, has continued to support "white privilege by rendering institutional racism invisible" (Berlak & Moyenda, 2001, p. 94). Correspondingly, it has not analyzed the power structures that are in place that continue to oppress already marginalized linguistically and culturally diverse communities in and out of school settings.

Thus, many theorists have distinguished themselves and departed from the general multicultural education paradigms by placing racism/classism/sexism/etc. or hierarchical structures at the forefront of their philosophies (for substantial discussion of these, see Kanpol & McLaren, 1995; May, 1999). For example, McCarthy (1995) states that critical multiculturalism "links the micro dynamics of the school curriculum to larger issues of social relations outside the school" (p. 43). Kanpol and McLaren (1995) state that critical multiculturalism has to depart from the traditional notions of multiculturalism because "justice is not evenly distributed and cannot be so without a radical and profound change in social structures in terms of a development of historical agency and a praxis of possibility" (p. 13).

This departure from liberal multicultural education into critical multicultural education has the following four components: "1. Critical reflexivity; 2. Critical analysis of class, corporate power, and globalization; 3. An analysis of empowering pedagogical practices within the classroom; and 4. A deeper analysis of language and literacy than evidenced in multicultural education literature" (Sleeter & Delgado-Bernal, 2004, p. 242).

Understanding the conceptual tools for critical reflexivity is the first important implication for critical multicultural educators to understand. These analytical tools include attention to voice, culture, power relations, and ideology. Incorporating Freire's (1998) idea of dialogical communication to examine *voice* allows one to begin to expose and (de)construct dominant ideologies that obscure marginalized ideologies and concepts from the dialogue, whether partially or entirely. Development of non-essentialist conceptions of *culture* (including distinguishing culture from ethnicity), cultural values, and practices are significant as these are linked to civism (not neutral) (May, 1999). Illuminating and defying *power relations* and how power is operationalized both structurally and culturally, and not simply as a matter of tolerance, is an integral part of understanding critical multicultural education (Sleeter & Delgado-Bernal, 2004). Finally the concept of *ideology* as a tool in critical multiculturalism for attaining critical reflexivity is important since it requires an examination of the dominant ideologies that are perpetuated in educational institutions and in society. Thus for critical multiculturalists, analyzing and problematizing underlying ideologies is an essential conceptual tool.

Critical multiculturalism can also contribute to multicultural education through its conceptual analyses of how social class power, global corporate power, and capitalism are interconnected. Bringing these analyses into multicultural education's central focus of social class identity is an important contribution from critical multiculturalism (Sleeter & Delgado-Bernal, 2004). Doing so will illuminate how differences (along lines of race, class, gender, sexual orientation, disability, etc.) and power are interconnected and impact students in schools.

The role of power in the classroom and how it is embodied in empowering the pedagogical process is another contribution critical multiculturalists have made to multicultural education. For critical pedagogues, knowledge is produced by acknowledging and fostering students' agency and credit. Critical multiculturalists view the teacher—student role as a partnership and not authoritarian in nature. While the exchange and production of knowledge is reciprocal, it is students' sociopolitical and historical experiences that serve as the foundation for grounding the relationship and forging a curriculum.

The fourth and final implication is how critical multiculturalists examine language and literacy. The role of critical literacy and language in examining students' experiences as narrated by them serves as another significant practice in multicultural education (Sleeter & Delgado-Bernal, 2004). Emphasizing and valuing students' lived experiences are at that core of creating democratic public spaces to engage in dialogue (Freire, 1998).

In short, critical multicultural education has advanced the field by advocating an activist orientation to teaching and learning and recognizing the post-modern orientations around identity and culture as dynamic (Grant & Sachs, 1995). Critical multicultural education also names explicitly the power structures that continue to create and support racism, sexism, and other types of inequities and privileges in our society.

Critical Multiculturalism and Social Justice

A clear connection to critical multicultural education are the links it has to social justice pedagogy since it seeks to combat sexism, classism, racism, ableism, homophobia, etc., and end all forms of oppression through activism. Although social justice is at the core of education in a democratic society when understood from a progressive lens, it is often overshadowed by mainstream efforts such as top-down school reform and high stakes accountability (to name two).

We embrace the three principles for social justice education defined by Ayers, Quinn, and Stovall (2009): (1) Equity, (2) Activism, and (3) Social literacy. *Equity* rests on "equal access to the most challenging and nourishing educational experiences, the demand that what the most privileged and enlightened are able to provide their children must be the standard for what is made available to all children" (Ayers, Quinn, & Stovall, 2009, p. xiv). That is, equity goes beyond equality by providing authentic possibilities of achieving rigorous educational outcomes. *Activism* is a democratic goal which promotes "full participation by preparing youngsters to see, understand and when necessary, to change all that is before them" (Ayers, Quinn, & Stovall, 2009, p. xiv). Activism entails providing students an opportunity to develop their citizenship skills through critique as well as the opportunity to actively change their schools and communities (see chapters 14 and 16 for examples). *Social literacy* is the "principle of relevance, resisting the fattening effects of materialism and consumerism and the power of the abiding evils of white supremacy, patriarchy, homophobia-nourishing awareness of our own identities and our connection with others, reminding us of the powerful commitment, persistence, bravery and triumphs of our justice-seeking forebears, reminding us as well of the links between ideas and the concentric circles of context—economic condition, historical flow, cultural surround—within which our lives are negotiated" (Ayers, Quinn, & Stovall, 2009, p. xiv). Social literacy in this sense refers to providing students with opportunities to critique and analyze how their role and existence in our global society are interconnected with others' lives.

Fortunately, we are heartened by those educational professionals for whom enacting critical multicultural education with social justice pedagogy is not new and thus present a path of possibility for those interested in pursuing such a pedagogy. As just one example of national efforts, the team at *Rethinking Schools* (see http://www.rethinkingschools.org/) has been successful in producing helpful curriculum materials and engaging scholarship while acknowledging the complexity, the difficulty of doing this type of work. An example of a local effort is the work of the Raza Studies Program at the Tucson Unified School District (Cammarota & Romero, 2009). This program provides a space for students to be actively involved in their own learning, to center that learning in their (and their families' and communities') own struggles against oppression, and to forge academic skills within a social activist framework. Note that both groups have faced intense opposition just to survive in the current conservative climate. Power concedes nothing!

Concepts and Connections: From Critical Multiculturalism to Social Justice

There is an urgent need for critical multicultural education and social justice pedagogy to define key terms and make explicit the links between praxis and activism. Otherwise these efforts will fall into the same cycle that multicultural education has been criticized for (e.g., superficial notions of power, diversity, culture, etc.). The following are specific lessons that we have learned from the past and should take into account as we move away from noncritical notions about multicultural education and move toward enacting multicultural education within a critical, social justice framework.

First, lack of definitions has created tensions around practice. Thus it is important to define multiple terms and to have critical and concise terminology when referring to multicultural education, power, activism, social literacy, equity, diversity, ethnicity, social justice, etc., in order to avoid the simplistic and superficial ways of enacting critical multicultural education and social justice. However, to honor the dynamic nature of language, which is constantly changing given the sociocultural contexts, we believe terms need to be defined when using them so there are no assumptions or misunderstandings about the meaning(s) being attributed to them.

Second, our nation requires citizens capable of critique and activism, both of which are democratic values. Students should be exposed to the various ways that language can be used to critique and to be active in a democracy. In addition, students need to be provided with opportunities for social action, both by challenging their own oppression but also in opposing the oppression of others. Making specific pedagogical links to the complexity of this work is essential if teachers are going to be able to engage in social activism. Praxis (critical thinking leading to informed social action) *is* an important part of learning.

Third, critical and deep understanding of multicultural education and social justice can't happen in single activities, nor in single classes. It needs to include students and adults, as well as the school-wide and the surrounding local community. Schools cannot operate in isolation from the communities they serve or from the context of the larger society otherwise they will continue to be superficial, separated from real life and lack equity, activism, and social literacy in deep thoughtful ways.

In teacher education, for example, broad critiques and approaches to teaching for social activism are offered in educational foundations classes, but are then left unaddressed in methods classes, exacerbating the conceptual/practical divide.

Fourth, there is a need to recognize that whatever we do in education in general, and more specifically in multicultural education, is guided by ideological underpinnings and includes political implications for how we think about questions of equity. For that reason, we acknowledge Sales and García's (1997) analysis of approaches to multicultural education that are couched, very explicitly, as "political perspectives" in an effort to make clear the political nature of our approaches to diversity.

Finally, there is nothing quite as practical as a good theory. Still, unless critical multicultural education, within a social justice framework, is able to articulate pedagogical implications of its work, it will fail and be implemented superficially (May, 1999). We agree with Nagda, Gurin, and Lopez (2003) about the dialectical relationship between theory and practice when considering diversity efforts:

> The integration of content and pedagogical process is a theoretical prescription for success. Yet, it is practically difficult. Many educators focus on one or the other rather than their joint process. Content without a transformative pedagogy may be rhetorical, intellectualizing, and divorced from reality. An active and engaging pedagogy without a critical knowledge base may result in temporary 'feel good' emotions. (p. 168)

One promising practice helpful in extending critical multicultural education and social justice in education is Nieto and Bode's (2008) most recent definition of social justice in education. They offer pedagogical implications and attempts to be clear about their language within a critical multicultural education framework. Nieto and Bode (2008) define social justice as "a philosophy, an approach, and actions that embody treating all people with fairness, respect, dignity, and generosity" (p. 11). Nieto and Bode (2008) emphasize that social justice in education goes beyond "*being nice*" to students or praising them.

Specifically, Nieto and Bode (2008) offer four principles of social justice education. "First, it challenges, confronts, and disrupts misconceptions, untruths, and stereotypes that lead to structural inequality and discrimination based on race, social class, gender, and other social and human differences" (p. 11). This principle emphasizes that teachers with a social justice standpoint deliberately include subject matter that can open the discussion to issues of inequality in the curriculum and encourage students to actively strive for equality and fairness both in and out of the school context. Nieto and Bode's (2008) second principle emphasizes "providing all students with the resources necessary to learn to their full potential. This includes *material resources* such as books, curriculum, financial support, and so on. Equally vital are *emotional resources* such as a belief in students' ability and worth; care for them as individuals and learners; high expectations and rigorous demands on them; and the necessary social and cultural capital to negotiate the world" (p. 12). They emphasize that responsibility rests not solely on teachers and schools, but rather it includes restructuring of school policies and practices in order to provide all students an equal chance to learn. Their third principle of a social justice perspective is "*drawing on* the talents and strengths that students bring to their education. This requires a rejection of the deficit perspective that has characterized much of the education of marginalized students, to a shift that views all students—not just those from privileged backgrounds—as having resources that can be a foundation for their learning. The resources include their languages, cultures, and experiences" (p. 12). Their fourth essential component of social justice is "creating a learning environment that promotes critical thinking and supports agency for social change" (p. 12). Creating such classroom environments can provide students with an opportunity to practice democracy, which is essential in preparing them as citizens for social change.

Nieto and Bode's principles for social justice in education are clearly articulated and offer guidance in terms of praxis. With this in mind we argue that critical multicultural education and social justice pedagogy are frameworks that merge in various ways. Nieto and Bode (2008) illuminate seven principles that define and embody the essence of multicultural education (described earlier). Two of the seven principles described by Nieto and Bode (2008) are social justice and critical pedagogy exemplifying how they correspond to each other. In fact, critical multicultural education is strongly linked to social justice as they both critique structural institutional inequalities, promote equity pedagogy, and aim for anti-discriminatory practices. Nieto and Bode (2008) actually extend these links explicitly by rejecting a deficit perspective towards marginalized students and explicitly stating that activism is essential for social change. These frameworks can work effectively together while keeping in mind the need for impacting institutional structures and promoting activism among students and their communities. Social justice according to Nieto and Bode (2008) cannot be effective if only practiced in the confines of the classroom. Furthermore, they explicitly state that it is to serve all students and involves all elements of schooling while linking to larger societal concerns. However, in the next section we have raised some questions and challenges about the disconnect between theory and practice.

Conclusion: Questions, Challenges, and Points of Praxis

We raise the following questions that we have been grappling with in anticipation that through a collective dialogue we can move closer to understanding the issues that fuel the disconnect between theory and practice. First, we wonder how to create transformational experiences so that teachers will seriously deconstruct their existing ideologies/theories and be open to and ready for new theories? Second, what would be the impact of other progressive theories (decolonizing, indigenous, feminist, critical race, etc.) on the advancement of multicultural education? That is, what other theoretical lenses would help extend the work of multicultural education from a critical, social justice perspective and how would that shape the field differently? Finally, we ask what is the role of researchers and research in ensuring that the foundations of critical multicultural education are furthered? Implied is the question of whether or not current educational research is assuring that critical elements are part and parcel in the dialogue around education from a multicultural perspective.

In sum, we want to come back to the most critical issues that we hope this chapter advances. Here are three points that we would like to highlight. First, it is essential that we move beyond superficial and liberal pluralist notions of multicultural education. These serve to perpetuate pedagogical practices and curriculum that advocate for color-blind frameworks, fashion, folklore, or food as culture and diversity as a commodity. Second, the primary issue of superficial approaches to multicultural education lies in practice, in integrating it in teacher preparation programs, as well as in the broader sociopolitical context. Third, teaching is an activist profession; it is not politically neutral.

We wish to be clear that we recognize the tremendous pressure teachers are facing currently which make pursuing multicultural education with a social justice framework all the more difficult and complicated. These pressures include the broader conservative agenda and the attack on public education and its teachers. It includes a narrow curriculum, scripted pedagogies, and standardized assessments to pressure teachers to toe the line. We also acknowledge that to fully understand the concepts and practices of multicultural, social justice-oriented teaching takes time and requires a strong network of mentors, coaches, and critical friends—all too often lacking in most schools. Still, teachers have a moral obligation to use all of their professional expertise and influence to work side by side with students (and their caregivers) to eliminate social inequalities and institutional oppression in pursuit of a more robust democracy.

In light of these pressing issues we also call to action students and parents to advocate for critical multicultural education approaches and policies in schools. We call to action teachers to be active agents of change in their schools so that this shift becomes part of the school culture. Doing so can push school administrators to implement professional development opportunities for teachers to learn how to "put it into practice." We also call to action teacher education programs to integrate critical multicultural education theory into all courses. Finally, we call to action scholars to further advance the field with research that illuminates successful teachers who engage in critical multicultural education pedagogical practices.

Points of Inquiry

* The term "multicultural education," the authors claim, has been co-opted and revised according to political climates: How did this happen and, as important, why did this occur?
* The authors refer to neoliberalism as a political and policy orientation that has impeded the implementation of MCE in policy and practice. What examples can you cite from the research literature, your experiences and observations that support this idea?

- E. D. Hirsch, Linda Chavez, and Diane Ravitch are authors who believe that the route to a unified, democratic United States is through a common core of knowledge or curriculum. How are the changes and critiques they present different from a critical MCE approach to knowledge, its value and production?
- What evidence can you find in the research literature that illustrates the efficacy of an MCE practice on high expectations for student achievement and academic rigor?
- How have other scholars, beyond those cited in this chapter, conceived of social justice and its relation to multicultural education? What would they suggest it must also include? What would they take exception with?

Points of Praxis

- How does your site, your philosophy, and/or your context define the purposes of education?
- What elements of critical MCE relate to your teaching philosophy? How do you implement these elements? What impedes implementation? What elements challenge your teaching philosophy?
- What is the relationship between your practices as an educator (as well as those of your colleagues) and state and federal policies? How do you relate these to the principles of critical multiculturalism?
- In your setting and/or experience, what does MCE look like? Which elements are critical? Which are liberal pluralist? Which are assimilationist?
- How would multicultural education from a critical perspective lead to increased student learning? How would it lead to increased academic achievement as measured by traditional (standardized) assessments? Why or why not? What are the implications of this for implementation of multicultural education?
- What about math, science, art, music, and any of the content areas: do some lend themselves more to critical MCE? Why is this? Is there such a thing, for example, as mathematics or biology taught from a critical multicultural perspective? Why or why not?

Notes

1 With the election of Barack Obama and a legislature controlled by Democrats, it is likely that this act will be renamed. It remains to be seen what substantive policy changes may or may not take place to the NCLB policies at the same time.
2 At the time of writing, proponents of this proposition are gearing up to place it on the ballot once again for the next election cycle in Arizona.
3 Liberal pluralism, as summarized by Daniels (2008) is concerned with celebrating diversity within current social and political structures, with the belief that understanding differences allows others to appreciate diversity more fully. While acknowledging inequality, it refuses to examine the structural causes (such as capitalism, racism, and

patriarchy) of that inequality that might eventually lead to transformation of unequal power relations. Liberal pluralism posits that minority groups should not have special protections under the law and that questions of why some groups are marginalized and some groups are privileged should not be asked. Analysis of poverty, for example, would not critically examine existing economic structures nor would it address exploitation and marginalization based on socio-economic class.

References

Ayers, W., Quinn, T., & Stovall, D. (Eds). (2009). *Handbook of social justice in education.* New York: Routledge.

Banks, J. A. (1975). *Teaching strategies for ethnic studies.* Boston: Allyn & Bacon.

Banks, J. A. (2003). Approaches to multicultural curriculum reform. In J. A. Banks and C. A. McGee Banks (Eds.), *Multicultural education: Issues and perspectives* (pp. 225–246). New York: Wiley.

Banks, J. A. (2004). Multicultural education: Historical development, dimensions, and practice. In J. A. Banks and C. A. McGee Banks (Eds.), *Handbook of research on multicultural education* (2nd ed.), (pp. 2–29). San Francisco: Jossey-Bass.

Banks, J. A. (2009). *Teaching strategies for ethnic studies* (8th ed.). Boston: Pearson/Allyn & Bacon.

Berlak, A., & Moyenda, S. (2001). *Taking it personally.* Philadelphia: Temple University Press.

Bohn, A., & Sleeter, C. (2000). Multicultural education and the standards movement. *Phi Delta Kappan, 82*(2), 156–159.

Bennett, C. (2001). Genres of research in multicultural education. *Review of Educational Research, 71*(2), 171–218.

Brazzel, M. (2007). Deep diversity, social justice, and organization development. Paper presented at the OD Network Conference, October, Baltimore, MD.

Cammarota, J., & Romero, A. (2009). The social justice education project: A critically compassionate intellectualism for Chicana/o students. In W. Ayers, T. Quinn, & D. Stovall (Eds.), *Handbook of social justice in education,* (pp. 465–476). New York: Routledge.

Chapman, T., & Hobbel, N. (2005). Multicultural education and its typologies. In S. Farenga, and D. Ness (Eds.), *Encyclopedia of education and human development,* Vol. 1. (pp. 296–301). New York: M. E. Sharpe.

Daniels, C. L. (2008). From liberal pluralism to critical multiculturalism: The need for a paradigm shift in multicultural education for social work practice in the United States. *Journal of Progressive Human Services, 19*(1), 19–38.

Freire, P. (1973). *Education for critical consciousness.* New York: Seabury Press.

Freire, P. (1998). *Pedagogy of freedom.* Boulder, CO: Rowman & Littlefield.

Friedberg, J. (2004). *Granitos de Arena* [Motion Picture, Documentary; Jill Friedberg, Director]. United States: Corrugated Films.

Gay, G. (1992). The state of multicultural education in the United States. In K. Adam Moodley (Ed.), *Education in plural societies: International perspectives* (pp. 47–66). Calgary, Alberta, Canada: Detselig Enterprises.

Gay, G. (1995). Mirror images on common issues: Parallels between multicultural education and critical pedagogy. In C. E. Sleeter and P. McLaren (Eds.), *Multicultural education, critical pedagogy and the politics of difference* (pp. 155–198). Albany, NY: SUNY Press.

Grant, C., & Sachs, J. M. (1995). Multicultural education and postmodernism: Movement toward a dialogue. In P. McLaren and B. Kanpol (Eds.), *Critical multiculturalism: Uncommon voices in a common struggle* (pp. 89–105). Westport, CT: Bergin & Garvey.

Kanpol, B., & McLaren, P. (Eds.). (1995). *Critical multiculturalism: Uncommon voices in a common struggle.* Westport, CT: Bergin & Garvey.

Ladson-Billings, G. (2004). New directions in multicultural education. In J. A. Banks and C. A. McGee Banks (Eds.), *Handbook of research on multicultural education* (2nd ed.), (pp. 50–65). San Francisco: Jossey-Bass.

Ladson-Billings, G. (2009). Just what is critical race theory and what's it doing in a nice field like education? In E. Taylor, D. Gillborn, & G. Ladson-Billings (Eds.), *Foundations of critical race theory in education* (pp. 17–36). New York: Routledge.

McCarthy, C. (1988). Rethinking liberal and radical perspectives on racial inequality in schooling: Making the case for nonsynchrony. *Harvard Educational Review, 58*(3), 265–279.

McCarthy, C. (1995). Multicultural policy discourses on racial inequality in American education. In R. Ng, P. Staton, & J. Scane (Eds.), *Anti-racism, feminism, and critical approaches to education* (pp. 21–44). Westport, CT: Bergin & Garvey.

McDonald, M., & Zeichner, K. M. (2009). Social justice teacher education. In W. Ayers, T. Quinn, & D. Stovall (Eds.), *Handbook of social justice in education* (pp. 595–610). New York: Routledge.

May, S. (Ed.). (1999). *Critical multiculturalism: Rethinking multicultural and antiracist education.* New York: RoutledgeFalmer.

Nagda, B. A., Gurin, P., & Lopez, G. E. (2003). Transformative pedagogy for democracy and social justice. *Race, Ethnicity and Education, 6*(2), 165–191.

Nieto, S. (1992). *Affirming diversity: The sociopolitical context of multicultural education.* White Plains, NY: Longman.

Nieto, S. (1994). Affirmation, solidarity and critique: Moving beyond tolerance in education. *Multicultural Education Magazine, 1*(4), 9–12, 35–38.

Nieto, S. (2004). *Affirming diversity: The sociopolitical context of multicultural education* (4th ed.). Boston: Allyn & Bacon.

Nieto, S., & Bode, P. (2008). *Affirming diversity: The sociopolitical context of multicultural education* (5th ed.). Boston: Allyn & Bacon.

O'Donnell, J., Pruyn, M., & Chávez Chávez, R. (2004). *Social justice in these times.* Greenwich, CT: Information Age Publishing.

Sales, A., & García, R. (1997). *Programas de educación intercultural.* Bilbao: Desclée de Brouwer.

Sleeter, C. (2001). Preparing teachers for culturally diverse schools. *Journal of Teacher Education, 52*(2), 94–106.

Sleeter, C. E. (2000–2001). Diversity vs. white privilege. [Electronic version]. *Rethinking schools, 15.* http://www.rethinkingschools.org/archive/15_02/Int152.shtml

Sleeter, C., & Delgado-Bernal, D. (2004). Critical pedagogy, critical race theory, and antiracist education: Implications for multicultural education. In J. A. Banks and C. A. McGee Banks (Eds.), *Handbook of research on multicultural education* (2nd ed.), (pp. 240–258). San Francisco: Jossey-Bass.

Sleeter, C., & Grant, C. (1988). *Making choices for multicultural education: Five approaches to race, class and gender.* Columbus, OH: Merrill Publishing.

Sleeter, C., & Grant, C. (2009). *Making choices for multicultural education: Five approaches to race, class and gender* (6th ed.). Hoboken, NJ: Wiley.

Tellez, K. (2002). Multicultural education as subtext. *Multicultural Perspectives, 4*(2), 21–26.

Yosso, T. (2002). Toward a critical race curriculum. *Equity and Excellence in Education, 35*(2), 93–10.

Chapter 8

After Poststructuralism

Rethinking the Discourse of Social Justice Pedagogy

Robert J. Parkes, Jennifer M. Gore, and
Wendy Elsworth

It is common for poststructural analyses of curriculum and pedagogy to question per-
ceived pedagogical truths as part of a strategy of challenging injustices produced
through the institutions, practices, and knowledge structures of education. However,
poststructuralism itself has often been subject to the criticism that it is incapable of
offering anything other than critique, that it fails to provide pedagogical and curricular
alternatives or direction for educational reform.

In this chapter we explore the implications and inherent contradictions of poststruc-
tural analyses for pedagogy in general, and for social justice pedagogy more specifically.
Throughout this discussion, we elaborate the efficacy of poststructural analyses in and
for social justice education, arguing that poststructural theory can inform a productive
rethinking of social justice pedagogy. In its concern with local manifestations of
inequality and injustice, we argue that poststructuralism offers new spaces of freedom
for the enactment of a social justice agenda in education.

This chapter sets out to clarify an important role for poststructural theory in
addressing, practicing, and achieving the goals of social justice pedagogy. Such clarity will emerge however only after considerable problematizing of the key terms in
our opening sentence: poststructural theory, social justice, pedagogy, and "the
goals of social justice pedagogy." We acknowledge that other chapters in this volume are informed to varying degrees by poststructuralism and thus draw back from
a specific focus on any single area of social justice concern. Instead, we focus
on 'social justice' at a more conceptual level, exploring what specific insights
poststructural theory might provide in understanding and enacting social justice
pedagogy.

Theorizing Poststructuralism

Arguably emerging in the second half of the twentieth century as a French form of
methodological postmodernism (Breisach, 2003), and a reaction against both phe-
nomenology and structuralism (Dreyfus & Rabinow, 1982), poststructuralism is
neither a systematic theory, nor a unified discourse. It is perhaps best understood as
a continuum of critique that shares similar skepticism towards claims to truth in the
human and social sciences. The late 1980s and early 1990s marked a particular

moment of significance in the emergence of poststructural theory in educational discourse, with important critiques of curriculum (Cherryholmes, 1988; Daignault, 1992) and pedagogy (Davies, 1993; Gore, 1993; Lather, 1992; Whitson, 1995) alike. Drawing on the work of French social theorists such as Michel Foucault, Jacques Derrida, Jacques Lacan, and Gilles Deleuze to the greater extent, and Jean Francois Lyotard and Jean Baudrillard to a lesser extent, contemporary poststructuralist theorists share a number of relatively consistent orientations. These orientations have been most carefully articulated in the work of Foucault— although not named as such—and thus many of our explanations will draw on his particular formations of these concepts. In drawing on Foucault in this way, we inevitably commit a form of symbolic violence (Spivak, 1988), reducing poststructuralist theory to a single trope. We are aware of the growing development of Deleuzian scholarship in the field of education (Semetsky, 2006, 2008), and philosophical work exploring the educational implications of Derrida (Peters & Biesta, 2008; Trifonas & Peters, 2004), Lyotard (Dhillon, 2001), and others (Peters, 1998; Peters & Burbules, 2004). However, there is neither the scope, nor the necessity, to attempt a synoptic reading of the field of poststructural theorizing in this chapter, and the take up of Foucault's work in education makes him the poststructural theorist of choice for many scholars publishing in the field of curriculum and pedagogy (see the prominent place of Foucauldian scholarship in edited collections by Baker & Heyning, 2004b; Ball, 1990; Brennan & Popkewitz, 1997; Peters & Besley, 2006, 2007; Popkewitz, 1999).

There is also another important reason why Foucauldian poststructuralism might speak to social justice pedagogy. Dominick LaCapra (2000) has argued that Foucault wanted "to write the history or trace the archaeology of what they [the medical, penal, psychiatric, or pedagogical establishment] silenced, repressed, or excluded in constituting themselves and the institutions that house them" (p. 130). That is, Foucault's (1965/1988) work on the history of madness, and his work that followed on the clinical and medical perception (1975), punishment and the prison (1977), and sexuality (1980a), can all be seen as histories that call for social justice by challenging any notion that things in the present are inevitable or natural. Foucault's work, as LaCapra (2000) notes, "was forceful in bringing into prominence the ways in which marginalization, subjection, and abjection could take place even in the seemingly most liberal or enlightened policies and practices" (p. 16). For the purpose of understanding poststructuralism as social justice pedagogy then, Foucauldian theorizing is well placed in terms of its impact on the field of pedagogical inquiry; its predisposition towards counter-histories that expose how discourse functions to name, coerce, constitute, include, and exclude; and the clarity of its theoretical apparatus. We begin then by outlining three common orientations underpinning Foucauldian-influenced poststructuralist theorizing.

The Critique of Universalism

One orientation that is shared by poststructuralist theorists is a rejection of 'totalizing discourses' that attempt to explain diverse phenomena by appeal to a single concept or grand explanatory narrative. Poststructuralists remain suspicious of concepts such as 'progress' and 'the scientific quest for truth' that are used to explain historical changes across human social systems, in terms that suggest a movement towards emancipation and a utopian future (Kvale, 1992). In contrast, poststructural accounts of historical change are characterized by a respect of that which might be described as specific, local, different, and peculiar, and a rejection of theories that propose a general, global, uniform, or norm as if it were a universal, natural, or foundational fact of human existence. Where explanations are provided they are at best given tentatively, cautiously, and reluctantly, as descriptions from the author's own praxis or position, or as a set of self-proclaimed fictions (Foucault, 1980b), rather than as absolutes. The poststructural critique of 'master narratives' thus challenges educators to approach knowledge as problematic. The curriculum, far from being a set of truth-statements, is read from a poststructuralist perspective as a discourse that constitutes and constructs, incites and induces, rather than simply documents and describes, reality.

Discourse has become, as Sara Mills (1997) has argued, "common currency" as a concept in a variety of disciplines, so much so that it is "frequently left undefined" (p. 1). However, as an important concept in poststructural theorizing, the meaning of 'discourse' requires some attention in this chapter. While 'discourse' remains somewhat fluid as a concept, it does draw on everyday meanings such as "holding forth on a subject" (Mills, 1997, p. 2), as well as being inflected by more technical or theoretical meanings arising within particular disciplinary formations. Just as there are multiple conceptions and definitions of 'discourse' circulating in contemporary theory (Mills, 1997), there have been a wide variety of ways in which 'discourse analysis' is taken up as a practice in educational theory specifically (MacLure, 2003; Poynton & Lee, 2000), and this often serves to confuse things further. It would seem that almost the full range of possible conceptions of 'discourse' have been mobilized within the field of curriculum and pedagogical studies. Any historically oriented study of the concept of 'discourse' reveals a complex genealogy, emerging from the interaction of ideas across the domains of structuralism, poststructuralism, linguistics, post-Freudian psychoanalysis, neo-Marxism, and the field of cultural studies (Sawyer, 2002). It is important to note that although a great deal of contemporary research credits Foucault with the origination of the widespread adoption of the term 'discourse', there has been a rather convincing argument put forward by Sawyer (2002) that it is not the strict Foucauldian definition that is mobilized in contemporary scholarship, but a hybrid. Sawyer (2002) claims that the more probabilistic origin of the 'broad usage' of the term, particularly if we look at how it is being used, is with two other French theorists, the Marxist Michel Pêcheux and psychoanalyst Jacques Lacan, and many of the theorists who worked in the emerging field of British cultural studies during the 1960s and 1970s. Foucault (1969/1972) has added to the confusion himself, stating in *The Archaeology of Knowledge* that, despite his own formal definition, he has used 'discourse' in a range of ways: "treating it sometimes as the general domain of all statements, sometimes as an individualizable group of statements, and sometimes as a regulated practice that accounts for a number of statements" (p. 80). Certainly we should recognize that "a great deal of what he [Foucault] wrote can be seen as a response to Marxism" (Olssen, 2006) and that this may account for the way in which the various meanings of 'discourse' bleed into each other. However, it is perhaps enough for our purposes to announce that Foucault's most important contribution to this discussion was to define discourse as a series of statements that form the objects of which they speak (Sawyer, 2002). Reynolds (2003) has argued that, for Foucault, discourse consisted "of words spoken or written that group themselves according to certain rules . . . that make their existence possible" (p. 76). The "rules" that form the "conditions of existence" of a discourse are not conceptualized by Foucault (1968/1996) as the constraints and affordances of a linguistic grammar: they are instead rules of formation for objects, operations, concepts, and theoretical options; or the conditions that broker the limits and forms of expressibility, conservation, memory, reactivation, and appropriation. These rules determine not only what can and cannot be said, but also what may be considered true or false, within a given discipline, community, or institution, at a specific historical moment; or as Foucault (1980a) expresses it, "discourse can be both an instrument and an effect of power" (p. 101).

Importantly, Foucault's concern with discourse centres on what he describes as "the archive", the sum total of authoritative statements that have actually been made in a given field, discipline, or institution, although he is careful to suggest that these need not be obligatory domains for analysis (Foucault, 1969/1972, p. 195). 'Discourse analysis' in a Foucauldian sense is, however, most often the study of the disciplinary archive, or what Popkewitz, Franklin, and Pereyra (2001), call "knowledge systems." These knowledge systems are constituted by "*serious* speech acts: what experts say when they are speaking as experts" (Dreyfus & Rabinow, 1982, pp. xx, emphasis in the original); or what is articulated and accepted within a given discipline, community, or society. If 'discourse' operates as a synonym for sets of 'authoritative statements', then it is important to note that these authoritative statements stand in 'intertextual relationship' with one another. Texts thus instantiate and are constituted by and as 'discourse,' or sets of 'authoritative statements.' These 'authoritative statements' or 'master narratives' not only inscribe particular relations of power, but are so seductive that it is often impossible, difficult, or dangerous to think otherwise (for a well-articulated discussion of how this plays out in teaching, see McWilliam, 1999). Understood in this way, we might suggest that 'discourse' functions as a kind of 'scaffolding' within which particular forms of reasoning are constructed (Popkewitz, 2001). Such 'authoritative statements' discursively construct the boundaries of what can be considered 'intelligible.'

Practically, Foucault's discourse analytics attempts to "define the play" between intradiscursive, interdiscursive, and extradiscursive dependencies (Foucault, 1991, p. 58); "between the objects, operations and concepts of a single formation" (p. 58), "between different discursive formations" or disciplines (p. 58); and "between discursive transformations and transformations outside of discourse . . . and a whole play of economic, political and social changes" (p. 58), respectively. Knowledge from a poststructuralist perspective is thus no longer the neutral content of pedagogy, or a statement of universal truth, but must be considered a site of conflict, contestation, and negotiation, in which power relations construct "regimes of truth" (Foucault, 1969/1972). As one of us has noted elsewhere, these discursive regimes have both political and ethical aspects (Gore, 1993). Discourse, from a poststructuralist perspective, acts at the political level as a legitimating force that defines the limits of what can be considered 'truthful' and worthy of consideration. At the ethical level, discourse acts as a disciplinary force, providing the means by which individuals become subjects through legitimated practices of self-styling. Because of the political and ethical operations of discourse, the idea of a universal meaning or truth is jettisoned in poststructural theory, and recast through the idea that what we consider to be true is always an artifact of the functioning of discourse. According to Grosz (1995), Foucault's description of contemporary power suggests that the subject is constructed in specific ways by a range of competing discourses that enact "epistemic and coercive relations" (p. 35). There is, to put a Foucauldian spin on Derrida, no outside of discourse. We are always operating within one or more discursively constructed knowledge systems, whether we acknowledge it, know it, or not. From within a Foucauldian poststructuralist position, we are inscribed within particular discourses, and those discourses shape our subjectivities.

The Critique of Foundationalism

Closely related to the rejection of universalism is the critique of foundationalism. This second orientation held by the majority of poststructuralist theorists has been defined by Roland Barthes (1968/1977) as "the death of the author." A much more complex problematic that overlaps and intersects with the other orientations addressed in this chapter, "the death of the author" symbolizes a range of border crossings, in which a series of modernist dualities are collapsed as their definitional restraints are relaxed, released, or reconstructed, and their dividing lines transgressed. One reading of the death of the author is derived from Derrida's (1976) argument that our dependency on the conventions of language makes it necessary for one text to always refer to other texts in order to make sense—resulting in a series of interdependent or intertextual relationships between both authors and texts. Another reading concludes that the author is no longer the sole giver of meaning to a text, and therefore not its sole author, since readers, as they engage with a text, re-author it for themselves. There are certainly voices in the academy that argue texts both constrain and enable certain kinds of readings. However, there is little to stop a cultural critic using Lacanian psychoanalytic, Foucauldian poststructuralist, or Hallidayean grammatical analyses and arriving at what is to them meaningful, deeply meaningful, or meaningless interpretations of a single text. The point is that the meaning readers gain from a text involves a process of 're-authoring' the text for themselves, as a consequence of their own past experiences, expectations, reading positions.

A third reading of "the death of the author" relates to the complex way in which authorship or the origin of ideas gets attributed to particular individuals, and is perhaps Foucault's unique contribution to our understanding of this motif. Consider the following example. Had an unpublished university student, or an out-of-work plumber, written *The Satanic Verses* rather than Salman Rushdie (the famous author), it is uncertain whether the Ayatollah Khomeini would have felt the need to declare a fatwa. Further, if this hypothetical student or plumber had stolen Rushdie's idea and beaten him into print with *The Satanic Verses*, forcing Rushdie to declare his own fatwa, it is questionable whether such a declaration would have had the same authority as that of an ayatollah's. When looking at the question of the author, these concerns are not as trivial or unproblematic as they might first appear. Indeed, they highlight the way in which authors, far from being simple "empirical realities" (Close, 1990), are in fact textual productions, the constructions of particular discursive regimes, whose power and authority resides in their strategic locations in discourse. Foucault (1969/1977) argues that authorship "is not defined by the spontaneous attribution of a text to its creator, but through a series of precise and complex procedures" (p. 130). The procedures Foucault discusses relate once again to the workings of discourse in which the 'authority' of an author is constructed discursively, through a set of rhetorical devices, textual strategies, and strategic manoeuvres. From a poststructural perspective, there is no authoritative meaning that can be anchored in a text outside of the discursive establishment of an author's ethos, or authority to speak. Likewise, there is no truth or meaning that can be derived from a text that does not involve some interpretation (or re-authoring) on the part of the reader; and no meaning in a text that does not in part derive its construction from reference to other texts. Thus, poststructural theorists find no ground upon which to privilege one interpretation as a singular truth, with a single point of origin, leaving them without an absolute foundation or platform from which to cast their own authoritative statements. This should not be understood as a descent into relativism however for, as Falzon (1998) has argued, it is impossible for us not to pass judgment on the statements we encounter, and we must understand our judgment to arise out of the discourses in which we are located. Thus, we find ourselves engaging as poststructuralists in a kind of reflexivity that resists any self-righteous claims to innocence (Gore, 1993).

The Critique of Essentialism

A third orientation shared by poststructural theorists involves a rejection of the idea of a universal human subject that is divorced from history, culture, and society, most famously announced by Foucault (1970/1994) at the conclusion to *The Order of Things: An Archaeology of the Human Sciences*. While most poststructuralist theorists appear to be in agreement over the problem and definition of totalizing discourses, there appears to be much wider variation in the meaning they ascribe to the notion of "the death of the subject." Although Heller (1992) has identified more than 20 different uses of the term in contemporary continental philosophy, it is not possible to review them all here. Rather, the most significant reading for an understanding of the poststructuralist position derives from poststructuralist feminist theorizing, where it is argued that the death of the subject means the birth of subjects (Luke & Gore, 1992). Such a reading recognizes 'the [masculine] subject' as the main participant in the grand narratives of the modernist paradigm. By rejecting the privileged status of the singular, white, masculine subject, this poststructuralist feminist reading simultaneously mounts an attack on the grand narratives of Anglo-European patriarchal cultures. What is being rejected is the transcendental self, the disembodied rational hero-norm of the Enlightenment, who masquerades as ahistorical, asexual, acultural, and classless, while simultaneously masking a (socially constructed) white masculine middle-class subjectivity.

In place of the metaphysical or transcendental subject, poststructuralists propose decentered, fragmented, material subjects, producers and products of the discursive practices of their unique historical circumstances. Not only are these subjects argued to lack an underlying ahistorical unity, they are also considered to be split or fragmented within themselves (Mansfield, 2000), as a consequence of their participation in contradictory discursive practices. For poststructuralism, the self is fluid, understood only across categories. For the pedagogue, this fluid subject violates particularly the developmental narratives (or stage theories) so often applied in educational psychology (Morss, 1990, 1996). There can no longer be certainty about what is appropriate pedagogy for an 8 year old when the child becomes redefined as a unique intersection of discourses and disciplinary practices related to their gendered, classed, and ethnic inscriptions (MacNaughton, 1995). Thus, both what Freire (1970) has called transmissionist "banking" pedagogies that presuppose "docile" human subjects who are constructed as receptacles for the grand narratives of the official curriculum, and psychological approaches that locate the subject in grand biological narratives, fail to address the complexities and contradictions of the human subject. Standpoint theories that define subjects by their class, race, ethnicity, or gender, are also approached cautiously by poststructuralist theorists, as they frequently derive from a form of essentialism that defines the subject in too rigid categories. In the same way that discourse legitimates particular truth claims, or constructs one's authority to speak, discourse operates as a means by which individuals may be interpellated (Althusser, 1971); literally 'hailed' or 'called upon' to behave or be understood in particular ways by the categories they are inscribed within. Thus, just as discourse constructs the objects of which it speaks, so too does discourse construct the subject of which it speaks. What is being rejected by poststructuralism is not the use of these categories altogether—though one would always remain suspicious of their limitations—but a universal unchanging self. It is with this in mind that Foucault (1982/1994) notes: "We have to promote new forms of subjectivity through the refusal of this kind of individuality which has been imposed on us for centuries" (p. 216).

Rethinking Social Justice Pedagogy after Poststructuralism

The three orientations described above inform a range of approaches to engaging in poststructuralist critique. Baker and Heyning (2004a) identify three particular approaches to using Foucault's ideas in Anglophone educational scholarship, including: (1) Historicization and philosophizing projects aimed at revitalizing the object of inquiry; (2) Denaturalization projects aimed at opening up diversity through the use of counter-history; and (3) Critical reconstruction projects aimed at providing new solutions to old problems. Such projects are underpinned by the critiques of universalism, foundationalism, and essentialism described above. Drawing on Foucault's archeological, genealogical, and problematization approaches, designed to unearth the rules of discourse, its historical transformations, and challenge its naturalized constructions respectively, these approaches form the methodological means by which discourses, such as those mobilized in the name of social justice and pedagogy, may be interrogated.

Before discussing social justice pedagogy, it is worth considering what poststructuralism offers in terms of understanding social justice (and) pedagogy specifically. From a poststructural perspective, the concept of social justice must be problematized, rather than accepted uncritically as a universal truth or desire. Poststructural theory requires us to engage with 'social justice' as a thoroughly historical concept. As a consequence of its skepticism towards universalism and totalizing discourses, poststructural theory prompts us to question and even reject any discourse that positions social justice as a universal good without explicit identification of the specific, local, different, and particular ways in which social justice is both conceptualized and enacted. What discourses are invoked in the name of social justice? What kinds of dominations occur? Who has defined 'justice?' How far does activism in the name of social justice take us? What is gained through social justice agendas? What is lost? These are some of the questions that poststructuralism prompts us to ask. The poststructural critique of foundationalism reminds us to question on what grounds, and with what assumptions, do we claim the high ground by advocating our specific conceptions of social justice pedagogy (see Gore's 1993 critique of feminist and critical pedagogies as "regimes of truth"). Poststructuralism's concern with essentialist discourses make us skeptical of any account that promises universal liberation for a specific social, ethnic, racial, linguistic, or gendered group, without recognizing the injustices done to particular parties as a result of categorizing and naming them in particular ways. Foucault's well-documented resistance to the construction of 'gay' identity, on the basis that homosexuality was a historical construct, and black feminist critiques that identify the symbolic violence performed on African American women by well-meaning white feminists who inadvertently assumed the universal character of female suffering, are both examples of the kind of insight poststructural critique can provide.

We take this illustration of poststructuralism's contribution to understanding social justice pedagogy further by engaging with Nieto and Bode's (2008) conceptualization of social justice. First, Nieto and Bode suggest that social justice challenges, confronts, and disrupts misconceptions, untruths, and stereotypes that lead to structural inequality and discrimination based on race, social class, gender, and other social and human differences. Certainly there is little in this definition that is not consistent with a poststructuralist stance. However, the question arises: Why, despite understanding the dangers of stereotyping, do structural or systematic inequalities for particular groups in education continue? For example, racist assumptions have meant that students of color in American schools, and Indigenous students in Australian schools, have often been treated as inferior and have been subjected to lower expectations than white students. Identifying students by a social category can often result in one group of students being favored by a teacher (as better behaved, or more capable, intellectual, or talented), while another group may be treated as less well behaved and less capable. Ruge (1999) has documented how expectations of students as high or low achievers results in the differential treatment of students, such that low achievers receive little feedback, little praise, are called on less often, are seated further away from the teacher, are provided less wait time when asked questions, and are interrupted and criticized more often by the teacher. There is also evidence that when a teacher is placed in a school whose community has been identified as having low socio-economic status, they more often will make modifications to the curriculum that "dumb it down" or "slow it down" (Ruge, 1999). In each of these cases, students are receiving more impoverished forms of curriculum and pedagogy based on the ways in which students are inscribed within the discourses that circulate among the teachers in a community or school, or society at large. While a social justice pedagogy would aim to take action that ameliorated the disadvantage experienced by these students, the discourses that circulate everyday among teachers and the community may construct difference as deficit without any intention to do so.

Such discourses are also perpetuated in preservice teacher education, despite the efforts of teacher educators. That is, most teacher educators will have had the experience—particularly where the course adopts a smorgasbord approach to instruction by focusing on social class one week, gender the next, and ethnicity the week after—of students graduating from a sociology of education course who believe that the lack of academic achievement among students of color in American schools or Indigenous students in Australian schools is the result of some inherent capability on the part of the white students, and an inherent inferiority on the part of Indigenous students or students of color. This is not the intended message of the sociology professor when discussing the social categories within which students are inscribed. The professor wants to point out that students' social class, race, gender, sexuality, religion, culture, etc., all impact on their readiness to adapt to, and succeed within, the white patriarchal middle-class institution of schooling. The professor wants his or her students to leave the course with the understanding that because the white middle class invented schooling, it privileges its own forms of knowledge and thus children from white middle-class homes seem 'smarter' and 'more capable' when they enter school. However, it is easy to move from a use of social categories like class, race, ethnicity, and gender, to a situation where our understanding of each of these categories means that we understand difference as deficit rather than a factor in structural disadvantage, particularly where we are ourselves white middle-class educators. White privilege remains invisible unless we do hard reflexive work to make it otherwise. All too often, a student who has rejected the social justice message will either ignore difference in their classroom, treating all students as if they were already members of the white middle classes, irrespective of their cultural and linguistic backgrounds; or if they have misunderstood the message, will read difference as deficit and alter their expectations so that less is expected of particular groups of students. Instead of seeing the disadvantage students experience as: (1) a socio-politico-historical artifact of their inscription within discourses of race, class, ethnicity, and gender; or (2) the location of a student in an institution whose discourses privilege a different social class or ethnic group and attribute the differential success of some students to inherent characteristics related to the students' class, race, ethnicity, gender, sexuality, linguistic heritage, etc.

From a poststructuralist perspective, it becomes clear that the solution to educational inequality is not as easy as saying that we should hold the same expectations of all students, at least not without some caveats. Simply holding the same expectations of all students may overlook what Sennett and Cobb (1972) call the "hidden injuries" of class, and others have now identified as the 'hidden injuries' of race, ethnicity, and gender which students bring into the classroom. These 'hidden injuries' are the lived experience of structural disadvantage that surfaces when a student from the margins encounters a school system which privileges their counterparts from the dominant group that has set the protocols and norms for behavior, desire, and communication. The work of Bourdieu and Passeron (1977) in the late 1970s documented how students from the working class brought into their middle-class schools a way of being, behaving, and communicating (habitus) that was interpreted by their middle-class teachers as inferior to the way of being, behaving, and communicating of their middle-class peers. Without even realizing it was happening, educators made judgments about students based on these outward signs of their social class, and entertained a deficit discourse that assumed the working-class students were less capable. The consequence was structural disadvantage that resulted in inequitable outcomes from schooling. Bourdieu and Passeron's (1977) verdict was that the French school system was a class-based filtering system, and not the 'great leveller' that it had pretended to be. Failure to acknowledge that white middle-class children are privileged by the institution of western schooling, and therefore will 'appear' to be 'naturally' more capable, fails to acknowledge the ways in which complex and diverse histories, cultures, and societies have shaped our students' lives. Clearly we do need to recognize that without pedagogical intervention, some of our students will do better than others because of the privilege they carry or the hidden injuries with which they live.

If we turn again to Nieto and Bode (2008), we note that they raise three further points in defining social justice. First, they suggest that a social justice perspective means providing all students with the resources necessary to learn to their full potential. While few poststructuralists would dispute Nieto and Bode's emphasis on providing students with available material and emotional resources to support them as they learn to negotiate the world, a poststructuralist analysis would interrogate the very notion of 'full potential,' or indeed any 'potential' that can be measured, assumed, or implied. The notion of 'full potential' is itself conceived within a totalizing discourse which serves to construct perceptions of students' capacity to learn, rather than to question whether or not we are capable of even imagining the limits or limitlessness of student learning. Second, Nieto and Bode (2008) suggest that social justice pedagogy should draw on the talents and strengths that students bring to their education by rejecting deficit perspectives that have characterized much of the education of marginalized students. Such framing views all students—not just those from privileged backgrounds—as having resources that can be a foundation for their learning. A danger of this claim, however, is that it resembles a kind of totalizing discourse that suggests that the different resources students bring to their learning serve as equally beneficial starting points for learning. However, schooling and school systems have traditionally valued some 'talents and strengths' over others, and the responsibility rests with those teaching for social justice to draw upon students' 'talents and strengths' and support them in developing the resources they need to enable them to succeed in schooling, however that is defined. The popularity of approaches to pedagogy that, in the name of 'multiple intelligences,' rely on students' quasi-diagnosed preferred form of 'intelligence' and then adapt teaching and learning activities to the specific intelligences in any given classroom is also borne of a discourse of 'talents and strengths.' Blind adherence to such pedagogy is unlikely to lead to successful learning for students, as long as that success is partly or wholly defined by assessment of outcomes at any level beyond the individual student. Institutional logistics and educational and political agendas generally dictate assessment regimes in which students are not assessed according to the same ostensibly preferred intelligence by which their learning was constructed. Nor are students likely to opt for education and workplace pathways beyond schooling that allow them to exclusively engage with society in what was once diagnosed as their preferred learning style. At the social group level, these dangers intensify. When groups of students who have been traditionally disadvantaged by schooling and school systems are taught by one means and assessed in school and life by another, the result is that typical trends of advantage and disadvantage are reinforced, potentially exponentially.

Nieto and Bode (2008) also propose that in order to achieve social justice the pedagogue must create a learning environment that promotes critical thinking and supports agency for social change. This principle for social justice pedagogy is less open to the charge that it in some way universalizes or essentializes the nature and potential of students, and although the concept of 'agency' derives from a structuralist discourse that presupposes an uneven distribution of power, it does open possibilities for a poststructuralist account of social justice pedagogy that avoids foundationalism, universalism, and essentialism. The critical pedagogy movement, linked to the work of Giroux, McLaren, and others, has worked around the concept of 'agency' and 'critical engagement' with the social world. However, 'critical pedagogy,' as a significant tradition in the promotion of social justice pedagogy, has been subject to substantial poststructuralist critique. Indeed, critical pedagogies, derived from Frankfurt School critical theories, but supplemented by elements of French social theory, were among the first manifestations of Foucault's influence in education. These particular forms of critical pedagogy, underpinned by an emancipatory project and structuralist views of power, sustained considerable criticism from a number of feminist poststructuralist researchers, working within explicitly Foucauldian frameworks, during the early 1990s, leaving the possibility of critical pedagogy in question (Ellsworth, 1989; Gore, 1993; Lather, 1992). Critical pedagogy has been accused of using rhetoric that "give[s] the illusion of equality while leaving the authoritarian nature of the teacher/student relationship intact" (Ellsworth, 1989, p. 306); of overstating the power of 'rationality' to free the subject from constraining metanarratives (Lather, 1992; Yates, 1992); of narrowly identifying power with forces of exploitation and repression (Shapiro, 1995); of not getting beyond the "missionary position" (McWilliam, 1997). Ellsworth (1989) argued in the late 1980s that the technical lexicon of 'critical pedagogy' such as "'empowerment,' 'student voice,' 'dialogue,' and even the term 'critical'—were repressive myths that perpetuate relations of domination" (p. 298), since "the intrinsically asymmetrical conditions of classrooms precluded the sort of dialogue envisioned by critical pedagogy" (Stanley, 1992, p. 142), given that the form of dialogue envisioned is often an idealized form, one that ignores the material circumstances of speakers, and unwittingly imposes its own set of particular communicative norms (Burbules, 2000). Gore (1992) has likewise questioned the notion of a pedagogy of 'empowerment' as it appears to privilege those doing the 'empowering,' and thus fails to avoid the very relations of power it proposes to subvert. Further, Gore (1991) argues that "radical pedagogy discourses have tended to hold traditional [zero-sum] conceptions of power and knowledge" that overly simplify power relations and "risks the replacement of one orthodoxy with another," particularly through "tendencies to create grand narratives" of its own (Gore, 1993, p. 122).

Enacting Poststructuralism: Pedagogy as the Practice of Freedom

The idea of social justice pedagogy analyzed through a poststructural lens thus raises a number of questions. Who is positioned to benefit from social justice pedagogy? Who decides who benefits from social justice pedagogy and what constitutes justice? How can pedagogy impact on social justice and in what ways does social justice impact on pedagogy? Does social justice pedagogy mean educating students to achieve greater tolerance for diversity? Does it mean achieving equal outcomes for students from different social backgrounds? Does it mean attention to one (or more) categories of non-dominant social grouping? Which categories count and who decides? If social justice pedagogy is about practice, then what does it look like? Is it different to regular pedagogy? What is regular pedagogy? If social justice pedagogy primarily depends of the skills and dispositions of the teacher, then what work on themselves must teachers do in order to deliver socially just teaching or outcomes? Such questioning can leave readers with the view that poststructural analyses offer nothing other than critique, even when they contribute to important historicization, denaturalization, and critical reconstruction projects. In the remainder of this chapter, we turn to a discussion of ways in which poststructuralism can be useful in not only conceptualizing but also enacting social justice pedagogy.

Poststructuralism clearly challenges any social justice pedagogy founded on an assumption that specific well-intentioned commitments or actions will necessarily yield the desired outcome. As Sawicki (1988) asserts, "there are no inherently liberating or repressive [pedagogical] practices. . . . Evaluating the political status of [pedagogical] practices should be a matter of historical and social investigation, not a priori theoretical pronouncement" (pp. 185–186). Poststructuralism problematizes the possible effects of particular actions and strategies and challenges both arrogant assumptions of empowerment and the authority of knowledge. While some educators may feel paralyzed by the poststructural recognition that everything is dangerous, including social justice pedagogy, we argue that a poststructuralist stance can actually free agents/teachers from current forms of paralysis arising out of the despair and perceived failure that follow from totalizing adherence to a particular pedagogical regime. Hence, the view that poststructuralism is a theoretical position with no positive thesis misrepresents the insights poststructuralism provides.

Recognizing complexity, embracing uncertainty, and overcoming pedagogical paralysis can begin with acceptance of Foucault's (1985) important view on the pedagogical relation of teacher and student:

> I really can't see what is so objectionable in the practice of those who know more in a given truth game than another participant and tell the latter what he must do, teach him, and pass on knowledge and explain techniques to him. The problem arises much more in knowing how, when using these practices (in which power is neither avoidable nor intrinsically unacceptable), to avoid the effects of dominance. Such effects would make a small boy subservient to the pointless and arbitrary authority of a primary school teacher, or make a student dependent upon the professor who abuses his position etc. I believe this problem must be understood in terms of the relevant laws, rational methods of control, and also ethics, practice of the self and freedom. (p. 44)

Two things strike us as important within this quotation. First, Foucault states that there is nothing inherently unacceptable about explanation and instruction. In fact, Foucault is describing a point which underpins many approaches to social justice pedagogy, that the educator's goal should be to let the student in on the secrets of the game, and that direct instruction is often the vehicle for such learning. There is a second series of points that Foucault is also making, namely that power cannot be avoided, that it is not intrinsically a problem, and that educators will need to figure out how to use their teaching position and strategies to "avoid the effects of dominance" (Foucault, 1985, p. 44). Whether pedagogy without dominance is indeed possible is an open question. One might argue that a pedagogical relation is intrinsically a form of subjection and subjugation. Certainly Bernstein (1990) recognized that pedagogy is more than a relay for power relations external to itself. He also made the case that many attempts to alter pedagogical relations in the classroom simply made a visible pedagogy invisible (Bernstein, 1990). However in Foucault's later work, in his re-articulation of Nietzsche's genealogical method (Foucault, 1971/1994), and his discourse on the ethics of self-creation as a practice of freedom (Foucault, 1984/1996), there is some hope for an answer to the problem of social justice pedagogy.

Foucault's work is often described as moving through a number of phases, associated with the advance of different theoretical tools (Heikkinen, Silvonen, & Simola, 1999; Kendall & Wickham, 1999). According to Foucault (1969/1996), his reconceptualized archeological technique involves the investigation of "the mass of things spoken in a culture, presented, valorized, re-used, repeated and transformed," with a view to understanding them as the components of "a practice which has its rules, its conditions, its functioning and its effects" (Foucault, 1969/1996, pp. 65–66). Thus, the task of archeology is to determine what can and cannot be said at a given historical moment. If we stop at archeological analysis, change can seem like a hopeless prospect. We can seem at the mercy of discourse, its rules, operations, and effects, with little chance of resistance. However, it was Foucault's shift to a genealogical method that opened up the possibility for theorizing resistance by exploring "spaces of freedom" within any regime of truth. Foucault has affirmed that genealogy—widely conceptualized as the second of his 'methods'—"must record the singularity of events outside any monotonous finality" (Foucault, 1971/1994, p. 367). Avoiding the pitfalls of totalization, genealogy must seek "to re-establish the various systems of subjection: not the anticipatory power of meaning, but the hazardous play of dominations" (Foucault, 1971/1994, p. 376). In other words, the task of genealogy is to uncover the constitution of subjectivity in a web of power relations; or as Foucault (1971/1994) states most succinctly, "its task is to expose a body totally imprinted by history" (p. 376), and document "a history of the different modes by which, in our culture, human beings are made subjects" (Foucault, 1983, p. 208). Thus, genealogy works to challenge the idea of an essential human subjectivity, or the universality of a particular cultural practice, by tracing its historical emergence. O'Leary (2002) makes clear what this means for human freedom:

> When the genealogical method is applied to this entity [the human], when the subject is treated as a phenomenon with a history in which the complex interplay between relations of truth, power and self is evident, then the subject loses its foundational status. As soon as the subject becomes natural, as opposed to a metaphysical or a transcendental, phenomenon, it is not only given a history but—crucially for ethics and politics—it is given a *future*. (p. 108, emphasis in the original)

The future that Foucault's genealogical investigations open up is the possibility to be other than who we are now; to be able to refuse the self that has emerged out of our collective and personal histories. This goal underpins Foucault's strategic move toward the articulation of technologies of the self.

According to Foucault (1984/1996), those processes which begin as social practices very quickly become "technologies of the self" as individuals apply those social practices to themselves. These technologies of the self through which subjectivities are constituted, "make the body [or subjectivity] into a particular kind of body [or subject]—pagan, primitive, medieval capitalist, Italian, American, Australian" (Grosz, 1990, p. 65). Foucault (1984/1996) defines freedom throughout his later work as refusing who we are. This makes sense, because if human subjectivity is constituted within discourse, then to be free would mean being other than how we have been constituted within discourse. Pedagogy in its broadest form is the sociohistorical process through which we have become who we are, and through which we may become other than who we are. If it is the case that pedagogy is implicated in the historical process of subjectivity formation, then at least one ethical position an educator can adopt is to engage in teaching as a practice of freedom. That is not to say that teaching should become an 'anything goes' practice but rather, that an ethical imperative emerges out of taking Foucault seriously, and that is one in which students are provided with tools that allow them to disassemble their own subjectivities, and reconstitute themselves in new forms. It is a form of pedagogy in which knowledge is approached as if it is problematic, historically and culturally situated, socially constructed, and politically motivated; and the self is approached as a historical being with a complex past and an uncertain future. If we are to resist who we are, or become other than who we are, then we need to appropriate practices that embody alternative ways of being and behaving, or that assist us in deconstructing our existing practices and forms of knowledge. As pedagogues this means approaching teaching and learning as acts of autopoesis, as moments of self-formation, in which the self is understood as the material to be worked on (O'Leary, 2002). We can assist our students in this task when we make available mediating artifacts that can act as tools to serve our practice of freedom, in the same way that discourses may have acted as constitutive agents in our social construction.

Poststructuralism highlights the dangers of universalizing and essentializing faced by those who are committed to social justice in and through pedagogy. It refuses a position of innocence, recognizing how we are all implicated in the practices of the present, and that there is no escape from discourse. It resists generic solutions that commit acts of symbolic violence against the lived experience of different social groups. However, as Foucault (1983) has stated, the acknowledgment of the dangers inherent in even well-meant practices, does not have to lead to pessimism but rather to an acceptance that there is always more to do. Through perpetual problematization, we can resist the tendency towards complacency. Through engaging in the pedagogical act as a process of knowledge problematization and concomitant self-creation, we can open up the possibility of refusing who we are. The analysis we have provided should refine and enhance social justice efforts through its recognition of the messy complexity that characterizes pedagogical and social reality. Using poststructuralist approaches, it becomes possible to identify spaces of freedom for our own actions as educators that will allow us to work toward practices of freedom through which students can become other than who they are by refusing their inherited inscriptions. Engaging in pedagogy with all the insights that poststructuralism offers may make the project of social justice pedagogy less grand, but it also equips us with insights that may be marshalled to refuse and resist those discourses that erase difference and naturalize disadvantage.

Points of Inquiry

- The authors have considered poststructuralism's contribution to understanding social justice pedagogy. What explanations can you offer for the structural and systematic inequalities for particular groups in education that continue to pervade social justice agendas?
- How can social justice pedagogy overcome the challenges presented by those who subscribe and those who totally resist deficit discourses?
- What categories of people are important in education research? What might be historical reasons (genealogical reasons) for this?

Points of Praxis

- Consider a social justice agenda in your community. What have been the perceived benefits? What injustices can you identify as a result of this agenda?
- In what ways has white privilege been made visible in your teaching and learning experiences?
- How can you make the complexities of poststructural analysis accessible to your students, to people at your site and/or community?

References

Althusser, L. (1971). Ideology and ideological state apparatuses (Notes towards an Investigation) (B. Brewster, Trans.). In L. Althusser (Ed.), *Lenin and philosophy and other essays* (pp. 127–186). New York: Monthly Review Press.

Baker, B., & Heyning, K. E. (2004a). Introduction: Dangerous coagulations? Research, education, and a traveling Foucault. In B. Baker, & K. E. Heyning (Eds.), *Dangerous coagulations? The uses of Foucault in the study of education* (pp. 1–79). New York: Peter Lang.

Baker, B., & Heyning, K. E. (Eds.). (2004b). Dangerous coagulations? The uses of Foucault in the study of education. New York: Peter Lang.

Ball, S. J. (Ed.). (1990). Foucault and education: Disciplines and knowledge. London: Routledge.

Barthes, R. (1968/1977). The death of the author (S. Heath, Trans.). In R. Barthes (Ed.), *Image–music–text* (pp. 142–148). London: Fontana.

Bernstein, B. (1990). *The structuring of pedagogic discourse*. London and New York: Routledge.

Bourdieu, P., & Passeron, J. C. (1977). *Reproduction in education, society and culture*. London: SAGE Publications.

Breisach, E. (2003). On the future of history: The postmodernist challenge and its aftermath. Chicago: University of Chicago Press.

Brennan, M., & Popkewitz, T. S. (Eds.). (1997). *Foucault's challenge: Discourse, knowledge, and power in education*. Columbia: Teachers Press.

Burbules, N. (2000). The limits of dialogue as critical pedagogy. In P. P. Trifonas (Ed.), *Revolutionary pedagogies: Cultural politics, instituting education, and the discourse of theory* (pp. 251–273). New York: Routledge Falmer.

Cherryholmes, C. H. (1988). Power and criticism: Poststructural investigations in education. New York: Teachers College Press.

Close, A. (1990). The empirical author: Salman Rushdie's "The Satanic Verses". *Philosophy and Literature, 14*, 248–267.

Daignault, J. (1992). Traces at work from different places. In W. Pinar, & W. Reynolds (Eds.), *Understanding curriculum as phenomenological and deconstructed text* (pp. 195–215). New York: Teachers College Press.

Davies, B. (1993). *Poststructuralist theory and classroom practice.* Melbourne: Deakin University Press.

Derrida, J. (1976). *Of grammatology.* Baltimore, MD: John Hopkins University Press.

Dhillon, P. (Ed.). (2001). *Lyotard: Just Education.* New York: RoutledgeFalmer.

Dreyfus, H. L., & Rabinow, P. (1982). *Michel Foucault: Beyond structuralism and hermeneutics.* Brighton, Sussex: Harvester Press.

Ellsworth, E. (1989). Why doesn't this feel empowering? Working through the repressive myths of critical pedagogy. *Harvard Educational Review, 59*(3), 297–324.

Falzon, C. (1998). Foucault and social dialogue: Beyond fragmentation. London: Routledge.

Foucault, M. (1965/1988). Madness and civilization: A history of insanity in the Age of Reason (R. Howard, Trans.). New York: Vintage Books.

Foucault, M. (1968/1996). History, discourse and discontinuity (A. M. Nazzaro, Trans.). In S. Lotringer (Ed.), *Foucault live: Interviews, 1961–1984* (pp. 33–50). New York: Semiotext(e).

Foucault, M. (1969/1972). *The archaeology of knowledge.* London: Routledge.

Foucault, M. (1969/1977). What is an author? (D. F. Bouchard, & S. Simon, Trans.). In D. F. Bouchard (Ed.), *Language, counter-memory, practice: Selected essays and interviews* (pp. 113–138). Ithaca, NY: Cornell University Press.

Foucault, M. (1969/1996). The birth of a world (L. Hochroth, & J. Johnston, Trans.). In S. Lotringer (Ed.), *Foucault live: Interviews, 1961–1984* (pp. 65–67). New York: Semiotext(e).

Foucault, M. (1970/1994). The order of things: An archaeology of the human sciences. New York: Vintage Books.

Foucault, M. (1971/1994). Nietzsche, genealogy, history (D. F. Brouchard, & S. Simon, Trans.). In J. D. Faubion (Ed.), *Essential works of Foucault 1954–1984* (Vol. 2: *Aesthetics*, pp. 369–391). London: Penguin Books.

Foucault, M. (1975). *The birth of the clinic: An archaeology of medical perception* (A. M. Sheridan Smith, Trans.). New York: Vintage Books.

Foucault, M. (1977). Discipline and punish: The birth of the prison. New York: Pantheon.

Foucault, M. (1980a). *The history of sexuality: Volume 1: An introduction* (R. Hurley, Trans.). New York: Vintage.

Foucault, M. (1980b). Power/Knowledge: selected interviews and other writings 1972–1977. London: Harvester Press.

Foucault, M. (1982/1994). The subject and power (P. Rabinow, & H. Dreyfus, Trans.). In J. D. Faubion (Ed.), *Essential works of Foucault 1954–1984* (Vol. 3: *Power*, pp. 326–348). London: Penguin Books.

Foucault, M. (1983). The subject and power. In H. Dreyfus, & P. Rabinow (Eds.), *Michel Foucault: Beyond structuralism and hermeneutics* (2nd ed.). Chicago: University of Chicago Press.

Foucault, M. (1984/1996). The ethics of the concern for the self as a practice of freedom (P. Aranov, & D. McGrawth, Trans.). In S. Lotringer (Ed.), *Foucault live: Interviews, 1961–1984* (pp. 432–449). New York: Semiotext(e).

Foucault, M. (1985). *The history of sexuality, Volume 2: The use of pleasure* (R. Hurley, Trans.). New York: Pantheon Books.

Foucault, M. (1991). Politics and the study of discourse. In G. Burchell, C. Gordon, & P. Miller (Eds.), *The Foucault effect: Studies in governmentality.* London: Harvester Wheatsheaf.

Freire, P. (1970). *Pedagogy of the oppressed.* New York: Penguin Books.

Gore, J. M. (1991). Neglected practices: A Foucauldian critique of traditional and radical approaches to pedagogy. Paper presented at the the the Liberating Curriculum Conference, University of Adelaide.

Gore, J. M. (1992). What we can do for you! What can "We" do for "You"?: Struggling over empowerment in critical and feminist pedagogy. In C. Luke, & J. Gore (Eds.), *Feminisms and critical pedagogy* (pp. 54–73). New York: Routledge.

Gore, J. M. (1993). The struggle for pedagogies: Critical and feminist discourses as regimes of truth. New York: Routledge.

Grosz, E. (1990). Inscriptions and body-maps: Representations and the corporeal. In T. Threadgood and A. Cranny-Francis (Eds.), *Feminine, masculine and representation.* Sydney: Allen & Unwin.

Grosz, E. (1995). *Space, time and perversion.* New York: Routledge.

Heikkinen, S., Silvonen, J., & Simola, H. (1999). Technologies of truth: Peeling Foucault's triangular onion. *Discourse: Studies in the Cultural Politics of Education, 20*(1), 141–157.

Heller, G. (1992). Death of the subject? In G. Levine (Ed.), *Constructions of the self* (pp. 269–284). New Jersey: Rutgers University Press.

Kendall, G., & Wickham, G. (1999). *Using Foucault's methods.* London: Sage Publications.

Kvale, S. (1992). Postmodern psychology: A contradiction in terms? In S. Kvale (Ed.), *Psychology and postmodernism* (pp. 31–57). London: SAGE Publications.

LaCapra, D. (2000). *History and reading: Tocqueville, Foucault, French studies.* Carlton South: Melbourne University Press.

Lather, P. (1992). Post-critical pedagogies: A Feminist reading. In C. Luke, & J. Gore (Eds.), *Feminism and critical pedagogy* (pp. 120–137). London: Routledge.

Luke, C., & Gore, J. (1992). Introduction. In C. Luke, & J. Gore (Eds.), *Feminisms and critical pedagogy* (pp. 1–14). London: Routledge.

MacLure, M. (2003). *Discourse in educational and social research.* Buckingham, UK: Open University Press.

MacNaughton, M. (1995). A post-structuralist analysis of learning in early childhood settings. In M. Fleer (Ed.), *DAPcentrism: Challenging developmentally appropriate practice* (pp. 36–53). Canberra: Australian Early Childhood association.

McWilliam, E. (1997). Beyond the missionary position: Teacher desire and radical pedagogy. In S. Todd (Ed.), *Learning desire: Perspectives on pedagogy, culture, and the unsaid* (pp. 217–235). New York: Routledge.

McWilliam, E. (1999). *Pedagogical pleasures.* New York: Peter Lang.

Mansfield, N. (2000). *Subjectivity: Theories of the self from Freud to Harraway.* Sydney: Allen & Unwin.

Mills, S. (1997). *Discourse.* New York: Routledge.

Morss, J. R. (1990). *The biologising of childhood: Developmental psychology and the Darwinian myth.* New Jersey: Erlbaum.

Morss, J. R. (1996). *Growing critical: Alternatives to developmental psychology.* London: Routledge.

Nieto, S., & Bode, P. (2008). *Affirming diversity: The sociopolitical context of multicultural education* (5th ed.). Boston: Allyn & Bacon.

O'Leary, T. (2002). *Foucault and the art of ethics*. London: Continuum.

Olssen, M. (2006). *Michel Foucault: Materialism and education*. Westport, CT: Paradigm.

Peters, M. A. (Ed.). (1998). *Naming the multiple: Poststructuralism and education*. New York: Bergin & Garvey.

Peters, M. A., & Besley, T. A. C. (Eds.). (2006). *Why Foucault?: New Directions in Educational Research*. New York: Peter Lang.

Peters, M. A., & Besley, T. A. C. (Eds.). (2007). *Subjectivity and truth: Foucault, education, and the culture of self.* New York: Peter Lang.

Peters, M. A., & Biesta, G. (Eds.). (2008). *Derrida, deconstruction, and the politics of pedagogy*. New York: Peter Lang.

Peters, M. A., & Burbules, N. C. (2004). *Poststructuralism and educational research*. Lanham, MD: Rowman & Littlefield.

Popkewitz, T. S. (Ed.). (1999). Critical theories in education: Changing terrains of knowledge and politics. New York: Routledge.

Popkewitz, T. S. (2001). The production of reason and power: Curriculum history and intellectual traditions. In T. S. Popkewitz, B. M. Franklin, & M. A. Pereyra (Eds.), *Cultural history and education: Critical essays on knowledge and schooling* (pp. 151–183). New York: Routledge Falmer.

Popkewitz, T. S., Franklin, B. M., & Pereyra, M. A. (2001). History, the problem of knowledge, and the new cultural history of schooling. In T. S. Popkewitz, B. M. Franklin, & M. A. Pereyra (Eds.), Cultural history and education: Critical essays on knowledge and schooling (pp. 3–44). New York: Routledge Falmer.

Poynton, C., & Lee, A. (2000). Culture & text: An introduction. In A. Lee, & C. Poynton (Eds.), *Culture & text: Discourse and methodology in social research and cultural studies* (pp. 1–18). St Leonards, NSW: Allen & Unwin.

Reynolds, W. M. (2003). *Curriculum: A river runs through it*. New York: Peter Lang.

Ruge, J. (1999). *Raising expectations: Achieving quality education for all*. Darlinghurst, NSW: Priority Schools Funding Program, Equity Programs and Distance Education Directorate, NSW Department of Education and Training.

Sawicki, J. (1988). Identity politics and sexual freedom: Foucault and feminism. In I. Diamond, & L. Quinby (Eds.), *Feminism and Foucault: Reflections on resistance*, (pp. 177–92). Boston: Northeastern University Press.

Sawyer, R. K. (2002). A discourse on discourse: An archaeological history of an intellectual concept. *Cultural Studies, 16*(3), 433–456.

Semetsky, I. (2006). *Deleuze, education and becoming*. Rotterdam: Sense Publications.

Semetsky, I. (2008). *Nomadic education: Variations on a theme by Deleuze and Guattari*. Rotterdam: Sense Publications.

Sennett, R., & Cobb, J. (1972). *The hidden injuries of class*. New York: Knopf.

Shapiro, S. (1995). The end of radical hope? Postmodernism and the challenge to critical pedagogy. In P. McLaren (Ed.), *Postmodernism, postcolonialism and pedagogy* (pp. 187–204). Sydney: James Nicholas.

Spivak, G. C. (1988). Can the subaltern speak? In C. Nelson, & L. Grossberg (Eds.), *Marxism and the interpretation of culture*. Urbana: University of Illinois Press.

Stanley, W. B. (1992). *Curriculum for utopia: Social reconstructionism and critical pedagogy in the postmodern era*. New York: State University of New York Press.

Trifonas, P. P., & Peters, M. A. (Eds.). (2004). *Derrida, deconstruction and education: Ethics of pedagogy and research*. Hoboken, NJ: Wiley-Blackwell.

Whitson, J. (1995). Post-structuralist pedagogy as counter-hegemonic practice. In P. McLaren (Ed.), *Postmodernism, postcolonialism and pedagogy* (pp. 121–144). Sydney: James Nicholas.

Yates, L. (1992). Postmodernism, feminism and cultural politics: Or if master narratives have been discredited, what does Giroux think he is doing? *Discourse, 13*(1), 124–141.

Chapter 9

Indigenous Knowledges and Social Justice Pedagogy

Bryan McKinley Jones Brayboy and
Teresa L. McCarty

Schooling and its processes make value judgments about what kinds of knowledge(s)
count. Indigenous knowledges tend to be misunderstood and marginalized in the con-
text of Western schooling. These misunderstandings can "count" against Indigenous
students in profoundly negative ways. The goal of this chapter is to provide insights
from research, theory, and practice on Indigenous knowledges as a means of informing
education policy and practice for Indigenous students. Our focus is on ways of knowing
for Indigenous peoples in the United States and Canada—a highly diverse group who
nonetheless share certain experiences and values.

We begin by outlining what we mean by Indigenous ways of knowing, emphasizing
that Indigenous knowledges are: (1) emplaced within distinctive physical landscapes
and social networks; (2) rooted in community; (3) systematic; and (4) lived in everyday
social practice. We then explore relationships, responsibility, and reciprocity as anchor-
ing principles for the transmission, acquisition, and expression of Indigenous knowl-
edges. Recognizing that teaching and learning are integrally connected and that social
justice too must be lived, we examine three case examples that demonstrate the possi-
bilities for "doing" social justice pedagogy in ways that embrace Indigenous ways of
knowing, learning, and teaching for the benefit of all students.

> I grew up in a home where only Navajo was spoken. . . . We lived in a one-room
> *hooghan* (a traditional earth and log dwelling), with no modern amenities. I
> learned to greet people by kinship. We never called each other by our English
> names, only by our Navajo names. . . . At an early age I learned the values, beliefs,
> and traditions of my people. For instance, in Navajo we begin prayers with *shimá*
> *hahasdzáán, shitaa yáh dilhil*. By this we mean we have the same relationship to
> mother earth (*shimá nahhasdzáán*) as we have to the person who gave birth to us.
> The passing on of these values and of history, ritual, and family traditions was
> done through oral tradition.
>
> (Dick, 1998, pp. 23–24)

This introductory epigraph, taken from the language autobiography of Navajo
bilingual educator Galena Sells Dick, illuminates the different ways of conceptualizing what knowledge is and who (re)produces it. It also suggests the ways in which

Indigenous knowledges, though they differ among themselves, as a whole tend to be misunderstood and marginalized in the context of Western schooling. As Galena Dick continues her account:

> My "formal" education began at the age of seven in a boarding school 35 miles from home.... It was confusing and difficult; we had to struggle.... the Navajo word for school is *ólta'*, meaning "a learning place associated with the white man's world." But the treatment we received in school gave us little to admire about the white man's world or his language. (1998, pp. 23–24)

In this segment of her autobiography, Galena Dick refers to the physical and psychological abuse Native students endured for speaking their mother tongue in school. Colonial schooling for Native American students was aimed at what one federal official called "blotting out" Indigenous languages, lifeways, and identities (Adams, cited in Crawford, 1992)—practices that, in new contexts and guises, continue to this day.

In this chapter we expand on the lessons in Galena Sells Dick's account to offer a theoretical and epistemological orientation to Indigenous knowledges and ways of knowing, which, we argue, encompass ways of being, teaching, learning, and valuing. Our focus is on ways of knowing and being for Indigenous peoples in what is now the United States and Canada—a diverse group of peoples (there are more than 560 Native nations in the U.S.A. alone) who are nonetheless distinguished by certain shared experiences and values. As we will see, a primary understanding is that Indigenous knowledges are lived and embodied within particular people and communities—that is, they are *emplaced*. We also explore the ways in which Indigenous ways of knowing and being are linked through principles of *relationality, responsibility, reciprocity*, and *respect*.

With this groundwork in place, we move to the relationship between Indigenous ways of knowing and social justice pedagogy. In keeping with the understanding that, like Indigenous ways of knowing and being, social justice too must be lived, we devote this portion of the chapter to concrete examples of the possibilities for "doing" social justice pedagogy in ways that embrace Indigenous ways of knowing, learning, and teaching.

Indigenous Ways of Knowing

A great deal of research on Native peoples and Western education highlights cultural differences or "mismatches" between Native students and the culture of the schools. While this research has been immensely valuable in countering fallacious notions of inherited, racialized "intelligence," too often culture is conceived as static and monolithic (see, e.g., Eisenhart's 2001 discussion of these problems). This reduces culture to a superficial list of traits or artifacts, and learners to one-dimensional proportions, as in the widespread myth that Native American students are "silent," "non-analytical," or "right-brained" learners. (For critiques of these approaches, see Foley, 1996; Lomawaima & McCarty, 2006, pp. 20–21; McCarty,

Wallace, Lynch, & Benally, 1991). By examining Indigenous ways of knowing and being, we aim to offer a more nuanced and accurate analysis of pedagogical issues when Indigenous children enter largely non-Indigenous schooling environments. Another way of thinking about these ways of knowing is to view them as the threads, which, when woven together, make up the cultural cloth of particular communities (Meyer, 2001). This theoretical frame is one presentation of a cultural weaving together of many communities and diverse Indigenous scholars. These threads do not reside in libraries or museums, but are "embedded in the cumulative experiences and teachings of Indigenous peoples" (Battiste, 2002, p. 2).

These knowledges form a coherent sense of how to view the world, and the passing on and acquisition of these knowledges informs the everyday existence of Indigenous peoples. Mi'kmaq scholar Marie Battiste (2002) writes that, "Indigenous knowledge is systemic, covering both what can be observed and what can be thought. It comprises the rural and the urban, the settled and the nomadic, original inhabitants and migrants" (p. 7). Combined with her observations that Indigenous knowledges and ways of knowing are context-specific and rooted in the lived experiences of individuals and communities, the notion of Indigenous knowledge as an all-encompassing system accounts for the range and variation in the knowledge possessed by many Indigenous peoples.

Our discussion of Indigenous knowledges and ways of knowing is thus intentionally plural. Lomawaima and McCarty (2006) caution of the dangers of reducing our understanding of Indigenous learners to single dimensions. Yet, it is the very multidimensionality of Indigenous knowledges that presents rhetorical difficulty. In attempting to reduce the many dimensions of embodied, lived knowledge to this two-dimensional medium, much is lost. But, perhaps there is also a gain; in the process the complexity of lived Indigenous experiences and communities becomes apparent.

Indigenous Knowledge is Emplaced

> American Indians hold their lands—place—as having the highest possible meaning, and all their statements are made with this reference point in mind. . . .
>
> Place or space is concrete and palpable. It is in a profound sense where one discovers . . . self . . . as opposed to the casual sense of where one just happens to find one's self.
>
> (Deloria & Wildcat, 2001, p. 144)

The connection between people and place is central to understanding Indigenous knowledges. A sense of place frames and textures the oral traditions that, for millennia, have carried the histories of Native peoples, rooting them within distinct landscapes and social networks. As Acoma writer Simon Ortiz describes his early socialization:

> It was the stories and songs which provided the knowledge that I was woven into the intricate web that was my Acoma life. In our garden and our cornfields

I learned about the seasons, growth cycles of cultivated plants, and what one had to think and feel about the land; and at home I became aware of how we must care for each other: all of this was encompassed in an intricate relationship which had to be maintained in order that life continue. (1993, pp. 29, 38)

This "intricate relationship" has, in the course of Anglo-European colonization, been steadily assaulted, appropriated, and displaced. Yet, as we discuss throughout this chapter, the nexus of place and peoplehood remains central to contemporary Indigenous ways of knowing and being (for international accounts that illustrate this point, see Villegas, Neugebauer, & Venegas, 2008). The land, the history, and the community of a place are the agents of knowledge discovery and use. Every place is defined by all these factors, and assuming the specificity of such a reality is to assume that universality is a rather weak concept, not paying heed to all that makes a place a unique instantiation of creation and creative endeavor.

According to Manuelito, "Land exists as sacred space. . . . For Navajos, life is a journey through sacred landscape" (2005, p. 81). Like the *hooghan* (home) in Galena Sells Dick's account, "land is a place of birth, growth and development, and death" (Manuelito, 2005, p. 81). Cradled in the context of specific landscapes, knowledge is raised (see, e.g., Kawagley's [2006] discussion of this for the Yupiaq of present-day Alaska). The landscape—the places where teaching and learning take place—is not just a blank backdrop for the journey, but the locus of the power to move through a knowledge-seeking journey. It is an active space, not a neutral, insignificant one.

Indigenous Knowledge is Rooted in Community

At the heart of Indigenous ways of knowing and being are notions of community and communal survival. We simply cannot understand these issues without a deep and abiding understanding of how, for many Indigenous peoples, community is at the core of existence. The survival of Indigenous community is more important than a single individual. Individuals, through self-discovery and selflessness, become whole, thereby insuring community survival. Lomawaima and McCarty (2006) write, "The ultimate test of each human educational system is a people's survival" (p. 30).

This sentiment is captured through Brian Yazzi Burkhart's (2004) insightful reworking of the Cartesian Principle. Descartes based his philosophies of knowing and being on the principle that says, "I think, therefore I am." This belief in the individual is evidenced in myriad policies, court decisions, and laws that serve as the foundation of the present-day United States. But consider Burkhart's reworking of the Cartesian Principle when he writes that an Indigenous version is, "We are, therefore I am." At its core, then, the knowledge systems, ways of being, and teaching philosophies for many Indigenous peoples are focused on community and survival.

Similarly, Deloria (1992) notes that the freedom to think and act in ways governed by individual will, promoted in some other epistemologies, is most detrimental. It allows one to conceive of reality in whatever way a person finds beneficial, which encourages a person to disregard others and be blind to the repercussions of her thoughts and actions on those around her. Community-based ways of knowing require individuals to be concerned with the welfare of others, whereas those tied primarily to the individual only call for a concern for self and—potentially—those whom one births. Progenitors are often myopically focused on their own children—this is not the broad concern demonstrated by those who are focused on the survival and sustenance of a community. A healthy community is both the purpose and litmus test of knowledge.

Indigenous Knowledge is Systematic

We know that these knowledge systems are systematic and systemic. Notwithstanding Galena Dick's use of the term "formal" to characterize her schooling experience, we caution against reproducing the formal/informal dichotomy. As Lomawaima and McCarty write,

> This popular but artificial dichotomy fails to describe the complexity of American education [both] inside and outside of schools. Its failure regarding Native educational systems is even more profound because it communicates that they are "accidental" or "unplanned." . . . The label "informal" is another one-dimensional strategy used to denigrate and marginalize Native education. (2006, p. 27)

As many Indigenous accounts attest, the lived curriculum and pedagogy in Indigenous communities are often quite formal in that they are planned, transferred, and acquired in very systematic ways with the end goal being one of sustenance and continuation/survival. The four-day Navajo *kinaaldá* or girls' puberty ceremony, for instance—still practiced today—is designed to help girls "make themselves strong" by running each morning toward the dawn light (Begay, 1983; Markstrom, 2008). Through formalized learning experiences such as this ceremony, and through everyday social practice, Navajo young people are both prepared and tested for what lies ahead. As these and many other Native accounts testify, Indigenous peoples learn, know, and do things (an application of knowledge) for the purposes of survival (Kawagley, 2006). There is nothing informal about survival.

Indigenous Knowledge is Lived

Indigenous ways of knowing view knowledge as both embodied and intensely intellectual. Medicine remarks that, "Elders are repositories of cultural and philosophical knowledge and are the transmitters of such knowledge" (2001, p. 73), reminding us that when an elder dies, it is like a library burning. These sentiments suggest that Indigenous ways of knowing and being are embedded in the lived lives of real people and evolve and adapt over time. They are not static—although the past greatly influences their present incarnations—but rather are dynamic instantiations specific to particular groups of people and places (Basso, 1996; Battiste, 2002).

In contrast to this emphasis on lived and embodied knowledge, Western definitions of knowledge tend to emphasize the development of professional skills and credentials for which one is financially compensated, suggesting the degree to which mainstream conceptions of knowledge value "book smarts" over lived experience (Deloria, 2001). At the same time as we recognize these differences, thinking in terms of a dichotomy between Western and Indigenous ways of knowing is not particularly useful in that it erases complexities, nuances, and closes off spaces of possibility. Battiste (2002) makes this point vividly, writing:

> Indigenous scholars discovered that Indigenous knowledge is far more than the binary opposite of western knowledge. . . . Indigenous knowledge fills the ethical and knowledge gaps in Eurocentric education, research, and scholarship. By animating the voices and experiences of the cognitive "other" and integrating them into educational processes, it creates a new, balanced centre and a fresh vantage point from which to analyze Eurocentric education and its pedagogies. (p. 5)

As we illustrate with the pedagogical examples in the second part of this chapter, these knowledges can be—in fact, must be—configured in a way that is complementary, rather than contradictory.

Related to this more nuanced view of knowledges, even within a particular community (and like human communities around the world), not everyone will operate from the same epistemological foundation. Battiste (2002) reminds us of this reality:

> Within any Indigenous nation or community people vary greatly in what they know. There are not only differences between ordinary folks and experts, such as experienced knowledge keepers, healers, hunters, or ceremonialists, there are also major differences of experiences and professional opinion among the knowledge holders and workers, as we should expect of any living, dynamic knowledge system that is continually responding to new phenomena and fresh insights. (p. 12)

The diversity of knowledges and ways of knowing is fundamental to the dynamism of knowledge systems and the survival of communities.

This holistic knowledge is evidenced in our attempts to present a picture of what Indigenous ways of knowing and being offer. The interconnectedness of our knowledges, experiences, and sources of knowledge is critical to understanding how Indigenous peoples have survived well over 500 years of genocide. These are peoples who have adapted and adjusted to their situations and the threats aimed at their extinction. As an Indigenous student once said to Brayboy, "I am the descendent of a people who would not die." This survival and unwillingness to die is directly connected to moving outside traditional categories and recognizing the interconnected nature of all things in the world.

Knowledge is contextual and contextualized; it is lived and is an integral part of survival; truth and knowledge cannot be ends in themselves. These conceptualizations are often at odds with school-based notions of knowledge as a noun, rooted in things or possessions, passive, or so abstract as to not be seen. From an Indigenous perspective, knowledge is seen and active, and those who possess it must be active in their acquisition and use of it. Burkhart (2004) continues along this vein, writing that, "Knowledge is what we put to use" (p. 21).

In this way, we see a definitive connection between ways of knowing and being. If knowledge is lived, then the process of living demonstrates what one knows. Ways of being become so intimately linked to ways of knowing that separating the two is impossible. We can see what one knows by what one does; what one does, or puts to use, demonstrates one's knowledge.

Relationships and Responsibility: Twin Pillars of Indigenous Knowledges

In his book, *The American Indian Mind in a Linear World*, historian Donald Fixico begins with this:

> "Indian Thinking" is "seeing" things from a perspective emphasizing that circles and cycles are central to the world and that all things are related within the universe. For Indian people who are close to their tribal traditions and native values, they think within a native reality consisting of a physical and metaphysical world. . . people raised in the traditional ways of their peoples see things in this combined manner. (2003, pp. 1–2)

A circular worldview that connects everything and everyone in the world to everything and everyone else, where there is no distinction between the physical and metaphysical world, and where ancestral knowledge guides contemporary practices is the premise of American Indian philosophies. This holistic worldview is fundamental because it shapes all other understandings of the world.

More specifically, holistic understandings do not draw separations between the body and mind, between humans and other earthly inhabitants, or between generations of humans. Instead, connections, are central for knowledge production and the responsible uses of knowledge. Responsibility is a logical outgrowth of these philosophical understandings. When everything and everyone are connected, a person has a responsibility to act according to his or her surroundings. S/he understands that one's actions affect everything else. S/he is invested in maintaining balance. These connections are also central to how Indigenous peoples view their own places within the larger cosmos of all living things. For example, Meyer (2001) shows how Hawaiian educators articulate relationships between the body and mind, describing knowledge as "felt" and "in pulse. Without heart we don't have sense" (pp. 141, 143). That body sense has profound implications for action.

Greek philosophers who were engaged in humanistic studies came to understand that humans were superior to other natural physical entities, which was later used to justify manipulation of the earth for selfish ends. Contrary to these Western epistemologies, however, "Indian people did not [sic] believe that they were greater than nature, and they altered their cultural norms to fit the cycles of the seasons" (Fixico, 2003, p. 44). We would argue that many Indigenous people presently do not believe that they are greater than nature and that they adapt and adjust to all changing systems and structures. Thus, Indigenous peoples' relationship to the earth is often one of humility and responsibility. Among others, Battiste (2002), Medicine (2001), Marker (2003), Stoeffle, Zedeno, and Halmo (2001), Fixico (2003), Grande (2000), Deloria (1992), and Meyer (2001) point out that responsible use of knowledge in building, nurturing, and maintaining relationships is a fundamental value among Indigenous peoples.

Reciprocity: Completing the Circle

A reciprocal relationship exists where communities act to support individuals and individuals act with the best interests of their communities in mind. What do we mean by reciprocity? Reciprocity, as we use it here, is not simply a quid pro quo or a sense of "you scratch my back and I'll scratch yours." Instead, it is a sense that individuals act outside of their self-interests for those of the community and work toward their own betterment for the community's sake (see, for example, the way that Deloria [1992] explains the idea of self-development as an integral part of Indigenous communities). The point here is that individual development occurs for the betterment of community. Additionally, those who are given gifts of guidance, shared wisdom, and teachings are expected to pass this on to others. As McCarty et al. (1991) write in their analysis of Navajo theories of individual growth and development: "Knowledge . . . is intended to be shared and used, for good or valued ends. This is the essence of *k'é* [kinship, clanship]: knowledge should be used, not for narrow individual purposes, but to benefit the social group (the family or clan) as a whole" (p. 51). If we consider the connections between the past, present, and future, these values come into deeper clarity.

For community members or allies who are given gifts, their responsibility is to ensure the community's survival. One way of doing this is by responding to the needs of the youth and sharing that knowledge (and its concomitant power, where appropriate) with the next generation. Simply stated, reciprocity is guided by the mantra, "We give so that others can take, for our survival. We take so that we can give to others. Those who receive must give what they have to others." Only through reciprocity is community survival possible. This simple fact points to one of the reasons for the centrality of the community rather than the individual. Individuals play a role in the survival of communities; they can never come before it. Thus, the purpose of knowledge, first and foremost, is to ensure personal growth, rooted in relationships with other members of the community and with the places the community inhabits. Whitt (2004) describes knowledge sharing as gift giving. As such, she contends, "It is, after all, the givers of gifts who must determine when, to whom, and how the gifts are to be given" (p. 209). Further, she argues that the recipient of a gift has a responsibility to that gift and the person or community who shared it with him/her. This gift giving relies on principles of reciprocity.

Applying the Principles: Indigenous Knowledges in Action

In the previous section, we overviewed the "building blocks" of Indigenous ways of knowing and their concomitant ways of being and valuing: a rootedness in place, the centrality of community, and the guiding principles of relationality, responsibility, and reciprocity. It is now time to link our discussion of Indigenous knowledges to social justice pedagogy and to consider what this might look like in practice.

First, some definitions. Expanding on Nieto and Bode's (2008) definition of social justice "as *a philosophy, an approach, and actions that embody treating all people with fairness, respect, dignity, and generosity,*" we add that social justice pedagogy is the *process of engaging in and creating a social-educational system that allows us to move toward equity and fairness for all.* Social justice is both a theoretical and philosophical stance and an active engagement with the world. Just as Indigenous knowledges do not exist in isolation or the abstract, social justice too must be lived. From this perspective, pedagogy is more than simply the act of teaching; it too is an active and critical engagement with the world. Thus, teaching and learning are coterminous; one cannot truly engage in teaching without also being a learner.

What might these understandings of Indigenous knowledges and social justice pedagogy look like in practice? In the remainder of this section, we explore three illustrative examples that suggest the possibilities for "doing" social justice education in ways that embrace Indigenous ways of knowing, learning, and teaching. The examples were selected both for their distinctive qualities (i.e., they are models of pedagogical practice) and their inclusiveness across American Indian, Alaska Native, and Native Hawaiian contexts. As we detail these case examples, we ask readers to consider the ways in which they exemplify the conjoined pedagogical principles we have highlighted in the foregoing sections: place, community, relationships, responsibility, reciprocity, and equity and fairness for all.

Bahidaj High: "Our Alumni are Going to be Tribal Leaders"

Bahidaj High (a pseudonym) is located in an urban metropolitan area of the southwestern U.S.A. Bahidaj is a particularly relevant case for our purposes, as its mission is to serve as an academically rigorous, bicultural, community-based high school for Native American youth. "By infusing all aspects of the educational experience with elements of [Native] language and Native history," a school brochure reads, "the school will nurture individual students, helping them become strong and responsible contributors to their communities."

Approximately 150 students in grades 9 through 12 attend Bahidaj High; many are bused in daily from their home villages on reservation lands some 70 miles away. A former church, repainted in vibrant colors, the school facility is sur-rounded by working gardens and native desert trees planted by students and their teachers that are part of Bahidaj High's ethnobotany and permaculture curriculum. The gardens and a traditional Native outdoor kitchen serve as a gathering place for students, teachers, neighborhood residents, and parents. Inside the school, the organization of space is equally distinctive, with student projects and the Native language evident throughout the building.

Bahidaj High teachers, many of whom are Native American, frequently use the metaphors of family, home, and community to describe their school: As one teacher noted in a 2003 interview with McCarty, the school is "more of a commu-nity school which just happens to be located in an urban setting." A sense of com-munity also grows out of the school's unique mission. Bahidaj educators clearly articulate the social justice dimensions of their work and the belief that schools can be agents of positive social change:

> [E]ducation can enable social change and political change, but . . . with our stu-dent population, it becomes less abstract. Most of our students are [name of tribe] and the [tribal] Nation is very small . . . if we create tribal leaders in the school . . . we have to give them as many responsibilities [and] tools as we can to make decisions in the future. . . . [M]any of our alumni . . . are going to be tribal leaders.
>
> (Bahidaj High educator interview, 2005)

Bahidaj High's curriculum combines Native language and culture with conven-tional courses. English literature courses, for example, emphasize poets and writers of color, including Native American authors. The U.S. history text is Howard Zinn's (2003 [1980]) *A People's History of the United States*, which begins with a cri-tique of the Christopher Columbus story: "Even allowing for the imperfection of myths, it is enough to make us question . . . the excuse of progress in the annihila-tion of races, and the telling of history from the standpoint of the conquerors and leaders of Western civilization" (Zinn, 2003, p. 22). This critique is evident in the writings of Bahidaj High School students: "My teacher doesn't teach us out of a textbook," one student states, "because . . . they're often too one-sided. Instead, she tells us both sides of history"—

> It makes me think of [the Chiricahua Apache leader] Geronimo and what they did to him when he was captured. They dressed him up and made him dance like crazy, just to give the public the idea that Indians acted like that. After learning all that it makes me wonder about what else people lied about.
>
> (Juan, 2003, p. 27)

In addition to Spanish, students' tribal language is taught; even non-Native speak-ing teachers at Bahidaj High take classes in the language. "I choose to learn about my culture," a student states, "so I can know where I come from, and know who I am" (Juan, 2003, p. 29). The primary purpose of these and Native culture classes is to develop a respect for them based on first-hand experience. Of the ethnobotany curriculum, a teacher says: "The presence of a garden in a struggling neighborhood can be a wellspring for building pride and self-esteem" (Woelfle-Erskine, 2003, p. 72).

This experiential, community-based learning is central to the Bahidaj School philosophy and curriculum. Senior capstone projects investigate important issues in students' communities using human as well as textual resources, and including an action component. During a recent school year, one student was researching sweatshops. Another was investigating diabetes in the local Native community and organizing a health fair for younger Native students. Other student projects have included a volunteer mission to Chiapas, Mexico, to help build a school and regular field investigations in the surrounding desert region to learn about the use and terminology of local flora in the Native language and English (Tirado, 2001).

Bahidaj High has consistently demonstrated academic excellence, by its own standards as well as those of the state. Perhaps even more important are students' expressions of the empowerment gained through an education steeped in Indigenous knowledge and social justice pedagogy. "I can always look toward the future," a student writes, "while still looking back at the past to find out who I am. As long as I know my background, I can have some sense of pride, and can know that I won't get lost" (Juan, 2003, p. 29).

Culturally Responsive Schooling in Alaska: "A Firm Grounding in the Language and Culture Indigenous to a Particular Place Is Fundamental"

Treating all people "with fairness, respect, dignity, and generosity" and "moving toward equity and fairness for all" requires new approaches to assessment that hold schools and educators accountable to the children and communities they serve. In Alaska, a statewide initiative has created a parallel set of Native cultural standards and guidelines intended to complement those for mainstream schooling adopted by the state. These cultural standards

> are predicated on the belief that a firm grounding in the heritage language and culture indigenous to a particular place is a fundamental prerequisite for the development of culturally-healthy students and communities associated with that place, and thus an essential ingredient for identifying the appropriate qualities and practices associated with culturally-responsive educators, curriculum, and schools.
>
> (Assembly of Alaska Native Educators [AANE], 1998, p. 2)

The standards grew out of a collaboration between the University of Alaska Fairbanks and the Alaska Federation of Natives, who created the Alaska Native Rural Systemic Initiative (AKRSI), a statewide network of 20 partner school districts representing 176 rural schools and 20,000 primarily Alaska Native students (Barnhardt & Kawagley, 2005). According to Ray Barnhardt and A. Oscar

Kawagley, university-based educators who were instrumental in forming the partnership:

> The activities associated with the AKRSI have been aimed at fostering connectivity and complementarity between the Indigenous knowledge systems . . . and the formal education systems imported to serve the educational needs of rural Native communities. The underlying purpose of these efforts has been to implement research-based initiatives to systematically document the Indigenous knowledge systems of Alaska Native people and to develop pedagogical practices and school curricula that appropriately incorporate Indigenous knowledge and ways of knowing into the formal education system. (2005, p. 15)

The *Alaska Standards for Culturally Responsive Schools*—one outcome of this unique partnership—are guidelines for students, educators, curriculum, and communities intended to ensure that students achieve state standards "in such a way that they become responsible, capable and whole human beings in the process" (AANE, 1998, p. 3). The emphasis is on fostering strong connections between students' in-school and out-of-school lives, recognizing multiple ways of knowing and worldviews.

Within this framework, culturally knowledgeable students are expected to assume responsibilities for the well-being of their communities, recount their family histories, understand the role of the heritage language in their identities, and determine the place of their Native community within wider state, regional, national, and international economic systems (AANE, 1998, p. 5). Culturally responsive educators recognize the validity and integrity of traditional knowledge systems, incorporate the expertise of elders in their teaching, and "continually involve themselves in learning about the local culture" (AANE, 1998, p. 9). A culturally responsive curriculum reinforces the Indigenous knowledge students bring to school, drawing on substantive elements of that knowledge while tapping local languages and oral traditions to plumb deeper meanings. Schools and communities are expected to demonstrate respect for Native elders by providing multiple pathways for them to interact with students and "a place of honor in community functions" (AANE, 1998, pp. 17, 21).

Accompanying the standards are guidelines for preparing culturally responsive teachers, strengthening Indigenous languages, nurturing culturally healthy youth, respecting cultural knowledge, and developing cross-cultural orientation programs. Teacher preparation guidelines, for example, call for developing "a philosophy of education that is able to accommodate multiple world views" (AANE, 1999, p. 4). Further, "teachers should build on students' prior knowledge . . . learn about the local language[s] and culture[s] of the community in which they are situated," and be able to apply local knowledge in the delivery of academic content (AANE, 1999, pp. 4, 8). They should use multiple instructional strategies grounded in local ways of teaching and learning, and a broad assortment of assessment tools "that maximize the opportunities for students to demonstrate their competence"

(AANE, 1999, pp. 12–13). Finally, teachers should work as partners with parents, elders, families, community members, and local school board members, and "engage in critical self-assessment," participating in and learning from local community events in culturally appropriate ways (AANE, 1999, p. 16).

All of these guidelines draw upon the power of place and the principles of community building, reciprocity, responsibility, relationality, and respect. "In the course of implementing AKRSI initiatives," Barnhardt and Kawagley state, "we have come to recognize that there is much more to be gained from further mining the fertile ground that exists within Indigenous knowledge systems" (2005, p. 15). (For more on culturally responsive schooling, see Castagno and Brayboy's [2008] literature review.)

Nāwahī okalani'ōpu'u Laboratory School: "Holding Hawaiian Language and Culture High"

Our final example comes from the U.S. state of Hawai'i. Native Hawaiians face many of the same challenges as American Indians and Alaska Natives, including a history of forced linguistic and cultural assimilation through English-only, Anglo-American schooling. In this context, Nāwahīokalani'ōpu'u Laboratory School (called Nāwahī for short), is making a difference for this Indigenous population.

Nāwahī is a Hawaiian-medium, early childhood through high school affiliation of programs featuring a college preparatory curriculum rooted in Native Hawaiian language and culture. Named for a major nineteenth-century figure in Hawaiian-medium education, the school grows out of the 'Aha Pūnana Leo (Hawaiian "language nest") movement that began in the 1980s. In 1983, a small group of parents and educators established the Pūnana Leo non-profit organization and then its preschools, which enable children to interact with fluent speakers entirely in Hawaiian. The goal is to cultivate children's fluency and knowledge of Hawaiian language and culture, much as occurred in the home in earlier generations. The movement entered the public schools and added a grade a year, reaching intermediate school in 1994, when Nāwahī was founded.

The school teaches all subjects through Hawaiian language and values. According to William H. Wilson, cofounder of the Pūnana Leo and Nāwahī School, English instruction begins in fifth grade with a standard English language arts course; students enroll in such a course every semester through grade 12. Elementary students also study Japanese, and intermediate students study Latin—opportunities for contrastive linguistic analysis with Hawaiian and for building students' multilingual-multicultural skills. And, similar to the ethnobotany curriculum at Bahidaj High, Nāwahī includes a horticulture program emphasizing respect for and sustainability of Native plant life.

Some 2,000 Native Hawaiian students now attend a coordinated set of schools, beginning with Pūnana Leo preschools and moving through Hawaiian immersion elementary and secondary programs. The state of Hawai'i has established a Hawaiian Language College within the University of Hawai'i-Hilo to continue teaching through Hawaiian at the tertiary level; Nāwahī is the university's laboratory school.

Hawaiian-medium schooling has yielded impressive academic results. Nāwahī students, 60 percent of whom come from reduced and free lunch backgrounds, not only surpass their non-immersion peers on English standardized tests, they out-perform the state average for all ethnic groups on high school graduation, college attendance, and academic honors. The school has a 100 percent high school gradu-ation rate and a college attendance rate of 80 percent. School leaders Kauanoe Kamanā and William Wilson attribute these outcomes to an academically chal-lenging curriculum that applies lived experience rooted in Hawaiian identity and culture. Reflecting the principles of place, reciprocity, relationality, and respect, the school has succeeded by "holding Hawaiian language and culture high through the hard work so highly valued by Hawaiian elders. . . . [T]hat hard work means apply-ing oneself in academics to outperform those in mainstream schools to move the Hawaiian people forward" (William H. Wilson, personal communication, July 23, 2008, and September 8, 2008; see also Wilson & Kamanā, 2001, 2006).

Critical Pedagogy, Social Justice, and Indigenous Knowledges—Working Beyond the "Indigenous versus Western" Divide

> If education could do all or if it could do nothing, there would be no reason to speak about its limits. We speak about them, precisely because, in not being able to do everything, education can do something. As educators . . . it behooves us to see what we can do so that we can competently realize our goals.
>
> (Freire, 1993, p. 25)

Critical pedagogue Paulo Freire recorded these thoughts in an interview during his first year as Minister of Education in São Paulo, Brazil. To rephrase Freire's words, recognizing the systemic limits of schooling, it nonetheless "behooves us to see what we can do" to transform the practices that continue to exclude Indigenous knowledges from the schooling experience of Indigenous (and non-Indigenous) youth. In this chapter, we have explored key epistemological, philosophical, and pedagogical "threads" which, when woven together, make up the cultural cloth that we have pluralized with the labels of Indigenous knowledges and ways of knowing. We have also provided examples of how such cultural weavings can be activated in real, live(d) classrooms and schools. Although we have focused on a few key exam-ples, there are many others we might cite that demonstrate the ways in which edu-cation practitioners are bridging the pedagogical divides portrayed in our opening epigraph.

These examples illustrate the spaces of possibility in which Indigenous students are supported in achieving academically by mainstream standards *and* those of their communities. Without ever calling them epistemologies, the educators and communities in the cases profiled here have clearly put into action that which we have spent this chapter describing. These hopeful pedagogical demonstrations point the way beyond the Indigenous—Western divide. In Freire's words, they illuminate "what we *can* do" (our emphasis) to create a critically conscious, socially just, and uplifting education for all learners.

Points of Inquiry

- Given the definition of Indigenous knowledges in this chapter, how might social justice be a "lived pedagogy" for teachers?
- How would you define "place, community, relationships, responsibility, reciprocity, and equity and fairness for all" in your life and community? How do your definitions resonate with or differ from those Brayboy and McCarty discuss for Indigenous knowledges?
- In what ways are "standards for learning" culturally defined? Who creates them? How do they affect the ways diverse students approach "standards for learning" in school?

Points of Praxis

- Ask students to define how culturally based knowledge works in their lives and communities.
- When teaching lessons that reflect particular cultural experiences or worldviews, include a reflective component that allows for comparison among these worldviews.
- Assist students in connecting with a school (public, federal, private) that has a significant Native population. In collaboration with teachers and students at the school, design learning activities and experiences of mutual benefit to all.
- Take advantage of the human and material resources available through community-based American Indian centers, institutions of higher education, and Native American tribal offices to provide accurate and authentic materials and referrals to people who are willing to speak with students on Native American issues. Invite community resource people from diverse communities to participate regularly in learning—teaching experiences in and out of the classroom.

References

Assembly of Alaska Native Educators (AANE). (1998). *Alaska standards for culturally-responsive schools.* Anchorage: Alaska Native Knowledge Network.

Assembly of Alaska Native Educators (AANE). (1999). *Guidelines for preparing culturally responsive teachers for Alaska's schools.* Anchorage: Alaska Native Knowledge Network.

Barnhardt, R., & Kawagley, A. O. (2005). Indigenous knowledge systems and Native Alaska ways of knowing. *Anthropology and Education Quarterly, 36*(1), 8–23.

Basso, K. H. (1996). *Wisdom sits in places: Landscape and language among the Western Apache.* Albuquerque: University of New Mexico Press.

Battiste, M. (2002). Indigenous knowledge and pedagogy in first nations education: A literature review with recommendations. Ottawa: Indian and Northern Affairs Canada.

Begay, S. M., with Clinton-Tullie, V., & Yellowhair, M. (1983). *Kinaaldá: A Navajo puberty ceremony.* Rough Rock, AZ: Navajo Curriculum Center Press, Rough Rock Demonstration School.

Burkhart, B. Y. (2004). What coyote and thales can teach us: An outline of American Indian epistemology. In A. Waters (Ed.), *American Indian thought: Philosophical essays* (pp. 15–26). Oxford: Blackwell.

Castagno, A. E., & Brayboy, B. M. J. (2008). Culturally responsive schooling for Indigenous youth: A review of the literature. *Review of Educational Research, 78*(4), 941–993.

Crawford, J. (Ed.). (1992). *Language loyalties: A source book on the Official English controversy.* Chicago and·London: University of Chicago Press.

Deloria, V., Jr. (Ed.). (1992). American Indian policy in the twentieth century. Norman: University of Oklahoma Press.

Deloria, V., Jr. (2001). Higher education and self-determination. In V. Deloria, Jr., & D. Wildcat, *Power and place: Indian education in America* (pp. 123–133). Golden, CO: American Indian Graduate Center and Fulcrum Resources.

Deloria, V., Jr., & Wildcat, D. R. (2001). *Power and place: Indian education in America.* Golden, CO: American Indian Graduate Center and Fulcrum Resources.

Dick, G. S. (1998). I maintained a strong belief in my language and culture: A Navajo language autobiography. *International Journal of the Sociology of Language, 132,* 23–25.

Eisenhart, M. (2001). Educational ethnography past, present, and future: Ideas to think with. *Educational Researcher, 30*(8), 16–27.

Fixico, D. (2003). *The American Indian mind in a linear world: American Indian studies and traditional knowledge.* New York: Routledge.

Foley, Douglas E. (1996). The silent Indian as a cultural production. In B. A. Levinson, D. E. Foley, & D. C. Holland (Eds.), *The cultural production of the educated person: Critical ethnographies of schooling and local practice* (pp. 79–91). Albany: State University of New York Press.

Freire, P. (1993). *Pedagogy of the city.* New York: Continuum.

Grande, S. (2000). American Indian geographies of identity and power: At the crossroads of Indígena and Mestizaje. *Harvard Educational Review, 70*(4), 467–498.

Hinton, L. (2001). An introduction to the Hawaiian language. In L. Hinton, & K. Hale (Eds.), *The green book of language revitalization in practice* (pp. 129–131). San Diego, CA: Academic Press.

Juan, M. J. (2003). Modern nomad. *110°,* September, pp. 26–30.

Kawagley, A. O. (2006). *A Yupiaq worldview: A pathway to ecology and spirit* (2nd ed.). Prospect Heights, IL: Waveland Press.

Lomawaima, K. T., & McCarty, T. L. (2006). *"To remain an Indian": Lessons in democracy from a century of Native American education.* New York: Teachers College Press.

McCarty, T. L., Wallace, S., Lynch, R., & Benally, A. (1991). Classroom inquiry and Navajo learning styles: A call for reassessment. *Anthropology and Education Quarterly, 22*(1), 42–59.

Manuelito, K. (2005). The role of education in American Indian self-determination: Lessons from the Ramah Navajo Community School. *Anthropology and Education Quarterly, 36*(1), 73–87.

Marker, M. (2003). Indigenous voice, community, and epistemic violence: The ethnographer's "interests" and what "interests" the ethnographer. *Qualitative Studies in Education, 16*(3), 361–375.

Markstrom, C. A. (2008). *Empowerment of North American Indian girls: Ritual expressions at puberty.* Lincoln: University of Nebraska Press.

Medicine, B. (2001). *Learning to be an anthropologist and remaining "native."* Chicago: University of Illinois Press.

Meyer, M. A. (2001). Our own liberation: Reflections on Hawaiian epistemology. *Contemporary Pacific, 13*(1), 124–148.

Nieto, S., & Bode, P. (2008). *Affirming diversity: The sociopolitical context of multicultural education* (5th ed.). Boston: Allyn & Bacon.

Ortiz, S. (1993). The language we know. In P. Riley (Ed.), *Growing up Native American: An anthology* (pp. 29–38). New York: William Morrow.

Stoefle, R., Zedeno, M., & Halmo, D. (2001). *American Indians and the Nevada test site.* Washington, DC: U.S. Government Printing Office.

Tirado, Michelle (2001). Left behind: Are public schools failing Indian kids? *American Indian Report,* (September), 12–15.

Villegas, M., Neugebauer, S. R., & Venegas, K. R. (Eds.). (2008). *Indigenous knowledge and education: Sites of struggle, strength, and survivance.* Harvard Educational Review Reprint Series No. 44. Cambridge, MA: The President and Fellows of Harvard College.

Whitt, L. A. (2004). Biocolonialism and the commodification of knowledge. In A. Waters (Ed.), *American Indian thought: Philosophical essays* (pp. 188–213). Malden, MA: Blackwell.

Wilson, W. H., & Kamanā, K. (2001). *"Mai ioko mai o ka 'Iini:* Proceeding from a dream." The 'Aha Pūnana Leo connection in Hawaiian language revitalization. In L. Hinton, & K. Hale (Eds.), *The green book of language revitalization in practice* (pp. 147–176). San Diego, CA: Academic Press.

Wilson, W. H., & Kamanā, K. (2006). "For the interest of the Hawaiians themselves": Reclaiming the benefits of Hawaiian-medium education. *Hūlili: Multidisciplinary Research on Hawaiian Well-Being, 3*(1), 153–178.

Zinn, H. (2003). *A people's history of the United States: 1492–present.* New York: HarperCollins. (Original work published 1980.)

Chapter 10

Welcoming the Unwelcome
Disability as Diversity

David J. Connor and Susan L. Gabel

This chapter claims disability as a form of human diversity integral to social justice education and multicultural curricula. Using Disability Studies (DS), we confront widespread misconceptions and stereotypes about how disability is conceived in relation to social judgments of human difference. We then relate these notions of difference to implications for education and social justice pedagogy. First, we look at limiting, oppressive conceptualizations of disability that circulate within the dominant discourse of special education. Second, we briefly narrate the origins of DS, and its development of the social model(s) that radically reconceptualized disability. Third, we focus on the value of Disability Studies in Education (DSE) in unlearning pervasive, damaging stereotypes in order to rethink and reteach disability. Fourth, we sample DSE in action. In closing, we make a case for interdisciplinary research and pedagogy, and focus on the growth of DSE as a tool to be used by all social justice educators.

If asked to identify examples of "diversity" cast large, many readers of this book might respond that race, gender, sexual orientation, ethnicity, nationality, social class, and so on, constitute diversity. Civil rights movements have resulted in increased awareness of diversity and increased access to all aspects of society for various groups, although admittedly, we are still a far cry from true equality. In addition to African-Americans, women, gay/lesbian/bisexual/transgender/ queers (GLBTQ), people with disabilities[1] and their allies have also forged a civil rights movement, in an attempt to move them from the margins to center stage. Comprised of an estimated 15 percent of the population (U.S. Census, 2005–7), members of this group have proven to be resolute and subversive. They are resolute because the movement continues to challenge both material and abstract obstructions in the form of physical barriers and human attitudes. They are subversive because although disability has historically been associated with stigma, devaluation, shame, and self-loathing (Goffman, 1963; Stiker, 1999), it now cultivates celebration, value, pride, and self-love (Barnes, Oliver, & Barton, 2002).

Linton (1998) illustrates the resolute and subversive aspects of disability in her classic work *Claiming Disability* where she urges us to think critically about disability, as "a juncture that can serve both academic discourse and social change" (p. 1). In doing so, she identifies academia as complicit with the rest of society stating, "The enormous energy society expends keeping people with disabilities sequestered and in subordinate positions is matched by the academy's effort to justify that isolation and oppression" (p. 3). Why is it, we must ask, "in many progressive spaces where commitments to social justice are real and enduring, the lives and experiences of people with disabilities are sometimes overlooked?" (Hamre, Oyler, & Bejoian, 2006, p. 91). This question becomes even more compelling when considering the fact that disability is experienced by some members of all other identity groups. Recognizing resistance to this reality, Erevelles (2006) notes,

> ... theorists of race, class, gender, and sexual orientation, rather than seeing some commonality with disability have, instead, actively sought to distance themselves from disability, fearing that associating with disability will imply that their difference would equate with a biological deviance/deficit—an association they assume will be even more difficult to critique. (p. 367)

For various reasons including misunderstanding, fear, and ignorance, disability has traditionally been turned away from the table of diversity or has been ignored even as it sits at the table. When disability has been claimed as part of diversity or multiculturalism, critics often counter with: "scholarship on disability will 'water down' the diversity requirement"; "it's not valid scholarship"; "its purpose is to increase self-esteem, or capitulate to interest group pressure"; and "It's not valid or rigorous scholarship" (Linton, Mello, & O'Neill, 1995, p. 9). While some progress in this regard has been made since Linton et al. first made this claim, it is too little progress from our perspective. Of course it has been said that the oppressed are also oppressors, and so it is not altogether unsurprising that "the criticisms previously heard from proponents of the traditional canon are now being used against the inclusion of disability in curriculum transformation efforts" (ibid.). Disability raises an important question: How much diversity can you take (Connor & Baglieri, 2009)?

Rethinking "Special"

Until recently, any reference to disability and education immediately triggered associations with special education, which has largely served as the default box into which all disability issues have been placed (Connor, Gabel, Gallagher, & Morton, 2008). Indeed, special education did offer hope to countless families whose disabled children stayed at home or were placed in institutions because public schools were not required to educate them until 1975 (Safford & Safford, 1996). Over 30 years later, special education is deeply implicated in maintaining racial segregation in schools (Blanchett, 2006; Ferri & Connor, 2006; Losen & Orfield, 2002); stigmatizing difference (Harry & Klingner, 2006; Keefe, Moore, & Duff, 2006; Reid & Valle, 2004); diluting the curriculum (Brantlinger, 2006); segregating, assimilating, and educationally impoverishing many migrant and indigenous children (Gabel, Curcic, Powell, Khader, & Albee, 2009); and contributing to the "school-to-prison pipeline" in which three-quarters of those incarcerated have significant struggles in literacy (Karagiannis, 2000).

For decades, scholars critical of special education[2] have questioned its foundations and the practices they undergird, including: labeling (Carrier, 1986), structuring (Gartner & Lipsky, 1987); segregation (Dunn, 1968; Wang, Reynolds, & Walberg, 1986), pedagogy (Heshusius, 1989, 1995; Iano, 1986, 1990), professionalization (Skrtic, 1991), and institutionalization (Bogden & Taylor, 1989). The work of these scholars has paved the way for other critical special educators who came to find the discipline of DS as more compatible with their beliefs and values. Subsequently, critiques of special education have encompassed: its basis in positivism (Danforth, 1999; Gallagher, 2001); the professionalization of school failure (Ferguson, 2002); an overreliance on interventions aimed at deficits (Hehir, 2005); intelligence testing (see classic analysis by Gould, 1981); segregation (Allan, 1999); and the medicalization of disabled people (Abberley, 1987; Barton, 1996). Taken together, these critiques reveal the limiting, oppressive conceptualizations of disability within special education. Instead, critical special educators situate disability within a sociological context—implicating society as actively disabling people through social practices, beliefs, attitudes, and expectations (Shakespeare, 1994). When this thinking is applied by DSE scholars to schools (Brantlinger, 1997; Danforth, 1997; Gallagher, 2006), the field of special education becomes angry, defensive, and even hostile in its response, dismissing critiques as "scurrilous" (Kauffman, 1995, p. 245) and "foppery" (Kauffman & Sasso, 2006, p. 109). Despite this, we urge that points of contention between "disability fields" be seen as sites rich in potential for generating productive dialogue (Andrews et al., 2000; Gabel & Connor, 2009; Gallagher, 2006). At the same time, we must recognize that special education has traditionally resisted understanding disability outside of medical, scientific, and psychological frameworks—collectively creating a "clinical" disposition (Reid & Valle, 2004). As a result, the field has become static and insular, with little tolerance for non-medicalized framings of disability (Baglieri, Gallagher, Valle, & Connor, in press) or those that shift the focus from the individual to society. In the following section, we illustrate what it means to view disability within a social context, why this reframing radically shifts ways in which disability comes to be understood, and ultimately why this is an issue of social justice.

Alternatives to the Medicalized Master Narrative of Disability

Linton (1998) argues that disability studies arose as the basis from which to examine the construction and function of "disability" in social, cultural, and political terms. Confronting inaccurate and damaging conceptualizations of disability within academic inquiry, disability studies scholars have generated a powerful body of work that was united in its critique of disability conceptualized predominantly as a medical condition or individual experience (Barton, 1996; Davis, 1995, 2002; Garland Thomson, 1997; Oliver, 1990, 1996; Zola, 1982). Many of these scholars are themselves disabled people. As Linton (1998) notes,

> By refusing the medicalization of disability and by reframing disability as a des-
> ignation having primarily social and political significance, disability studies
> points to the inadequacy of the entire curriculum with respect to the study of
> disability. The fault lines that have been exposed stretch from one end of the
> curriculum to the other: from cultural studies to American studies, from
> women's studies to African American studies, from biology to literary criticism,
> from history to psychology, and from special education to philosophy. (p. 3)

Disability, therefore, is not viewed as an individual unit of analysis in the form of a
personal deficit, but rather it is understood within a social model and as located
within "the social world" comprised of human values, beliefs, relationships among
people, and (im)positions of power throughout history. As such, disability is cast as
a social phenomenon, a status ascribed to "others" who do not adhere to required
culturally defined standards of sensory, cognitive, behavioral, and physical
conformity. Priestley (1998) refers to this perspective on the social model as the
"cultural version" in which disability is the "product of specific cultural conditions" (p. 81). In sum, within the social model the ascribed "difference" represented
by disability is not automatically relegated to dysfunction, disorder, or deficit.
Instead, it is understood to be how natural *differences* among humans are
interpreted. The definition of disability, like beauty, is in fact, largely subjective.

In countering the medical model as the master narrative of disability, DS scholars on both sides of the Atlantic and around the rest of the world have developed
eclectic ways of conceptualizing and representing disability. Within this eclecticism, two main fluid strands of thought have emerged from within the United
States (the minority group model) and the United Kingdom (the social model).
These are both worth explaining. Over 30 years ago, borrowing from terminology
of the Civil Rights Movement, Bogdan and Biklen (1977) created the term "handicapism" (consistent with the terminology of the time) to refer to "a set of assumptions and practices that promote the differential and unequal treatment of people
because of apparent or assumed . . . differences" (p. 15). Observing similar circumstances and experiences with other groups, Hahn (2002) notes that disabled people
"have been plagued by . . . high rates of unemployment, poverty, and welfare
dependency; school segregation; inadequate housing and transportation; and
exclusion from many public facilities that appear to be reserved exclusively for the
non-disabled majority" (pp. 171–172). Although Hahn references the social limitations placed upon disabled Americans during the 1970s and 1980s, conditions and
opportunities over 30 years later are still very limited.

It is fitting that the social model of disability has been formulated by Oliver
(1990) in response to *The Fundamental Principles of Disability* (UPIAS, 1975), a
publication generated by members of the Union of Physically Impaired Against
Segregation (UPIAS), an organization in the Disabled People's Movement in the
UK. This document states:

> In our view, it is society which disables physically impaired people. Disability
> is something that is imposed on top of our impairments by the way we are

unnecessarily isolated and excluded from full participation in society. Disabled people are therefore an oppressed group in society. (p. 3)

Clarifying the difference between impairments (functional limitations, or what Danforth calls "bodily differences that matter," personal communication) and disability (a form of social oppression) is the trademark characteristic of the social model of disability (Abberley, 1987; Humphrey, 2000). However, this distinction is debated within Disability Studies. For example: Finkelstein (2003) has argued that it is not a model per se, but an idea stolen from the grassroots Disabled People's Movement by self-serving academics who use it for elitist purposes. Corker and Shakespeare (2002) have argued for the full diversity of *individual* experiences to be recognized, understood, and accepted. Gabel and Peters (2004) speculate on contentious and amorphous ideas that may have outlived their time, yet recognize the value of eclecticism, while urging scholars to clearly define when and how they use "the social model perspective" of disability.

Irrespective of adherence to a minority group or social model (or some other social interpretation of disability), scholars who identify as working within DS are concerned with the inequities that exist for children and adults with disabilities. In particular, they are troubled by general cultural values which inform practices that continue to actively disable people. One major area is that disability is invariably seen as a negative characteristic, a tragedy, and ultimately, an abnormality (Stiker, 1999)—all ableist assumptions (Hehir, 2005). Ableism—analogous to racism, sexism, heterosexism, and so on—is the belief that people with disabilities are inferior to those without them; the former are always perceived to be "lacking" a characteristic (physical, cognitive, sensory, and/or emotional) that robs them of their full humanity. Rausher and McClintock describe ableism as

> A pervasive system of discrimination and exclusion that oppresses people who have mental, emotional, and physical disabilities. . . . Deeply rooted beliefs about health, productivity, beauty, and the value of human life, perpetuated by the public and private media, combine to create an environment that is often hostile to those whose physical, mental, cognitive, and sensory abilities . . . fall out of the scope of what is currently defined as socially acceptable. (1996, p. 198)

The overall devaluation of people with disabilities within the macro level of the larger society is quite transparent in the micro level of policies and practices of schooling. Hehir (2003) notes,

> attitudes that uncritically assert that it is better for a child to walk than roll, speak than sign, read print than read Braille, spell independently than use a spell check, and hangout with nondisabled children rather than with other disabled children. (p. 15)

In sum, attitudes toward and beliefs about disabled people arise from a myriad of negative associations with disability, experienced daily throughout our lives. These associations become inscribed upon people who are deemed outside the realm of normalcy, causing great stigmatization. In his classic text on stigma, Goffman (1963) claims that, "the normal and the stigmatized are not persons but rather perspectives" (p. 138). Furthermore, we agree with Davis's (2002) assertion that "the body is never a physical thing so much as a series of attitudes toward it" (p. 22). It can be argued that attitudes toward those deemed abnormal, whether it be indifference or denigration, play a significant role in preventing access to all aspects of society for people with disabilities.

Disability Studies in Education: Undoing Pervasive Stereotypes

While broad, the work of scholars within DSE is united by a desire to unlearn longstanding stereotypes through critiquing the status quo. Recent scholarship includes: confronting ableism (Danforth & Gabel, 2006); pushing for increased access to mainstream schools and classrooms (Brantlinger, 2004); helping parents of children and youth with disabilities to navigate unfriendly school bureaucracies (Ferguson & Ferguson, 2006); using assistive technology and universal design (Brown & Brown, 2006); disrupting normalcy (Mutua & Smith, 2006); creating a more dynamic, accessible curriculum (Baglieri & Knopf, 2004); teaching disability as a natural part of human diversity (Connor & Bejoian, 2007) and an ethical responsibility (McLean, 2008); connecting international concerns of disability and schooling (Gabel & Danforth, 2008); providing alternatives to medicalized histories of disability (Danforth, 2009); forging interdisciplinary alliances (Ware, 2008); developing qualitative methodologies (Narian, 2008); examining ideologies embedded within language (Danforth, 2008; Broderick & Ne'eman, 2008); challenging the knowledge base of special education (Gallagher, 1998); investigating social policies in relation to disability (Bjarnason, 2008); advocating activism in the policy domain (Gabel, 2008); focusing on the overrepresentation of students of color (Ferri & Connor, 2005); linking medicalized discourses to eugenics (Smith, 2008); and unraveling the myth of the typical child (Baglieri, Bejoian, Broderick, Connor, & Valle, in press). Such a recent burst of activity around disability and education has been a welcome change to the glacial pace of developments in theory, research, and practice within the field of special education.

Within these eclectic works, however, are common strands that unify them into a field. In addition to undermining the euphemism of "exceptionality," and foregrounding material ways in which ableism operates at individual, institutional, societal, and historical domains of education, they also disrupt any comfortable notions of "normalcy." Just as Critical Race Studies serves to unite and clarify issues of race according to those for whom race is usually defined and positioned as inferior, it is equally an educational tool for the dominant group (Whites) to learn about how power operates in invisible/unrecognized ways to privilege some citizens' perceived biological characteristics over others. Similarly, DS foregrounds the concept of disability, allowing those defined as disabled to become the definers, thereby educating the dominant (non-disabled) group to learn how power operates to privilege some citizens over others according to perceived physical, cognitive, emotional, or sensory characteristics.

By questioning the very concept of "disability," Disability Studies forces us to look at, and question, the concept of normalcy—ultimately viewing it as a social construction, subject to many cultural influences including beliefs of difference and societal expectations as to what a body ought to look like and should be able to do. That the number of children and youth with disabilities in schools has grown enormously due to more disabilities being "identified" (a special education perspective) or disability being "manufactured" (a Disability Studies perspective), a distinction for the reader to contemplate. Regardless of perspective, the implications are the same in that the notion of an idealized American citizen has remained remarkably constant—and does not encompass "the disabled." In his study on stigma published in the early 1960s, Goffman notes that, "in an important sense there is only one complete unblushing male in America: a young, married, white, urban, northern, heterosexual Protestant father of college education, fully employed, of good complexion, weight, and height, and a recent record in sports" (p. 128). Being "all American" paints almost the exact same picture in the mind's cultural eye, maintaining most, if not all, of these characteristics. This concept of an ideal citizen promises full status within normalcy and guarantees admittance (and usually acceptance) into all domains of society. Yet such idealization is fundamentally challenged on many levels by disability. As pointed out by Murphy (1995),

> The pursuit of the slim, well-muscled body is not only an aesthetic matter, but also a moral imperative. . . . It hardly needs saying that the disabled, individually and as a group, contravene all the values of youth, virility, activity, and physical beauty that Americans cherish, however little most individuals may embody them. (p. 153)

Without a doubt, notions of an idealized, desirable citizen mirrored in a perfect, Greek God-like body undergird our society. Outside of these parameters, disability is viewed as an undesirable deviation from the norm, an aberration, an abnormality. Yet, positioned outside of the socially sanctioned norm, people with disabilities have rightfully asked: Who (re)creates that norm? Why has it been (re)created? Where was it (re)created? When was it (re)created? Who are positioned the "insiders" and who the "outsiders"? Who becomes advantaged and who disadvantaged by this arrangement? Indeed, we come to see that just as the world is racialized, gendered, and sexualized, it is also profoundly normalized. Garland Thomson (1997) has referred to the "normate," a non-stigmatized, desirable citizen, constructed through hundreds-upon-hundreds of daily acts that define and reinforce normalcy. Conversely, through relentless definitions of normalcy, abnormalcy becomes reified, reinforcing normalcy. As Davis (2002) points out,

> Whether we are talking about AIDS, low birth weight babies, special education issues, euthanasia, and the thousand other topics listed in the newspapers every day, the examination, discussion, anatomizing this form of "difference"

is nothing less than a desperate attempt by people to consolidate their normalcy. (p. 117)

What, then, are educators to make of normalcy in schools? How does general education and its domain of normalcy reinforce special education's position of abnormalcy, and vice versa? Rigid school operations such as standardized norms, age and grade level "appropriate" expectations, ability tracking, ritualized behaviors, heavily bureaucratized practices around documentation of disability, all pivot around the axle of normalcy, leading Baker (2002) to refer to such practices as "the hunt for disability" in classrooms. The ever-growing numbers of students labeled Behavior Disordered (BD), emotionally disturbed (ED), learning disabled (LD), Cognitively Impaired (CI), Attention Deficit Disorder (ADD), Attention Deficit Hyperactivity Disorder (ADHD), Oppositional Defiant Disorder (ODD), Speech and Language Disorder (S & L), Autistic Impairment (AI), and so on, are evidence of a fixation within education to locate, and then usually relocate, children who are not viewed by experts as sufficiently normal in terms of behaving, learning, focusing, following instructions, and speaking correctly. Disability studies believes instead of seeking purported "intrinsic deficits" within children and youth, more can be gained by holding a mirror up to the institution of schooling and commonplace practices within it. By doing so, what becomes revealed is "the ways that bodies interact with the socially engineered environment and confirm to social expectations [and] determine the varying degrees of disability or able-bodiedness, or extra-ordinariness" (Garland Thomson, 1997, p. 7). When thinking about how people's bodies interact with the environment, the dominant medical model of disability that upholds the pseudo-scientific discourse within schooling is revealed to be not only highly restrictive, but actually detrimental to students. In pathologizing human difference, education's relentless obsession with student weaknesses is at the expense of neglecting their strengths and talents, perpetuating inequalities and creating potential life-long stigmatization.

Regardless of whether they identify as special or general educators (a problematic "forced" choice in and of itself), critical educators recognize how disability presented within traditional special education is cast within scientific/medical/psychological (clinical) understandings complete with expectations of treatment, remediation, and cure—being restored, or at least approximating as close as possible, to normalcy. As Christensen (1996) observes, "schooling itself is disabling, that its lack of flexibility in accommodating a diverse range of learners creates disabled students" (p. 65). By focusing on the overall system rather than on the child as the site of responsibility, teachers and scholars in the field of DS engage in combating ableism and embracing human difference without stigmatizing it. In addition, they also seek maximum access to educational opportunities for *all* students. As Sapon-Shevin explains, "educators need to transcend discussions of diversity as a classroom problem and regard it as natural, desirable, and inevitable occurrence that enriches educational experiences for both teachers and students" (2000, p. 34). In keeping with this sentiment, we believe that educators can, and must, go beyond acceptance of disability as diversity; it is imperative that they actively teach about it, including its history, its culture, and the ways in which people are disabled by barriers. In the next section, we sample some ways in which educators can provide students with information and resources that help them learn about disability as diversity—and promote critical thinking that supports social change throughout the curriculum.

Actively Using DSE/Cripping the Curriculum

Of vital importance to DSE is having teachers to first recognize the dominant discourse about disability that circulates throughout education, or what Swartz (1992) calls "The Master Script." "Master scripting," he explains, "silences multiple voices and perspectives, primarily by legitimizing dominant, White, upper-class, male voicing's as the 'standard' knowledge students need to know" (p. 341). Other scripts are deliberately omitted, or reshaped within the master script for assimilationist purposes; the more contrary the other script, the greater likelihood of its exclusion or radical morphing, thereby ensuring a continuation of the dominant discourse. Scholars working within DSE commonly experience being subjected to master scripting by the major journals in the field of special education—highly medicalized in their understanding of disability (Gallagher, Heshusius, Iano, & Skrtic, 2004), resistant and generally unwilling to publish DSE scholarship. Indeed the deep and entrenched separation of "special" and "general" reveals how the master script of ability has cleft our *initial* conceptualizations of education. This arrangement is highly troublesome as it divides and labels teachers, resulting in one group being experts and having "ownership" of students with disabilities, while the other group comes to see these euphemistically labeled "special" children actually belonging to the realm of other "special" educators. In many cases, general educators are inculcated into a higher education discourse that largely absolves them from contemplating children labeled disabled in terms of their own responsibility. Indeed, many come to see disability-related issues as synonymous with "problems" only to be solved by specialists.

Rather than viewing students with disabilities as problem individuals who always need accommodations and modifications, i.e., creating extra work for teachers, we advocate for all teachers to develop their skills in Universal Design (UD).[3] Simply stated, Universal Design originated in terms of architecture, with the idea that environments should be created from their inception as accessible to all people. When applied to creating classroom environments, these principles become known as universal design for instruction (UDI) (Burgstahler & Cory, 2008) or universal design for learning (UDL, see www.cast.org). Guiding principles include creating a classroom with: equalizing the use of materials in varied formats; providing flexibility of pedagogical methods; engaging in simple and intuitive instruction; providing of perceptible information; tolerating error; minimizing fatigue; ensuring size and space for moving around and using materials; structuring multiple interactions to build a community of learners; instruction designed to be welcoming and inclusive.

Using a UD approach means educators arguably adopt a *proactive* stance toward instructing students with diverse abilities, instead of a *reactive* response that often translates into what is perceived as time-consuming retrofitting of classrooms and curricula. Instead of having a singular "average" student in mind, it is more beneficial to imagine a broad array of individual learners when teachers envision their classrooms. Although changes made through Universal Design were originally intended for people who have disabilities, they also benefit others in the population. One example is corner curb cuts for wheelchair users that become utilized by people who wheel strollers, roll luggage cases, and deliver large or heavy items that need to be rolled. Similarly, in classrooms, the simple premise of having instructions in writing, read out loud, and then discussed benefits the majority of students. Oftentimes, it is helpful to teachers' understanding of UD to simply convey that this approach provides *access* to the classroom and curriculum. Perhaps stating the obvious, it is also important to note that disability is merely one of many characteristics that also include learning styles, interests, talents, culture, and background knowledge, and the concept of "universal" applies to variation among *all* of us according to gender, social class, national status, racial and ethnic backgrounds, sexual orientation, and other markers of identity.

In addition to recognizing and then rewriting the master script, and creating classrooms built upon the premise of UD, it is vital that teachers develop ways in which to teach disability as diversity. Banks (1994) outlines five dimensions of multicultural education that are perfectly apt applied to disability: (1) diversity must be integrated into the content, not an additive approach; (2) the origins and construction of knowledge is made transparent, including how various ways of thinking have influenced scholars; (3) a proactive approach is used to reduce prejudice and helps cultivate positive attitudes to different groups; (4) equitable pedagogy is used that encourages diverse forms of social interactions; and (5) an empowering school culture is consciously developed. These dimensions guide and support a transformative approach to teaching and learning, including epistemological contributions of formerly marginalized groups, to ensure valuing a plurality of perspectives.

Implicit in UD and the five dimensions listed above is the need to rethink how we "do" education. The most important part of "doing" education is classroom practice, including how and what teachers teach about disability, and what and how students learn about disability. Due to the space restrictions of this chapter, we have limited the amount of suggestions available for "cripping the curriculum" (Connor & Bejoian, 2007) confining our comments to a sample of possibilities of teaching disability throughout the K-12 curriculum. For others, please see Gabel and Connor (2009), Ferguson (2001), and the Syracuse University-sponsored website (www.disabilitystudiesforteachers.org).

Generally speaking, children's literature featured within elementary schools has been critiqued for erroneously representing the lives of people (often children) with disabilities (Blaska, 2004; Worotynec, 2004; A. Shapiro, 1999; Ziegler, 1980), predominantly portraying them as "poor little things" and "brave little souls" designed to evoke admiration and/or pity (Ayala, 1999, p. 103). This trend can be countered by teaching within the broad context of diversity/difference using perennial favorites such as *Chrysanthemum* (Henkes, 1996), *Charlotte's Web* (White, 1952/2004), and *The Secret Garden* (Burnett, 1909). Student-centered discussions can focus on: In what ways is the character different? What do other characters think of her/him? What happens to the character because of her/his difference? In turn, how does that character respond? What can we learn and appreciate about the big idea of difference by coming to know this character?

Another way of teaching disability is to provide progressive representations to juxtapose with classic, stereotypical characters such as Tiny Tim in *A Christmas Carol* (Dickens, 1843/1986). Contemporary tales such as *The Fly Who Couldn't Fly* (Lozoff, 2002), *Mandy Sue's Day* (Karim, 1994), and *Lester's Dog* (Hesse, 1993) foster more nuanced, positive representations of disability. When doing this, it is important to avoid exaggeration in the opposite direction of the Tiny Tim stereotype—toward the "super crip." Both stereotypes are harmful. Bearing this in mind, Myers and Bersani (2009) advocate that teachers analyze all books for potentially ableist characters and plotlines that miseducate children, asking themselves questions such as: Does the book promote ableism by ignoring people with disabilities? Are characters with disabilities portrayed as three-dimensional people who belong or as flat, stereotyped outsiders? Are characters with disabilities ever in the role of hero, or are they always victims to be rescued by the hero?

While any grade level is a good level to address issues of language, middle school years are rife with putdowns by peers—said in both seriousness and in jest—revealing the widespread use of disability-related language with demeaning connotations. Examples include the ubiquitous refrain "that's retarded" (also widely used by educators), along with: "Are you blind?"; "Are you deaf?"; "That's dumb"; "He's crazy"; "She's nuts"; "I'm such a spaz"; "That's so lame"; "Moron," and so on. Students can discuss: What are the implications of these associations? What may people with disabilities think about able-bodied people using this language? Why is it socially permitted to use "retard" when other hateful words such as "bitch," "nigger," "faggot," and "dyke" are not tolerated? What does that tell us about the status of people with disabilities?

Whether in middle or high school, students learn about the Civil Rights Movements. Teachers must ask themselves: What groups are included or excluded—African-Americans? Women? GLBTQ? People with disabilities? Each group has organized at the grassroots level and forged onward despite considerable social and cultural opposition, to gain political power that ensures greater access to various rights and protections in terms of employment, education, health care, transportation, and community integration. When focusing on the Disability Rights Movement (a phenomenon that is often unrecognized and rarely included), emphasis can be placed on the activists who organized demonstrations, staged sit-ins, and argued vociferously to speak for themselves and finally be heard. From an activist's perspective, being able to *get on* a public bus was the first symbolic move (Fleischer & Zames, 2001). Students can evaluate in what ways the Disability Rights Movement is similar to and different from other important movements, in addition to describing the breadth and limitations of each.

Several middle school level texts feature interesting, progressive portrayals of main characters with disabilities/differences, and can be employed as a "read-aloud" to encourage student discussions. One example is *Stuck in Neutral*

(Trueman, 2001), in which the narrator is a teenager with multiple disabilities who is unable to speak, and comes to believe his father is preparing to carry out a "mercy killing" on him. Another example is *Freak the Mighty* (Philbrick, 1995), a tale of companionship between a large, awkward, cognitively impaired adolescent and a small, smart, physically frail child in a world that is hostile to both of them. Friendship is forged through respect of each other, including a mutual understanding of their differences/disabilities.

In high school, students' awareness of the complex nature of the world increases, and they create connections among multiple sources of information. At this age, students are able to understand the idea of disability as a minority status, and it can be explored with other "markers of identity" such as race, gender, ethnicity, and sexual orientation (Gordon & Rosenblum, 2001). Students can also contemplate: when people with disabilities claim kinship as a minority group, how might that change their self-perception, and how non-disabled people view them? Students can also explore some of the inequalities faced by people with disabilities that, until pointed out to the majority group, usually go "unseen" and therefore unacknowledged.

Finally, using film to teach disability is an excellent tool since this medium is the "text" with which students interact more than the written word. The vast majority of films portray people with disabilities inaccurately (Darke, 1998), and depictions can be explored and challenged through a rigorous analysis of ableism (Safran, 1998, 2002). For example, Al Pacino's Academy Award ® winning performance as a blind war veteran in *Scent of a Woman* is of a self-loathing, bitter, lonely, angry, socially estranged man (stereotype) who has an incredible sense of smell (myth), feels faces to "see" (myth), and is suicidal (myth). In what ways can students discuss blindness as an everyday experience in the world that is actually "normal" for some people? More accurate representations can be found in films such as: *Rory O'Shea Was Here* (young adults with disabilities assert their rights to live where they want); *The Station Agent* (a little person leading a "normal" life); and *Finding Nemo* (having a "gimpy" body part is only one aspect of a person).

Conclusion: Disability Studies in Education as a Tool for All Educators

Given the breadth of issues pertinent to disability studies, it is clear that there is great potential within the umbrella of social justice education for interdisciplinary theorizing and research. Ultimately, opportunities are only meaningful if they can influence changes in attitudes and policies that in turn transform structural arrangements and instructional classroom practices to promote equity among *all* citizens. Elsewhere, we have theorized about the value of intersectional approaches to understanding complex phenomena (as abilities and disabilities cannot exist free of context), and focusing on commonalities with and dissonance among DSE and Multiculturalism, Critical Race Studies, and Queer Theory (Gabel & Connor, 2009). We acknowledge that there is still much work to be done in exploring interdisciplinary scholarship within social justice, and believe that this edited book actively fosters such thinking. In many ways, it is important that all of us are receptive to, and see the value of, intersectional approaches. As previously mentioned, every one of us is raced, nationalized, ethnicized, gendered, dis/abled, sexualized, and so on. Disability studies scholar Vic Finkelstein asserts, "disabled people's control over their lives and disability is not a single issue" (Campbell & Oliver, 1996, p. 64). Disability is therefore inextricably combined with other markers of identity that influence human experience, these can never be entirely untangled. Altogether, Garland Thomson (1997) believes they constitute "related products of the same social process and practices that shape bodies according to ideological structures" (p. 136). Intersectionality with dis/ability requires us to think about ways in which multiple discourses together create multidimensional experiences, thereby enriching previously held notions of how we all come to know and understand our lives.

The historian Catherine Kudlick (2003) has made a compelling case for "Why we need another 'other'," foregrounding the concept of disability to help us address fundamental questions such as: "What does it mean to be human? How can we respond ethically to difference? What is the value of a human life? Who decides these questions, and what do these answers reveal?" (¶ 1). Disability, the formerly uninvited guest at the table of diversity in academia and all that it influences, now brings new ways of seeing where and how discrimination exists, and ways to counter social injustices based on physical, cognitive, behavioral, and sensory differences. Turning "normalcy" on its head by refuting its solidity and contesting its stability, DSE invites us all to rethink some of our most fundamental assumptions about where and how to educate everyone in a democracy.

Points of Inquiry

- Why would other oppressed groups distance themselves from the disabled? How do notions of deficit tied to biology work in the production of group identities? Research the history of representation of a racialized, gendered, or classed group.

- How can identity groups find points of affirmation and solidarity with one another? What points of structural and/or experiential intersection can you identify that would further this project?

- If, as Connor and Gabel claim, disability is frequently manufactured as a form of "othering" in schools, what reasons and evidence can you provide for this?

- Simi Linton claims that a critical look at disability can serve as a catalyst to social change. In what ways might this be true? In what ways is the argument problematic?

- In what ways does the Disability Rights Movement parallel other civil rights movements? How does it diverge?

- Why does disability "tip the scales" in how diversity is currently conceived in programs of education? What can be done to further dialogue around what "counts" as diversity?

- Will there always be competition among disenfranchised and oppressed groups? How can educators mediate issues of "who belongs" and how students come to better understand the histories, values, contributions, and experiences of one another?

Points of Praxis

- Critical Race Theory gives us the tool of counterstory to the majoritarian story, or master script. How can you engage your students in counterstories by and about people marked as "disabled"?
- Identify daily acts and procedures at your site that define and reinforce normalcy in terms of ability—as well as race, gender, sexual orientation, and so on. In what ways do these acts influence all individuals?
- In what ways does ableism operate unconsciously (or consciously) within your site? How might the instances that you identify be addressed?
- Describe the relationship(s) between and among students ("disabled" and "normal"), parents, administrators, aides, and teachers at your site. Who is responsible for what with whom? Who is integrated with whom, segregated from whom, and delegated responsibility for whom?
- How does master scripting influence curricular content in your experience and observation? What alternative curricular approaches exist?
- Who is responsible for providing access and equity at your site? Why?
- Transform standard(ized) content and/or curriculum using Universal Design for Instruction (UDI). You may want to start with a lesson or unit plan, or address broad literacy and numeracy goals.
- If you teach a "homogenous" group of students, none of whom are labeled as disabled, how can you raise the issues that Connor and Gabel describe effectively in your practice?
- What is the "language" of disability in your site? Where does it originate? Who uses it in what circumstances? What values are inherent in the language used? How does the language position people with (and without) disabilities? In what ways can language be rethought and taught?
- Given the widespread, and largely unrecognized characterization of people with disabilities, both in and out of school environments, is it a moral imperative to teach disability?

Notes

1   The term "people with disabilities" denotes people-first language. This choice is made to counter language that emphasizes deficits, such as "autistic boy" or "dyslexic woman,"

that emphasizes disability as *the* primary marker of identity. However, we acknowledge that the term "disabled people," emanating from a social model of disability is also valid, even preferable in many cases, as the term accurately describes how societal practices *actively disable* certain people because of their "differences" or impairments.

2   Many scholars who identify as working within DSE also self-identify as critical special educators.

3   It must be noted that for some students, accommodations may still be needed (or even legally required) within UD.

References

Abberley, P. (1987). The concept of oppression and the development of a social theory of disability. *Disability, Handicap, and Society 2*(1), 5–19.

Allan, J. E. (1999). *Actively seeking inclusion: Pupils with special needs in mainstream schools.* London: Falmer.

Andrews, J. E., Carnine, D. W., Coutinho, M. J., Edgar, E. B., Forness, S. R., Fuchs, L. S., Jordan, D., Kauffman, J. M., Patton, J. M., Paul, J., Rosell, J., Rueda, R., Schiller, E., Skrtic, T. M., & Wong, J. (2000). Bridging the special education divide. *Remedial and Special Education, 21*(5), 258–267.

Ayala, E. C. (1999). "Poor little things" and "brave little souls": The portrayal of individuals with disabilities in children's literature. *Reading Research and Instruction, 39*(1), 103–116.

Baglieri, S., & Knopf, J. (2004). Normalizing difference in inclusive teaching. *Journal of Learning Disabilities, 37*(6), 525–529.

Baglieri, S., Gallagher, D., Valle, J. W., & Connor, D. J. (in press). Disability studies in education: The need for a plurality of perspectives. *Remedial and Special Education.*

Baglieri, S., Bejoian, L., Broderick, A., Connor, D. J., & Valle, J. W. (in press). (Re)claiming "inclusive education" toward cohesion in educational reform: Disability studies unravels the myth of the normal child. *Teachers College Record.*

Baker, B. (2002). The hunt for disability: The new eugenics and the normalization of school children. *Teachers College Record, 104,* 663–703.

Banks, J. A. (1994). Transforming the mainstream curriculum. *Educational Leadership, 51*(8), 4–8.

Barton, L. (Ed.). (1996).*Disability and society: Emerging issues and insights.* London/New York: Longman.

Barnes, C., Oliver, M., & Barton, L. (Eds.). (2002). *Disability studies today.* Malden, MA: Blackwell.

Bjarnason, D. S. (2008). Private troubles or public issues? The social construction of "the disabled baby" in the context of social policy and social technological changes. In S. Gabel and S. Danforth (Eds.), *Disability and the politics of education: An international reader* (pp. 251–274). New York: Peter Lang.

Blanchett, W. (2006). Disproportionate representation of African American students in special education: Acknowledging the role of white privilege and racism. *Educational Researcher, 35*(6), 24–28.

Blaska, J. (2004). Children's literature that includes characters with disabilities or illnesses. *Disability Studies Quarterly, 24*(1). Retrieved from: http://www.dsq-sds.org/article/view/854/1029

Blaska, J. K., & Lynch, E. C. (1998). Is everyone included? Using children's literature to facilitate the understanding of disabilities. *Young Children, 53*(2), 36–38.

Bogdan, R., & Bicklen, D. (1977). Handicapism. *Social Policy, 7*(5), 14–19.

Bogdan, R., & Taylor, S. (1989). Relationships with severely disabled people: The social construction of humanness. *Social Problems 36*(2), 135–147.

Brantlinger, E. A. (1997). Using ideology: Cases of nonrecognition of the politics of research and practice in special education. *Review of Educational Research, 67*(4), 425–459.

Brantlinger, E. A. (2004). Confounding the needs and confronting the norms: An extension of Reid & Valle's essay. *Journal of Learning Disabilities, 37*(6), 490–499.

Brantlinger, E. A. (Ed.). (2006). *Who benefits from special education? Remediating (fixing) other people's children.* Mahwah, NJ: Lawrence Erlbaum.

Broderick, A., & Ne'eman, A. (2008). Autism as metaphor: Narrative and counter narrative. *International Journal of Inclusive Education, 12*(5–6), 459–476.

Brown, P. A., & Brown, S. E. (2006). Accessible information technology in education: Addressing the "separate but equal" treatment of disabled individuals. In S. Danforth & S. Gabel (Eds.), *Vital questions facing disability studies in education* (pp. 253–270). New York: Peter Lang.

Burgstahler, S., & Cory, R. (2008). Moving in from the margins: From accommodation to universal design. In S. L. Gabel & S. Danforth (Eds.), *Disability studies in education: An international reader* (pp. 561–581). New York: Peter Lang.

Burnett, F. H. (1909). *The secret garden.* New York: Harper Classics.

Campbell, J., & Oliver, M. (1996). *Disability politics: Understanding our past, changing our future.* New York: Routledge.

Carrier, J. G. (1986). *Learning disability: Social class and the construction of inequality in American education.* Westport, CT: Greenwood Press.

Christensen, C. (1996). Disabled, handicapped or disordered: "What's in a name?" In C. Christensen & F. Rizvi (Eds.), *Disability and the dilemmas of educational justice* (pp. 63–77). Buckingham: Open University Press.

Connor, D. J., & Baglieri, S. (2009). Tipping the scales: Disability studies asks "How much diversity can you take?" In Shirley Steinberg (Ed.), *Diversity: A Reader* (pp. 341–361). New York: Peter Lang

Connor, D. J., & Bejoian, L. (2007). Cripping school curricula: 20 ways to re-teach disability. *Review of Disability Studies, 3*(3), 3–13.

Connor, D. J., Gabel, S., Gallagher, D., & Morton, M. (2008). Disability studies and inclusive education—implications for theory, research, and practice. *International Journal of Inclusive Education, 12*(5–6), 441–457.

Corker, M., & Shakespeare, T. (Eds.). (2002). *Disability/postmodernity.* London: Continuum.

Danforth, S. (1997). On what basis hope? Modern progress and postmodern possibilities. *Mental Retardation 35*(2), 93–106.

Danforth, S. (1999). Pragmatism and the scientific validation of professional practices in American special education. *Disability and Society 14*(6), 733–751.

Danforth, S. (2008). Using metaphors to research the cultural and ideological construction of disability. In S. Gabel and S. Danforth (Eds.), *Disability and the politics of education: An international reader* (pp. 385–400). New York: Peter Lang.

Danforth, S. (2009). *The incomplete child: An intellectual history of learning disabilities.* New York: Peter Lang.

Danforth, S., & Gabel, S. L. (Eds.). (2006). *Vital questions for disabilities studies in education.* New York: Peter Lang.

Darke, P. (1998). Understanding cinematic representations of disability. In T. Shakespeare (Ed.), *The disabilities studies reader: Social science perspectives* (pp. 181–197). London: Cassel.

Davis, L. J. (1995). *Enforcing normalcy: Disability, deafness and the body.* London: Verso.

Davis, L. J. (2002). *Bending over backwards: Disability, dismodernism, and other difficult positions.* New York: New York University Press.

Dickens, C. (1843/1986). *A Christmas carol.* New York: Bantam Classics.

Dunn, L. M., (1968). Special education for the mildly retarded: Is much of it justifiable? *Exceptional Children, 35*(1), 5–22.

Erevelles, N. (2006). How does it feel to be a problem? Race, disability, and exclusion in educational policy. In E. A. Brantlinger (Ed.), *Who benefits from special education? Remediating (fixing) other people's children* (pp. 77–99). Mahwah, NJ: Lawrence Erlbaum.

Ferguson, P. M. (2001). *On infusing disability studies into the general curriculum. On Point . . . Brief Discussions of Critical Issues.* Washington, DC: Special Education Programs (ED/OSERS). Retrieved July 25, 2006, from: http://www.urbanschools.org/pdf/OPdisability.pdf?v_document_name=On%20Infusing%20Disability%20Studies

Ferguson, P. M. (2002). Notes toward a history of hopelessness: Disability and the places of therapeutic failure. *Disability, Culture and Education, 1*(1), 27–40.

Ferguson, P. M., & Ferguson, D. (2006). Finding the "proper attitude": The potential of disability studies to reframe family/school linkages. In S. Danforth & S. Gabel (Eds.), *Vital questions facing disability studies in education* (pp. 217–235). New York: Peter Lang.

Ferri, B. A., & Connor, D. J. (2005). Tools of exclusion: race, disability, and (re)segregated education. *Teachers College Record, 107*(3), 453–474.

Ferri, B. A., & Connor, D. J. (2006). *Reading resistance: Discourses of exclusion in the desegregation and inclusion debates.* New York: Peter Lang.

Finkelstein, V. (2003). *The social model of disability repossessed.* Retrieved September 15, 2004, from: http://www.leeds.ac.uk/disability-studies/archiveuk/finkelstein/soc%20mod%20repossessed.pdf

Fleischer, D. Z., & Zames, F. (2001). *The disability rights movement: From charity to confrontation.* Philadelphia: Temple University Press.

Flynn, J. (Producer), & O'Donnell, D. (Director) (2004). *Rory O'Shea Was Here.* [Motion picture]. Focus Features.

Gabel, S. L. (2008). A model for policy activism. In S. Gabel and S. Danforth (Eds.), *Disability and the politics of education: An international reader* (pp. 311–331). New York: Peter Lang.

Gabel, S., & Connor, D. J. (2009). Theorizing disability: Implications and applications for social justice in education. In W. Ayers, T. Quinn, & D. Stovall (Eds.), *Handbook of Social Justice* (pp. 377–399). New York: Lawrence Erlbaum.

Gabel, S. L., Curcic, S., Powell, J., Khader, K., & Albee, L. (2009). Migration and ethnic group disproportionality in special education: An exploratory study. *Disability & Society, 24*(5), 625–639.

Gabel, S. L., & Peters, S. (2004). Presage of a paradigm shift? Beyond the social model of disability toward a resistance theory of disability. *Disability and Society, 19*(6), 571–596.

Gabel, S. L., & Danforth, S. (2008). *Disability and the politics of education: An international reader.* New York: Peter Lang.

Gabel, S. L., & Connor, D. J. (2009). Theorizing disability: Implications and applications for social justice in education. In W. Ayres, T. Quinn, & D. Stovall (Eds.), *Handbook of social justice in education* (pp. 377–399). New York: Routledge.

Gallagher, D. J. (1998). The scientific knowledge base of special education: Do we know what we think we know? *Exceptional Children, 64*(4), 493–502.

Gallagher, D. J. (2001). Neutrality as a moral standpoint, conceptual confusion and the full inclusion debate. *Disability & Society 16*(5), 637–654.

Gallagher, D. J. (2006). If not absolute objectivity, then what? A reply to Kauffman and Sasso. *Exceptionality, 14*(2), 91–107.

Gallagher, D. J., Heshusius, L., Iano, R. P., & Skrtic, T. M. (2004). *Challenging orthodoxy in special education: Dissenting voices.* Denver, CO: Love.

Garland Thomson, R. (1997). *Extraordinary bodies.* New York: Columbia University Press.

Gartner, A., & Lipsky, D. (1987). Beyond special education: Toward a system of quality for all students. *Harvard Educational Review, 57*(4), 367–395.

Goffman, E. (1963). *Stigma: Notes on the management of spoiled identity.* New York: Simon & Schuster.

Gordon, B. O., & Rosenblum, K. E. (2001). Bringing disability into the sociological frame: A comparisson of disability with race, sex, and sexual orientation statuses. *Disability & Society, 16*(1), 5–19.

Gould, S. J. (1981). *The mismeasure of man.* New York: W. W. Norton.

Hahn, H. (2002). Academic debates and political advocacy: The US disability movement. In C. Barnes, M. Oliver, & L. Barton (Eds.), *Disability studies today* (pp. 162–189). Cambridge: Polity Press.

Hamre, B., Oyler, C., & Bejoian, L. B. (2006). Guest editors' introduction. Narrating disability: pedagogical imperatives. *Equity & Excellence in Education, 39*(2), 91–100.

Harry, B., & Klingner, J. (2006). *Why are so many minority students in special education?* New York: Teachers College Press.

Hehir, T. (2003). Beyond inclusion. *School Administrator, 60*(3), 36–39.

Hehir, T. (2005). *New directions in special education: Eliminating ableism in policy and practice.* Cambridge, MA: Harvard University Press.

Henkes, K. (1996). *Chrysanthemum.* New York: Harper.

Heshusius, L. (1989). The Newtonian mechanistic paradigm, special education, and contours of alternatives: An overview. *Journal of Learning Disabilities, 22*(7), 403–415.

Heshusius, L. (1995). Holism and special education: There is no substitute for real life purposes and processes. In T. M. Skrtic (Ed.), *Disability and democracy: Reconstructing (special) education for postmodernity* (pp. 166–189). New York: Teachers College Press.

Hesse, K. (1993). *Lester's dog.* New York: Crown.

Humphrey, J. C. (2000). Researching disability politics, or, some problems with the social model in practice. *Disability & Society, 15*(1), 63–85.

Iano, R. (1986). The study and development of teaching: With implications for the advancement of special education. *Remedial and Special Education, 75*(5), 50–61.

Iano, R. (1990). Special education teachers: Technicians or educators? *Journal of Learning Disabilities, 23*, 462–465.

Karagiannis, A. (2000). Soft disability in schools: Assisting or confining at risk children and youth? *Journal of Educational Thought, 34*(2), 113–134.

Karim, R. (1994). *Mandy Sue's day.* New York: Clarion Books.

Kauffman, J. M. (1995). Commentary: Today's special education and its messages for tomorrow. *Journal of Special Education, 32*(4), 244–254.

Kauffman, J. M., & Sasso, G. M. (2006). Certainty, doubt, and the reduction of uncertainty. *Exceptionality, 14*(2), 109–120.

Keefe, E. B., Moore, V., & Duff, F. R. (2006). *Listening to the experts: Students with disabilities speak out.* Baltimore, MD: Paul H. Brookes.

Kudlick, C. J. (2003). Disability history: Why we need another "other." Retrieved August 22, 2008, from: http://www.hostorycooperative.org

Linton, S. (1998). *Claiming disability.* New York: New York University Press.

Linton, S., Mello, S., & O'Neill, J. (1995). Disability studies: Expanding the parameters of diversity. *Radical Teacher, 47*, 4–10.

Losen, D., & Orfield, G. (2002). *Racial inequity in special education.* Cambridge, MA: Harvard University Press.

Lozoff, B. (2002). *The wonderful life of a fly who couldn't fly.* Charlottesville, VA: Hampton.

McLean, M. A. (2008). Teaching about disability: An ethical responsibility? *International Journal of Inclusive Education, 12*(5–6), 605–619.

Murphy, R. F. (1995). Encounters: The body silent in America. In B. Instad & S. R. White (Eds.), *Disability & culture* (pp. 140–157). Berkeley, CA: University of California Press.

Mutua, K., & Smith, R. M. (2006). Disrupting normalcy and the practical concerns of teachers. In S. Danforth & S. Gabel (Eds.), *Vital questions facing disability studies in education* (pp. 121–133). New York: Peter Lang.

Myers, C., & Bersani, H. (2009). Ten quick ways to analyze children's books for ableism. *Rethinking Schools, 23*(2), 52–54.

Narian, S. (2008). Institutional stories and self-stories: Investigating peer interpretations of significant disability. *International Journal of Inclusive Education, 12*(5–6), 525–542.

Oliver, M. (1990). *The politics of disablement.* Basingstoke: Macmillan.

Oliver, M. (1996). *Understanding disability: From theory to practice.* New York: St. Martin's Press.

Philbrick, P. (1995). *Freak the mighty.* New York: Scholastic.

Priestly, M. (1998). Constructions and creations: Idealism, materialism and disability theory. *Disability & Society*, pp.75–94.

Rauscher, L., & McClintock, J. (1996). Ablesim and curriculum design. In M. Adams, L. A. Bell, & P. Griffen (Eds.), *Teaching for diversity and social justice* (pp. 198–231). New York: Routledge.

Reid, D. K., & Valle, J. (2004). The discursive practice of learning disability: Implication for instruction and parent school relations. *Journal of Learning Disabilities, 37*(6), 466–481.

Safford, P. L., & Safford, E. J. (1996). *A history of childhood and disability.* New York: Teachers College Press.

Safran, S. P. (1998). Disability portrayal in film: Reflecting the past, directing the future. *Exceptional Children, 64*(2), 227–238.

Safran, S. P. (2002). Using movies to teach students about disabilities. *Teaching Exceptional Children, 32*(3), 44–47.

Sapon-Shevin, M. (2000). Schools fit for all. *Educational Leadership, 58*(4), 34–39.

Shakespeare, T. (1994). Cultural representations of disabled people. *Disability and Society, 9*(3), 283–299.

Shapiro, A. (1999). *Everybody belongs: Changing negative attitudes toward classmates with Disabilities.* London: Routledge Falmer.

Skrtic, T. M. (1991). *Behind special education: A critical analysis of professional culture and school organization.* Denver, CO: Love.

Smith, P. (2008). Cartographies of eugenics and special education: A history of the (ab)normal. In S. Gabel and S. Danforth (Eds.), *Disability and the politics of education: An international reader* (pp. 417–432). New York: Peter Lang.

Stiker, H. J. (1999). *A history of disability.* Ann Arbor, MI: Love.

Swartz, E. (1992). Emancipatory narratives: Rewriting the master script in the school curriculum. *Journal of Negro Education, 61*(3), 341–355.

Trueman, T. (2001). *Stuck in neutral.* New York: Harper Collins.

Unites States of America Census (2005–7): http://factfinder.census.gov

Union of Physically Impaired Against Segregation [UPIAS] (1975). *Fundamental principles of disability.* Retrieved July 5, 2004, from: http://www.leeds.ac.uk/disability-studies/archiveuk/UPIAS/fundamental%20principles.pdf

Wang, M. C., Reynolds, M. C., & Walberg, H. J. (1986). Rethinking special education. *Educational Leadership, 44*(1), 26–31.

Ware, L. (2001). Writing, identity, and the other: Dare we do disabilities studies? *Journal of Teacher Education, 52*(2), 107–123.

Ware, L. (2008). Worlds remade: Inclusion through engagement with disability art. *International Journal of Inclusive Education, 12*(5–6), 563–583.

White, E. B. (1952/2004). *Charlotte's web.* New York: Harper Trophy.

Worotynec, S. Z. (2004). Contrived or inspired: Ability/disability in the children's picture book. *Disability Studies Quarterly, 24*(1).

Ziegler, C. R. (1980). *The image of the physically handicapped in children's literature.* New York: Arno Press.

Zola, I. K. (1982). *Missing pieces: A chronicle of living with a disability.* Philadelphia, PA: Temple University Press.

Part III

Social Justice Pedagogy and Praxis

Chapter 11

Social Justice and Arts Education

Spheres of Freedom

Therese Quinn

Frederick Douglass famously observed in 1855 that, "knowledge unfits a child to be a slave" (1987, p. 92). Decades later the musicians Michelle Shocked and Fiachna O'Braonain made a similar claim when they named their 1996 album Artists Make Lousy Slaves. *Art, they seem to be saying, provides a kind of education that particularly unfits its practitioners for a constrained life. A wide range of theorists and practitioners of the arts and education have expressed similar ideas, noting how art stimulates participants, including both viewers and makers, against complacency and toward possibility. For example, in* Art as Experience *John Dewey (1934) claimed for art a central place in education, describing how "imaginative vision" and "the first intimations of a better future are always found in works of art" (pp. 345–346). Philosopher Maxine Greene has also written eloquently and often about the relationship of the arts to social transformation. "[T]he arts," she says, "will help disrupt the walls that obscure . . . spheres of freedom" (1988, p. 133). This chapter explores this and other ideas about the role of the arts in education and for social justice.*

All humans are innately artists. For at least tens of thousands of years we have crafted creative responses to our circumstances. Adornment, embellishment, representation, documentation, self-expression, persuasion, innovation; we have always, it seems, engaged with ourselves and our surroundings in these ways, enjoying, improving, and sharing what we see, know, and imagine. Of course, art has been, and continues to be, defined variously: It is the name we give to our common drive to note and create rhythm, harmony, and balance; it is how we express our experience of the mysterious and difficult to understand; it is the shapes, sounds, and movements we use to expose feelings, preserve the ephemeral, and suggest solutions. And humanity has also long debated the meaning and place of art in society. For example, Aristotle outlined one of the earliest arguments for art as a form of *civic education*, and in many parts of the world artists have been educated within guilds and associations and through apprenticeships where the goal was transmission of skills and attainment of traditional mastery (Efland, 1990). Art has also been posited as a *public good* that could and should be made widely available through common schools; a *significant form* that moves its viewers aesthetically (Bell, 1914); a means to *heightened experience* through which multiple senses may be engaged and the ordinary can come to seem extraordinary; a form of *cultural history* through which social values are expressed and shared; and as a means of *political action* or even an "artist's political manifesto" or the physical manifestation of each creator's commitments (Mortier, 2009). What holds across these evolving understandings is evidence that we are "born artists" (Dissanayake, 2009, ¶12)—artistry is a human birthright.

In fact, Ellen Dissanayake (2009) traces the origin of the arts to the earliest human interactions, communication between mothers and infants; she claims that these exchanges are "fundamentally aesthetic" (¶18), using sounds and movements to convey meanings.

> [W]hen ancestral humans began creating ceremonies, they drew upon their evolved sensitivities to the emotionally evocative and compelling features of mother-infant interaction and elaborated them further, into what we now call the arts. These became efficient means of arousing interest, compelling attention, synchronizing bodily rhythms and movements, conveying cultur-ally important messages memorably and with conviction, and ultimately indoctrinating and reinforcing "right" attitudes and behavior within the group. (¶19)

She goes on to point out that what those who are recognized as artists do is a for-malized and specialized extension of what all people do in our everyday lives; though not all of us make art, we regularly make aesthetic choices. This capacity—an awareness of beauty and the meanings conveyed by forms, sounds, and more—can be nurtured though an arts-rich education to the benefit of individuals and our societies.

The proposition that all people have artistic capacity and that this capacity is socially developed and valuable is important. Shared with students it can serve to counter the myths of special talent and artistic genius; this understanding, that arts skills are learned, is key to education of all sorts—with practice and work, all young people can gain important knowledge of whatever they are interested in learning, from writing computer code to decoding the meaning of an abstract painting, given the opportunity to do so. It is vital—a social justice concern, in fact—that all youth are offered an arts education, toward, as it states in the United Nations (1994) Convention on the Rights of the Child, the "development of the child's personality, talents, and mental and physical abilities to their fullest potential" (p. 185). As poet Gwendolyn Brooks has vividly shown in her writing, young people are always generative. Her poem, "Boy Breaking Glass," chal-lenges us to understand the consequences of undirected creative power by imagin-ing a boy,

> Whose broken window is a cry of art.
> —
> I shall create! If not a note, a hole.
> If not an overture, a desecration.
> (Brooks, 1987, ¶1, 2)

As teachers, we have both the pleasure and the responsibility of making sure our students have tools and skills they can use to construct through the arts, and we can get started by reminding them that humans have always been artists.

The Arts in Education

The arts stimulate cognitive development, in psychologist Lev Vygotsky's (1925/1971) view; he described how, in the act of creating or viewing art a "reply" is initiated—the viewer or creator's initial reaction to the work is transformed and along with it their understanding of limits. For example, each student in an elementary art class is presented with a photograph of the neighborhood, and invited to design a new streetscape. A girl begins by filling in the empty lots and vacant storefronts. She imagines and then draws a carnival, a bakery with cupcake-filled windows, a colorfully painted school with an orchard "where kids can eat apples right from trees," a swimming pool and outdoor track, and an outdoor café with umbrellas where she can meet her friends. Her "act of envisioning opens up new possibilities . . . for further envisioning" (Holloway & LeCompte, 2001, p. 395); the student asks her table-mates' opinions, adds more colors and details, and later walks around the room to see what other classmates are doing. One student has drawn bright murals on the front of each building and turned every open space into a park; another has expanded his apartment building to fill a full city block with its adjoining and new playgrounds, internet-wired recreation room, and gym. Some students caption their pictures; almost all mark where they live.

The class session closes with a short critique. "What do you see?" the teacher asks, and invites appreciative responses and questions directed to each young artist. Then, extending the project, the teacher arranges for his class to hang these drawings throughout the school; excited discussion bubbles and rolls through the hallways as students from other classrooms notice, admire, and expand on the city-planning ideas they present. This project is surrounded by related activities that extend and enrich the learning—students have talked and written about qualities of communities, done some image research online, and participated in group discussion that expanded their knowledge of formal arts discourse and the give-and-take of moderated discussion. In any school, this kind of art activity could benefit, as well, from connections to a range of subjects, including measurement and migration, weather patterns and demographics, city planning, and more.

While the arts are elastic and generous, art education and integrating arts across the curriculum takes thought and planning, an understanding of the learners in one's classroom and school, including the social context of their lives, an understanding of content and pedagogy, and understanding the conditions—constraints, opportunities, and possibilities—of one's workplace. Teachers who build relationships with their colleagues and in their teaching communities and are focused on and alive to their own learning, as well as the development of their students, will be able to see the opportunity that the arts provide, to not only engage all students (that's the easy part—art is fun), but, through the arts, to foster fertile grounds for intellectual growth in their classrooms.

The Arts and Social Justice

This capacity of art—to trigger more and new thought—makes it important for educators, but its potential is even more expansive; the arts provoke, and can open us to new and even surprising ideas. Gwendolyn Brooks reminds us that art is "not an old shoe," soft and comfortable (quoted in Gayles, 2003, p. 37). Often, she claims, "Art hurts. Art urges voyages—and it is easier to stay at home." Vygotsky (1925/1971) also described how the arts can "incite, excite, and irritate" (p. 252) people, pushing us to voyage in unknown, sometimes uncomfortable places, and also stimulating in us the prospect of dreaming and acting in novel ways. Similarly, in her book, *Releasing the Imagination,* philosopher Maxine Greene (1995) links the arts to the development of "social imagination: the capacity to invent visions of what should be and what might be in our deficient society, on the streets where we live, in our schools" (p. 5). Like Brooks, she points out that rather than lulling or soothing, "the arts stimulate the 'wide-awakeness' so essential to critical awareness, most particularly when they involve a move to the imaginary" (quoted in Paley, 1995, 7). Art, Greene suggests (1995), can lead to social change because, "to call for imaginative capacity is to work for the ability to see things as if they could be otherwise" (p. 19). Once seen, she argues, other worlds and ways of being can—and inevitably will—be made; the child who learns that she can create will continue to learn and create.

Like all good teaching, the community redesign project described earlier engaged a range of social justice themes and practices: It stimulated *self-awareness,* centering reflection on, "What is important to you?" It fostered *democracy* by proposing that everyone can participate and every contribution can be valued. It supported *collectivity,* or, a sense that we are all in it together and our experiences may be shared, and *activism,* or, choosing and acting. It offered experiences with *public space* by presenting the community as shared and co-created, and *history,* as in, we are always in it and making it, even in the midst of the seemingly mundane. Perhaps most important, it offered students a way to express *imagination* that exceeds limitation, or, as the poet Jayne Cortez described it, an opportunity to dream up "somewhere in advance of nowhere" (quoted in Kelley, 2002, p. xii).

While these ideas often recur in justice-focused pedagogy, there are many ways of conceptualizing "social justice" within education. First, teaching for social justice is "always more possibility than accomplishment" (Ayers & Quinn, 2005, p. viii); there is no one right way or "best practice" that suits all situations (Horton, 1990). Rather, attention to context is crucial; teachers for social justice must be students of communities, cultures, children, and much more as they review and revise their curricula, again and again.

Still, an education grounded in social justice is *for* something. Pauline Lipman (2004), for example, describes four "social justice imperatives": equity, agency, cultural relevance, and critical literacy (p. 16). Tamara Beauboeuf-Lafontant (1999) examined the idea of "cultural relevance" and countered with a call to "politically relevant teaching"; she argues that it is not the "cultural similarity" between teachers and students, but the "political clarity" of teachers that allows them to develop a pedagogy that is "'relevant' to the *political* experiences of inequity and disenfran-chisement of their students" (p. 705, emphasis in the original). Connie North has described a "robust . . . socially just" education as the quest for the multiple litera-cies—functional, critical, relational, democratic, and visionary—that will allow learners to "effect the kind of large-scale social and economic transformations nec-essary to grow muscles and tendons on the abstract, fragile bones of 'social justice' and 'democracy'" (North, 2009, pp. 162–163; see also Morrell, 2004). Kevin Kumashiro has called for a critique of normative standards and "common sense" and proposed an "anti-oppression education" framework (Kumashiro, 2000, 2004). While there are differences between them, each of these perspectives empha-sizes critical (or, attending to power) *analysis and action*, engaged in by both teach-ers and students. In other words, working for social justice through teaching requires practicing and fostering attention to the complexities and deep structures of daily life, and then, developing and implementing engaged responses aimed at change. The goal is dual—building in students expertise and rich knowledge and a "democratic vision of [the importance of] participation" (Kahne & Middaugh, 2007).

Social Justice in Art Education

Many theorists and practitioners have called for an arts education that clearly links the arts to social change. Historically, these perspectives have been articulated as social reconstructionist (Freedman, 1994; Hicks, 1994), multicultural (Cahan & Kocur, 1996; Stuhr, 1994), and critical art education, described as art education "explicitly in the service of social transformation" (Siegesmund, quoted in Holloway & Krensky, 2001, p. 361). In addition, social justice movements includ-ing feminism (Collins & Sandell, 1996), lesbian and gay liberation (Lampela & Check, 2003; Lampela, 2005, 2007), and disability rights (Blandy, 1994, 1999) are reflected in art education literature. More recently, educators have encouraged crit-ical, democratic, social theory and social justice engagements through visual and material culture approaches to an arts education; these are emphases that invite classroom consideration of all that surrounds us in daily life, including popular cul-ture and design (Amburgy, Knight, and Keifer-Boyd, 2004; Bolin & Blandy, 2003; Tavin, 2003). Arts projects inspired by visual and material culture approaches have focused on everything from school uniform redesign, and visual critiques of Native American sports mascots, to gender-bending Second Life avatar development.

According to artist and art educator Olivia Gude (n.d.), a strong art curriculum will always have the characteristics of a social justice education; it will necessarily be multicultural, exploratory, and rooted in life experiences. Also, it will focus less on art as product and solo endeavor, and more on collaborative work not (always) aimed at artifact creation, as do many contemporary artists who create temporary, activist, and online projects. Nato Thompson and Gregory Sholette (2004) describe some of these, such as the God Bless Graffiti Coalition, Inc., which "was founded in Chicago 'to combat growing national international anti-graffiti trends'" (p. 71) and the Critical Art Ensemble, which is a collective of artists who have recently explored biotechnology, in their catalog for an exhibition at Mass MoCA, The Interventionists; others, like RTMark (pronounced "artmark"), a project that questions the relationship between funding and creativity by inviting users to invest in user-proposed art projects, and Learning to Love You More, a project consisting of public responses to assignments given by artists Miranda July and Harrell Fletcher, can be found online and, at times, documented in books. These and similar arts practices connect ideas about art and culture to urgent social issues, and have been exciting starting points to strong and engaging curricula for many educators.

Examples of specifically justice-oriented analyses of visual and material culture for arts classrooms are numerous and include many of those just mentioned, as well as Nancy Pauly's (2005) powerful work exploring the images of Abu Ghraib, and Nancy Parks's (2008) discussions of the possibilities of using video games and other forms of new media in a "reconstructionist" arts education (p. 240); both of these include curriculum ideas for arts classrooms. What links these and similar projects is a goal to teach about the complex conditions of our world through the arts; at the same time, students participating in these experiences will have opportunities to learn how the arts classroom offers critical and practical skills students can use in many areas of their lives—to use Freire's (1987) phrase, a social justice-focused arts education offers more ways for students to experience "Reading the word and the world."

Despite the availability of these and many other examples, art education curricula in most U.S. schools are still dominated by "formalist/modernist model[s], in particular, Discipline-based Art Education [DBAE], in which aesthetics is taught disconnected from its social context" and separate from social movements for change (Alexander & Day, 1991; Holloway & Krensky, 2001, p. 359). Further, research consistently shows that schools nationwide, and in particular those serving the greatest numbers of low-income youth of color, have increased instructional time for tested subjects including reading/language, arts, and math and decreased it for untested ones, in particular, the visual arts and music (Au, 2008; Dillon, 2006). A narrowed curricular focus, however, isn't a new problem; debates about what and whose knowledge is of most importance are perennial and contested in public education (Schubert, 1986). Movements for justice have always sought to link social change efforts to these classrooms, including the anti-bias and anti-racism education movements, multiculturalism, gender equity, and sexual and gender identity "safe zone" awareness projects, all of which have affected what teachers learn in pre-service programs and both what and how teachers teach.

Still, despite these successes, it is clear that teaching for social justice is "teaching against the grain" (Cochran-Smith, 2004, p. 28); even teachers committed to this kind of pedagogy can feel fearful, alone, and unsupported (Salas, 2004). For this reason it is important that educators interested in developing an arts-based (or any) social justice curriculum make it a priority to build connections with others who will support their efforts, including colleague educators in their own and other subject areas, administrators, students, parents and community members, and activists—classrooms are not, should not, and cannot be islands. Rather, classrooms must be considered and created as hubs of inquiry and centers of action with links to every important topic, movement, and social concern. Teachers aiming to bring the world into their classroom through a justice-focused curriculum benefit from working in creative communication with the increasing numbers of progressive educator groups focused on social justice; the resources section at the close of this chapter includes contacts to some of these.

Concluding Thoughts

The arts participation of people in the United States has been measured by studying how frequently individuals visit art museums; perhaps not surprisingly, visitors to museums were more likely to have had art lessons than non-visitors (Hendon, 1990). This might be enough of a reason to support arts education—it may build in our youth a sense that they can visit and appreciate our public national culture institutions, and few would argue against the goods of access to public spaces and museum attendance. Yet, a bigger and more important goal for arts educators could be developing in students the knowledge that they make meaning when they make things, and that they are free when they can choose what to craft (not when they choose what to buy). Making art is powerful, in other words, and attainable for all.

The Action of Praxis

What follows are two vignettes of arts educators in action, matched to social justice themes identified earlier in this chapter.

Self-awareness

In one summer school class a group of girls, all there because they failed one or more classes during the fall-to-spring high school year, are watching a DVD of Lucille Clifton reading her poems. As the tape starts, the girls are squirming and loud. A few young women sit slumped, chests collapsed onto bellies, heads settled on arms crossed and resting on table-tops, eyelids firmly shut. Most are distractedly watching the monitor while they talk to friends. Then Clifton's voice rings out, and she is smiling as she begins:

> homage to my hips
>
> these hips are big hips.
> they need space to
> move around in.
> they don't fit into little
> petty places. these hips
> are free hips.
>
> . . .

The poem builds and Clifton's voice swells:

> . . .
> these hips are magic hips.
> i have known them
> to put a spell on a man and
> spin him like a top

The girls are listening now, and giggling. Like them, Lucille Clifton is brown-skinned and full-bodied. Like theirs, her hips are substantial. Clifton continues:

> *poem in praise of menstruation*
>
> if there is a river
> more beautiful than this
> bright as the blood
> red edge of the moon
>
> if there is a river
> more faithful than this
> returning each month
> to the delta
> . . .

Where just a moment before chairs had swiveled as girls chuckled appreciatively to each other, now the room erupted in a frenzy of disapproval.

> "That's nasty."
> "That is *not* right. Why would she write something like that?"
> "That's not poetry. It's ugly."

Clifton kept reading; she finished her praise-song, and then offered an elegy to her last period, "well, girl, goodbye . . ." and "*wasn't she beautiful?*" And finally, she closed with some "wishes for sons" which included the lines:

> i wish them cramps.
> i wish them a strange town
> and the last tampon.
> i wish them no 7/11.
> . . .

Now each girl was rapt. As Clifton finished with, "in the inner city/or/like we call it/home," the room was nearly quiet; a few girls talked softly to each other, a young mother of a baby son pulled his picture from her purse and sat appreciating it; a couple more girls were moving their pens over paper, and one asked who—what poet—are they going to hear next?

The educator in this classroom front-and-back ended the lesson with activities aimed at deepening her students' learning, including self-reflective writing and group discussion. What would you add to this project?[1]

Public Space

A young teacher surges down the street with a group of sixth grade boys and thousands of other people that are swiftly and steadily marching for immigrant rights through a large Midwestern city. Two of the boys are holding small video cameras, and the group occasionally stops so one of them can interview someone in the crowd. The others, like many at the massive march, are carrying hand-painted posters. In English and Spanish, these signs offer kids'-eye views of the march's many agendas.

> "We are not illegal people, we are America."
> "No more borders; no more discrimination."
> "*No deportan a los immigrantes.*"

And one points out that, "My parents work hard, they are not criminals."

Each of these posters is carefully lettered, most using a bubble-letter font style reminiscent of the graffiti of hip hop culture, *circa* 1980s, the timeframe of the teacher's early youth.

Back in their classroom, the boys watch and log the footage and start the edits that will result in a short video. They have already invited the whole school community to attend a screening in the school cafeteria because many parents couldn't go to the march, either because they had to work or were afraid they might be arrested and deported. What started as a class discussion about the students' lives and concerns has grown into a multi-part many-week project: First each of the art classes turned their ideas into block prints while learning about the history of political prints and posters; then they studied lettering styles, discussed past and current social movements, selected images and text, carved linoleum blocks, and printed a set of proofs. Finally, the students translated their small print images, using a gridding and transfer method, into large posters for the march. They documented and memorialized their participation in this event using digital video and edited the film on their teacher's laptop computer, and on the night of its showing, over a hundred people watched what these students had created.

Both the streets and the school served as public galleries for this art project. How might these students' work reach more people? What would you add to the project?

Points of Inquiry

- How are the practice, pedagogy, and theory of art, and what makes art, embedded in a context of sociopolitical history?
- What discourses are embedded in the study of art? How do these relate to identity politics, teaching, and schooling?

Points of Praxis

- How can you incorporate the social, environmental, and political contexts of your students' lives in your practice? What problems might you and your students pose that art can begin to answer?
- How can arts education offer "equity, agency, cultural relevance, and critical literacy" to privileged populations?
- Quinn describes several projects that make art public. What are approaches you can use to take art beyond the classroom?

Related Art Education Resources

- *Art Education 2.0: Using New Technology in Art Classrooms*—A wiki described as "a global community of art educators exploring uses of new technology"; also has profiles and blogs created by arts educators from around the world. (http://arted20.ning.com/)
- *Art 21: Art in the 21st Century*—Fantastic source for contemporary art images and project ideas. (http://www.pbs.org/art21/)
- *Critical Art Ensemble* (http://www.critical-art.net/)
- *Docs Populi: Documents for the Public*—This is the digital repository of radical librarian and artist Lincoln Cushings; it features collections of labor culture artifacts; Cuban and Chinese poster art; links to archives; and much more. (http://www.docspopuli.org/)
- *Green Museum: Online Museum of Environmental Art*—This online source for "green" art and artists offers a wealth of visuals and links. (greenmuseum.org)
- *Just Seeds: Visual Resistance Artists' Cooperative*—An excellent source for inexpensive examples of socially engaged art, including the wonderful "People's History Posters" series. (http://www.justseeds.org/)
- *Learning to Love You More* (http://www.learningtoloveyoumore.com/hello/index.php)
- *Poetry Foundation*—Wonderful site with poems by hundreds of writers and on every subject, and search tools that will help you find them. Includes fantastic audio and video readings, blogs, reading guides, and more.
- *RTMark* (rtmark.com)
- *Spiral Art Education*—This website, created by Olivia Gude of the University of Illinois at Chicago, has wonderful ideas for arts projects and all the materials a teacher will need to get started, from framing essays and artist images and bios, to examples of artwork made by students. (http://www.uic.edu/classes/ad/ad382/)

Related Teacher Organizations

- Association of Raza Educators (National; Chapters in California) (http://www.razaeducators.org/)

- Caucus of Rank and File Educators (Chicago) (http://coreteachers.org/)
- New York Collective of Radical Educators (http://www.nycore.org/)
- Teachers 4 Social Justice (San Francisco) (http://www.t4sj.org/templates/ System/default.asp?id=39669)
- Teachers for Social Justice (Chicago) (http://www.teachersforjustice.org/)

Note

1 "homage to my hips" is in *Good Woman*; "poem in praise of menstruation," "to my last period," and "wishes for sons" are in *Quilting: Poems 1987–1990*.

References

Alexander, K., & Day, M. (1991). Discipline-based art education: A curriculum sampler. Los Angeles: J. Paul Getty Museum.

Amburgy, P. M., Knight, W. B., & Keifer-Boyd, K. (2004). Schooled in silence. *Journal of Social Theory in Art Education, 24,* 81–101.

Au, W. (2008). Unequal by design: High-stakes testing and the standardization of inequality. New York: Routledge.

Ayers, W., & Quinn, T. (2005). Series foreword. In G. Michie, *See you when we get there: Teaching for change in urban schools* (pp. vii–ix). New York: Teachers College Press.

Beauboeuf-Lafontant, T. (1999). A movement against and beyond boundaries: "Politically relevant teaching" among African-American teachers. *Teachers College Record, 100*(4), 702–723.

Bell, C. (1914). *Art*. Retrieved July 12, 2009, from: http://www.csulb.edu/~jvancamp/ 361r13.html#Bibliography

Blandy, D. (1994). Assuming responsibility: Disability rights and the preparation of art educators. *Studies in Art Education, 35*(3), 179–187.

Blandy, D. (1999). A disability aesthetic, inclusion, and art education. In A. Nyman and A. Jenkins (Eds.), *Issues and approaches to art students with special needs*, Reston, VA: National Art Education Association.

Bolin, P. E., & Blandy, D. (2003). Beyond visual culture: Seven statements of support for material culture studies in art education. *Studies in Art Education, 44*(3), 246–263.

Brooks, G. (1987) Boy breaking glass. *Blacks* (p. 438). Chicago: Third World Press.

Cahan, S., & Kocur, Z. (Eds.). (1996). *Contemporary art and multicultural education*. New York: Routledge.

Clifton, L. (1987). *Good woman*. Brockport, NY: BOA Editions.

Clifton, L. (1991). *Quilting: Poems 1987–1990*. Brockport, NY: BOA Editions.

Cochran-Smith, M. (2004). *Walking the road: Race, diversity, and social justice in teacher education*. New York: Teachers College Press.

Collins, G., & Sandell, R. (Eds.). (1996). *Gender issues in art education: Content, contexts, and strategies*. Reston, VA: NAEA.

Dewey, J. (1934). *Art as experience*. New York: Minton, Balch, & Company.

Dillon, S. (2006). Schools cut back subjects to push reading and math. *New York Times*, March 26, pp. 1, 16.

Dissanayake, E. (2009). The birth of the arts. *Greater Good Magazine, 5*(3). Retrieved July 8, 2009, from: http://greatergood.berkeley.edu/greatergood/2009winter/Dissanayake453. php

Douglass, F. (1987). *My bondage and my freedom.* W. L. Andrews (Ed.). Urbana: University of Illinois Press. (Original work published 1855.)

Efland, A. (1990). *A history of art education: Intellectual and social currents in teaching the visual arts.* New York: Teachers College Press.

Freedman, K. (1994). About the issue: The social reconstruction of art education. *Studies in Art Education, 35*(3), 157–170.

Freire, P. (1987). *Literacy: Reading the word and the world.* Westport, CT: Bergin & Garvey.

Gayles, G. W. (2003). *Conversations with Gwendolyn Brooks.* Jackson: University Press of Mississippi.

Greene, M. (1988). *The dialectic of freedom.* New York: Teachers College Press.

Greene, M. (1995). *Releasing the imagination: Essays on education, the arts, and social change.* San Francisco: Jossey-Bass.

Gude, O. (n.d.). Rubric for a quality art curriculum. UIC Spiral Art Education. Retrieved July 12, 2009, from: http://www.uic.edu/classes/ad/ad382/sites/AEA/AEA_02/AAEA02a.html

Hendon, W. (1990). The general public's participation in art museums: Visitors differ from non-visitors, but not as markedly as case studies have indicated. *American Journal of Economics and Sociology, 49*(4), 439–457.

Hicks, L. (1994). Social reconstruction and community. *Studies in Art Education, 35*(3), 149–156.

Holloway, D, & Krensky, B. (2001). Introduction: The arts, urban education, and social change. *Education and Urban Society, 33*(4), 354–365.

Holloway, D. & LeCompte, M. (2001). Becoming somebody! How arts programs support positive identity for middle school girls. *Education and Urban Society, 33*, 388–408.

Horton, M. (1990). *The long haul: An autobiography of Myles Horton.* New York: Doubleday.

Kahne, J. & Middaugh, E. (2007). Is patriotism good for democracy? In J. Westheimer (Ed.), *Pledging allegiance: The politics of patriotism in America's schools* (pp. 115–126). New York: Teachers College Press.

Kelley, R. (2002). *Freedom dreams: The Black radical imagination.* Boston: Beacon.

Kumashiro, K. (2000). Toward a theory of anti-oppressive education. *Review of Educational Research, 70*(1), 25–53.

Kumashiro, K. (2004). *Against common sense: Teaching and learning toward social justice.* New York: Routledge.

Lampela, L. (2005). Writing effective lesson plans while utilizing the work of lesbian and gay artists. *Art Education, 58*(2), 33–39.

Lampela, L. (2007). Including lesbians and gays in arts curricula: The art of Jeanne Mammen. *Visual Arts Research, 33*(1).

Lampela, L., & Check, E. (Eds.). (2003). *From our voices: Art educators and artists speak out about lesbian, gay, bisexual and transgendered issues.* Dubuque, IA: Kendall/Hunt.

Lipman, P. (2004). *High stakes education: Inequality, globalization, and urban school reform.* New York: RoutledgeFalmer.

Morrell, E. (2004). *Becoming critical researchers: Literacy and empowerment for urban youth.* New York: Peter Lang.

Mortier, G. (2009). Art as political manifesto. Retrieved July 12, 2009, from: http://www.ispa.org/index.php/resources/ideasexchange/65-mortier

North, C. (2009). *Teaching for social justice? Voices from the front lines.* Boulder, CO: Paradigm.

Paley, N. (1995). *Finding art's place: Experiments in contemporary education and culture.* New York: Routledge.

Parks, N. (2008). Video games as reconstructionist sites of learning. *Studies in Art Education,* *49*(3), 235–250.

Pauly, N. (2005). Abu Ghraib (un)becoming photographs: How can at educators address current images from visual culture perspectives? *Journal of Social Theory in Art Education,* *25,* 158–187.

Salas, K. (2004). How to teach controversial content and not get fired. In *The New Teacher Book* (pp. 127–132). Milwaukee, WI: Rethinking Schools.

Schubert, W. (1986). *Curriculum: Perspective, paradigm, and possibility.* New York: Macmillan.

Shocked, M., & O'Braonain, F. (1996). *Artists make lousy slaves* [CD]. Michelle Shocked Online Music.

Stuhr, P. (1994). Multicultural art education and social reconstruction. *Studies in Art Education, 35*(3), 171–178.

Tavin, K. (2003). Wrestling with angels, searching for ghosts. *Studies in Art Education, 44*(3), 197–213.

Thompson, N., & Sholette, G. (2004). *The interventionists: User's manual for the creative disruption of everyday life.* North Adams, MA: Mass MoCA.

United Nations. (1994). *Human rights: A compilation of international instruments.* New York & Geneva: United Nations.

Vygotsky, L. (1925/1971). *Psychology of art.* Cambridge, MA: MIT Press.

Chapter 12

Writing in Academic Genres
Is Social Justice a Learning Outcome?

Nikola Hobbel and Thandeka K. Chapman

In this chapter we examine student outcomes from a critical multicultural education (MCE) curriculum that pushed students to think individually and collectively about the relationships between personal, communal, and global justice concerns. Our research question was: Using a critical MCE curriculum to explore issues of social justice for the individual, community, and world, how did students express their personal identities, group affiliations, and privilege and oppression? The researchers employed a textual analysis of high school students' writings from multiple three-week writing seminars to explore the rich ways that students experience and conceive issues of race, class, and gender. Students' assignments were the result of a social justice framework with multiple writing tasks that highlighted particular aspects of their identities, issues that mattered to them and their communities, and issues of world concern which may only indirectly affect the quality of their lives.

> "A critical perspective suggests that deliberate attempts to expose iniquity in the classroom and society need to become part of our everyday classroom life."
> —Vivian Maria Vasquez, 2004, p. xv

Background

In recent years, a significant amount of theoretical and conceptual work has been published validating the need for social justice curricula, with little empirical work demonstrating how these curricula appear in practical situations. In fact, much of the research discussing social justice orientations focuses on teachers' practices and philosophies, with astoundingly little work that illustrates what impact such practices and philosophies have on students' academic achievement. Moreover, the hammer blows of No Child Left Behind on how we think about student learning have reshaped the field of secondary English research considerably. Specifically, learning in secondary English has taken the shape of test scores and on-demand writing. Recently, on national and state levels, the teaching of writing has come back into focus, in part because of the insistent pressure of organizations like NCTE and NWP,[1] and also in part due to changes in high stakes tests, which now include on-demand writing tasks in addition to multiple-choice questions (the California High School Exit Exam and the SAT, to name two examples).

Understandably, much of the professional work in this resurgent interest in writing at the secondary level takes the approach of academic literacy. Academic literacy includes the teaching of Standard English as the proper language of the classroom, explicit instruction regarding formal grammar, and genre studies of argumentative, expository, and persuasive writing. While we do not in this chapter discuss the relationship of English education policies, standards, and classroom practices, they inform our work and the context in which it takes place.

Using empirical research as a focus of discussion, this chapter validates, extends, and critiques multicultural education for social justice. The standards movement provides prime examples of how content knowledge, skills, and dispositions have been placed at direct odds with social justice pedagogy: whether at the level of curriculum and instruction, or at the level of teacher education accreditation, social justice has been distanced or eliminated entirely as a guiding concept. Even so, we argue that a social justice orientation is necessary to avoid contributing to the continued erosion of what Christine Sleeter described over two decades ago as the original mission of multicultural education:

> to challenge oppression, and to use schooling as much as possible to help shape a future America that is more equal, democratic, and just, and that does not demand conformity to one cultural norm. And it must reaffirm is radical and political nature. (1989, p. 63)

In English education, much of social justice rhetoric has devolved to a mere politics of representation and identity construction that often overshadow both the unyielding yet sliding constructions of institutional racism, sexism, and classism in the U.S. and global contexts. Although these depoliticized rhetorical performances of multicultural education are documented in curriculum standards and other policy artifacts, no significant conceptual changes in learning outcomes have been linked to multicultural education for social justice.

In this chapter we examine student writing from a critical multicultural education curriculum that pushed us and our students to think individually and collectively about the relationships between personal, communal, and global concerns. While we entered into this teaching as confirmed multiculturalists in the critical tradition, we began to ask as we worked with our students to produce academic writing in the persuasive genre: Is social justice a learning outcome?

Conceptual Framework

Multicultural education (MCE) for social justice remains an espoused ideal for many critical educators who desire to see students understand and critique their communities and the greater society as a practice of democratic citizenship. Over the past 30 years, the terms multicultural education and social justice have undergone significant reinterpretations. For the purposes of this chapter, we employ Sonia Nieto's most recent definition: "a philosophy, an approach, and actions that embody treating all people with fairness, respect, dignity, and generosity" (Nieto & Bode, 2008). Nieto and Bode present four features of social justice education:

First, it challenges, confronts, and disrupts misconceptions, untruths, and stereotypes that lead to structural inequality and discrimination based on race, social class, gender, and other social and human differences.

Second, a social justice perspective means providing all students with the resources necessary to learn to their full potential. This includes *material resources* such as books, curriculum, financial support, and so on. Equally vital are *emotional resources* such as a belief in students' ability and worth; care for them as individuals and learners; high expectations and rigorous demands on them; and the necessary social and cultural capital to negotiate the world.

A third component of a social justice perspective is *drawing on* the talents and strengths that students bring to their education. This requires a rejection of the deficit perspective that has characterized much of the education of marginalized students, to a shift that views all students—not just those from privileged backgrounds—as having resources that can be a foundation for their learning. A fourth essential component of social justice is creating a learning environment that promotes critical thinking and supports agency for social change.

(Nieto & Bode, 2008, p. 11)

Although Nieto's definition provides the overarching framework here, we also draw on the rich work of multicultural theorists: Banks's transformational multicultural education (1995), Grant and Sleeter's MCE for social justice (1998), and Kanpol and McLaren's critical multiculturalism (1995). What remain unclear are the types of tangible outcomes teachers desire from their students. What do we expect students to know and be able to do in terms of social justice? Then, how do we know if students have reached the goals we set for them and those they set for themselves?

What Is an Outcome? Nieto, Bode, and Freire

Generally, one can define outcomes as things that measure and demonstrate a student's knowledge, skills, and dispositions. Of course, the notion of the outcome is embedded in a deep and problematic historical matrix of neoliberal politics, developmental psychology, and differential schooling for privileged and oppressed populations. In terms of social justice, though, what might outcomes mean? If we think about Nieto and Bode's definition, focusing particularly on those aspects which are directed at students, we might say that social justice outcomes in writing include evidence of "challeng[ing], confront[ing], and disrupt[ing] misconceptions, untruths, and stereotypes that lead to structural inequality and discrimination based on race, social class, gender, and other social and human differences." We might add that these outcomes would demonstrate a synthesis of students' own social and cultural capital, strengths and experiences, with critical thinking and an eye toward social change. The aspects of critical thinking and support for social change could be understood as including the complexities of collective *and* individual racial identities, among others. Again, we draw on Nieto to clarify; the demonstration of a social justice orientation must include affirmation, solidarity, *and* critique:

> *Affirmation, solidarity* and *critique* [emphasis in the original] represent the very highest level of multicultural education. It means accepting the culture and language of students and their families as legitimate and embracing them as valid vehicles for learning. It also means understanding that culture is not fixed or unchangeable, and thus one is able to critique its manifestations and outcomes. Because multicultural education is concerned with equity and social justice for all people, and because basic values of different groups are often diametrically opposed, conflict is inevitable. Passively accepting the status quo of any culture is inconsistent with multicultural education. . . . Multicultural education without critique implies that cultural understanding remains at the romantic or exotic stage. If we are not able to transcend our own cultural experiences through reflection and critique, we cannot hope to understand and critique that of others.
>
> (Nieto, 1992, p. 277)

The secondary English classroom is a place of reading and writing, of speaking and listening: these are the skills, broadly outlined, that constitute literacy. We know, as teachers of English, that we, for example, are to ask students to write essays, read novels, and give and evaluate oral presentations. However, literacy skills in and of themselves are no guarantee of a social justice orientation: no matter how controversial the subject of the essay may be, no matter the range of authors our students encounter. Indeed, too often research papers on illegal immigration or abortion and the beautiful texts of Zora Neale Hurston and Amy Tan pass for multicultural education in the English classroom. While it is possible to engage feminism, economic disparities, history, and oppression in the production of outcomes associated with such topics and texts, these assignments do not elicit affirmation, solidarity, or critique merely by their nature. Further, it is often the case that they are seen as 'enough' by teachers who do not themselves have the skills to open the dangerous gates of critique and walk into a realm that, by definition, asks them to enter into praxis alongside their students. We therefore argue that social justice as a learning outcome destabilizes traditional power relationships in classrooms in the way that Paulo Freire elucidated in his now-canonized meditation on critical pedagogy, *Pedagogy of the Oppressed* (2006). Reading between Nieto and Bode's definition of social justice and Paulo Freire's concept of problem-posing education, we noted mutuality in the thrust of their arguments. Freire claims,

> In problem-posing education, men [*sic*] develop their power to perceive critically the way they exist in the world with which and in which they find themselves; they come to see the world not as a static reality, but as a reality in process, in transformation. Although the dialectical relations of men with the world independently of how these relations are perceived (or whether or not they are at all), it is also true that the form of action men adopt is to a large extent a function of how they perceive themselves in the world. Hence, the

teacher-students and the students-teachers reflect simultaneously on themselves and the world without dichotomizing this reflection from action, and thus establish an authentic form of thought and action.

(Freire, 2006, p. 65)

While the congruence of challenging and confronting inequality are clear in both texts, Nieto and Bode's features of social justice extend the ideas of reflection and action to include explicitly the funds of knowledge (Moll, Amanti, Neff, & Gonzalez, 1992) that students bring to the classroom: their emotional and cultural resources. Learning to know and do social justice, then, depends on weaving a rich matrix of self and others, one that presses past boundaries and into new understandings of complex social and political contexts.

What We Know, What We Can Do

Using this working and albeit admittedly problematic definition of learning outcomes, we offer the following essays, written in our classroom, to illustrate and discuss those outcomes our students demonstrated in order to think through what came easily, what did not, and what was absent altogether in the analyses we entered into together, as a class. Using Freire's approach to understanding "consciousness" and "empowerment" to code for outcomes, we include good and not-so-good examples of outcomes that addressed:

o   Recognition of one's place in the world
o   Recognition of political contexts and institutional structures
o   Belief that as an individual and community citizen, one can promote change
o   Ability to pose solutions and organize around issues of concern
o   Ability to connect with others across lines of race, class, gender, and sexuality.

We consider this work not as a necessary example of best practice; rather, we are interested in building empirical examples that will lead us, as teachers, to create classroom environments and academic tasks with our students that act as instantiations, visible and demonstrable, of critical multiculturalism in practice.

A Bit of Context

The students—no longer docile listeners—are now critical co-investigators in dialogue with the teacher. . . . Students, as they are increasingly posed with problems relating to themselves in the world and with the world, will feel increasingly challenged and obliged to respond to that challenge. Because they apprehend the challenge as interrelated to other problems within a total context, not as a theoretical question, the resulting comprehension tends to be increasingly critical and thus constantly less alienated. Their response to the challenge evokes new challenges, followed by new understandings; and gradually the students come to regard themselves as committed.

(Freire, 2006, p. 64)

In order to examine student outcomes, our research question was: Using a critical MCE curriculum to explore issues of social justice for the individual, community, and world, how did students of color express their personal identities, claim group affiliations, and perceive both privilege and oppression? We employed a textual analysis of high school students' writings from multiple three-week writing seminars to explore the rich ways that students experience and conceive issues of race, class, and gender. Students' assignments were the result of a social justice framework with multiple writing tasks that highlighted particular aspects of their identities, issues that mattered to them and their communities, and issues of world concern which may only indirectly affect the quality of their lives.

Recognition of One's Place in the World

From a social justice understanding, recognition of one's place in the world means a recognition of one's own cultural complexities: the economic, racial and ethnic, gender, geographic features of our lives overlap and depend on each other to shape our realities and values. In order to affirm our own and our students' experiences, these experiences must enter the conversations of the classroom. While not a new idea, autobiography as a way to invite students' lives into the classroom is not enough to instantiate conversations across lines of difference. Indeed, it may lead to an attitude of "we are all the same because we are all different" (Sleeter, 1996, pp. 239), which remains inadequate as a tool of confronting and challenging iniquities. Still, it is the beginning of affirmation, and without it, no solidarity and no critique can come. Not surprisingly, those of our students who had immigrated or were the children of immigrants were most keenly aware of disparities in economic resources over continents and generations. They understood and wrote about poverty from highly personal points of view, and discussed economic attainment in terms of educational opportunities, family obligations, and transnational contexts:

> Education in my family is the most important thing, beyond all others. My dad always says to me that no matter what, education comes first. Education is really important to the Hmong culture. My parents didn't really get a chance to go to school and get an education, so this is why education matters to me so much. I want to go to school and get my education, so one day I can repay my parents for what they did for me. Once I find a good job, I will buy my parents a new house that I have already paid for. Also, in my family no one has ever finished or gone to college and I want to be the first one to do that. (Boon)

Boon entwines Hmong cultural values with American material acquisitiveness. In recognizing his place in the world, one aspect that matters to him greatly, according to this narrative, is to take up a traditional role as male breadwinner at the same time that he ventures into the realm of higher education beyond his parents' experiences.

> Education means success and money. My older sister and older brothers have gone through high school and have attended college for a couple of years now.

They make more money than my parents who have no education whatsoever and can hardly speak English. My parents work in a factory with a pay of eight to ten dollars an hour, and stand for eight hours straight working in an environment filled with abundant noise and hot temperatures. This living wage is barely enough to support our family of eleven. They have to work diligently, five days a week sometimes even more (overtime), in order to support us. When I think about the things they do for us (my siblings and me), I am flooded with guilt because I can't do anything to help them. The best I can do is go to school and work hard how they want me to so that I can someday show my gratitude and provide for them. My older siblings who work have bills and tuitions to pay and therefore have enough problems to deal with already. My family is the reason I will work industriously to make the most of my education in order to earn a good living wage. It's about time my parents get a rest and let someone else take care of them for a change. (Ia)

As does Boon, Ia relates educational attainment with economic gain. In addition, she paints a clear picture of her parents' working lives, and how their lives contrast with her possible future.

Communities that are made up of all kinds of different people who vary in ethnicity and come from different backgrounds who become a part of a higher social or economic class are highly affected by poverty. No matter who they are right now doesn't change where they originated. An example is my friend: she has family members back in Nicaragua where she herself is from and because of this, she shared her experience with me about her trip back there. I found her experience to be a very fascinating and an eye-opening story. She talked about the neighborhood in which her aunt and cousins lived and how it was a run-down place and the feeling of it was depressing. While she was there, she discovered that everything had to be done by oneself, such as washing clothes and doing the dishes by hands. She found this to be very difficult. This experience affected her in a way where she learned to not turn down opportunities presented to her and to not take things for granted. From this you can see that even in the U.S., we don't realize or appreciate the smallest things like a washing machine and a dishwasher. (Mai)

Mai draws on transnational and transgenerational connections in order to make sense of her own situation. In a sophisticated and critical manner, she is able to tie the two together and include how her friend's situation and experience matter to her.

Poverty is a big deal not just to the world and the community, but also to me—even though I'm very lucky to live in a country where everything I need is provided for me, my sister is in Thailand where it's very hard for her to provide for her family. She's unable to do that unless my parents and siblings here in the U.S. help her by sending her some money. This saddens me because while I'm living in luxury and do very little for my daily needs, my sister has to work hard everyday for her family's needs. My sister's life is also an example to me to not take anything for granted and to be thankful for every good thing in my life no matter how big or small they are. (Mai)

Clearly, in order to understand one's place in the world, our students argue collectively that this place is related to economic possibilities, national infrastructures, family values, friendship, and care.

Recognition of Political Contexts and Institutional Structures

If we wish to move into solidarity with each other to confront injustice, we must not only understand our own places and histories, but we must also understand ourselves as living within contexts and affected by structures. It is this sort of understanding from which springs the capacity to build coalition across lines of difference. When we enter into discussion about our values and differences, we hope to do so in a way that is meaningful. If we wish to address the oppression we experience under norms of patriarchy, for example, we must not only consider the effects of these norms on our own lives, but also on the lives of others, who may or may not be affected in the same ways that we are, nor interpret their experiences the way we do. Building solidarity must come, then, not merely from an affirmation of sameness and difference, but rather from a willingness to fully engage the experiences and lifeways of others. While conflict is inevitable, we should see that conflict can be productive and necessary in building a social justice agenda.

In the following excerpt, Jennifer draws on her understanding of historical and cultural ideals of beauty in order to critique actions taken by herself and her peers. Speaking to an audience of women, Jennifer's essay explores the sliding scale of beauty and its possible effects on life trajectories and ideas of the self.

> Why do we women want to be beautiful, pretty, or cute? We may not like to admit it, but beauty is a factor in many decisions we make about our lives; from hiring an employee to choosing a romantic partner. Our ideas on what beauty is adapts, it's not as if we are born with an exact sense of what beauty is to us. Images have spanned from ancient and renaissance art with the artists portraying chubby, plump, women who were considered to be beautiful. This changed to suffocating ourselves with corsets so that we created the image of having a thin waist, from the blond frenzy in the 50s to the waif look in models, and finally to the comeback of curves from celebrities like Jennifer Lopez. These popular images of beautiful women are a constant reminder seen in art and especially the media that are ever changing; the message coming across to us with "red is the new black", or white jeans are 'out', and as a result, leaving women forever trying to keep up at all costs. (Jennifer)

While Jennifer focuses primarily on the feminine aspects of her identity, Alex focuses on pointing out the prevalence of racism as an institution:

Racism is one of the horrible issues that occur around the world: "Racism refers to the way society as a whole is arranged, and how the economic, educational, cultural and social rewards of that society are distributed. It is about collective injustice" (Project Hip-Hop Voices, p. 5). It causes problems like violence, wars, and destruction in the world. I have examples about why racism is a problem to me. It can cause a spilt between the world like killing the communities and affecting the world. This issue is serious to me because I don't want my children to go through this issue. Racism makes me feel scared and frightened for my life. It makes me feel like I'm back in slavery because blacks were treated like dogs by their white slave owners. (Alex)

Ia wrote about economic structures, pointing out disparities within and without the United States:

In the United States the minimum wage is around five dollars and fifteen cents, but it can vary depending on the type of job. For example, sometimes waitresses or waiters make lower than minimum wage but they get to keep tips. The pay for doctors is determined by the type of doctor and level of schooling he/she has undergone. In the United States, the level of education determines the level of pay; the higher the degree, the bigger the numbers on the paycheck. This is why Democrats in America are fighting for a higher living wage of seven dollars and twenty-five cents. This situation, where education leads one to a better pay, is also present in many other countries around the world. Although education is important and is the source to earning a good living wage, some countries are poor and efficient education is not possible for most of the population. This type of situation leads to an increase in workers in sweatshops as an attempt to at least earn some type of income regardless of the pay. (Ia)

Recognizing political contexts and institutional structures is necessary not only in order to affirm personal and group experiences, but also in order to build solidarity. Freire's argument that, in problem-posing education, a belief that as an individual and a community citizen, one can promote change, aligns with Nieto's argument that solidarity must be in play in order for social justice to flourish.

Belief that as an Individual and Community Citizen One Can Promote Change

For young people set in institutions of secondary schooling, the belief in one's own ability to promote change is a radical belief. Most of secondary schooling mitigates and governs the desires of its students in order to ensure safety, control, and the maintenance of hierarchical relationships. The excerpts that follow illustrate that it is not necessarily school that promotes solidarity and change.

I am affected by natural disasters also. When I was five years old there was flood that happened and our house was ruined. We had to take out all of our carpets and reline them and we had to fix the damage that was done to the house. Luckily our region wasn't as bad as the others. The feeling that cousins or family have to go through natural disasters like tornados or hurricanes make me scared for them. This year my family took in two survivors of hurricane Katrina they had to move to Baton Rouge so that they could go to school they were two very studious boys that had their homes and lives were ripped away in a blink of an eye. (Corey)

In this instance, Corey shows that it is her family that supports action, based on their own prior experiences. While this narrative does not illustrate institutional change, it does show that Corey has learned that people can help each other.

Even though we can aim higher and do so much more than we think we can, we don't because we don't realize how lucky we are until we're put into a situation like poverty. However, in the end, we become someone we thought we could never become by achieving our goals or sometimes the outcome could be that we may have given up and is deeply lost we don't know who we are anymore. (Mai)

Mai's insight shows that she understands the forces of structure as limiting action and consciousness, even when the intent to change is present. While Mai is describing a commonly experienced if rarely explicated problem of rising through the class structure, she is not posing a solution.

Ability to Pose Solutions and Organize around Issues of Concern

Writing about immigration, schooling, and human trafficking, the following three authors offer the impetus to pose solutions and build solidarity. Whether Bao writes about teaching her friends about her culture and language, or Chuncky points out the vagaries of trying to learn in stifling situations, or Talicia gives a call to arms to end human trafficking, all three ask their audiences to engage solutions.

Immigration affects me because of the negative things that happen. The unique part about people immigrating to the United States is because there are so many different kinds of people and so many cultures that we all learn each day. I myself am teaching other friends that are not Hmong to speak in my language and what Hmong do. It is a great way to have people came together from different part of the world but it also causes a lot of negative things too. (Bao)

I think the schools need to be upgraded. The upgrade is that they have to start teaching different ways, so that everyone knows what's going on in the classrooms. Also they need to make school a lot more fun. Instead of sitting listening to the teacher talk we should be active. It seems that half the class doesn't know what is going on when the teacher lectures for a long time. There should be more visuals and hands on materials to help us understand and stay

246 Nikola Hobbel and Thandeka K. Chapman

interested. Not everyone learns the same. Schools don't seem to realize that kids are bored and not learning. Because lots of people skip school and if they just change it and make it fun, then most of the people that skip school, won't skip school anymore. I don't think they get that the world is changing, not everyone will sit in a chair, listen, and learn. These days there are only some like that. So if they can change/upgrade our school, we would be better off. (Chao AKA Chuncky)

Why can't we stop this? We know what is going on, yet we fail to notice it. Pretending the problem is not there makes it worse. We need to take a stand for human rights in trafficking, because what if they were our children or even our parents? (Talicia)

Posing solutions remains a most complex endeavor; indeed, if solving such concerns were simple, perhaps they would already be moot. We found that one of the most difficult aspects of this sort of work was to continue the problem-posing with each other in order not to produce glib solutions for the sake of a rhetorical move in writing.

Ability to Connect with Others across Lines of Race, Class, Gender, and Sexuality

While posing solutions proved difficult, our students were ready, willing, and able to connect with other people. Alex discussed his own experiences as a young black man and connected to the experiences of Middle Eastern people in arguing against racism:

Additionally racism causes problems in the world. Problems like America treating people from Iraq. This all started when the twin towers were attacked on 9/11. Bush was mad and told U.S soldiers to fight in Iraq. When some Iranians moved to the U.S to be safe from the war, they were treated like trash and like they weren't important to us. Middle Easterners get checked as if they have weapons or they are stealing something. . . . I think it is unfair that many Middle Easterners are getting punished for someone else's actions. Some are being punished for nothing or something they didn't do. I hope the U.S gets its act together and gives them respect like it does its own U.S citizens. (Alex)

Edith wrote about religious intolerance:

I decided to write about religion because I felt that is important topic to reflect on it. If you do not agree with other religions that are not yours, you still have to respect them, and ask the same of them. (Edith's reflection)

Ia, ever mindful of connections and complexity, sought solidarity with workers around the world:

In many countries where people work in sweatshops, workers don't earn enough to provide for personal and family uses. In the Dominican Republic, workers that sew pants for JC Penney only make sixty cents per hour, which isn't even one-third of the living wage that Dominicans are supposed to make to support their families. In Indonesia, sweatshop workers who work for Nike only make ten cents per hour, and that puts them in poverty. In China, Chinese workers for Ralph Lauren work fifteen hours a day, six days a week, making only twenty-three cents an hour. These underpaid people do not want more money to become rich, but so that they can live a life of comfort where they don't have to worry each day whether there will be food on the table, whether their children will have clothes to wear, or whether there will be enough blankets to stay warm. Living wage is not just a problem in these countries, but in others as well. (Ia)

Lastly, Jennifer showed that struggles continue over the decades, and that understanding the history of a particular struggle can inform the present:

We say we want to be 'original'. Does being original mean buying the same clothes at the same stores as your friends? Decades ago, until now people have been molding themselves into what their community considers acceptable and expected. We think that bound feet, neck elongation and inserting a plate into our lip are extreme? It may be so, but going to the mall and spending more than 100 dollars on jeans that look the exact same as the jeans you see on the sales rack is senseless. Right now, fashion and beauty-wise, we are tending to follow rather than lead while young women who grew up in the 1970s and 80s were encouraged to fight sexism by shrugging off the beauty hierarchy, and many obeyed orders, purposefully disregarding their weight, rejecting makeup and avoiding any clothing that would emphasize their femininity. The exact opposite of what we are doing now. (Jennifer)

We were delighted at our students' willingness to connect struggles across boundaries of race, class, gender, and sexuality, even when they (nor we) could not offer easy solutions to these struggles. Consciousness and empowerment, affirmation, solidarity, and critique: none of these ideas pose facile answers within their arguments. In fact, they continually remind us of how difficult work in social justice really is.

Work still to be Done

Problem-posing education affirms men as beings in the process of becoming—as unfinished, uncompleted beings in and with a likewise unfinished reality.

(Freire, 2006, p. 66)

While it is clear that our students' work varied greatly in terms of critique, it is also the case that as teachers, we must continue to push students' understandings of political contexts, myths, and beliefs in meritocracy. We don't believe that these examples are uniformly critical, nor do we argue that other teachers should do as we do, lock-step. Rather, the praxis we enter into with each other, as teachers, and with our students must be understood as on-going and unfinished. Of course, this approach negates the very notion of a static "outcome." Learning is dynamic, and that is its radical possibility.

Conclusions

> With this class I started to like writing a little more. I liked this class because I got to write what I wanted. It didn't matter how long it was, as long as I wrote it. At first I was just going to write something short, but I got into what I was writing. That never happened to me before. (Chuncky's reflection)

Our indicators of successful social justice education ask students and teachers to move beyond representations in texts and beyond only bringing students' voices and lives into the classroom. We argue that these are not enough to address social inequality; in fact, by remaining at the representational curricular level, these pedagogical approaches may serve to empty multiculturalism of its transformative power. We offer this discussion in order to expand the empirical work done in multicultural education, and to revivify the promise of earlier curricular movements that sought to restructure education. By using the trope of the learning outcome, we hope to convince readers that social justice can be an outcome, and that we must question and resist efforts by policy makers to impose upon our students and ourselves an overly narrow version of learning. Lastly, we believe that Nieto's guiding philosophy regarding affirmation, solidarity and critique may be applied in any classroom, not just in English classrooms. Continuing this work through research will build a broad base of evidence that content learning and social justice are complementary goals. If we are to take seriously the project of participatory democracy, the features of an education for social justice are essential.

Points of Inquiry

- Outcomes are traditionally framed as "knowledge, skills, and dispositions." Should social justice be a learning outcome? How does it compare with other content-based or knowledge outcomes? With skills and dispositions outcomes?
- What is the history of the now-ubiquitous standards movement? What are the political aspects that shape its expression at your site or in your state?
- How have teachers, students, and schools responded to the high-stakes testing era? How do these responses shape the possibility of doing social justice work?

Points of Praxis

- The authors mention the component of critique and the inevitability of conflict as a part of teaching and learning. How do you create an environment at your site that can support these components in a productive manner?
- In examining the content you teach, whether based on state standards, available textbooks and resources, or your own philosophy, what parallels and contradictions do you note between the authors' concepts of social justice as content and your approach?
- The authors created a simple prompt for their expository writing course: *Think about things that matter to you. Now, tell your audience why it matters to you, why it matters to your community, and why it matters to the nation or the world.* Create curriculum that directly incorporates content with social justice.

Note

1 NCTE: the National Council of Teachers of English. NWP: The National Writing Project.

References

Banks, J. A. (1995). Multicultural education: Historical development, dimensions, and practice. In J. A. Banks (Ed.), *Handbook of Research on Multicultural Education* (pp. 3–24). New York: Macmillan.

Freire, P. (2006). *Pedagogy of the oppressed: 30th anniversary edition.* New York: Continuum.

Grant, C. A., & Sleeter, C. E. (1998). *Turning on learning: Five approaches for multicultural teaching plans for race, class, gender, and disability.* Columbus, OH: Merrill.

Kanpol, B., & McLaren, P. (Eds.). (1995). *Critical multiculturalism: Uncommon voices in a common struggle.* Westport, CT: Bergin & Garvey.

Moll, L.C., Amanti, C., Neff, D., & Gonzalez, N. (1992). Funds of knowledge for teaching: Using a qualitative approach to connect homes and classrooms. *Theory into Practice, 31*(2), 132–141.

Nieto, S. (1992). *Affirming diversity: The sociopolitical context of multicultural education* (1st ed.). New York: Addison Wesley Longman.

Nieto, S., & Bode, P. (2008). *Affirming diversity: The sociopolitical context of multicultural education* (5th ed.). Boston: Allyn & Bacon.

Sleeter, C. E. (1989). Multicultural education as a form of resistance to oppression. *Journal of Education, 171*(3), 51.

Sleeter, C. E. (1996). Multicultural education as a social movement. *Theory Into Practice, 35*(4), 239.

Vasquez, V. M. (2004). Negotiating critical literacies with young children. New York: Routledge.

Chapter 13

Writing, Pedagogy, and Social Justice

Korina M. Jocson

Several years ago I was a guest speaker in a tenth grade English class and, there, I asked, "Who is Alice Walker?" Students raised their hands with fervor. As they muttered responses to each other, I proceeded to follow up with another question. "Who is June Jordan?" This time, not one hand came up and the room grew silent. Some seemed curious, while others seemed uninterested. Then I held up a poster with Jordan's picture and read the accompanying text, "Inaugural June Jordan Poetry Prize Contest for 9th and 10th graders sponsored by Alice Walker and the Westside Unified School District. Submit your poem."[1] The teacher of this tenth grade class had invited me into her classroom to introduce the contest and to discuss with students the historical relevance of a new effort in urban classrooms. The year was 2003.

The story I tell here highlights the work of Jordan and Walker to offer a particular perspective on teaching for social justice, that is, using the power of words to transform representations of historically denied populations in literature (and larger social discourses) while assisting young people to further develop academic and critical literacy skills associated with the English language arts. The story I tell focuses on culturally responsive pedagogy to understand not only Jordan's and Walker's work, but also the work of teachers and other educators who recognize the value of creating learning environments that promote social justice. The emphasis is on literacy and its link to the construction of knowledge in classrooms to reflect and challenge larger social, historical, and cultural issues.

Challenging the Difference in Literacy and Education

The Nation's Report Card on *reading* indicate that literacy achievement gaps based on race and gender continue to exist; the difference, for example, between African American and Hispanic students and their White counterparts marks the latter as having scored higher, on average, than the former in both the fourth and eighth grades. Similarly, the Nation's Report Card on *writing* indicates that, while results show higher average scores across racial groups than in 1998, White students outperformed Black and Hispanic students in both fourth and eighth grades (National Assessment of Educational Progress, 2009). In this era of No Child Left Behind, these differences more than beg the question of how to close existing gaps in test scores; they demand giving attention to an educational crisis and addressing issues of literacy among adolescents.

What does this mean for literacy educators? From my experience as a former high school teacher and a current collaborator in urban schools, the difference in scores implies an urgent call for an improved pedagogy, a culturally responsive pedagogy that continues to build on the academic and cultural strengths of students as they enter the classroom. Various terms have been coined to emphasize the need for a pedagogy that addresses cultural diversity in the classroom in nuanced ways, ranging from cultural mismatch to culturally relevant or responsive pedagogy (Au & Jordan, 1981; Banks & Banks, 1995; Gay, 2000; Ladson-Billings, 1994; Moll & Gonzalez, 1994). Recent studies have also accounted for cultural politics and difference in ways that promote teaching for social justice (Ayers, 1998; Cammarota, 2007; Nieto & Bode, 2008) and value intersections of history, culture, and education through an anti-oppressive lens (Kumashiro, 2001). In particular, researchers in adolescent literacy learning identify culturally responsive pedagogy as connoting practice that is "intimately tied to relationships, activities, spaces, and times" whether it is in subject content areas in classrooms or in after-school programs (Moje & Hinchman, 2004). Manifesting this practice is certainly not an easy task. For teachers and other literacy educators, a culturally responsive pedagogy at the very least means expanding definitions of reading and writing to account for multiple differences situated in particular sociocultural contexts. It means paying attention to the wide variety of literacy events and literacy practices that stem from different communities and cultures, and treating literacy as linked to structures of power (Heath, 1982; Street, 1984). From these perspectives, it is my contention that culturally responsive pedagogy not only takes into consideration the myriad existing literate practices of students but also makes explicit their connections to the possibilities of empowerment and social justice. The connections are often made through informed experimentation in and out of the classroom.

Artistic and Political Empowerment

June Jordan's Poetry for the People is an accredited poetry program at the University of California, Berkeley. In its fifteenth year of existence, the program led by its current director maintains its course offerings in the African American Studies department on the university campus as well as continues its efforts in the larger community through outreach and writing workshops. One of these efforts is a flagship partnership with a local high school, in consultation and collaboration with English language arts teachers (Jocson, 2005).

Poetry for the People's pedagogical objectives are two-fold: (1) to create a safe medium for artistic and political empowerment, and (2) to democratize the medium of poetry and include "the people" or populations who have been historically denied equal access and representation. Along with these objectives are teaching principles:

1. That students will not take themselves seriously unless we who teach them, honor and respect them in every practical way that we can.

2. That words can change the world and save our lives.
3. That poetry is the highest art and the most exacting service devoted to our most serious, and most imaginative deployment of verbs and nouns on behalf of whatever and whoever we cherish.

In promoting teaching and writing for social justice, Poetry for the People has developed a curriculum that centers on multicultural poets and writers from the U.S.A. and abroad. Their works are included in printed readers and other publications used for instruction. Their works often serve as primary texts during instruction—either through individual reading at home or small to large group discussions in class. They also serve as models for writing as students explore an array of perspectives, traditions, forms, and styles. In addition to established authors, Poetry for the People utilizes the works of emerging writers, including those of college student-teacher-poets and other students in the program (both recent participants and alumni). This deliberate mixture of texts brings multicultural and multi-generational experiences of different peoples into one common space, an approach important to Poetry for the People's educational project.

More specifically, Poetry for the People's curriculum exposes students to provocative writing topics as well as specific writing guidelines, with emphasis on precision and intensity of language. These guidelines contain a pretext that also names the particular tradition the program follows.

(Note): Numerous traditions and ideas about poetry coexist in the world today. Poetry for the People is one specific program founded and directed by the (late) poet and professor June Jordan. Studies with other poets/in other poetry programs may very well disagree, even emphatically, with these rules: well and good! But for now, stick with these:

- **Read it aloud.**
  If anything sounds weak or wrong, change it!
  Listen to the language of every line; hear what you've written and change or retain your carefully chosen words carefully.

- **What is your purpose?**
  What do you want to happen as a consequence of this poem?
  Do not forget the near universal regard of language as a sacred medium, an expression of faith, a pre-requisite to community.
  Does every line and stanza serve the same, governing purpose of the poem or not?

- **Is it a poem?**
  Poetry is a medium for telling the truth.
  Poetry reaches for maximal impact through the use of minimal number of words.
  Poetry demands utmost precision word by word. That painstaking precision delivers the intensity and the density of language that separates poetry from prose.

- **What is the distinguishable subject of the poem throughout?**
  Does each line and stanza follow logically from the one before it?
  Is the poem a complete dramatic event? Does the poem have a beginning, middle, and an end?
  Does the poem create and/or discover connections among otherwise apparently unrelated phenomena?
- **Identify the strengths and weaknesses of the poem** (cf. Technical Checklist)
- **Suggest ways to improve the poem.**
- **Read it aloud!! Repeat your critical passage through these guidelines.**

Embedded in Poetry for the People's selection of writing topics are progressive ideals toward social change and social justice. Topics such as racial profiling and self-affirmation tap into the power of writing as a vehicle for transformation and addressing social, cultural, historical, and political issues relevant to marginalized populations, including youth in low-income urban schools. Sometimes, as I have found in my teaching experience with Poetry for the People, the pre-selected writing topics also challenge students to take up Chinese and Japanese poetic forms such as haiku, tanka, and t'ang. These forms become an added yet fun challenge for students to make every word (and syllable) count.[2] Other writing topics and assignments deemed worthy by students include love and ode. One Latina student named Yerna identified the former as a "good way to remember . . . to show your appreciation to those you care about." Yerna with a strong affinity for Pablo Neruda wrote many poems for and about her father whom she did not get a chance to know (and vice versa). Additional topics with guiding questions and subsequent writing assignments are as follows:

- **Profiling:** What is profiling? What are the different types of profiling? What are your experiences with profiling? *Write a 'profiling' poem.*
- **Democracy:** What is democracy? How does it manifest in American society. *Write a 'democracy' poem.*
- **Home:** What is your notion of Home? What does it mean to be Home? *Write a 'Home' poem.*
- **Self-Affirmation:** What is affirmation? How does affirmation relate to self? *Write a 'self-affirmation' poem.*
- **Ode (or Love):** What is an ode? What does it mean to praise or pay close attention to something or someone? *Write an ode.*

Discussions on the uses of literary devices such as rhythm and rhyme, repetition, alliteration, metaphors, and similes are also incorporated into the topic discussions and lessons about writing poetry. College student-teacher-poets familiar with Poetry for the People's writing guidelines use their knowledge and training to scaffold high school students' incorporation of particular techniques; also, they provide feedback on student work during small-group writing workshops. At the end of any collaboration with a host teacher, a public reading event is held along with an anthology publication consisting of student poems produced during the collaboration. The selection of the anthology's title such as *What We Must Say* from 2001 or *Speak On It* from 2002 often falls in the hands of students themselves—a declaration of their collective naming and, thus, collective message to the public. Until recently, the work of Poetry of the People remained at one high school serving ninth to twelfth grade students. It has now grown and reached other school sites.

Calling on Youth Poets

The June Jordan Poetry Prize Contest began in the spring of 2003 as an extension of earlier efforts in urban public schools. The Prize aims to build the voices of young people through writing and to provide a fresh way of teaching and learning about multicultural poetry. Alice Walker established this annual award largely for budding poets in the San Francisco Bay Area to continue a vision of empowerment within the literary world. As revealed on the night of the inaugural awards ceremony in 2004, it is Walker's five-year gift in memory of her colleague and friend of thirty years. On that same night, Walker shared with the audience her hopes that students would be inspired to continue a legacy by expressing themselves through

Table 13.1 Call for Submissions—Themes and Prompts

	Theme	Prompt(s)
Year 1	Inspiration	Students are required to submit two poems:
		POEM #1: June Jordan said, "We are the ones we have been waiting for." What did she mean? Write a poem inspired by these words or write a poem about a country that she loved. Read her poetry to find out more about what she stood for and had to say about the world.
		POEM #2 prompt: Write a poem from your heart about something that inspires or enrages you! Or, write about someone or some place you love. Submit your best poem and express the depth of your emotion without profanity.
Year 2	Empathy	Write a dedication poem to a person or group of people who are outside your personal world or experience. Submit your best poem showing empathy and expressing the depth of your emotion without profanity.
Year 3	Danger	Write a poem about danger or a specific danger in the world as created by nature or humans. Consider the following questions as you write your poem:
		• What is danger? • How does danger affect your own life or the lives of others?
		Submit your best poem that expresses the depth of your emotion without unnecessary profanity.

words and using the power of words to incite change in the world. For her as it was for Jordan, poetry is "a commitment born of passion, love with unrelenting vision."

Audience for and Evaluation of Student Work

A critical component of the Prize is evaluation, which consists of reading and assessing poems based on Poetry for the People's writing guidelines (see rubric in Table 13.2). A team of teachers and other members of the contest's steering committee, including me, score and tabulate all student poetry entries. After this initial step, approximately 50 poems (and the respective names of semi-finalist poets) are then forwarded to Alice Walker for a final evaluation.

Table 13.2 Writing Guidelines and Rubric for Assessing Poetry Submissions

June Jordan Poetry Prize Rubric										
Criteria	Needs work————————WOW									
Purpose There is a purpose to this poem. The poem is driven by ideas. Every line and stanza serves the same, governing purpose of the poem.	1	2	3	4	5	6	7	8	9	10
Is it a poem? The words speak some truth. The poem is dense and the writer uses a minimal number of words to achieve maximal impact.	1	2	3	4	5	6	7	8	9	10
Subject Each line and stanza follows logically from the one before it. The poem is a complete dramatic event. It has a beginning, middle, and end. The poem creates and/or discovers connections among otherwise apparently unrelated phenomena.	1	2	3	4	5	6	7	8	9	10
June Jordan's Craft Checklist: • Strong descriptive verbs used • Adjective use is limited • Singularity and vividness of diction • Clarity of each stanza, and overall • Specific details • Visual imagery • Defensible line breaks • Abstractions and generalities avoided • The poem makes music • The poem fits into a tradition of poetry • The poem is not predictable or cliché • Limited use of punctuation	1	2	3	4	5	6	7	8	9	10

As one form of external assessment, the evaluation process, is consistent with the current national focus on testing, standards, and accountability. It lends a particular perspective to English language arts standards related to: (1) *application of concepts* such as theme, purpose, and audience in students' production of poetry; (2) *use of spoken and written language* in various forms to communicate knowledge; (3) *reading a wide range of poems* written by multicultural authors from various traditions as a consistent activity for scaffolding student work; and (4) adhering to specific writing guidelines as a means to teach about the importance of *revision in the writing process* (International Reading Association/National Council of Teachers of English, 1996). Notable in the case of this district-wide contest was a chance for students, teachers, members of the steering committee, and Alice Walker to become part of a larger, authentic audience for students' poetry. The audience, of course, grew in size as parents, friends, and other community members later became part of the awards ceremony, a place where each also received a complimentary anthology to take home. For students it was a chance to share their words and their worlds outside of a classroom setting. It was a chance to engage a real audience.

While the rubric serves as a tool for evaluation, it is also important to mention several teachers' reflection on their participation in the Prize. For example, during the second year of the contest, the prompt involved a call for writing about empathy. A group of ten teachers who responded to an open questionnaire revealed that the topic of empathy pushed students to what one called *a shift from the "I" stance and into the "other."* What ensued in the examination of empathy was an opportunity for students to envision character and voice in their writing. According to a follow-up focus group interview with these teachers, the teaching and learning process required plenty of scaffolding, particularly for the younger ninth grade students than their older counterparts, to emerge out of the "I" and write from another stance or place. It was important to explicitly investigate what it meant to be in another person's shoes or to see with someone else's lens. Some of the strategies these teachers used to scaffold students included:

1. collectively reading and deconstructing poems from the printed reader
2. identifying common and uncommon themes
3. using examples from everyday social worlds
4. building on imagination and exploring different possibilities.

As noted by teachers, emerging out of the "I" was a critical element of teaching and writing poetry with a social justice agenda. This process of emerging out of the "I" resulted in student-produced poems relating experiences of individuals from poor and working-class backgrounds, the struggles and plights of immigrant families, topical issues such as everyday racism, sexism, criminalization, imprisonment, and a satirical representation of President George W. Bush and his policies, among others. The process offered students a means to examine issues relevant in their lives; it also offered them a chance to (begin) see(ing) themselves as agents of change through writing. The following excerpt from a poem entitled "I Wanna Understand," written by ninth grade African American female student named

Shannon, exemplifies the use of details to imagine and explore something different, while incorporating writing guidelines set forth by Poetry for the People.

. . . I wanna understand, make me understand

The bedroom window is broken
The baby catching pneumonia
Without a phone to call 911
Waiting in the 45 degree weather
For the next bus to run
Tubes from here on out
Needles in her arms
Air support in her mouth
A victim of second hand smoke
Her last breath of air
The baby starts to choke
She's gone to rest with our heavenly father
Who knows we can overcome this lesson of life

I wanna understand, please make me understand

If only the whole world can relate
What did you do to deserve this?
Working so hard like you have a debt to pay
Slaving off the blocks
Hunting for change as you play
The olda brotha and sista
Never had a night to themselves
Waiting for their siblings to go to sleep
To enter the game on their midnight creep
Sista got kidnapped and raped
Nearly killed
Brotha went down the wrong alley and jacked
For everything he didn't have
Not even a best friend to have his back

I wanna understand, make me understand . . .

The value of empathy in teaching for social justice cannot be underestimated. Shannon's "I Wanna Understand" captures the potential of emerging out of the "I" and into the other and reminds us of the power of words in the movement toward individual and social transformation—a movement toward social justice. Shannon's poem was highly regarded by the steering committee and went as far as the semi-finals round of the Prize. According to Shannon, the details in the poem echoed her observations and provided her a chance to "speak on what is happening around us, around me, because change doesn't just happen like that." Several other students affirmed instances when writing provided the necessary reflection to contemplate change. In fact, African American male student, Eddie, penned a short poem entitled "Time for a Change" encapsulating forms of inequality and inflecting a call to action. Eddie reeled the message home in these lines: "Look at that man who will never get a job/because of his race/the color of his face/that obligates him to catch another case/ . . . people used to say that man's a failure/look at that man now/dead."

Elsewhere, two other collaborators and I discuss our experience extending students' poems from the inaugural Prize contest to reach an even larger audience through new media production (Jocson, Burnside, & Collins, 2006). The result was a student-produced video documentary about students' individual and collaborative projects, including their processes and end products, relating to the theme of inspiration. This work demonstrates a type of innovative practice that stemmed out of our common interest to use poetry as a form of empowerment while intertwining written, oral, and visual modes of communication in the English classroom. The video documentary project pushed us as educators to do more in the following year, asking students to adapt poems like Shannon's "I Wanna Understand" or Eddie's "Time for a Change," for example, to create visual narratives that could impact audiences multimodally. What they created were individual and collaborative digital poems based on written poems that had been partly shaped by Poetry for the People and the Prize.

Some Lessons and Possibilities

The two pedagogical approaches described in this chapter—one through a university—school partnership and the other through a district-wide contest—demonstrate a kind of innovation in literacy and subject matter instruction that is linked to teaching and writing for social justice. In my examination of Poetry for the People's work in various school classrooms, I found that relevant and provocative prompts were integral to creating poetic texts that focused neither on a right or wrong answer nor on structure and grammar. To begin from a reader- and writer-response standpoint provided a place where students could see themselves and relate the sociocultural contexts with which they are familiar. It provided a place for both celebrating and building youth voice, and to foreground everyday knowledge and produce new forms of knowledge. Most notable were pedagogical approaches espoused by Poetry for the People and the Prize that created spaces for students to (1) use character or character-building as a strategy into someone else's world through topical discussions and assignments such as empathy poems; (2) begin connecting literary devices and techniques such as sensory details to other writing genres; and (3) appreciate and identify the craft of "good writing" within various traditions of multicultural literature.

Indeed, the expansion of literacy instruction is about the expansion of pedagogy. The partnership and subsequent contest provided a space for students and teachers in the San Francisco Bay Area to encounter multicultural literature *by* and *with* acclaimed authors. This encounter was not only about an understanding of various texts, but also about an understanding of the historical relevance of producing works that continue a legacy, of writing and representing the experiences of historically denied populations, of making words matter in the world. What it implies is the importance of studying and expanding literature while also challenging traditional notions of what and who makes up the literary canon. At the very least, it implies the importance of representation (both ethnically and linguistically) in the movement toward teaching *and* writing for social justice.

There are many possibilities in literacy and culturally responsive pedagogy. The Poetry for the People program and the Prize may be unique, but their pedagogies offer us myriad ways to rethink what is possible in twenty-first-century classrooms. For those interested in critical literacy, Poetry for the People's approach to writing as a form of artistic and political empowerment may be worth exploring in English language arts and across content areas. Or perhaps the extension of learning beyond classroom walls through writing workshops and activities with members of the community may also be worth considering. For others it might be worthwhile to see what happens when students choose their best work for publication in class anthologies and examine along with students what it means to write for a real audience. Those involved in project-based learning approaches might also find it worthwhile to incorporate evaluation that is not solely based on testing and grades. Perhaps there might be a consideration for including assessments of student portfolios and other performance-based work across time, place, and genres. Or perhaps even forms of external assessment with input from parents and other community members might be included. There are no limits to effective literacy instruction as there are no limits to shaping innovative practice. Culturally responsive pedagogy offers a way to develop innovative practices that build on the strengths of every child and every young person in school.

Points of Inquiry

- How can the writing and performance of poetry by students affect test scores? What literacy practices are congruent between these two different arenas?
- Why is literacy so intimately connected to social justice pedagogy? Draw together research and practice to argue your point.

Points of Praxis

- What generative themes would be apt for your classroom? Design a series of inquiry-based lessons that allow students to design their own poetry projects.
- Using the guidelines described by Jocson, write a poem about what it's like to teach at your school. Share it with your students.
- How might contemporary multicultural poetry be incorporated into your curriculum? Who and what works would be most relevant? Authors for your consideration include Ethelbert Miller, James Weldon Johnson,

Nikki Giovanni, Audre Lorde, Cornelius Eady, Haas Mroue, Naomi Shihab Nye, Nicolás Guillen, Lorna Dee Cervántes, Martín Espada, Li Young Lee, Janice Mirikitani, and Jessica Hagedorn.

Resources

* June Jordan: http://www.junejordan.com
* Muller, L., & the Poetry for the People Blueprint Collective (Eds.). (1995). *June Jordan's Poetry for the People: A revolutionary blueprint.* New York: Routledge.
* Poetry for the People, Department of African American Studies, University of California at Berkeley: http://africam.berkeley.edu/p4p.html

Notes

1 All names are pseudonyms, except for Alice Walker, June Jordan, and the University of California, Berkeley.
2 Different from a haiku or a tanka, a t'ang poem consists of four lines with five one-syllable words per line, each word either a verb or a noun.

References

Au, K., & Jordan, C. (1981). Teaching reading to Hawaiian children: Finding a culturally appropriate solution. In H. Trueba, B. Guthrie, & K. Au (Eds.), *Culture and bilingual classroom: Studies in classroom ethnography* (pp. 139–152). Rowley, MA: Newbury.

Ayers, W. (Ed.). (1998). *Teaching for social justice: A democracy and education reader.* New York: New Press.

Banks, J., & Banks, C. (Eds.). (1995). *Handbook of research on multicultural education.* New York: Macmillan.

Cammarota, J. (2007). A social justice approach to achievement: Guiding Latina/o students toward educational attainment with a challenging, socially relevant curriculum. *Equity and Excellence in Education, 40,* 87–96.

Gay, G. (2000). *Culturally responsive teaching: Theory, research and practice.* New York: Teachers College.

Heath, S. B. (1982). What no bedtime story means: Narrative skills at home and at school. *Language in Society, 11*(2), 49–76.

International Reading Association/National Council of Teachers of English. (1996). *Standards for the English language arts.* Urbana, IL: National Council of Teachers of English.

Jocson, K. M. (2005). "Taking it to the mic": Pedagogy of June Jordan's Poetry for the People and partnership with an urban high school. *English Education, 37*(2), 44–60.

Jocson, K. M., Burnside, S., & Collins, M. (2006). Pens on the prize: Linking school and community through contest-inspired literacy. *Multicultural Education, 14*(2), 28–33.

Kumashiro, K. (Ed.). (2001). *Troubling intersections of race and sexuality: Queer students of color and anti-oppressive education.* Lanham, MD: Rowman & Littlefield.

Ladson-Billings, G. (1994). *The dreamkeepers: Successful teachers of African American children.* San Francisco: Jossey-Bass.

Moje, E., & Hinchman, K. (2004.). Culturally responsive practices for youth literacy learning. In T. Jetton, & A. Dole (Eds.), *Adolescent literacy research and practice* (pp. 321–350). New York: Guilford.

Moll, L., & Gonzalez, N. (1994). Lessons from research with language-minority children. *Journal of Reading Behavior, 26*(4).

National Assessment of Educational Progress. (2009). *The nation's report card.* Washington, DC: U.S. Department of Education/National Center for Education. Retrieved on December 6, 2009 from: http://nces.ed.gov/nationsreportcard/

Nieto, S., & Bode, P. (2008). *Affirming diversity: The sociopolitical context of multicultural education* (5th ed.). Boston: Allyn & Bacon.

Street, B. (1984). *Literacy in theory and practice.* Cambridge: Cambridge University Press.

Chapter 14

Mathematics Education for Social Transformation

Eric (Rico) Gutstein

Framing mathematics as a weapon in the struggle for social justice and making explicit the political nature of mathematics education in particular, and school in general, directly responds to the question students in math class (and school) perennially ask: "Why do I need to know this?" This chapter gives concrete examples of teaching mathematics for social justice from a Chicago public high school as well as evidence that students can develop sociopolitical consciousness in such a class; it also provides a theoretical framing for this practice, based on the work of Paulo Freire. This broader awareness that students develop, in part through the political experience of learning to read and write the world with mathematics, can support them in becoming effective change agents in the larger historical motion. Their mathematics education can contribute to this process.

No oppressive order could permit the oppressed to begin to question: Why?
(Freire, 1970/1998, p. 67)

The purpose of this chapter is to provide concrete examples of what Paulo Freire (Freire & Macedo, 1987) termed *reading and writing the world*—specifically, its meaning with respect to mathematics education.[1] Mathematics knowledge, with its valorized status, often serves the needs and goals of capital, the financial and corporate elites who largely control (although contested) our world (Apple, 2004). But that is not the only possibility for mathematics. Like any knowledge, it can be used to benefit the few or the many. Educators and students (at *all* grade levels) can collaborate to re-envision and re-create mathematics classrooms supporting social justice and an end to oppression and exploitation. In this chapter, I provide a brief conceptual framework and concrete examples of what this looks like at the classroom level, drawing on years of teaching for social justice in Chicago public schools. I hope to support teachers, teacher-candidates, researchers, curriculum developers, and teacher educators in creating mathematics curricula, pedagogies, and classroom cultures that foster students to do what no oppressive order wants them to do—to question why.

Learning from Paulo Freire

Freire left us a rich body of work upon which to draw in "reinventing" him (his word). Foremost is that education should explicitly serve the oppressed against capitalism and neoliberalism (1970/1998, 1994, 1998, 2004). Though Freire acknowledged the limitations of education alone in changing society, he believed it played an important, essential role. For him, education needed to be for liberation rather than for domination, social reproduction, and submission, which is its current role in U.S. schools (and elsewhere). His terms, *reading the world* (developing a deep sociopolitical consciousness about power relations and structural oppression), and *writing the world* (taking one's own destiny into one's hands to make history), situate education as a way to grasp the essence of, and transform, social reality.

Freire created educational programs that tapped into and built on what he called "popular knowledge" (which others refer to as community knowledge). He argued "the starting point for organizing the program content of education or political action must be the present, existential, concrete situation, reflecting the aspirations of the people" (1970/1998, p. 76). In his work, educators and organizers uncovered and learned about these by studying the people's *generative themes* (the dialectical interrelationship between key social contradictions in their lives and how they understand and interact with them, Freire, 1970/1998). They then created and taught curriculum, in both in- and out-of-school settings. Although Freire's work covered many other ideas, the most central for me is that political experiences are essential to develop political consciousness. This, in turn, is central to learning to read—or to do mathematics. Freire argued that engagement in political struggles and social movements can lead to a deeper comprehension of our role in making history, and this politicization addresses the question of why should people learn mathematics. That is, when people realize that disciplinary knowledge (like mathematics) is key to understanding the genesis of the oppression and marginalization they experience, they will more deeply engage in learning that knowledge. It takes on genuine meaning, relevance, and power. Furthermore, this increased awareness can then lead us to become more active and committed to transforming society.

How are these ideas relevant to mathematics education in a U.S. urban context? Freire worked mainly with adults, who were volunteers, in economically developing countries, in community settings, on literacy campaigns, with no high-stakes tests, and the freedom to design curriculum from learners' generative themes. In contrast, I work with youth in a Chicago public high school, who are mostly not volunteers, in an "advanced" capitalist country, on mathematics, with high-stakes tests, and, mostly, with mandated, irrelevant curricula. Our task in understanding Freire is to learn from his experiences and from those who have tried to actualize his theory and principles, and apply this to our contexts. This is not to "export" Freire, but to reinvent him in our lives.

Teaching Mathematics for Social Justice: Providing Opportunities for Political Experience

I have worked with Chicago public schools for the last 15 years. I first worked with "Rivera" elementary school for 10 years, in a low-income Mexican immigrant community. During that time, I taught seventh and eighth grade mathematics for about four years (one class a year) as part of how I defined my work as a university professor. Since late 2003, I have worked with a new high school in a similar community, whose students are 30% African American (from neighboring North Lawndale) and 70% Latino, mainly of Mexican descent (from Little Village), and 98% low income. That school is the Greater Lawndale/Little Village School for Social Justice (or "Sojo"), and I support the mathematics teachers, work with students, develop social justice mathematics curriculum, and co-teach social justice mathematics projects (ranging from a few days to two weeks). This year (2008/9), I currently teach a twelfth grade math class, in which *all* contexts are about students' social reality. In both schools, I have studied the process as it unfolds, with students and teachers as co-researchers. And, although space precludes my discussing it here, the larger sociopolitical context of mathematics education and its role in global economic competition is central to my analysis and practice (Gutstein, 2009).

Briefly, I understand social justice mathematics education to be when teachers and students work together to provide students the opportunity to read and write the world with mathematics (Gutstein, 2006). These ideas owe much to my interpretation of both Freire's work and of the history and tradition of African American liberatory education (e.g., Anderson, 1988; Perry, 2003). My goals include that students learn both mathematics and about the world. They should develop deep sociopolitical consciousness of their immediate/broader contexts and a *sense of social agency* (see themselves as capable of changing the world). In the process, they should develop strong cultural and social identities, be rooted in who they are as a people, and develop the confidence to stand up for their beliefs. They should learn important mathematics so that they have opportunities to study, pursue meaningful lives, and support their families and communities, but even more, so that they can use mathematics to fight injustice and improve society (my data over the years suggest that mathematical sophistication and maturity supports the development of political awareness). And finally, I want students to change their orientations toward mathematics, to realize that it has real meaning in life and can be specifically used to read and write the world.

At Sojo and Rivera, I am well aware that, as a white male monolingual professional with the associated baggage, I am an outsider to students' communities, languages, and cultures. However, I am a close outsider because I have a good deal of life experience in such communities, and I consciously try to stand in solidarity with the people there. I am actively involved in local struggles in Chicago against gentrification, school closings, and the exclusion from the city of low- and moderate-income people (mainly, but not exclusively, of color). Also, I am an anti-Zionist Jew with the memory of the Holocaust and anti-Semitic racism in my being, and thus have empathy for other people's suffering. Nonetheless, teaching for social justice is complicated enough, and to try to do so while teaching "other people's children" (Delpit, 1988) and crossing lines of social class, race, age, gender, culture, language, ethnicity, experience is even more complex.

There is solid evidence from Rivera and Sojo that the above goals can be partially realized—youth can *begin* to read and write the world with mathematics, while also learning conceptual mathematics—and the work is complicated, slow, and difficult. Our data suggest that Sojo's current seniors (the class on which I have focused since they were ninth graders, now about 75 students) have normalized learning mathematics for social justice.

We think this is so for two reasons. First, Sojo has an explicit mission about social justice, although that means different things, in theory and practice, to various administrators, teachers, parents, and students. Second, and perhaps primary, the senior class I refer to here has completed three or four social justice math projects since they started school. We frame this work as "using mathematics as a weapon in the struggle." These projects have evidently been sufficiently meaningful and memorable to students that in our focus group interviews, none reported it as unusual to hear that particular framing of mathematics.

Examples of Social Justice Mathematics Projects

When students were ninth graders (2005/6, the year Sojo opened), they completed a mathematics project about racial profiling, a topic with which many students were familiar or had personal experience. During the project, students used calculators to simulate "random" traffic stops that police made in an area for which we had the real data. Before we began, we explained that we would "use mathematics to check up on the police" to verify if they had conducted unbiased stops. Our framing was explicit: to use mathematics to collect and analyze data to evaluate police behavior, to pose other questions (e.g., is racism a factor and how do you know?) and possible further investigations, and to fight for social justice.

As students entered eleventh grade in Fall 2007, we started with a two-week project about the criminalization of youth of color, specifically about the Jena Six, six African American male high school students from Jena, Louisiana (Sia & Gutstein, 2007). In December 2006, the Jena Six were charged with attempted murder in a schoolyard fight that developed out of a racist incident a few months earlier. In June 2007, an all-white jury convicted Mychal Bell (the first of the six to be tried) of lesser charges, and he awaited sentencing in September 2007 as we began school. Our project's focus question was: Given Jena's demographics (2,154 adults and 85.6% white as of the 2000 census), what was the probability of randomly choosing an all-white (12-person) jury for Mychal Bell? The ninth and tenth grade math teachers picked up, modified, and also taught the project, and thus the whole student body learned about the Jena struggle through their mathematics classes—unusual to say the least. The project contributed to students taking action—dozens walked out of school and organized an impromptu protest on a nearby corner on Mychal Bell's sentencing day.

When students were tenth graders in the 2006/7 school year, they completed a project, "Reading Hurricane Katrina with Mathematics." Students examined data, graphs, and photos to understand who was unable to leave the city—and why, specifically in terms of race and class. The final part of the assignment was:

> Now that you've done all this investigation, it's time to pull together the story that your data tell. Write a good, solid essay explaining your analysis of Hurricane Katrina on the people of New Orleans. You *must* use mathematical arguments from your work here and create one (or more) *well-labeled* graphs to present your data/mathematical arguments. Here are some questions to help you:
>
> (a) What data are most convincing and what do they tell you? Why are these data convincing to you?
> (b) How do the data help explain the story? Could there be other explanations?
> (c) What other data would you need to know or do you want to know? What questions do *you* have?

Students' essays were emotional, strongly worded, and uneven. Although the mathematics was essentially proportional reasoning and not overly challenging, making sense of the graphs and data was quite difficult. Students had to understand that the ratio of *poor-African-Americans-with-no-car* to *poor-whites-with-no-car* was relevant and key to arguing why more African Americans, both numerically and proportionately, were stranded in New Orleans versus whites. For the most part, students used mathematics to argue their points, although there were weaknesses and errors. Guadalupe, a Latina, wrote in her essay:

> It was 3.2 times more likely for a black person to be poor than a white person in New Orleans. The question we really need to ask is did the African American people get left behind for their skin color?.... A large percent of the people that got left behind were poor & Black. [There was a] 14 to 1 ratio of not having a car for poor Black person vs. a poor white person. It was 8 more times as likely for a Black person [regardless of income] not to have a car.

And Gregory, an African American male wrote:

> The most convincing piece of data was that it was 3.2x more likely to be a poor black in New Orleans than white. This basically tells me that it is more likely for you to see a poor black than a poor white [in the Superdome]. This data is the most convincing because I saw a lot of this on TV. This helps to tell the story because when you look at the pictures, that is all you see.

Vanessa, a Latina, made a few points that were mathematically not totally accurate:

> Another ratio that is very unfair is that for every one white household, there are 14 black households w/out no car [this is actually the ratio of poor Blacks without cars to poor whites without cars]. So there are more black people in

New Orleans, but still there are more whites w/ cars [actually true, but she may have confounded rates with actual numbers].

She continued, suggesting that despite some confusion, she learned from the project:

> From this project, I found out that in New Orleans, racism is going on. I really never thought of there being such things around. This opened my eyes to see that math helps us find REAL percentages of what really happens. This showed me that I don't need no one to come tell me and lie to me about who are being left behind when I can do it myself.

Challenges in Enacting Social Justice Mathematics Education

Although we can point to both possibilities and learning in this work, there are significant difficulties and obstacles (see Gutstein, 2006 for further discussion). It is important to examine these honestly to support others in doing similar work. A significant issue is how to reconcile the contradiction between using a mostly mandated curriculum with high-stakes assessments (e.g., the ACT exam), and developing and teaching social justice mathematics that builds on students' generative themes. An alternative framing is: How can we build on students' community (popular) knowledge while simultaneously supporting the development of critical (mathematical) knowledge and classical (academic) knowledge (Gutstein, 2007b)?

This dialectic has numerous complexities. First, there is no social justice mathematics curriculum that I know of. There are several collections of social justice mathematics projects, units, and lessons (e.g., Gutstein & Peterson, 2005; Mistrik & Thul, 2004; radicalmath.org, 2006; Shan & Bailey, 1991; Stocker, 2006; Thul, 2004; Vatter, 1996), but no comprehensive, coherent social justice mathematics curriculum actually exists. Second, a *published* social justice mathematics curriculum is, in part, an oxymoron because it could not stem directly from students' generative themes, although one could develop social justice mathematics units to be "reinvented" by teachers, as well as a general framework for creating such a curriculum (though again, no such framework exists as far as I know). Third, building curriculum from students' lives and knowledge is difficult and time consuming. Fourth, writing quality mathematics curriculum is daunting. Each of the 13 "reform" mathematics curricula (aligned with the National Council of Teachers of Mathematics, 1989) took millions of dollars and years of work. One way to address these quandaries has been to use good, conceptually based mathematics curricula and intersperse, as coherently as possible, social justice mathematics projects, while working with students to co-create an environment that supports political relationships between students and teacher (Gutstein, 2006). But much remains to be done. At Sojo, we are studying the twelfth-grade mathematics class that I have been developing and teaching. It blends pre-calculus and quantitative literacy, and students and I collectively determined the social justice contexts. While we are learning a lot, our analysis is just beginning, as I write this in March 2009 with three months to go in the year.

A second issue is the complexity of teaching—as opposed to developing—social justice mathematics curriculum. The literature is clear that even experienced teachers need time to learn new, challenging mathematics curricula (Fennema & Scott Nelson, 1997). One should expect that teaching mathematics for social justice would be even harder given the interdisciplinary complexity and the background knowledge teachers need. At Sojo, the mathematics teachers are dedicated, but also young and inexperienced. They have had to learn to teach, to teach mathematics, to teach a standards-based curriculum (new units each year), and to teach mathematics for social justice, all in the context of a new, complex school. None of it has been easy. Freire (1994) argued that conscientization grew from, in part, political experiences, implying that teachers will need to develop, in myriad ways, the necessary sociopolitical consciousness to teach for social justice and build political relationships with students (Gutstein, 2008).

A third challenge has been to support students in using mathematics to present and defend their views and analyses about social justice issues and to take actions they deem appropriate. For example, we wanted them to use mathematics to argue whether Mychal Bell's jury selection was fair or biased. Teaching students to use mathematical argumentation and justification is not simple, especially given what they report to be their lack of experience with this in elementary school. Furthermore, on one project, students proposed several actions to effect change— but almost none used mathematics. In other words, students might be learning to write the world—but not necessarily *with* mathematics. This contrasts with our data that show students beginning to *read* the world with mathematics. Does it really matter if students advocate mathematical ways to change the world, as long as they use mathematics to make sense of social reality and act as historical actors however they see fit? We are ambivalent but will continue to study this and support students in defending their ideas with mathematics and with words, and in taking suitable actions.

Finally, some have asked: Where is the mathematics? I consistently address this question in my work because, as I note above, mathematics is essential for equity and access concerns *and* because students must understand mathematics well to read and write the world with it. In the Jena Six project, students derived a formula (for $n\, C\, r$) that they did not know and which was necessary to solve the problem as we framed it (Sia & Gutstein, 2007). I explicitly told students that they had to "think like mathematicians" and "develop mathematical generalizations." This challenging work is aligned with the mathematics education philosophy of *realistic mathematics education* (Freudenthal, 1991) in which teachers support students to "reinvent" significant mathematics.

These complexities may give prospective social justice mathematics teachers pause, so our (Gutstein & Peterson, 2005) advice is to start small. Teachers can take mathematical ideas they are teaching and find related social justice mathematics curriculum through the resources available (see supplemental resources). Listening to students and their families, knowing their communities, and being tuned to the media are all ways to extend "regular" classroom math. Try it and learn from the experience, work with others in mathematics and different subject areas, and continue to grow and develop as a professional and social justice advocate.

Conclusion

The formal mathematics education of Sojo youth, I believe, has always been divorced from their lives. We all know the perennial question students ask mathematics teachers: "When am I ever going to need this?" The vague answer is usually something like "sometime in the future." Engagement, commitment, perseverance, and motivation in learning mathematics, and more generally, in school, clearly matter. Why should students who have been excluded, marginalized, criminalized, and discriminated against spend the time and effort to commit to school?

Framing mathematics as a weapon in the struggle for social justice and making explicit the political nature of mathematics education in particular, and school in general, is a way to address the above question. The process can contribute to students becoming social change agents and participating in social movements. One can create opportunities for youth to be politically involved, in appropriate and various ways, both directly and vicariously (Gutstein, 2007a). In 12 years of creating and teaching social justice mathematics projects, although not all students loved them or were enthralled, some things are clear. I never heard a student ask, "When will I ever need this math?" Instead, as Antoine, a student in the math and social justice class I currently teach recently explained about the work we do in our class:

> Reading and writing the world with mathematics for me is interpreting and making our judgment of the social and political reality of our community and the world we live in. . . . We do it because it helps us understand and combat against oppression and injustice in our communities and in the world. But more importantly, we do it to be educated in knowing what we are fighting against. (February 2009).

Overall, Sojo and Rivera students have consistently been more engaged in the projects than in other mathematics. This may be because the projects are "linked to and address one's status as a member of a historically oppressed people" (Perry, 2003, p. 19). The projects position learning mathematics as a liberatory tool that provides students deeper understandings of Hurricane Katrina, racial profiling, conditions of immigrant agricultural workers, disparity in mortgage rejection rates, wealth inequality, the cost of the Iraq War, the impact of different world map projections, gentrification in their neighborhoods, and many other issues that we studied. These matter to Sojo and Rivera students because of the righteous anger and powerful sense of justice that they bring with them into school due to their location in an oppressive society. Furthermore, the projects at times give them ways to begin to see themselves as agents of change, whether through demonstrating in support of the Jena Six, attending city hall hearings about displacement, speaking at conferences, or just coming to know that, although they have the capacity to do so, their prior schooling has prepared them *not* to read and write the world.

Along the way, some students have begun to understand that they were profoundly "miseducated" (Woodson, 1933/1990) in U.S. schools that prepare them mostly for low-skill service-sector jobs, prison, gangs, the military, or the grave (Lipman, 2004). In North Lawndale, the mathematics is grim—two males for every three females, because, to quote a male student from the community, "all the brothers are locked up or in the ground." One student wrote, on a project that examined world maps in sociopolitical context, "It makes me feel like I was lied to all these years." This broader consciousness, gained in part through the political experiences of learning to read and write the world with mathematics, will be necessary for Sojo and Rivera students, and youth like them, to become effective change agents in the larger historical motion. Their mathematics education *can* contribute to this process.

Points of Inquiry

- Review the national math curriculum standards (NCTM, 1989, 2000). How do they relate to social justice education?
- How might teaching mathematics for social justice differ from other subjects? What are the points of similarity?
- This article is about middle and high school mathematics—what is the relevance to primary grades?
- What are some commonalities and overlaps between the history of African American education for liberation and Paulo Freire's work?

Points of Praxis

- Considering the Jena Six and Hurricane Katrina, generate other themes and topics that would be appropriate starting points for your students to begin constructing their own generative themes. Reflect on how your own knowledge and experiences influence your choice of topics/themes.
- Gutstein discusses critical math education in schools populated predominantly by members of marginalized groups. How can we build critical mathematics curricula if we are working in privileged schools and communities?

Resources

- http://www.radicalmath.org RadicalMath is a resource for educators interested in integrating issues of social and economic justice into their math classes and curriculum.
- *Rethinking mathematics: Teaching social justice by the numbers.* Edited by Eric Gutstein and Bob Peterson. Published by Rethinking Schools, Milwaukee (2005).

- *Radical equations: Math literacy and civil rights.* By Bob Moses and Charles Cobb. Published by Beacon Press, Boston (2001).
- *Math for a world that rocks* (3rd ed.). Edited by Robert C. Thul. Published by St. Ignatius College Prep, Chicago (2004).
- *Math for a change* (5th ed.). By Kevin J. Mistrik and Robert C. Thul. Published by the Mathematics Teachers' Association of Chicago and Vicinity (2004).
- *Maththatmatters: A teacher resource linking math and social justice.* By David Stocker. Published by Canadian Center for Policy Alternatives, Ottawa (2006).
- *Civic mathematics: Fundamentals in the context of social issues.* By Terry Vatter. Published by Teacher Ideas Press, Englewood, CO (1996).
- *Multiple factors: Classroom mathematics for equality and justice.* By Sharan-Jeet Shan and Peter Bailey. Published by Trentham Books, Stoke-on-Trent, U.K. (1991).

Acknowledgment

I would like to acknowledge the students at "Rivera" Elementary School and the teachers and students at the Greater Lawndale/Little Village School for Social Justice in Chicago, especially the student co-research team. The work and knowledge production I describe here regarding the schools was genuinely collaborative.

Note

1 Portions of this chapter are from talks at the fifth Mathematics Education and Society Conference (Albufeira, Portugal, February 2008) and the annual meeting of the American Educational Research Association (New York, March 2008).

References

Anderson, J. (1988). *The education of Blacks in the south, 1860–1935.* Chapel Hill, NC: University of North Carolina Press.

Apple, M. W. (2004). *Ideology and curriculum* (3rd ed.). New York: RoutledgeFalmer.

Delpit, L. (1988). The silenced dialogue: Power and pedagogy in educating other people's children. *Harvard Educational Review, 58,* 280–298.

Fennema, E., & Scott Nelson, B. (Eds.). (1997). *Mathematics teachers in transition.* Mahway, NJ: Erlbaum.

Freire, P. (1970/1998). *Pedagogy of the oppressed.* (M. B. Ramos, Trans.). New York: Continuum.

Freire, P. (1994). *Pedagogy of hope: Reliving Pedagogy of the Oppressed.* (R. R. Barr, Trans.). New York: Continuum.

Freire, P. (1998). *Pedagogy of freedom: Ethics, democracy, and civic courage.* (P. Clarke, Trans.). Lanham, MD: Rowman & Littlefield.

Freire, P. (2004). *Pedagogy of indignation.* Boulder, CO: Paradigm Publishers.

Freire, P., & Macedo, D. (1987). *Literacy: Reading the word and the world.* Westport, CT: Bergin & Garvey.

Freudenthal, H. (1991). *Revisiting mathematics education: China lectures.* Dordrecht, NL: Kluwer Academic.

Gutstein, E. (2006). *Reading and writing the world with mathematics: Toward a pedagogy for social justice*. New York: Routledge.

Gutstein, E. (2007a). "And that's just how it starts": Teaching mathematics and developing student agency. *Teachers College Record, 109*, 420–448.

Gutstein, E. (2007b). Connecting *community*, *critical*, and *classical* knowledge in teaching mathematics for social justice. *Montana Mathematics Enthusiast, Monograph 1*, 109–118.

Gutstein, E. (2008). Building political relationships with students: What social justice mathematics pedagogy requires of teachers. In E. de Freitas, & K. Nolan (Eds.), *Opening the research text: Critical insights and in(ter)ventions into mathematics education* (pp. 189–204). New York: Springer.

Gutstein, E. (2009). The politics of mathematics education in the US: Dominant and counter agendas. In B. Greer, S. Mukhopadhyay, S. Nelson-Barber, & A. Powell (Eds.), *Culturally responsive mathematics education*. Mahway, NJ: Erlbaum.

Gutstein, E., & Peterson, B. (Eds.). (2005). *Rethinking mathematics: Teaching social justice by the numbers*. Milwaukee, WI: Rethinking Schools.

Lipman, P. (2004). *High stakes education: Inequality, globalization, and urban school reform*. New York: Routledge.

Mistrik, K. J., & Thul, R. C. (2004). *Math for a change* (5th ed.). Chicago: Mathematics Teachers' Association of Chicago and Vicinity.

National Council of Teachers of Mathematics (NCTM) (1989). *Curriculum and evaluation standards for school mathematics*. Reston, VA: Author.

National Council of Teachers of Mathematics (2000). *Principles and standards for school mathematics*. Reston, VA: Author.

Perry, T. (2003). Up from the parched earth: Toward a theory of African-American achievement. In *Young, gifted, and black: Promoting high achievement among African-American students* (pp. 1–108). Boston: Beacon Press.

Shan, S-J., & Bailey, P. (1991). *Multiple factors: Classroom mathematics for equality and justice*. Stoke-on-Trent, U.K.: Trentham Books.

Sia, J., & Gutstein, E. (2007). Detailed mathematics unit. In A. Mangual & B. Picower (Eds.), *Revealing racist roots: The 3 R's for teaching about the Jena 6* (pp. 21–25). New York: Teacher Activist Groups. (available from: http://www.nycore.org/curricula.html).

Stocker, D. (2006). *Maththatmatters: A teacher resource linking math and social justice*. Ottawa: Canadian Center for Policy Alternatives.

Thul, R. C. (Ed.). (2004). *Math for a world that rocks* (3rd ed.). Chicago: St. Ignatius College Prep.

Vatter, T. (1996). *Civic mathematics: Fundamentals in the context of social issues*. Englewood, CO: Teacher Ideas Press.

Woodson, C. G. (1933/1990). *The mis-education of the Negro*. Trenton, NJ: Africa World Press.

Chapter 15

Science Curricular Materials through the Lens of Social Justice

Research Findings

Mary M. Atwater and Regina L. Suriel

The purpose of this chapter is to provide a practical snapshot of social justice in action with science curricula—what it looks like, why it matters, and how teachers might envision practices and orientations for their science classes. To accomplish this, the authors focus on the results and implications of studies of teachers that designed multicultural science curriculum and their results of implementing some of the activities in their science classrooms. The implications of research on multicultural science curricula have the potential for future impact on student science learning, science teacher education programs, and research. It even has more to say about the difficulty of maintaining a social justice agenda in science education.

Introduction

With the printing of Science for All Americans (SFAA) in 1990 by the American Association for the Advancement of Science (AAAS), scientists, mathematicians, engineers, physicians, philosophers, and historians called for high school graduates to be scientifically literate with the return of Haley's comet in 2061. To be scientifically literate under the SFAA ideals, students need to understand not only the tenets and approaches of science, but they also need to be literate in mathematics and technology. Then in 1993, AAAS published Benchmarks for Science Literacy as a tool for educators to use to fashion their own curricula in every state and school district. Elementary, middle school, and high school teachers, school administrators, scientists, mathematicians, engineers, historians, and learning specialists participated in the development of the benchmarks that were to be reached by students at specific grade levels, so that all students in the United States would become literate in science, mathematics, and technology. In 1996, the National Research Council published the National Science Education Standards, "a vision of science education that will make scientific literacy for all a reality in the 21st century" (p. ix). With these standards for science teaching, professional development for teachers, assessment, K-12 science contents, science education programs, and school systems, the science education community was poised to begin its work on ensuring science literacy for all students in the United States. However, the authors of this chapter do not believe that any of these documents provide philosophical and theoretical lenses to accomplish this literacy for all.

Hence, the purpose of this chapter is to provide a practical snapshot of social justice in action with science curricula that will begin to ensure science literacy for all students in the United States. Since there is very little ongoing research about science curricula, especially with an emphasis on social justice, the emphasis of this chapter will be on why social justice is important in science curricula, what social justice looks like in science curriculum materials, and how science teachers might envision social justice orientations and practices.

First, we need to define some terms such as "science literacy," "all students," "science curriculum," "critical science multiculturalism," and "social justice." People define science literacy in many ways—what a person knows, what a person can do, and what kinds of careers a person pursues. For example, SFAA (1990) delineates a scientifically literate person as

> one who is aware that science, mathematics, and technology are interdependent human enterprises with strengths and limitations; understands key concepts and principles of science; is familiar with the natural world and recognizes both its diversity and unity; and uses scientific knowledge and scientific ways of thinking for individual and social purposes. (p. xvii)

According to SFAA, a scientifically literate high school graduate (a) understands the nature of science, mathematics, and technology as a human enterprise, (b) possesses the basic knowledge about the world from the perspectives of scientists, mathematicians, and technologists, (c) understands about some of the great episodes in the history of the scientific endeavor and crosscutting themes that can serve as tools for thinking about how the world works, and (d) possesses habits of the mind. The science knowledge includes knowledge of the biophysical environment and social behavior that explains the dependency of living things on each other and the physical environment and the nature of systems, the importance of feedback and control, the cost-benefit risk relationships, and the inevitability of the side effects of technology that impact the environment and the microcultures found in the United States. Scientific habits of the mind help people from all "walks of life" (p. xiv) to deal with problems that involve evidence, quantitative considerations, logical arguments, and uncertainty. Scientifically literate people can participate with others to build and protect an open and just society.

No Child Left Behind (NCLB) legislation defines who *all* students are in U.S. school systems that garner federal funds. NCBL's purpose is to ensure "all children have a fair, equal, and significant opportunity to obtain a high-quality education and reach, at a minimum, proficiency on challenging State academic achievement standards and state academic assessments" (U.S. Department of Education, n.d., Section 1001, ¶ 1). "All," then, includes students from the following groups of students: low-achieving children in the highest-poverty schools, limited English proficient children, migratory children, children with disabilities, Native American children, neglected or delinquent children, and young children in need of "reading assistance in the United States" (U.S. Department of Education, n.d., Section 1001, ¶ 3). The purpose of the law is to close the achievement gap between high- and low-performing children, especially the achievement gaps between White students and students of color, and between underserved children and their better served peers.

In order to meet the goals of NCLB, it is necessary to focus on the curriculum. Jackson (1992) defines curriculum as all of the educative experiences of students in schools and under the guidance of their teachers and other school personnel. Bybee and DeBoer (1994) view science curriculum as what is to be learned by students in schools. Using this definition of the science curriculum, the focus of science curriculum is then on the science knowledge to be learned, the processes or methodologies that scientists use, and the applications of science, especially the relationship between science and society and science–technology–society. However, Bybee and DeBoer's definition for science curriculum limits what questions can be raised about science curriculum issues. We would broaden the definition of science curriculum so that it includes all the educative experiences that students have related to science, mathematics, technology, and society in schools.

To broaden the questions that can be raised about science curricula, the theoretical lens of critical multiculturalism proves useful. Critical multiculturalism is a philosophical perspective that critically analyzes institutions and societal structures and examines conformity, oppression, and subjugation as the result of different cultural groups (Thomson, Wilder, & Atwater, 2001). These cultural groups are formed as a result of people's ages, social classes, disabilities, ethnicities, genders, sexual identities, geographical locations, languages, places of residences, races, and religions in the United States. Critical science multiculturalism as it relates to science education is a philosophical perspective we can use to analyze and examine the inclusion of *all* students in the learning process of science so they *all* obtain a quality science education. These analyses and examinations can help us ensure that we engage antiracist science curricula so that social justice emerges. Boyer and Baptiste, Jr. (1996) believe that a curriculum is not multicultural if social justice is not the foundational base of the curriculum. Banks (1995, 2004) defines the dimensions of multicultural education and then proposes four levels of multicultural integration into curricula: contributions approach, the additive approach, the transformation approach, and the social action approach. Level 1, the *contributions approach*, focuses on heroes, heroines, holidays, and discrete cultural fundamentals, while Level 2, the *additive approach*, includes the insertions of content, concepts, themes, and perspectives without changing the structure of the curriculum. Level 3, the *transformation approach* occurs when the very structure of the curriculum is altered so that students can view concepts, issues, events, and themes from the perspectives of many others, that is, no longer is the Eurocentric perspective the dominant view of the curriculum. Finally, in Level 4, the *social action approach*, social justice is central in that students use their knowledge and skills to make decisions about important social issues and take action to help solve problems, including their own. Atwater (2003) delineates science examples related to Banks's dimensions of multicultural education, but until now, there have not been any research findings based on Banks's levels of multicultural integration into science curriculum materials.

According to Nieto and Bode (2008), social justice is a philosophy, an approach, and actions that embody treating all people with fairness, respect, dignity, and generosity. On a societal scale, this means affording each person the real—not simply a verbalized—opportunity to reach their potential by giving them access to the goods, services, and social and cultural capital of a society, while also affirming the culture and talent of each individual and the group or groups with which they identify. It challenges, confronts, and disrupts myths, misconceptions, untruths, stereotypes, and cultural assumptions that lead to structural inequality and discrimination based on human differences. Banks (1993) and Grant (1994) have addressed myths about multicultural education, illustrating that untruths can be based on cultural assumptions, ideas that are taken for granted to be true about members of a cultural group or the culture of individuals. Assumptions can take the form of commonplace, generally accepted statements, such as, "Middle Eastern people support terrorism," "people living in urban communities deserve to be living in these poor areas," or "teenagers should be paid minimum wage." These assumptions derive from cultural frames of reference that are based upon an individual's experiences. Most people have developed rationalizations for their cultural ideas and positions. However, most of their cultural assumptions are really beliefs with little or no evidence that they are true. As teachers, we come with cultural assumptions, and we act upon them sometimes in detrimental ways and sometimes in a manner that benefits our students and the lives of others in our communities. In science classrooms where social justice is paramount, it becomes possible for students to make changes in their lives.

For instance, science teachers with a social justice perspective are committed to providing all students with the necessary resources to learn to their full potential. Kohl (1998) describes such a teacher as "one who cares about nurturing all children and is enraged at the prospects of any of her or his students dying young, being hungry, or living meaningless and despairing lives. . . . They go against the grain and work in the service of their students" (p. 285). These resources include material resources such as science books and other science curricular materials.

Equally vital are emotional resources such as a belief in students' ability and worth; care for them as individuals and learners; high expectations and rigorous demands on them; and the necessary social and cultural capital to negotiate the world. Science teachers' commitment to social justice is impacted by the school and community environments. Science teachers not only give their students resources, but draw on the talents and strengths of their students. Hence, they do not embrace a deficit perspective that has characterized much of the education of marginalized students, but shift their views to all students—not just those from privileged backgrounds—as having cultural capital that can be a foundation for their learning. It includes their languages, cultural knowledge, connections to their culture, and experiences (Bourdieu & Passeron, 1990).

Understanding Social Justice and Science Curriculum Issues

Studies in this area have focused on either teacher beliefs or multicultural educational material alone or together using various combinations of instruments measuring beliefs and student performance (Lee, 2004; McLaughlin, Shepard, & O'Day, 1995). In a study of the relationship of science teachers' beliefs and science curricula, Lee (2004) indicated that the establishment of instructional congruence depends on successful integration of student language and culture in addition to science and literacy instruction. Furthermore, Lee found that science teachers' ability to practice instructional congruence—the integration of the nature of science with students' languages and cultures (Lee, 2003)—is a gradual process that depends in large part on teacher professional development and support. In a study that focused on the nature of teacher beliefs as determinants of teaching practices and pedagogies, Brand and Glasson (2004) showed that preservice teachers' experiences with diversity confirmed or challenged pre-existing beliefs. The findings in the study of Latino paraprofessionals (Monzó & Rueda, 2003) expand upon and confirm Brand and Glasson's findings (2004).

When teachers attempt to integrate multicultural content into science curricula, the level of integration is well intentioned but not well informed; integration is typically at a superficial level. Using Banks's (1995) approaches to multicultural curriculum reform, Key (2000) showed that most of the participating preservice teachers were able to integrate (a) culturally relevant examples, such as data and information, to illustrate key concepts and ideas in their academic discipline in the content integration or contributions approach and (b) content, concepts, and lessons into their curriculum without changing its structure in what Banks refers to as the additive approach. However, few of the teachers in this study transformed the curriculum to enable students to examine content from multiple ethnic and cultural perspectives (the transformation approach), and none of the teachers provided opportunities for the students to make decisions and take actions concerning civic duties (the action approach).

A critical examination of ideas about learning and curricular and instructional practices does extend its focus to preservice teachers currently enrolled in teacher education programs; Van Hook (2002) reports preservice teachers' attitudes toward the implementation of multicultural science curricula and suggests that their identified barriers to teaching ethnically diverse classrooms are manifestations of their negative attitudes toward these learners. Gay (1990) maintains that multicultural teachers must (a) be able to conceptualize equity as comparability or equivalence of learning opportunities for students of color instead of the same treatment for everyone, (b) be aware of their routine teaching behaviors that militate against educational equity, and (c) learn how to make regular instructional procedures more accommodating to students of color.

Using research methods to assess teachers' philosophies, we can identify science teachers' ideas about multicultural education and the effect these ideas have on science curriculum material development and the implementation of multicultural science activities in their classrooms. In the next section, you will find science activities that are examples of science teachers' attempts to incorporate multicultural education into science curriculum units and their classroom teaching.

Practical Applications of Social Justice to Science Curricula

This section of the chapter focuses on some examples of science curriculum materials created by science teachers enrolled in a Master's level science curriculum course. The following exercises are excerpted from the science lesson plans of the participants in a longitudinal qualitative study and serve as examples of their attempts to incorporate multicultural education.

Exercise I. What culturally based assumptions are being made in the following activities?

1.   From an Earth Science lesson:
     Students will listen to the chorus students singing the water cycle song to the tune of "She'll Be Coming 'Round the Mountain".
     Water travels in a cycle, yes it does (yes it does).
     Water travels in a cycle, yes it does (yes it does).
     It goes up as evaporation,
     Forms clouds and condensation,
     Falls down as precipitation, yes it does (yes it does).
2.   From a lesson on sound:
     The students are to listen to a classical music piece.
3.   From a January 2008 N.Y. Regents Physics examination:
     While riding a chairlift, a 55-kilogram skier is raised a vertical distance of 370 meters. What is the total change in the skier's gravitational potential energy?
4.   From a science lab lesson:
     For a group activity, the teacher asks:

     a   All Latino students to group together
     b   Females to be the recorder.

Exercise II. Which of Banks's four approaches to multicultural education (Contribution, Additive, Transformative, and Action) is used in each example? If more than one approach is applicable, state why.

1.   Mrs. Mary wants her students to question their image of scientists. Students are asked to draw a picture of a scientist. Mrs. Mary then conducts a discussion through a PowerPoint presentation depicting pictures of scientists from different ethnicities and cultural backgrounds.
2.   In his Biology class, Mr. Harris assigns his students to construct a food web. Students can choose from any area around the world, conduct research, and then construct a food web. Students present their food web to the class.
3.   As part of a graphing laboratory exercise, students are asked to read an article explaining the history of chewing gum. The article highlights ancient use by the Greeks and Native Americans. It goes on to the development and introduction of modern gum by the Mexican general Antonio Lopez de Ana to the U.S.

entrepreneur Thomas Adam, Sr., who then began the mass marketing of chewing gum. Students are then asked to collect chewing time data from their lab assistants and construct a graph.

4. For a class covering the concept of the ecological footprint, students will research relevant information then take an ecological footprint quiz that surveys their habits (http://www.ecofoot.org/). After all of the students have received their scores, the class will discuss ways to improve on their own ecological footprint. Over the next five days, students will keep a journal on what they waste each day (how long they have the water running when they brush their teeth, how long it took them to take a shower, check to see if lights or computers were on and for how long, how much food did they throw away, etc.). The class will set a goal as to what the average should be for the ecological footprint. The students will then develop and distribute a newsletter containing facts on ecology, conservation, and local student change. A student club will be formed to discuss further issues with an eye toward interaction with the larger community. A club website will serve as a means of communication between the students and the community. The ultimate goal will be for the community to take action and reduce water and electricity use. This action may include the enactment of legal measures to enforce this decision.

5. In a unit on cells, Mrs. Roberts designs ten interactive, inquiry-based lessons explaining, discussing, exploring and investigating cells, cell theory and diversity, cell design and structure and ethnobotany. Lesson number eight is designed so students discover the many uses of plants by different people around the world. Students are asked to choose a plant to research and describe/explain how indigenous groups have used it for their benefit. Students are then to produce an artifact describing the plant and the culture of the indigenous group to place on the classroom bulletin board.

Exercise III. A teacher develops a unit on ecology for a students enrolled in a Life Science course. The first three inquiry-based lessons are designed to develop an understanding of the structure, function, and relationships found among ecosystems. The fourth lesson focuses on human population dynamics, characteristics, and impact. The following is an excerpt of an agenda included in the lesson design for Human Populations and Immigration.

1. Activating thinking strategy—Human population curve over the last one hundred years or a graph of the number of immigrants into the U.S.A. over the last one hundred years.

    a. Ask students discussion questions such as: What is a population? How can a population grow? What does the word immigration mean? Why is there an increase in the number of immigrants in 1910? Why is there a decline in 1930 and 1940? What new wave of immigration is currently happening?

2. Application of population dynamics/ecology to current event

   a.   Students will watch carefully selected segments of a recent roundtable discussion about U. S. immigration policy, reform, and assimilation from an online base website.

   b.   As students watch segments, review key components of the major bills/proposals in Congress and how they differ.

3.   Congressional Town Hall Meeting—U. S. immigration policy

   a.   Students placed in groups randomly through colored/numbered index cards, such as politicians, small business, big business, National Council of La Raza, undocumented immigrants, "patriotic" Americans, documented immigrants, Middle East immigrants, school officials, or teachers, and within that group they develop a stance on local immigration.

   b.   Students outline group stance, develop questions for other groups and develop "rebuttal" answers to anticipated questions/points from other groups.

   c.   Each group will make their case to a panel, with teacher acting as a member of Congress and moderator seeking public opinion/input on controversial issue in order to hopefully develop a comprehensive bill that can be approved by the House and Senate.

   d.   Each group has 3 minutes to present their stance to the member of Congress and 1–2 minutes of questions from other groups. While each group presents, moderator must maintain a professional and respectful environment in which each group listens to stance of others, without personal attacks or disrespectful comments.

   e.   At the conclusion of the meeting, students are asked to think about how the ever-growing population will affect local, national, and global environments (Prompting questions: Where will all the people live? How may this population boom impact the environment?).

   f.   Students will be assigned a minimal half-page reflection in which they must defend their personal stance on immigration policy and how population growth/immigration relates to ecological issues.

Questions for Reflection and Discussion

1.   What are the multicultural approaches and strategies used in this lesson?
2.   In what way would the lesson outcomes lead to instilling a sense of social justice in the students?
3.   What is the role of multicultural education in the promotion of social justice?

Note: suggested answers to Exercise II—Banks's multicultural curriculum approaches

1.   Contribution
2.   Additive
3.   Contribution
4.   Action
5.   Additive-Transformative

Points of Inquiry

- Read the documents "Science for All Americans," "Benchmarks for Science Literacy," and the "National Science Education Standards." What kind of students do these documents imagine? What kinds of knowledge, skills, and dispositions do they privilege? Atwater and Suriel question the documents' philosophies and theories—what do you think?
- Often, people talk about scientific knowledge as neutral and logical: Free from political constraints and social issues. What kinds of historical and sociocultural evidence can you find to problematize this approach to scientific knowledge?
- Review Banks's levels of multicultural education and compare them to the science program in the school you work: What different levels are in play? Why?
- How could you and your colleagues create a professional development environment that supports Lee's idea of instructional congruence?

Points of Praxis

- What kind of curriculum could you design that both meets the standards and places scientific knowledge in a sociocultural and social justice context?
- What activities could your students engage in that would allow them to see that scientific knowledge has been used simultaneously as a language of power, giving access to marginalized people, and also a tool of oppression that has been used to marginalize people?
- Rewrite definitions of science literacy to reflect a social justice orientation.
- What knowledge do your students already have? Design a series of activities to elicit their family, community, and intellectual funds of knowledge.

References

American Association for the Advancement of Science (AAAS). (1990). *Science for All Americans.* New York: Oxford University Press.

Atwater, M. M. (2003). Race and gender in science education: A reconceptualization. In R. Revere (Ed.). *Gender, race and science: Transforming the curriculum* (pp. 12–23). Baltimore, MD: Institute for Teaching and Research on Women.

Banks, J. A. (1993). Multicultural education: Development, dimensions, and challenges. *Phi Delta Kappan, 75*(1), 22–28.

Banks, J. A. (1995). Multicultural education: Historical development, dimensions, and practice. In J. A. Banks (Ed.). *Handbook of research on multicultural education* (pp. 3–24). New York: Macmillan.

Banks, J. A. (2004). Multicultural education: Historical development, dimensions, and practice. In J. A. Banks, & C. A. M. Banks (Eds.), *Handbook of research on multicultural education* (2nd ed.).(pp. 3–29). San Francisco: Jossey-Bass.

Bourdieu, P., & Passeron, J. C. (1990). *Reproduction in education, society, and culture.* (R. Nice, Trans.). Thousand Oakes, CA: Sage.

Boyer, J. B., & H. P. Baptiste, Jr. (1996). *Transforming the curriculum for multicultural understandings: A practitioner's handbook.* San Francisco: Caddo Gap Press.

Brand, B. R., & Glasson, G. E. (2004). Crossing cultural borders into science teaching: Early life experiences, racial and ethnic identities, and beliefs about diversity. *Journal of Research in Science Teaching, 41*(2), 119–141.

Bybee, R. W., & DeBoer, G. E. (1994). Research on goals for the science curriculum. In D. L. Gabel (Ed.), *Handbook of research on science teaching and learning* (pp. 357–387). New York: Macmillan.

Gay, G. (1990). Teacher preparation for equity. In H. P. Baptiste, Jr., H. C. Waxman, J. W. de Felix, & J. E. Anderson (Eds.), *Leadership, equity, and school effectiveness* (pp. 224–243). Newbury Park, CA: Sage.

Grant, C. A. (1994). Challenging the myths about multicultural education. *Multicultural Education, 2*(2), 4–9.

Jackson, P. W. (1992). Conceptions of curriculum and curriculum specialists. In P. W. Jackson (Ed.), *Handbook of research on curriculum* (pp. 3–40). New York: Macmillan.

Key, S. G. (2000). Applications of "multiculturalism" demonstrated by elementary preservice science teachers. Paper presented at the Annual Meeting of the American Educational Research Association, April, New Orleans, LA.

Kohl, J. (1998). Afterword: Some reflections on teaching for social justice. In W. Ayers, J. A. Hunt, & T. Quinn (Eds.), *Teaching for social justice* (pp. 285–287). New York: Free Press and Teachers College Press.

Lee, O. (2003). Equity for culturally and linguistically diverse students in science education: Recommendations for a research agenda. *Teachers College Record, 105*(3), 465–489.

Lee, O. (2004). Teacher change in beliefs and practices in science and literacy instruction with English language learners. *Journal of Research in Science Teaching, 41*(1), 65–93.

McLaughlin, M. W., Shepard, L. A., & O'Day, J. (1995). Improving education through standard-based reform: A report by the National Academy of Education Panel on Standard-based Education Reform. Stanford, CA: The Academy.

Monzó, L. D., & Rueda, R. (2003). Shaping education through diverse funds of knowledge: A look at one Latina paraeducator's lived experiences, beliefs, and teaching practice. *Anthropology & Education Quarterly, 34*(1), 72–95.

National Research Council. (1996). *National science education standards.* Washington, DC: National Academy Press.

Nieto, S., & Bode, P. (2008). *Affirming diversity: The sociopolitical context of multicultural education* (5th ed.). Boston: Allyn & Bacon.

Thomson, N., Wilder, M., & Atwater, M. M. (2001). Critical multiculturalism and secondary teacher education programs. In D. Lavoie (Ed.), *Models for science teacher preparation: Bridging the gap between research and practice* (pp. 195–211). New York: Kluwer.

U.S. Department of Education. (n.d.) *Title I: Improving the Academic Achievement of the Disadvantaged.* (Retrieved April 18, 2008, from: http://www.ed.gov/policy/elsec/leg/esea02/pg1.html).

Van Hook, C. W. (2002). Preservice teachers' perceived barriers to the implementation of a multicultural curriculum. *Journal of Instructional Psychology, 29*(4), 254–264.

Chapter 16

Critical Media Inquiry as High School Social Studies for Social Justice

Doc Your Bloc

David Stovall and Daniel Morales-Doyle

The following chapter describes a critical media inquiry project with high school students in Chicago. Borrowing from Duncan-Andrade and Yang's work with high school youth in Oakland, California, our Chicago interpretation of their "Doc Ur Bloc" (DYB) urban sociology class is a tangible example of translating broad constructs into concrete collaborative projects with youth. Given the context of the institution where we teach, we thought the Oakland DYB project enabled us to engage in a collective process to engage the real-life conditions of young people in their communities. As process, more than a conclusive exercise, the intent of our course was to initiate a broader dialogue with young people around how their communities are viewed in the larger world.

As the community of social justice educators in K-12 public schools grows nationally, ideas on how to engage urban youth in meaningful and relevant ways are exchanged in education conferences, professional development sessions, staff retreats, and community forums. In the spirit of this expanding community, the following pages describe an attempt to replicate the work of our comrades through a collaborative project with students.

Because our work concentrates on the use of generative themes in curriculum development, the chapter is structured to describe the steps taken in a collaborative process. Beginning with the description of the Oakland Doc Your Block urban sociology class we hope to illustrate authentic collaboration with students in classrooms. Then, we will show how we and our students used the tenets of Participatory Action Research (PAR) in creating a Chicago version of the Oakland DYB project. We share the overall mission of our high school (The Greater Lawndale/Little Village School for Social Justice—SOJO), and we describe our attempt to create a space for young people to critically analyze their worlds through a year-long video documentary project. Utilizing the concepts of PAR, we borrow from Cahill's (2004) understanding of the process as a

> Collective approach to research in which the participants look critically at their social and/or environmental contexts and develop proposals to address the problems raised by the research. PAR takes lived experience as the starting

point for investigation, places emphasis upon the research process, and reconsiders the value of research as a vehicle for social change.

(Cahill, 2004, p. 275)

Beginning with our working definition of social justice, in each section we will speak to the challenges inherent to our project—some of which are common in urban school spaces and others that are unique to our context.

A Brief Note on Social Justice in Education

A common worry of those who position their work to challenge systems of power is the threat of commodification or co-optation of the term "social justice." In many instances social justice exists as a broad term, which can lead to reducing the concept to describe work that is not intended to challenge our thoughts and actions. In this vein "social justice" can be used to depict one-time "community service days" or improvement in college acceptance rates. To address such concerns, we use the concept of social justice in education to speak to the day-to-day processes and actions utilized in classrooms and communities centered in critical analysis. This investigation is "critical" in that our work is intentional in its focus on changing the individual and collective conditions of our neighborhoods, cities, nation, and larger world. Such processes include the critical examination of power as it relates to race, class, gender, sexual orientation, and disability. While our work does not seek to offer the definitive example of social justice in education, it should be understood as an attempt to politically, socially, and pedagogically ground our work.

The Lawndale/Little Village Multiplex and the School for Social Justice

Central to our process is the narrative of the high school. Our existence as a social justice high school requires us to constantly revisit our educational practice in the attempt to engage our students as valuable members of our school and larger community. As facilitators of the DYB colloquium, we would be remiss in refusing to recognize the fact that without the efforts of community members, our course (and the school) would not exist.

Little Village, the Mexican-American neighborhood where the high school is located, is on Chicago's Southwest Side. Beginning as early as 1995, members of the Little Village community, through grassroots organizing, began to place pressure on Chicago Public Schools (CPS) to create a high school to address issues of overcrowding.

Under the request of elected officials for the neighborhood, community members first sought to address the problem through CPS protocols. When this process proved ineffective, members of the Little Village community decided to stage a hunger strike. The protest lasted 19 days, beginning on May 13 and ending on June 2, 2001. Due to the community-driven initiative, coupled with national media coverage and substantial support throughout the city, CPS decided to approach negotiations with the community members from Little Village. The ensuing series of interactions resulted in the community being granted its original demand for the high school. Four schools are housed in the structure, each with its own theme: (1) visual and performing arts, (2) math, science, and technology, (3) world languages, and (4) social justice. Both authors teach at the school for social justice. We have been open since the summer of 2005. The population of our school is African-American and Latino/a (around 70% Latino and 30% African-American). Students from our school come from the communities of Little Village and North Lawndale.

Beginnings—Building on the work of our Oakland Comrades

Borrowing from Duncan-Andrade and Yang's work with high school youth in Oakland, California (Duncan-Andrade and Morrell, 2008), our Chicago interpretation of their "Doc Ur Bloc" (DYB) urban sociology class is a tangible example of translating broad constructs (e.g., social justice, critical pedagogy) into concrete collaborative projects with youth. Given the context of the institution we teach in, we thought the Oakland DYB project enabled us as researchers (both facilitators and students) to engage in a collective process to engage the real-life conditions of young people in their communities. As process, more than a conclusive exercise, the intent of our course was to initiate a broader dialogue with young people around how their communities are viewed in the larger world. From the outset we operated on Duncan-Andrade and Morrell's assertion that "If urban schools have been derided for decades as 'factories of failure' (Rist 1973), then their production of failures mean they are in fact successful at producing the results they were designed to produce" (p. 5).

Through several conferences and personal interactions, we became familiar with the Oakland DYB project. We saw it from its initial stages of incorporating critical pedagogy in a high school classroom to its final documentary projects. While we were amazed with the quality of film production and the depth of analysis, even more impressive to us was the way in which students began to raise their own awareness and use their newly acquired skills to engage other justice-oriented work. Despite the unfortunate closing of East Oakland Community High School (EOC) in the spring of 2007, the work of students from the DYB project continues to influence media justice work with youth around the country.

Key Concepts in the Oakland Model

The Duncan-Andrade and Yang class at EOC was centered in the practical application of theoretical concepts. Included in these ideas was a central focus on the terms: hegemony, counter-hegemony, social degradation, social reproduction, and habitus. All were used to analyze the material conditions and social forces in their students' neighborhoods. From these concepts the central purpose of the project was to "put tools of critical thinking, research, and intellectual production in the hands of young people so they could counter-narrate pathological stories of their families and communities" (Duncan-Andrade & Morrell, 2008, p. 147).

As we observed the ability of their students to process concepts we struggled with in graduate school, it amazed us as to how freely they were able to apply them to their daily lives. In thinking about our own students, we felt they could do similar work. Providing additional inspiration for our Chicago version of the project, we were able to attend a presentation by EOC students at the American Educational Research Association's annual meeting. At one point in the panel an EOC student commented on what she felt the power of DYB to be, "Black and brown people controlling and producing their own stories, this is counter-narrative. The importance of this is that these are truthful stories about Oakland, and this will lead to counter-hegemony" (p. 148). Key to her comments are the terms counter-narrative and hegemony. As stories that challenge deficit assumptions about African-American and Latino/a youth, they stand to "counter" such views. In "countering" hegemony, they saw the DYB project as a means to interrupt negative entities (e.g., criminalization of youth, police brutality, lack of youth employment, substandard educational systems, etc.) that have the potential to dominate their existence.

The sociological concepts used by Duncan-Andrade, Yang, and their students are powerful tools for deconstructing the complex set of conditions and forces that shape their lives. Additionally, using these dense theoretical concepts develops students' academic literacy in a way that both provides them with confidence and helps them develop an intellectual identity that is directly tied to deconstructing elements of their everyday lives. In the summer institute described by Morrell (2008, p. 121), he considers showing the "university that students who were not gaining entry into the university could indeed perform the literacy tasks associated with university coursework" to be one of the explicit goals of conducting PAR with youth. While our project was not centered on a university campus as was Morrell's summer institute, we consider this to be an important goal in any academic undertaking with urban youth.

Colloquium Structure—Adjusting the Oakland Model

Where Andrade and Yang taught their class three times a week, ours took place in a once-a-week structure called colloquium. The current principal, during his research as a member of the design team to create SOJO, observed a structured-day innovation that provided students with a self-selected course that explored an issue relevant to their lives. Although the colloquium structure provides an opportunity to enhance student knowledge of subject matter in a non-traditional setting, it has its own limitations.

Specifically, students do not receive grades or course credit for colloquium. Instead, they have the opportunity to earn service-learning hours—40 of which are required for graduation from a CPS high school. Also, the meeting schedule for colloquiua is significantly different from that of traditional classes. Our class was offered once a week on Wednesdays (totaling eight sessions during the fall semester and eleven for the spring) for two and a half hours. The number of sessions was limited by the fact that colloquia were only held during weeks where there were no holidays or system-mandated institute days (e.g., report-card pick-up, staff development, etc.). Our students, unaware of our motivations for developing the course, chose our colloquium by ranking their preferences on a list of a dozen or so offerings. These colloquia last for one semester and students make new selections at the beginning of the following semester. Because we held the same colloquium for the entire school year, this chapter will discuss the course in the fall semester of 2007 and the spring semester of 2008. In light of students' ability to choose their colloquia each semester, four students chose the course for both semesters.

Given the nature of our once-a-week structure, our version of DYB required significant modifications. Despite our expected adjustments to accommodate time constraints, our project called for us to make more changes than were originally anticipated. In addition to the time constraints, keeping the interests of high school students for that amount of time requires a different type of lesson planning. For us, this was centered in challenging ourselves on what would be needed in making each session relevant. Upon consulting with Duncan-Andrade and Yang, they informed us that the bulk of our planning would have to be constructed collectively with our students. Central to PAR, this type of lesson planning contradicts traditional notions of teacher preparation in that our subsequent sessions would be based on the decisions made by the group (students and teachers) in the previous class. Because there could be weeks in between colloquium sessions, note-taking and reflection were critical to our process.

Borrowing a concept from the Duncan-Andrade and Yang model, we noticed that students in the EOC documentaries were always holding a composition book. When Duncan-Andrade and Yang were asked about the composition notebooks, they informed us that they were field- note logs. Understanding that the documentation of our process as teachers and students would be critical, we provided everyone (teachers included) with composition notebooks that would act as our field-note logs. Throughout our process we would have to rely on student field notes as much as our own to plan each session. As a collaborative course, the process of reviewing field notes provided students with a sense of ownership as they were able to physically visualize their contributions to the course. Without them we would have no record of the planning process and the various decisions made in previous classes. Discussed in the following section, we believe the key to understanding the challenges and successes of this course design lie in the details of its implementation.

From the First Day Onward

We began the first day of class by explicitly communicating our motivations and goals for the course. Given that colloquia are not academic classes, students often expect to do a minimal amount of "schoolwork" in them. In other words, they do not anticipate difficult reading and serious writing to be a significant component of their colloquium experience. However, because one of our motivations for teaching the course was to develop academic literacy through an investigation of their

realities, some "traditional" schoolwork skills were needed to making dense theoretical concepts relevant. In this sense we were asking students to do the unex-
pected—to do a significant amount of reading and writing in colloquium. We were
very upfront about this within the first few minutes of class and we gave students the
option to choose a different colloquium if they were not up to the challenge. No students took that option as that time. One did transfer out before the second meeting,
but several additional students also signed on upon hearing the focus of our
colloquium.

When we introduced the project for the course we framed it as an opportunity to
speak back to society about the realities of urban youth. Currently the vast majority
of mainstream media criminalizes African-American and Latino/a youth while
either excluding or minimizing the voices of the youth themselves. In posing a
counter-narrative, we informed our students that their video is an opportunity to
tell their own stories and truths. To that end, our first class activity was for students
to respond in composition books/field note logs to the prompt: *What do you think
the mainstream society says about you as young people?* The following response is
from Norma, one of our students.

> I think society thinks of teenagers as rebellious. People think of us like we don't
> care about anything or anyone, just ourselves. The (larger) society has a nega-
> tive image of us. (From) the way we dress, talk, walk, and people we hang with,
> society assumes we are doing bad things.

After students were given several minutes to write, we asked them to share their
ideas with the class. When Norma shared her insights, many agreed. Critical to the
process was our listening to the group, as opposed to arguing with them. Listening
allowed for deeper conversation into how they see themselves in the world. During
this discussion we made a list on the board that listed prevalent stereotypes of
African-American and Latino/a youth. Included in this discussion was the idea that
youth do not get involved in issues, young Black and Latino men being viewed as
criminals, and young women as likely to get pregnant. We used this list of stereotypes to introduce the concept of hegemony. We wrote it on the board next to the
list of stereotypes and defined it as "the total and complete domination of an individual or a group through the use of ideas and thoughts." We asked students to
write this definition in their composition books. Even this early in class, responses
like Norma's alerted us to the understanding that they were clear on developing a
counter-narrative.

Adjusting the Readings

Because the Oakland model provided more time for students to digest readings on
hegemony, habitus, and social-reproduction, our time constraints called for us to
reduce the number of readings. Our reduction led us to focus our work on the concept of hegemony. Instead of beginning with the writings of Antonio Gramsci, we
decided to introduce students through a more practical example. In borrowing

from the EOC syllabus we decided to begin with Malcolm X's speech *A Message to the Grassroots* (1965, pp. 3–17) and decided to add the speech *To Mississippi Youth* (1965, pp. 137–46). Following the Malcolm X reading, we included an excerpt from Antonio Gramsci's *Selections from the Prison Notebooks* (1999, pp. 259–61). Both served as starting points to theoretically ground our documentary. The following quote had a particular significance to our class: "One of the first things I think young people, especially nowadays, should learn is how to see for yourself and listen for yourself and think for yourself. Then you can come to an intelligent decision for yourself" (p. 137).

Where Malcom X's offerings are clear, we also felt that it was important to communicate to the class the context of the work. The speech was delivered to a group of youth community organizers in Mississippi in 1965 during an intense struggle for the right to be counted as citizens. By offering this suggestion, he was intentional in his stance against hegemony. As young people throughout the state were being viciously attacked for supporting the right to vote and attaining a quality education, his words spoke to the power of young people to "talk back" to the world. In this sense "thinking for oneself and listening" was key in that it addressed how young people could go about doing the work in class and living their lives.

We decided to use Malcolm X before Gramsci because we felt it offered a practical example of why they needed to tell their stories. It offered a perfect segue way to introduce hegemony because it allowed us to have an open discussion around what they were facing in the world.

In setting the stage for Gramsci, we introduced the passage informing our students that Gramsci did much of his writing from prison and that he had to find a way to get his subversive writings past the prison guards. From introducing the context, we asked students how did they think he got the letters past the prison guards. One student quickly suggested, "You could write it in code." We affirmed this response and encouraged students to think of Gramsci's dense language as a code of sorts. The following passage was used as a prompt to have our students think about Gramsci's code.

> There is no human activity from which every form of intellectual participation can be excluded: *homo faber* cannot be separated from *homo sapiens*. Each man, finally, outside his professional activity, carries on some form of intellectual activity, that is, he is a "philosopher," . . . has a conscious line of moral conduct, and therefore contributes to sustain a conception of the world or to modify it, that is, to bring into being new modes of thought.
>
> (Gramsci, 1999, p. 259)

As we read, we would stop frequently and check for understanding or clarify terms. Sometimes we would stop as frequently as two or three times per sentence. Terms that were pulled out from the larger passage included "*homo sapiens*," "*homo faber*," "bourgeoisie," and "strata." The complete passage focuses on the false division of people into thinkers and workers and explains how these groups are reproduced by the type and style of education offered to different classes of students. To connect this theory to concrete examples to which our students could relate, we asked if anybody knew the full name of Farragut, a high school just down the street from ours. A student quickly responded, "Farragut Career Academy." We then asked for the full name of the high school named after football great Walter Payton. Just as quickly, a student responded, "Walter Payton College Prep." For those unfamiliar with this second school, we explained that it is a selective enrollment or magnet school in one of the city's most affluent neighborhoods (nicknamed the "Gold Coast"). We then asked for the difference between these two schools, a student combined his own language with Gramsci's: "Payton offers a classical education, while Farragut prepares you for a job!" We went on to ask who attends both of these schools and emphasized that while Gramsci was writing about Italy decades ago, his ideas are applicable to Chicago today.

To deepen the connections between the concept of hegemony, Gramsci's writing, and our list of stereotypes about urban Black and Brown youth, we passed out issues (dating from 2005–2007) of several popular magazines including *Rolling Stone, URB, XXL, SLAM, The Fader,* and *The Source.* We asked students to rip out three images that represented stereotypes of youth. The pictures they chose included those of scantily clad African-American and Latina women next to fully clothed men of the same ethnicity. Some had bare-chested African-American and Latino men holding platinum or gold chains while scowling to project a "hard" image. Others had blank-faced Black and Latino males in photos, projecting another form of a "hard" image. Upon reviewing the photos as a group, we asked the students "do these images represent every aspect of your lives as Black and Latino/a youth?" When they responded with a resounding "no," we returned to the importance of the documentary in creating a counter-narrative with respect to popular stereotypes, while presenting an alternative perspective.

This idea that students need to be given opportunities to go beyond analyzing or critiquing dominant ideas within the walls of the classroom by creating their own counter-narratives is at the heart of this project. In his book, *Critical Literacy and Urban Youth* (2008), one of Morrell's central arguments about critical literacy pedagogy is that it must include opportunities for students to not only analyze texts, but to produce critical texts themselves. He also argues that there must be authentic opportunities for students to disseminate these texts.

> Critical literacy instruction needs to fundamentally be concerned with the consumption, production, and distribution of texts; counter-texts that not only name the workings of power, but critical texts that serve as the manifestation of an alternate reality or a not-yet-realized present that only enters into the imagination through the interaction with new and authentically liberating words that are created by writers as cultural workers.
>
> (Morrell, 2008, p. 115)

He also argues that we need to conceive of texts broadly, in a way that includes both analysis and production of documentary films and other new media texts. In sharing these beliefs, we decided to focus our course in the production of a short documentary film and, for the spring semester, a written article. Both forms allow the students to engage video and print as text to be shaped, debated, and configured to reflect their understandings of the larger world.

PAR as Collaborative Video Production

In developing the ability to engage media, collaboration with outside participants with expertise in research methods and video production was critical to our project. Documentary filmmakers and university faculty assisted the class with developing the structure of the documentary and our interview protocols. As a collaborative effort, we (teachers and students) created a situation where we would be in constant discussion concerning how to shape the project and what should be included. Our choice to begin with the students' lived experience as our baseline for what counts as "expert" knowledge enabled us to develop points of relevance with academic texts. Coupled with the selected writings, we were also able to incorporate researchers whose work was relevant to our project.

PAR often speaks to the "messiness" of creating and executing a curriculum built around a broad framework and the steps taken to implement our collective ideas. As an African-American male facilitator and a male facilitator with Irish-American and Latino heritage working with a class of African-American and Latino/a students, it was imperative for our process to include the real and often harsh realities of the intersections of race, class, and gender in our lives. In this sense our work was not meant to be objective. Instead, we understand ourselves as "part of the situation" we were investigating (McNiff and Whitehead, 2006, p. 5). Our own observations and experiences in communities similar to those of our students informed the construction of the course. We also recognize that we each brought to the classroom our own sets of experiences that are very different from each other's and from the students'. Specifically, both of us are also constantly aware of the power and privilege we hold as men and as professional educators. Also, Morales-Doyle works to be constantly aware and critical of his white privilege while also being proud and aware of his complicated Irish and Latino identities.

By being self-reflective and engaging the PAR process, we were able to educate each other through the exchange of ideas. Instead of "helping" our students to understand the function of research and analysis of our communities, we saw ourselves as standing in solidarity with our students as co-researchers throughout the development and implementation of the course. Whereas traditional research would suggest establishing distance between researcher and subject, our work stands as close and exposed. By confronting the realities of young people coupled with our own experiences, we were constantly challenged to "make it all make sense."

Fostering Expert Knowledge

Because one of the authors is a professor at a research university, we used our relationships with other faculty members to assist us in developing our work. We consulted with sociology professors Lorena Garcia and Kerry Ann Rockquemore about how to incorporate ethnographic and urban frameworks for our study. As Dr. Garcia reminded us of the process of "studying up," we began to pick out areas in the city that contrasted with ours demographically. This included a discussion that directed our focus toward the terms socio-economic status (SES), race/ethnicity, class, and gender.

During the second semester, we consulted with Dr. Rockquemore on ethnography and the processes needed to develop a question set for the documentary. As a group we developed a set of questions using a deductive process, with the first step being the creation of a master list of questions. From the master list, we engaged a collective process where students selected ten questions that would be used as the interview protocol for the documentary (see below). In addition to selecting the interview protocol, we also practiced interviewing techniques. All of these processes are important in PAR, in that we were able to use collaborative techniques to complete the project. For our course our process led to the following questions:

- Please state your name, age, race and gender.
- How long have you lived in the community?
- What does community mean to you?
- Do you think people who live in the community plan for the future?
- Where do you see this community in ten years?
- What are some of the problems of our community?
- How has police been a problem in our community? Who do they work for?
- Who should we trust to build our community?
- Do we trust the destiny of the community to the future generation?
- What can we do to make our community better for the next generation?

In addition to our collaborative work on qualitative research methods, we were also advised by documentary filmmaker Gabriel Cortez. During our class session he provided the group with the basics of documentary filmmaking. Upon viewing examples of his work he advised students to "pick your shot" and to "keep the camera moving." After reviewing his films, students understood more about how camera angles and music could be incorporated to enhance their work.

While most of the interviews the students conducted were videotaped, they also recorded responses to their questions in their composition books/field note logs. One of our most informative interviews was recorded only in this way because the interviewee was an undocumented day-laborer, wary of being videotaped. As it was in the Oakland Doc Ur Block project that informed and inspired our work, using notebooks as a space for reflection, note-taking, and composition were central to our PAR process. As instructors, we modeled the practice and habit of taking detailed field notes and we asked the students to do the same. This practice reinforced the idea that we were engaging in PAR with our students. Several times during each semester, students asked us, "Are you writing down what I just said?" In each case, their surprise quickly turned to pride as they recognized that adults were taking seriously the task of learning from them and with them. In the end, these field notes provided us with most of the data used to write this chapter—but more importantly, it demonstrated to our students not just good learning and research habits, but also that their ideas were to be taken seriously and considered deeply.

Going to the Block—Noting the Centrality of Fieldwork

In order to stay true to the name and idea of "Doc Your Block," we had to spend time gathering data off campus in the North Lawndale and Little Village communities and in other parts of Chicago. We did this during one full class session during each semester and also during a few Saturday trips. All of the sessions were informative in that they allowed students the opportunity to voice their insights on the situations they encounter on a day-to-day basis.

Law Enforcement and "the Right to be here"

In each of our weekday outings during the school day, we were stopped by police. During our first day of collecting footage and data during the fall semester, we were told we were not allowed to film in the neighborhood branch of the public library. Upon leaving the library, one of our students spotted two uniformed Chicago female police officers perusing the selection of knock-off "high-end" fashion purses at a street vendor's stand. The student became angry complaining that the police were shopping rather than doing their job. She quickly crossed the street, camera in hand, and began filming the officers. In response, they quickly met our student in the street and sternly informed her that she did not have permission to film them. The police officers were clearly upset and approached our group of one instructor (Morales-Doyle) and about 6–8 students. Morales-Doyle explained that the students were conducting a school research project. The officers' response was to ask for identification and to demand that any footage of them be erased. Once the officers were satisfied that this was a legitimate school group, led by a real teacher, and were also convinced that our footage of them had been erased, they allowed us to continue walking through the neighborhood, only to stop our other group of 6–8 students with Stovall on the next block.

In our experience the same officers noticed us with our notepads and camera. Where we didn't pay attention to the car at first, students in the group alerted me that the officers were close by. As the squad car approached us, I alerted the group to keep the camera rolling (with the idea that we could use it for the documentary—if the camera wasn't confiscated). Being the only adult in the group, I responded to the officer's request to approach the car. They opened their conversation by asking me who we were. I alerted them that we were a research team of high school students and a college professor investigating numerous aspects of the community. In the attempt to think quickly, recognizing the fact that I didn't have a high school teachers' identification card, the most valuable form of capital available to me (in my thought process) was my university affiliation. Although this usually doesn't work for an African-American male in the inner-city, I think the experience with the previous group toned the officers down. Nevertheless, in the attempt to pre-empt their request for proof, I showed them my university identification card and continued by explaining that the young people were all students at a local high school. Probably because of their most recent experience with the first group, they seemed less inclined to approach us with hostility. Still, they had me write down my work address and a telephone number. During the entire experience, our students kept the camera rolling. In the final video, one of our students gives a play-by-play of the encounter, referencing the encounter as "what the police always do." Her remarks also offered the comments "don't they know we're trying to do a project? They think we're bad kids, but we're just trying to do a project." Ironically, as my conversation with the officer ended, we noticed the other group of students directly across the street.

As mentioned earlier in the chapter, students decided to interview day-laborers who gather outside of the neighborhood hardware store every morning looking for odd jobs. While three groups of students conducted interviews and spoke with an organizer attempting to unionize the workers, a squad car from the police department of a neighboring suburb approached. Without getting out of the car, the police officers asked what we were doing. They were quickly satisfied with our explanation and left us alone.

The mistreatment of youth by police was one of the most common issues raised by students during both semesters of our class and distrust between community and police became one of the focal points that students chose to include in the spring semester documentary. Our experiences with the police while we were gathering data and footage demonstrated the constant suspicion and harassment that our students are subject to everyday in their own neighborhood. Do our youth not have a right to walk together in their own neighborhood without being stopped by police? We could speculate how the reaction of the officers may have been different had we (instructors) not been present, but it is more useful to consider what even these brief interactions say about police–youth relations and commonly held beliefs about Black and Latino/a youth and their education. Of the many people and groups of people out and about on both of these mornings, our group caught the attention of the police. While the neighborhood has more than its fair share of gang activity and other crime, nothing about our group suggested that we were up to no good. In fact, the video cameras and composition books that we carried suggested that we were involved in some sort of school project. This indiscriminate suspicion of Black and Latino/a youth frustrates our students and builds feelings of mistrust between the community and police. Luckily, in this case, nothing more than a conversation and display of identification by the facilitators was required to prevent further harassment. Because these attitudes of police are common in urban centers, we have to be aware that these sorts of encounters are likely when we bring our students off campus for learning projects that are centered in their lived experiences. In another off-campus data-gathering project in a park in another part of Chicago, one of the facilitators and his students were approached by detectives in an unmarked police car who explained that they had received a call about suspicious activity involving young people. Apparently, dealing with law enforcement is one of the challenges we must face if we want to push the boundaries of the classroom literally and figuratively.

"Studying Up"

"Studying up" as a concept means studying groups with different racial and socio-economic backgrounds. Although the term implies a hierarchy of groups, we utilized the concept to engage the process of investigating a different group. When the concept was reintroduced to the group to guide our video data collection, our students responded by informing us that they wanted to go to the "richest part of the city." During one of our Saturday sessions, the group decided to collect video footage in a neighborhood called "Streeterville" and a specific area known as the "Magnificent Mile." This particular strip of retail stores and hotels grosses the highest income revenue in the city. Its relationship to our students' lives is significant in that the commercial strip that grosses the second highest revenue is the 26th Street area in Little Village. Although the two communities are vastly different in race/ethnicity and socio-economic status, this relationship intrigued our students.

During our Magnificent Mile trip, our students filmed high-end retail stores, exotic cars, women in expensive furs, and new skyscraper construction. In contrast, students filmed family-owned restaurants, locally run businesses where they themselves shopped and local hangouts on 26th Street. Reflecting on both experiences at dinner with our students, they talked about how different the places were and how it was hard for them to conceptualize how much revenue was exchanged in their community in relationship to the Magnificent Mile. Despite the stark differences, they continued to talk about how footage is important in showing the differences in both spaces.

Interviewing

One of the most important interviews that took place was in a parking lot among a group of day-laborers. Across the bridge from our school is a shopping mall that houses two major home improvement stores (Home Depot and Lowe's). In the parking lot, many documented and undocumented workers wait for contractors to pick them up to work for the day. As some of the labor would be skilled or menial, we felt it was an important place for students to get a perspective on how different groups understand their community and what is happening in the larger world. Where our interviewees did not want to be videotaped, they were kind enough to let us record them through our field notes. The following excerpt is from one of our interviews.

Luis: Where do you see the community in ten years?
Miguel: More crisis, less jobs, and more gang problems.
L: Do you think people who live in the community plan for the future?
M: No. Most people are stuck in the present and don't think about the future.
L: What are some problems in the community?
M: Gas prices and government policies.
L: Who should we trust to build our community?
M: Not the government. They just look for things that help them(selves).
L: What can we do to make our community better for the next generation?
M: More protection. Pay more attention to the kids. . . . More after-school programs.

Where many in the mainstream media might not expect the previous responses from someone working as a day-laborer, Miguel's insights were critical to our project in that they shed light on the critical awareness of many community members. Critical to our goal of establishing a counter-hegemonic narrative, students were able to connect their understandings to a larger audience.

Reflections—Challenges and Successes with PAR

Reflection is required for any process centered in critical analysis. For our process, this included evaluation from ourselves (facilitators) and students to ascertain what worked well in our class. Because we were a small group, we chose not to use surveys to evaluate the course. Instead, our dialogue and field notes from the ensuing conversation were used to improve the course.

The biggest challenges we faced with this project were related to the inconsistent nature of the colloquium schedule. We believe that consistency is one of the most important qualities of a teacher, especially in a setting like ours. Many of our students have been let down by educational institutions and the people who work in them time and time again. Above all else, a good teacher is one that is unwavering in his or her commitment to the young people with whom he or she works. Consistency is also crucial to helping our students develop the habits and skills that will be necessary for them to develop the academic prowess they need to navigate educational institutions that are not generally set up for their success. Unfortunately, our colloquium met only during regular five-day weeks, and then only on Wednesday. This means that we had only seven sessions in the fall and twelve in the spring and that there was sometimes more than a month between these sessions. It is extremely difficult to build the type of classroom culture and demonstrate the type of consistency that both of us aim for with this sort of intermittent meeting schedule. However, we did take advantage of our initial meetings and of the months where we met four times to make our intentions of working hard and working collaboratively extremely clear.

During the fall semester, we had two mini-digital video cameras for the class and no access to the school computer lab during class time. Because of these technological limitations combined with having only seven scheduled meetings, we consolidated the original small groups we formed (four students each) into more whole-class sessions and, in the end, produced one video as a class. While we had access to more cameras and had more meetings in the spring, we decided to still produce only one video and one article as a class. But, in the second semester, we did work more in small groups by taking advantage of individual students' strengths and interests. Some students focused on writing the article and others became experts at conducting videos. Other groups worked outside of class as editors of video footage while still others contributed graffiti-style artwork for the title screen. Upon reflecting on this strategy, we believe that working in small groups more intentionally (with the possibility of several films and several articles) may have been more effective in terms of maximizing each student's ownership of the final products.

While recent developments in software (such as iMovie and Final Cut Pro) and dropping prices in hardware (cameras and fast computers with large hard-drives) have truly democratized the art of filmmaking, it remains an extremely time-consuming process. Given our limited class time, we asked students to volunteer to do much of the editing work outside of class. These students then presented this work to the class so that everybody could participate in key decisions about the film. During the first semester, it took hours upon hours just to upload the footage from our mini-DV cameras to the computer because this process must happen in real time. We thought we had found a solution to this problem in the spring semester in the form of cameras with built-in hard-drives which would allow movie files to be copied quickly to computer hard-drives. Unfortunately, the format of the files on the camera was not compatible with the software program we were using and we spent significant time converting the file types. Then, days before we were scheduled to present our film to the entire school, the server where all of our footage was stored went down and we thought for a day or two that we might not have any film to present. Luckily, we were able to regain access to our footage and students and facilitators alike put in a few late nights at the school to finish the film in time. While technology can be a powerful pedagogical tool, teachers who make it an integral piece of their curriculum must be ready to roll with the punches and think on their feet when there are technical difficulties. In the end, the benefits of this technology certainly outweigh the risks, but frequent back-ups and written accounts of all data are important practices for both youth and teachers.

At the end of each semester, students presented their film to an audience that included the entire faculty and student body of the school and numerous community members and others including graduate students and community organizers. Both videos were also uploaded to YouTube and the links were disseminated widely to youth and adults via email, MySpace, and via the authors' presentation at a teachers' conference in Arizona. The article that students wrote during the spring semester will likely be published in a journal whose audience is primarily teachers. According to Duncan-Andrade and Morrell (2008, pp. 124–125), distributing student-produced texts is an important part of the PAR process because it positions students as public intellectuals and provides authentic motivation for students to revise and improve these texts. Duncan-Andrade and Morrell also argue that the audiences of these student texts also stand to gain and learn from this distribution because of the students' positions as experts on the social and material conditions in their cities and neighborhoods. The response from teachers, community members, and other students supports this argument. People without direct involvement in the DYB project (including students, a school social worker, and teachers from other cities) have posted links to our students' videos on their MySpace pages or blogs.

Where our Chicago version of DYB was rife with challenges, the successes are an important factor in creating relevant learning environments for young people. Our attempt at libratory practice in high school classrooms should be considered part of the numerous acts of solidarity with teachers who have made the conscious decision to do such work.

Points of Inquiry

- What aspects of PAR and the DYB Colloquium align with the National Council for Social Studies (NCSS) curriculum standards? What social studies and history practices are congruent between these two different arenas?
- What policies (school, district, state, and federal) create the conditions for learning in your area? If you live in a rural area, or a suburban one, how do these differ or align with those outlined by Stovall and Morales-Doyle?

Points of Praxis

- What generative themes would be apt for your classroom? Design a series of inquiry-based lessons that allow students to design their own PAR projects. Consider local history, geography, how people came to live there and the work they do.
- Using the history textbook assigned to your students, create a collaborative critique with your students: What kinds of knowledge are promoted in the "regular" curriculum? How does it affect us as teachers and students (or not)?
- What other research techniques could you and your students use to create public access to community knowledge?

References

Cahill, C. (2004). Defying gravity? Raising consciousness through collective research. *Children's Geographies, 2*(2), 273–286.

Duncan-Andrade, J. R., & Morrell, E. (2008). *The art of critical pedagogy: Possibilities for moving from theory to practice in urban schools.* New York: Peter Lang.

Gramsci, A. (1999). Intellectuals and hegemony. In C. Lemert (Ed.), *Social theory: The multicultural and classic readings.* Boulder, CO: Westview. (Reprinted from *Selections from the Prison Notebooks,* New York: International Publishers Co., 1971.)

McNiff, J., & Whitehead, J. (2006). *All you need to know about action research.* London: Sage.

Morrell, E. (2008). *Critical literacy and urban youth: Pedagogies of access, dissent, and liberation.* New York: Routledge.

Reason, P., & Bradbury, H. (Eds.). (2006). *Handbook of action research.* London: Sage.

Weis, L., & Fine, M. (2000). *Construction sites: Excavating race, class, and gender among urban youth.* New York: Teachers College Press.

X, M. (1965). *Malcolm X speaks.* New York: Grove Press.

Chapter 17

Second Language Education

With Liberty and Languages for All

Raquel Oxford

The notion that second language education programs in the United States have often been divided into English as a second language (ESL), bilingual education, and foreign language education is well established (Davis, 1999). These differences exist for multiple reasons including the traditional separation of world language and English departments and the purposes of the constituencies for learning language. Differences or divisions in language education in terms of history, position, power, and privilege in turn affect the preparation and practices of teachers in these disciplines. However, such divides in practice, perceptions of the mission and vision of the others, and historical lack of collaboration between areas can be overcome. By doing so, advocacy for language learners can better be achieved for all. Working to alleviate tensions and better understand content expectations can help better prepare us for teaching and learning as well as provide practical opportunities for action in the realm of social justice.

Corson affirms that "Social justice has much to do with ideas about legitimacy, about fairness and impartiality, about welfare and mutual advantage, and about political and social consensus" (1993, p. 27). Teachers of second languages should be unified in their roles as language advocates, and world language teachers should be more sensitive to their traditional position of privilege (Muirhead, 2007) and the attack on bilingual education in the United States today spurred by anti-immigrant sentiments and the English-only movement which seeks to make English the official and only language in our country. This chapter aims to define social justice in world languages and English as a second language (ESL) while detailing examples of social justice pedagogy in language settings and the challenges for implementing appropriate curricula and critical design work in the field.

Defining Social Justice in Language Education

If Nieto (Nieto & Bode, 2008) "defines social justice as *a philosophy, an approach, and actions that embody treating all people with fairness, respect, dignity, and generosity*," then we should examine the prevailing philosophies and approaches within the fields of world languages and English as a second language (ESL). This examination should take into consideration the components of social justice in education: Challenging stereotypes, providing resources, drawing on students' funds of knowledge (Moll, Amanti, Neff, & Gonzalez, 1992), creating a supportive environment (Nieto & Bode, 2008) and how they apply to the context of second language teaching and learning in the United States.

Ruth Simmons, the first African American to lead an Ivy League institution, chose to study languages in the 1960s as a way of overcoming racial ignorance, and she has "argued persistently in favor of language study as an essential element of any long-term strategy for abating conflict and sustaining peace" (Simmons, 2004, p. 682). Learning not only language but culture and societal conditions of other peoples can build bridges and new relationships. Yet not all teachers involved in our field embrace the same potential for the teaching and learning of language. We must begin to think more critically about the curriculum, methodology, and assessments in the language classroom to maximize the potential for social justice. A significant framework for organizing such an exploration are the national standards for both ESL and world languages, which emerged in the late 1990s as part of the larger Standards movement.

Since language and culture are deeply interconnected elements, both serve as important resources for teachers and learners. Along with content area instruction, the primacy of these elements is indicative of recent trends in the field. Standards for English language learners, developed by the Teachers to Speakers of Other Languages (TESOL) organization, present five language proficiency standards which include both social and academic uses of the language students must acquire for success in and beyond the classroom. The English language proficiency standards are as follows:

- *Standard 1*: English language learners *communicate* for *social, intercultural, and instructional* purposes within the school setting.
- *Standard 2:* English language learners *communicate* information, ideas, and concepts necessary for academic success in the area of *language arts.*
- *Standard 3:* English language learners *communicate* information, ideas, and concepts necessary for academic success in the area of *mathematics.*
- *Standard 4:* English language learners *communicate* information, ideas, and concepts necessary for academic success in the area of *science.*
- *Standard 5:* English language learners *communicate* information, ideas, and concepts necessary for academic success in the area of *social studies.*

Thus, the expectation is clear for the teachers of English language learners (ELLs) to engage their students in multiple content areas while mastering communication skills in English. Additionally, tenets of best practice in programs serving English language learners include valuing first language and culture, maintaining high content area standards, integrating language and content objectives, using sheltered content area strategies that make language and academic content comprehensible, utilizing students's prior knowledge, and building bridges with family and community. These components echo Nieto's definition of social justice in education with a holistic and fair approach by respecting a student's first language while empowering them with English.

A school-wide approach to social justice can be seen in various two-way bilingual education programs throughout the nation. One such program is La Escuela

Fratney, a public school in Milwaukee, Wisconsin, that features two-way bilingual education—all students learn in both English and Spanish—and a curriculum that emphasizes anti-racist, multicultural social justice education. Since the school opened in 1988, the belief system, school rules and policies reflect the multicultural/anti-racist perspective and school-wide themes: We Respect Ourselves and Our World, We are Proud to be Bilingual/Multicultural Learners, We Can Make a Difference on Planet Earth, and We Share Stories of the World. These themes serve as the framework for the social studies curriculum and are integrated into other content areas as well. The fact that the school is a two-way bilingual model speaks to the advocacy for both English language learners and second language learners in one of the preferred models for language learning. Featured in *Teaching Tolerance* and multiple articles and books, the daily work of social justice at the school continues non-stop; one recent example is a fifth grade classroom's putting Columbus on trial for mistreatment of the indigenous peoples of the Americas. This concept of "putting Columbus on trial" is part of a curriculum ideas presented in Rethinking Columbus: The Next 500 Years, a volume from Rethinking Schools applicable to WL and ESL classrooms as teachers and their students explore resources for learning about the impact of the arrival of Columbus in the Americas. This is only one example of a learner-centered curriculum which, when fully developed and tilted to action, can be considered a step toward social justice.

Historically, within world languages, *Standards for Foreign Language Learning in the 21st Century* focused the profession on five goal areas or the 5Cs—communication, cultures, connections, comparisons, communities—often represented as interlocking rings and incorporated into various state curriculum guides (Standards, 1999). The national standards for world language teachers provide an important, beginning structure to consider issues of social justice, as language, culture, and community play significant roles in the curriculum. This framework is explored in Osborn's seminal work *Teaching World Languages for Social Justice: A Sourcebook of Principles and Practices* (2006) in which the author provides examples of social justice applications as he reinforces the concept that social justice is a journey of process and inquiry: Not a destination. National standards have provided a unifying agenda for curriculum and instruction and position world languages for interaction with other languages and content areas. Following are the professional Standards for World Languages:

- *Communication.* Communicate in languages other than english
- *Cultures.* Gain knowledge and understanding of other cultures
- *Connections.* Connect with other disciplines and acquire information
- *Comparisons.* Develop insight into the nature of language and culture
- *Communities.* Participate in multilingual communities at home and around the world.

National standards also provide a basis by which we can examine our progress as teachers and also our students' learning. With the focus on backloading curriculum, or beginning with the final assessment and working backwards in planning instruction, as well as a focus on what students should know and be able to do, performance assessments can form an important part of assessment and the standards reinforce this process (Sandrock, 2002).

What can this look like in a beginning level world language class? In a recent action research project, one field experience preservice teacher wanted to explore how to teach culture through authentic materials. Can teaching authentic literature in the target language effectively develop students' cultural competence in the culture(s) of the target language in a way that challenges student beliefs and viewpoints and stimulates sophisticated mental processes (evaluating, giving opinions, judging, connecting ideas to self)? The poem *Balada de los dos abuelos* in which the author Nicolás Guillén wrote of his black and white grandfathers and how they unite in him, and how it is a metaphor for the general Cuban culture and history was used in multiple activities to engage students with issues of social justice. Students' knowledge and responses regarding Cuban culture and history were limited and nonspecific. After the analysis of the literal and figurative meaning of the poem and discussion of issues such as slavery, race relations, and colonialism, students showed more analytical understanding of the poem. Some students made connections between the poem and their own families and issues of being biracial. These linkages, particularly regarding identity, can be woven into the world language curriculum at multiple levels, and embody the spirit of Nieto's definition of social justice.

Uniting Second Language Education

The notion that second language education programs in the United States have often been divided into English as a second language (ESL), bilingual education, and foreign language education is well established (Davis, 1999). Differences or divisions in language education in terms of history, position, power, and privilege in turn affect the preparation and practices of teachers in these disciplines. However, such divides in practice, perceptions of the mission and vision of the others, and historical lack of collaboration between areas can be overcome. Working to alleviate tensions and better understand content expectations can help better prepare us for teaching and learning and the important work in our classrooms. Teachers in second language should be unified in their roles as language advocates for all learners, particularly for English learners to be able to keep and strengthen their native language. English learners should also be encouraged to study additional languages to better position them for opportunities in higher education or a global economy. World language teachers should be more aware of, and sensitive to, their traditional position of privilege (Muirhead, 2007) due to the marginalization of bilingual education in the United States today. Bilingual education is taunted with anti-immigrant sentiments and the English-only movement which seeks to make English the official and only language in our country. These attitudes often influence the approaches to language learning in a district and which world languages are privileged in the curriculum.

Although the history of multilingualism in the United States can be seen as early as the sixteenth-century Manhattan Island, where at least 18 languages were spoken, the vestiges of monolingualism continue in our classrooms today. In addition, the history of high Native American literacy rates beginning in the 1700s, as well as the predominance and preeminence of Spanish in the Southwest in the 1800s, show us historical facts about our nation that have been overshadowed by the more widely accepted sentiment: If one speaks three languages, one is trilingual; if one speaks two languages one is bilingual, and if one speaks one language, one is an American. The Bilingual Education Act of 1968 was primarily construed as a remedial or compensatory model that devalued a child's native language. The idea was to move children as quickly as possible out of a bilingual setting into English-only instruction. In such subtractive, meaning negative, bilingualism, a child's second language is learned with the expectation that it will replace the mother tongue. This is in stark contrast to the case of additive bilingualism or the privilege of learning a world language: When a second language is acquired, it is only with the expectation that the native language will continue to be used. Appreciating the historical evolution of our fields of study might better help us engage with the sociopolitical realities of today. The U.S. English/English-only movements, and lead/mentor teachers who take advantage of the influence they hold as world language teachers, particularly in Spanish, can serve as advocates for English language learners, rather than purveyors of elite knowledge.

Fostering relationships among the areas of English as a second language, bilingual education, and foreign language learning can help teachers and teacher educators better address language equity and social justice issues within and outside of the classroom. Corson affirms that "Social justice has much to do with ideas about legitimacy, about fairness and impartiality, about welfare and mutual advantage, and about political and social consensus" (1993, p. 27). Thus, in the context of language education, we need to recall the general, public perception (and the real pedagogical condition) of bilingual education for English language learners as a subtractive model and learning a second language other than English as a case of additive bilingualism. Teachers of world languages are often consulted when there are new, non-English speaking students in a school and could be greater advocates for such students if equipped with a greater understanding of the sociopolitical issues involved. Immigrant and minority language learners face challenges in language maintenance or memory of native language as they enter American schools.

Certainly our goal as teachers is to equip and inspire our students to see issues that affect them or others in their communities and the larger global community and be involved. Much like the concept of community organizers who bring together people with common concerns who are mobilized to action in ideals of participatory democracy, student leaders can galvanize their peers and adults at the same time. In a simple yet moving example, an immigrant student in Seattle rallied fellow Hispanic students this year to address the issue of the dropout rate and path to college (Thompson 2008). The multifaceted plan of attack dealt with some basics of raising academic achievement, such as attending class and doing assignments, to seeking support from parents and investigating schools and strategies to successfully apply. They called themselves ELITES—Estudiantes Latinos Internacionales Trabajando por una Educación Superior—International Latino Students Working Toward Higher Education. The students themselves felt empowered to act on their own behalf, a significant step in self-advocacy.

As teacher and facilitator of learning in the classroom, we have an obligation to prepare ourselves for the role as advocate and activist. In her chapter "Literacy, Diversity, and Programmatic Responses," Bertha Pérez cautions that "the growing number of speakers of languages other than English and the current hostile political climate toward immigrants have created a dilemma for teachers. Not only must teachers provide the best instruction for increasingly diverse English language learners, but they also must do so in an increasingly restrictive political climate that is openly dismissive of native-language instructional support" (2004, p. 4). Students are often denied the use of their first language in the classroom, either because there is no bilingual aid or conversation is not allowed in their native language because adults misunderstand the communication as cheating or distracting. This dismissiveness often carries over to the personal level, resulting in professional exile or isolation for the teachers who serve English language learners—the sole ESL teacher in a high school working with content area teachers, for example—but in spite of this, that teacher can still be a change agent in the school community and an advocate for her students.

Beyond the building of self-advocacy, encouraging the development of advocacy for others is integral to building social justice awareness. An interesting trend in world language programs is to combine the traditional component of language study in a study abroad setting and experiences with service learning opportunities. One such example is the Panama Service Project (http://www.panamaservicepro-ject.com/) in which students have the opportunity to strengthen their language abilities while learning more about social issues and needs in Panama. These service connections often spur a greater interest once the students return home to engage with some of the parallel issues of poverty and child nutrition with a renewed sense of community involvement and leadership.

In *Power and Inequality in Language Education*, Tollefson conveys that

> until recently, most teacher-preparation programs in language education and English as a second language focused on second language acquisition, teaching methods, and linguistics, without placing these fields in their social, political, and economic context. The result was that many language teachers and other applied linguists lacked an understanding of how language-learning theory and common teaching practices are linked with broader sociopolitical forces. (1995, p. 1)

Indeed, these sociopolitical forces are at work, especially within recent accountability and high-stakes assessment movements as well as immigration confrontations, and are issues which teachers committed to social justice must confront in their classrooms.

Critical Social Justice work

In second language education we can often lack critical pedagogy and practical strategies and resources to implement a fully functional social justice curriculum. In addition, the instructional focus and demands in the classroom often default to the way we ourselves experienced language learning, in most cases grammar-focused rather than communicative and intercultural competence, with no comprehensive examination of "big questions" or social issues. However, with recent, notable shifts in practice and evidence of a growing number of teachers with an interest in incorporating aspects of a social justice curriculum within their classroom and instruction, there is hope.

Researchers and teachers alike can utilize critical design work in the exploration of issues in world languages and ESL as well as designing assessment procedures to help teachers chart their progress and their students' learning. Design research encourages the investigation of and reflection on the research process, including decisions that must be made and the learning opportunities that such present (Edelson, 2002). As Edelson further posits, design research can play a greater role in education research and reform because of the practicality of the unique lessons learned and that it involves researchers in the direct improvement of educational practice. Teacher researchers consider social justice implications, dealing with and finding solutions for complex sociocultural situations including school inequities, poverty, and academic achievement which can be addressed in critical design work as well as in action research. Indeed it is not enough simply to understand the issues facing diverse learners, in this case their level of language acquisition in informal learning environments, but to affect cultural change. Teachers are often not prepared to use their classrooms to change society, but yet as they focus on the learner and issues that impact their students, such can be a powerful outcome of instruction. Teachers' self-reflections as well as students documenting their learning in journals or in more traditional pre and post lesson measures can be meaningful assessments of progress.

Learner-centered environments, through their focus on the learner and issues that impact the students, can have a powerful outcome on instruction and have the additional advantage of lending themselves more readily to thematic units. Collaborative creation of curriculum, such as including students in decisions regarding thematic units, can empower and motivate student learning. Students also bring their experiences and skills to the classroom; in many cases this is their native language proficiency. The Center for Applied Linguistics (CAL) states that "As this nation faces a critical shortage of adults with proficiency in languages other than English, we need to develop our own rich linguistic resources, the languages spoken in communities across the United States" (CAL website) and heritage learners could help fill this need. In 1999, the National Foreign Language Center and the Center for Applied Linguistics began the Heritage Language Initiative "with the goal of building an education system that is responsive to heritage communities and national language needs and capable of producing a broad cadre of citizens able to function professionally in both English and another language" (Brecht & Ingold,

2002). Heritage language learners (HLLs) are students whose identity and/or linguistic needs differ from those of second language learners by virtue of having a family background in the heritage language (HL) or culture (HC) and who do not receive sufficient exposure to their language and culture to fulfill basic identity and linguistic needs (Carreira, 2004). Yet such heritage learners can provide a global link when they have instructional experiences that reinforce their language and identity. Jody Sokolower, a history teacher in Berkeley, California, provides a powerful example from her twelfth grade economics class which included all immigrants and all English language learners. She sought to connect the students' own experiences with an exploration of the complicated topic of globalization. Her definition is cutting: "Globalization—More than ever before in history, there is one world economy. This pressure toward one economy is called globalization. Globalization is the struggle for control of the earth's resources—natural resources, human resources, and capital resources" (2006, p. 46). She continues with eight elements of globalization which include migration, big companies are international companies, resources are international, free trade agreements, World Bank and International Monetary Fund (IMF), sweatshops, environmental problems, and increased communication among peoples—the basis for resistance. It is precisely these types of social justice issues that provide a rich learning environment across languages for both the ESL and Spanish teacher.

Service learning and community involvement opens students to opportunities for action and advocacy. Twice-nominated teacher of the year for the American Council on the Teaching of Foreign Languages (ACTFL), Nicolet High School (Glendale, Wisconsin) Spanish teacher Nina Holmquist embraces the fact that students and community members win when language study becomes a real-world experience. The benefits of work outside the classroom are touted for students as life-long learners of language but they also are better engaged citizens.

> At no time ever before has it been as important as today to be proficient in foreign languages and cultures. Our world is becoming smaller and smaller, and if we, as a country and individuals want to have a positive impact on the world, we *must* expand the language skills and cultural awareness of every American. It has been the case too often that our businessmen, tourists, and ambassadors went abroad full of goodwill, but without any understanding of the culture and language of the places they visited, and thus not reaping the success they had expected. This cannot be the case any longer. If we want to promote democracy, establish business relations, teach Aids prevention, etc., our mission will only be credible if we communicate with peoples in their language and are sensitive to what makes them tick. Today competition is fierce, and I am not necessarily speaking of the business world. Today we must educate youth that speak Pashtun to rebuild Afganistan, Russian to re-establish confidence in us, or Creole to promote understanding in Haiti, just to name a few.

It is this veteran teacher's call to action that can inspire new and experienced colleagues to find ways to integrate social justice into the curriculum. In the language classroom we challenge stereotypes and establish a climate of respect for individual differences, celebrating other languages, cultures, and backgrounds.

Points of Inquiry

- Why do the three different fields, ESL, bilingual education, and world languages have such distinct disciplinary approaches to curriculum and instruction?
- What are the commonalities the fields share (aims, politics, funding)?
- Which fields are privileged? Why?
- Historically, how have the fields emerged as disciplines and departments?
- How does each of these fields construe social justice pedagogy? Why?

Points of Praxis

- Using a world languages textbook, redesign a lesson or series of lessons to incorporate an explicit emphasis on social justice.
- Engage your students in a discussion of linguistic privilege: How can the learning of a particular language offer greater access? How can it restrict access? Does the language (English, Spanish, Hmong, etc.) itself determine this? How?
- How do people learn languages? What pedagogical approaches are most effective, and how can we incorporate problem-posing/critical pedagogy?
- With your students, critique the curriculum standards from a critical perspective.

References

Brecht, R. D., & Ingold, C. W. (2002). Tapping a national resource: Heritage languages in the United States. CAL Digest. Retrieved March 1, 2009, from: http://www.cal.org/resources/digest/0202brecht.html. EDO-FL-02-02

Carreira, M. (2004). Seeking explanatory adequacy: A dual approach to understanding the term "heritage language learner." *Heritage Language Journal, 2,*(1). Retrieved March 1, 2009, from: www.international.ucla.edu/languages/heritagelanguages/journal/article.asp?parentid=14647

Corson, D. (1993). *Language, minority education and gender: Linking social justice and power.* Bristol, PA: Multilingual Matters.

Davis, K. A. (1999). *Foreign language teaching and language minority education.* Honolulu, HI: Second Language Teaching & Curriculum Center, University of Hawai'i at Manoa.

Edelson, D. C. (2002). Design research: What we learn when we engage in design. *Journal of the Learning Sciences, 11*(1), 105–121.

Moll, L. C., Amanti, C., Neff, D., & Gonzalez, N. (1992). Funds of knowledge for teaching: Using a qualitative approach to connect homes and classrooms. *Theory Into Practice, 31*(2), 132–141.

Muirhead, Pablo. (2007). Culture in the world language classroom: A multiple case study.

Ph.D. dissertation, University of Wisconsin, Milwaukee. Retrieved January 16, 2008, from: ProQuest Digital Dissertations database. (Publication No. AAT 3244156).

Nieto, S., & Bode, P. (2008). *Affirming diversity: The sociopolitical context of multicultural education* (5th ed.). Boston: Allyn & Bacon.

Osborn, T. (2006). *Teaching world languages for social justice: a sourcebook of principles and practices.* Mahwah, NJ : Lawrence Erlbaum.

Perez, B. (Ed.). (2004). *Sociocultural contexts of language and literacy* (2nd ed.). Mahwah, NJ: Lawrence Erlbaum.

Sandrock, R. (2002). *Planning curriculum for learning world languages.* Madison: Wisconsin Department of Public Instruction.

Simmons, R. J. (2004). America's relationship with the world: How can languages help? *French Review, 77*(4), 682–687.

Sokolower, J. (2006). Bringing globalization home: A high school teacher helps immigrant students draw on their own expertise. *Rethinking Schools, 21*(1).

Standards for Foreign Language Learning in the 21st Century. (1999). Lawrence, KS: Allen Press.

Thompson, L. (2008). Hispanic students at Interlake pull together to graduate. http://seattletimes.nwsource.com/html/localnews/2004399964_osbaldo08e.html

Tollefson, J. W. (1995). *Power and inequality in language education.* Cambridge Applied Linguistics Series. Cambridge: Cambridge University Press.

Resources

Barab, S., Dodge, T., Thomas, M. K., Jackson, C., & Tuzun, H. (2007). Designs and the agendas they carry. *Journal of the Learning Sciences, 16*(2), 263–305.

Blackledge, A. (2000). *Literacy, power, and social justice.* Stoke-on-Trent, U.K.: Trentham Books.

Edelson, D. C., & Reiser, B. J. (2006). Making authentic practices accessible to learners: Design challenges and strategies. In R. Keith Sawyer (Ed.), *The Cambridge Handbook of Learning Sciences* (pp. 335–354). Cambridge: Cambridge University Press.

Frattura, E. M., & Capper, C. A. (2007). *Leading for social justice transforming schools for all learners.* Thousand Oaks, CA: Corwin Press.

Kumaravadivelu, B. (2003). *Beyond methods: Macrostrategies for language teaching.* Yale Language Series. New Haven, CT: Yale University Press.

Kumaravadivelu, B. (2008). *Cultural globalization and language education.* New Haven, CT: Yale University Press.

Petovello, L. R., Taranko, D., & Nichols, S. (1998). *The spirit that moves us: A literature-based resource guide: teaching about diversity, prejudice, human rights, and the Holocaust: Volume I, Grades kindergarten through four.* Gardiner, ME: Tilbury House.

Quenk, R. (1997). *The spirit that moves us: A literature-based resource guide, teaching about the Holocaust and human rights: Volume II, Grades 5–8.* Gardiner, ME: Tilbury House.

Reagan, T. G., & Osborn, T. A. (2002). *The foreign language educator in society: Toward a critical pedagogy.* Mawhah, NJ: Lawrence Erlbaum.

Sawyer, R. K. (2006). *The Cambridge handbook of the learning sciences.* Cambridge: Cambridge University Press.

Sleeter, C. E., & Grant, C. A. (2006). *Making choices for multicultural education: Five approaches to race, class, and gender.* New York: Wiley.

Afterword

The Power not yet in Power

Ira Shor

"How one person's abilities compare in quantity with those of another is none of the teacher's business."
—John Dewey, *Democracy and Education*, 1916, p. 172.

"We will only begin to get evidence of the potential power of pedagogy when we dare to risk and support markedly deviant classroom procedures."
—John Goodlad, *A Place Called School*, 1984, p. 249.

"It is astonishing that so few critics challenge the system. . . . The people are better than the structure. Therefore, the structure must be at fault."
—Theodore Sizer, *Horace's Compromise*, 1984, p. 209.

"Not since the Roaring Twenties have the rich been so much richer than everyone else."
—"It Didn't End Well Last Time," *New York Times*, April 4, 2007, p. A14.

"The United States has less than 5 percent of the world's population. But it has almost a quarter of the world's prisoners."
—"Inmate Count in U.S. Dwarfs Other Nations'," *New York Times*, April 23, 2008, p. A16.

Who will save school and society? Our Constitution is tattered, our democratic rights dissolving, our new President refusing to prosecute torture, detentions without trial, illegal eavesdropping, and secret renditions. Our looted economy remains in the hands of the looters, the Wall Street bankers appointed to vast power in Washington. Our productive industries are shuttering, with families thrown out of jobs, homes, pensions, and health plans, because business favors Wal-Mart wages here and starvation wages abroad. Our unwinnable wars are spreading to Afghanistan and Pakistan, with *$1 trillion* already down the rabbit hole of Iraq, where no threat to America ever emerged, but still 4,400 of our soldiers died along with tens of thousands of Iraqis. Our health care has become a privilege most can barely afford as Big Pharma charges $4,200 per dose of cancer medication and private insurers profit by denying and delaying benefits. Our infants die at an alarming rate in this great wealthy nation, 29th worst in the world, tied with Slovakia and Poland. Our children are at high risk of impoverishment, including some 34%

of all African-American kids. Our urban and rural youngsters attend underfunded public schools where they are tested more than taught and taught by underpaid teachers whose classes are too large and resources too few. Our collegiate adults mostly attend poorly budgeted public campuses with rising tuition and low graduation rates. Our hungry and homeless accumulate in rich cities like New York which spent hundreds of millions of dollars publicly financing a new Yankee Stadium built on a public park once used by poor Hispanic families nearby. I ask again, Who will save school and society?

The educators in this panoramic book have answered, "Count on us." Their brave, smart work comprises hopeful opposition to injustice in school and society. In wonderfully readable chapters, they insist that there are alternatives to the status quo, that another world is indeed possible. A path to that other world is named herein as "social justice education." That marvelous concept emerging in recent years—*social justice education*—brings together diverse trends and groups, offering a potential "big tent" to gather all those who dream of a humane world, a big tent of opposition in which to learn from each other's work, to mediate our differences, to imagine our options. This book, then, can be a tool for consolidating and advancing social justice forces whose work in classrooms, school systems, colleges, communities, and organizations inevitably involves the larger political system. Certainly, the need to consolidate democratic resistance is urgent in school and society. Consolidation across differences, across levels of work, and across sites of practice, is necessary for opposition forces to build the common ground that can amplify political consequence. Without consolidation on common ground, resistance to the status quo will remain dispersed, unable to stop the looting and abuse by the top against the rest of society.

Not only a tool for consolidation, this book also addresses a second need of democratic opposition, that of updating, situating, diversifying, and circulating knowledges of practice, the know-how accumulating in separate places which needs to circulate in a national space. Knowledges of practice—detailed in chapters here—are useful and inspiring. They can serve as tools for advancing the practice of others, a goal that can be called *cadre development* (advancing the political wisdom, critical practice and theory, oppositional desire, and organizational skills of democratic educators). This book can be used by diverse practitioners across the curriculum to raise critical teaching broadly in education—for people in preservice, inservice, and free-standing settings. These chapters' references to the roots of social justice education—in feminist, Freirean, multicultural, and other progressive foundations—deepens awareness of the multiple, mutual, and converging sources of opposition.

When the book's contributors update the roots and practices of opposition, the problem of power is never far from these chapters. "Power" was surely a theme that preoccupied Paulo Freire, who is also present on many of the preceding pages. This passionate man from Brazil liked to call the elite who dominate every society "the power now in power," with the emphasis on *now* to suggest the historical and changeable nature of the status quo. This status quo, operated by and for an elite minority, was to Freire an oppressive "limit-situation" for non-elite people and for democratic activists, against which we announce social justice practices and organ-izations that he named "the power not yet in power," anticipating the arrival of humane relations.

Connecting humane relations to the "big tent" character of this useful book, I can propose four supporting pillars of social justice learning: democracy, peace, equality, and ecology. These four values envision a nation at peace with itself and the world, an inclusive culture that subordinates and stigmatizes no group or iden-tity, a society of material security in all homes that neither impoverishes nor lav-ishes any community, a sustainable economy that exploits no one's labor and despoils no territory, and an education system that invests equally in all its children and citizens, where learning is not something done to students but something they do for themselves.

This agenda articulates for "the power not yet in power" some common goals for a humane nation. Another discourse for common ground could be sought in the alternative consciousness developed by social justice education. In general, "con-sciousness" (which I briefly define as intentionality-in-action, as learned ways of being and doing in the world, as the visible signs of human subjectivity) is a prod-uct of social experience (a constructivist idea in circulation since at least John Dewey). We are constructed by the material conditions in which we live. Our social experiences teach us how to make meaning in a world that is making us, as well as how to act on those meanings. This construction of self-in-society and society-in-self occurs unequally and locally depending on the sites and the subjects. At some social sites, say factories, everyday activities not only informally produce con-sciousness (who you are, where you fit in existing hierarchies, and what you can do or expect in such conditions), but also produce commodities like cars, TVs, cereal, shoes, sofas, MP3 players, etc. As we all know, such commodities are not produced by classroom activities, even though classrooms are surely sites for the social con-struction of the self and for the reproduction of already-existing inequities (with some high-status universities also producing research useful to the military and to corporations). This formation of human subjects in schooling is partly induced by pedagogical discourses which develop differentiated employees and citizens depending on the race, class, and gender of the students. Because of this differential development of students, education has always been contentious, regulated, and consequential: What kind of people and society do we want our classroom practices to construct? What kind of society would we live in if we spent as much on inner-city kids' schooling as we do on that of suburban youngsters, or as much on com-munity college students as we do on Harvard registrants? Mainstream education does not address its roles in reproducing inequities; its curriculum orients students and teachers to fit into the unequal status quo as it is. Social justice education ori-ents students and teachers to question the status quo in the name of democracy and equality, two key interests apparent in the preceding chapters.

Perhaps I can elaborate the alternate consciousness I see social justice education encouraging: It invites students and teachers to develop as citizen-activists, as critical readers of their world and its words, as community change-agents, as equality-advocates, as earth-stewards, as peacemakers, as constructive skeptics enabling group action, and as democratic partisans. Perhaps these alternate features of consciousness are worth further discussion as a common-ground agenda to help coalesce democratic groups and practitioners. We are moving in similar directions, seeking some similar outcomes, often by diverse paths and in disparate sites. Discourse on common ground is an idea whose time has come for advancing ideals of social justice.

All who work for social justice stand on the shoulders of those whose prior sacrifices and labor took us this far, so very far already, but not yet nearly far enough. The planet is writhing in crises that shelter and reward the powerful who caused them while punishing the victims. A tool called "social justice education" is now available to democratic partisans in the cultural arms race for the future. This book defines aspects of that tool which can help interfere with the descent into barbarism in school and society. Using such tools wisely, we can move along the path suggested years ago by a hopeful Paulo Freire: "In the last analysis, liberatory education must be understood as a practice where we challenge the people to mobilize or organize themselves to get power"(Shor & Freire, 1987, p. 34). We must teach as if our lives depended on gaining democratic power, because certainly many lives do.

July, 2009

Reference

Shor, I., & Freire, P. (1987). *A pedagogy for liberation: Dialogues on transforming education.* Westport, CT: Bergin & Garvey.

About the Contributors

Maurianne Adams is Professor of Education Emerita, Social Justice Education Concentration, at the University of Massachusetts-Amherst. She co-edited *Teaching for Diversity and Social Justice* (2nd edition, 2007), *Readings for Diversity and Social Justice* (2nd edition, 2010), and *Strangers and Neighbors: Relations between Blacks and Jews in the United States* (1999). Adams is editor of *Equity & Excellence in Education.*

Mary M. Atwater is a Professor in the Office of Research in the College of Education and an Adjunct Professor in the Social Foundations program at the University of Georgia. With a B.S. and Master's degree in chemistry, her research focuses on socio-cultural-political influences on science learning and teaching and multi-cultural science teacher education.

Bryan McKinley Jones Brayboy is Borderlands Associate Professor of Policy, Leadership, and Curriculum at Arizona State University. His research focuses on race and equity, and the experiences of Indigenous peoples in educational settings. Dr. Brayboy has been the recipient of the Distinguished Early Career Award from the American Educational Research Association and fellowships from the Ford and Spencer Foundations. He has published widely on Indigenous education, higher education, and Indian education policy.

Patricia D. Quijada Cerecer is an Assistant Professor of Educational Psychology at the University of Texas at San Antonio. Dr. Cerecer's research interests include Indigenous identity development in home, community, and school contexts, Indigenous epistemologies, and multicultural education in community and school contexts.

Thandeka K. Chapman is an Associate Professor of Urban Education in the Department of Curriculum and Instruction at the University of Wisconsin, Milwaukee. She has conducted research on policy implementation in desegre-gated schools, urban small school reforms, teaching and learning in racially diverse classrooms, and evaluating social justice curricula.

David J. Connor is an Associate Professor of Special Education at Hunter College, City University of New York. His research interests include inclusive education and social, cultural, and historical understandings of dis/ability. He is the author of *Reading Resistance: Discourses of Exclusion in Desegregation and Inclusion Debates* (with Beth Ferri) and *Urban Narratives: Life at the Intersections of Learning Disability, Race, and Social Class.*

Adrienne D. Dixson is an Associate Professor in the School of Teaching and Learning at the Ohio State University. Dr. Dixson's research focuses on race and racial and gender identities in urban schooling contexts. Her co-edited book with Celia K. Rousseau Anderson *Critical Race Theory in Education: All God's Children Got a Song* received the 2006 Critics Choice Award from the American Educational Studies Association.

Wendy Elsworth lectures in the School of Education at the University of Newcastle, Australia, and is Director of the Centre for Professional Learning and Education. Dr. Elsworth researches the transformative goals of critical multicultural education through her study of equity in education for Indigenous students and others who have been disadvantaged by schooling in Australia.

Susan L. Gabel is a Professor of Special Education and Disability Studies in Education in the National College of Education at National-Louis University. Her research focuses on disability and the politics and policies of education. With Scot Danforth, she is the editor of *Disability and the Politics of Education: An International Reader*, and *Vital Questions Facing Disability Studies in Education.*

Melissa L. Gibson is a doctoral student and teacher educator in the Department of Curriculum and Instruction at the University of Wisconsin, Madison. Her research focuses on teacher education and diversity, the purposes and philosophies of education in a multicultural democracy, and the connections between social justice and human rights in education.

Jennifer M. Gore is a Professor in the Faculty of Education and Arts at the University of Newcastle, Australia, where she is currently Dean of Education. Her scholarship has ranged across such topics as teacher socialization, alternative pedagogy, power relations in pedagogy, and reform in teaching and teacher education.

Carl A. Grant is Hoefs-Bascom Professor of Teacher Education in the Department of Curriculum and Instruction at the University of Wisconsin, Madison. His most recent publications include: *Teach! Change! Empower!* (2009); six volume set on the *History of Multicultural Education* (2008) (with Thandeka K. Chapman); and *Doing Multicultural Education for Achievement and Equity* (2008) (with Christine E. Sleeter).

Leticia Alvarez Gutiérrez is an Assistant Professor in the Department of Education, Culture and Society at the University of Utah. Her research is closely linked with issues of immigration, ethnic identity, race, class, and gender. Dr. Gutiérrez's passion centers on making a difference in the schooling experiences of linguistically and culturally marginalized youth.

Eric (Rico) Gutstein teaches mathematics education at the University of Illinois-Chicago. His work includes teaching mathematics for social justice, Freirean approaches to teaching and learning, urban education, and mathematics education policy. He supports mathematics teachers and students at Chicago's Social Justice High School where he has worked since 2003.

Nikola Hobbel is Associate Professor of English Education at Humboldt State University in Arcata, California. Teaching in the undergraduate, graduate, and credential programs, she centers her work on critical literacies, curriculum theory, and discourse studies. Her research focuses on multiculturalism, teacher education, and education policy, which garner her special attention, as do her inspiring students.

Korina M. Jocson is Assistant Professor of Education in Arts and Sciences at Washington University in St. Louis. Her research and teaching interests include literacy, youth culture, and ethnic studies in education. For the past decade, Jocson has collaborated with university programs, schools, and community-based organizations to engage students and promote literacy development. She is the author of *Youth Poets: Empowering Literacies In and Out of Schools.*

Lisa W. Loutzenheiser is an Associate Professor in the Department of Curriculum and Pedagogy at the University of British Columbia. Dr. Loutzenheiser's research is centered in sociology and anthropology in education, youth studies, qualitative methodologies, anti-oppressive education, and gender and queer theories. Her current research projects include the educational experiences of youth in foster care, and critical interrogation of identity with preservice teachers through autobiography.

Teresa L. McCarty is the Alice Wiley Snell Professor of Education Policy Studies and Professor of Applied Linguistics at Arizona State University. An educational anthropologist, she has worked with American Indian education programs throughout North America. Her books include *Language, Literacy, and Power in Schooling; A Place To Be Navajo;* and *"To Remain an Indian": Lessons in Democracy from a Century of Native American Education* (with K. T. Lomawaima).

Daniel Morales-Doyle is a chemistry teacher and science department chair at the Greater Lawndale Little Village School for Social Justice in Chicago. His interests include critical pedagogy, issues of race and class in science education, and connections between community organizing and urban schools.

Bekisizwe S. Ndimande is Assistant Professor of Curriculum and Instruction and with the Center for African Studies at the University of Illinois at Urbana-Champaign. His research interests include the politics of curriculum and examining the policies and practices in post-apartheid desegregated public schools, and also the implications of school "choice" for disadvantaged communities in South Africa. His current research examines children's rights and experiences of immigrant students and families in South Africa.

Raquel Oxford is Director of the World Language Teacher Certification Program at the University of Wisconsin, Milwaukee, and teaches courses in second language education including bilingual and English as a second language. Her research interests include second language teacher preparation and mentoring; technology integration in second language instruction; and multicultural education.

Robert J. Parkes is Deputy Head of School (Teaching and Learning), and Senior Lecturer in Curriculum Theory, History and Media Education, in the School of Education at the University of Newcastle, Australia. Robert's scholarship, drawing on poststructural, postcolonial, and hermeneutic approaches, is situated within an antipodean current of reconceptualist curriculum inquiry.

Therese Quinn is Associate Professor of Art Education at the School of the Art Institute of Chicago, where she directed the undergraduate teacher education program from 2002 to 2009. Quinn co-edits the Teachers College Press Series, Teaching for Social Justice, and blogs about public education at the Other Eye.

Francisco Rios is a Professor of Educational Studies at the University of Wyoming. He is the Senior Associate Editor of *Multicultural Perspectives*, the Journal of the National Association for Multicultural Education. Francisco was recently named as the first director of the University of Wyoming's Social Justice Research Center.

Ira Shor teaches at the City University of New York Graduate Center, where he started the doctorate in composition/rhetoric in 1993. He also teaches writing at CUNY's College of Staten Island. His books include the first volume Paulo Freire did with a collaborator, *A Pedagogy for Liberation* (1987), and *Empowering Education* (1992), widely used in teacher education. His son Paulo, now 6, works hard at raising his father. Ira grew up in the Jewish working class of the South Bronx and went to college in the sixties.

Christine E. Sleeter is Professor Emerita in the College of Professional Studies at California State University Monterey Bay, where she was a founding faculty member. Her research focuses on anti-racist multicultural education and multicultural teacher education. She has published over 100 articles in edited books and journals. Her most recent book is *Doing Multicultural Education for Achievement and Equity* (with Carl Grant). She is a recipient of the American Educational Research Association Social Justice in Education Award, and the American Educational Research Association Division K Legacy Award.

Jamila D. Smith is a third-year doctoral student in Adolescent, Post-Secondary, and Community Literacies at the Ohio State University. Her research interests include the oral and written narrative practices of adult Black women and Black female adolescents.

Regina L. Suriel is a doctoral student in the Department of Mathematics and Science Education at the University of Georgia. Ms. Suriel holds a B.S. and an

M.S. in Science Education from the City University of New York. She has taught high school science in bilingual classrooms in the NYC public school system for a number of years.

David Stovall is Associate Professor of Educational Policy Studies and African-American Studies at the University of Illinois at Chicago. Currently his interests include Critical Race Theory, school/community relationships, and concepts of social justice in education. He is also a volunteer social studies teacher at the Lawndale/Little Village School for Social Justice (SOJO).

Index

eBooks

eBooks – at www.eBookstore.tandf.co.uk

A library at your fingertips!

eBooks are electronic versions of printed books. You can store them on your PC/laptop or browse them online.

They have advantages for anyone needing rapid access to a wide variety of published, copyright information.

eBooks can help your research by enabling you to bookmark chapters, annotate text and use instant searches to find specific words or phrases. Several eBook files would fit on even a small laptop or PDA.

NEW: Save money by eSubscribing: cheap, online access to any eBook for as long as you need it.

Annual subscription packages

We now offer special low-cost bulk subscriptions to packages of eBooks in certain subject areas. These are available to libraries or to individuals.

For more information please contact webmaster.ebooks@tandf.co.uk

We're continually developing the eBook concept, so keep up to date by visiting the website.

www.eBookstore.tandf.co.uk